THE GENDER OF SEXUALITY

D1111180

THE GENDER LENS SERIES

Series Editors

Judith A. Howard
University of Washington

Barbara Risman
University of Illinois, Chicago

Joey Sprague
University of Kansas

The Gender Lens series has been conceptualized as a way of encouraging the development of a sociological understanding of gender. A "gender lens" means working to make gender visible in social phenomena; asking if, how, and why social processes, standards, and opportunities differ systematically for women and men. It also means recognizing that gender inequality is inextricably braided with other systems of inequality. The Gender Lens series is committed to social change directed toward eradicating these inequalities. Originally published by Sage Publications and Pine Forge Press, all Gender Lens books are now available from The Rowman & Littlefield Publishing Group.

BOOKS IN THE SERIES

THE GENDER OF SEXUALITY

Exploring Sexual Possibilities

Second Edition

Virginia Rutter and Pepper Schwartz

ROWMAN & LITTLEFIELD PUBLISHERS, INC.

Lanham · Boulder · New York · Toronto · Plymouth, UK

Published by Rowman & Littlefield Publishers, Inc.
A wholly owned subsidiary of The Rowman & Littlefield Publishing Group, Inc.
4501 Forbes Boulevard, Suite 200, Lanham, Maryland 20706
http://www.rowmanlittlefield.com

Estover Road, Plymouth PL6 7PY, United Kingdom

British Library Cataloguing in Publication Information Available

Library of Congress Cataloging-in-Publication Data

Rutter, Virginia.
  The gender of sexuality / Virginia Rutter and Pepper Schwartz.
    p. cm.
  Rev. ed. of: The gender of sexuality / Pepper Schwartz, Virginia Rutter. Thousand Oaks : Pine Forge Press, c1998.
  Includes bibliographical references and index.
  ISBN 978-0-7425-7003-0 (cloth : alk. paper) — ISBN 978-0-7425-7004-7 (pbk. : alk. paper) — ISBN 978-0-7425-7005-4 (ebook)
  1. Sex. 2. Sex (Psychology) 3. Sex differences (Psychology) 4. Sex role. 5. Gender identity. I. Schwartz, Pepper. II. Title.
  HQ21.S328 2012
  306.7—dc23
                                                                                              2011026638

Printed in the United States of America

Virginia: To John Schmitt

Pepper: To Fred, Cooper, and Ryder

Contents

Preface

THIS IS THE SECOND EDITION of *The Gender of Sexuality*, a book that has been a fun and informative guide for thousands of students and their professors for over a decade in how to think about the "joint social construction of gender and sexuality." We used that phrase when we originally wrote *The Gender of Sexuality* to focus attention on the fact that there are probably no two areas—gender and sexuality—with more taken-for-granted stereotypes and more armchair experts to expound upon them. Furthermore, there was only limited recognition that when people talk about gender, they often imply things about sexuality, and when they talk about sexuality, they can make assumptions about gender. You'll read definitions of gender, sex, and sexuality in chapter 1, but to guide you here in the beginning, keep in mind that in writing this book we sought to take the hot air out of unquestioned positions about gender and sexuality, especially deeply held "incorrigible" propositions that men and women are fundamentally and essentially different when it comes to sexuality.

What's New?

Over a decade has passed since we first wrote this book, and upon an intensive, detailed revision, we have added twenty-eight new tables, graphs, and images, and about a third of the book is completely new. When we talk about what's "new and improved" about the gender of sexuality—and *The Gender of Sexuality*—three things rise to the top of the list as having changed the most in the recent past: transgender, same-sex marriage, and gender differences.

Transgender. A decade ago, transgender was a topic in our University of Washington course on sexuality—we showed the remarkable documentary *What Sex am I?* to introduce students to a status that was pretty unfamiliar to mainstream students. We sought to dislodge simpleminded notions about the links between gender and sex and the familiar dichotomous ideas about sexuality. The conversations were aimed at helping mainstream students imagine that the relationship between gender and sex is not one-to-one and that there are not just binaries when it comes to sexualities. Even though we wrote a book about the complex relations between gender and sexuality, the topic of transgender was nearly invisible. When we reviewed the first edition we were stunned by the limited attention to transgender people and their experiences. Definitions of transgender identities are in chapter 1.

In this book, as in our world today, the broad array of people whom we refer to collectively as transgender have a small, but noticeable, presence. For example, in the spring of 2011, the documentary *Becoming Chaz*, about the transgender journey of Chaz Bono, the child of 1970s musical duo Sonny and Cher, met with great acclaim at the Sundance Film Festival and was covered in a feature article in the *New York Times*. College campuses everywhere no longer have a small gay and lesbian alliance, as was more likely the case a decade ago, and they now include communities for transgender, bisexual, questioning, as well as gay and lesbian students. The transgender experience in the United States and across the globe continues to be challenging. But since we last published this book, the transgender identity is no longer an "exotic outlier" that few people have heard about or feel any need to understand. Transgender is now more likely to be recognized as part of the human experience. Mainstream media, as well as researchers, are more likely to grapple with understanding the lives and rights of transgender people. Furthermore, growing communities of transgender people are freer than in the past to openly identify themselves and to work toward improved public awareness and resources for their needs as individuals and as a group.

Don't get us wrong: We understand the limits of the changes for transgender people—and it can hit close to home. A transgendered colleague in sociology has written movingly about looking for a job as a sociology professor. Questions like "what are you?" (by which the questioner typically means, "what's under your clothes?") were not only painful to endure for the person involved but also, more importantly, interfered with our friend's ability to find a job, despite stellar qualifications, because of stereotypes about how "some" transgender people are too "flamboyant." Our friend's story highlights the way that even people who are trained to understand "social construction" (in this case, sociology professors) can be uncomfortable about accepting someone based on an assessment of professional merit, because they still rely on simple binaries: "You are either a man or a woman, you are either straight or gay (or *maybe* bisexual)."

Same-Sex Marriage. In the mid 1990s, Pepper Schwartz was on the front lines of the nascent battles for same-sex marriage. She testified in the courts in Hawaii and provided background for lawyers seeking to build cases around the country for marriage rights for same-sex couples throughout the United States. We were familiar with the legal circumstance of same-sex marriage but also the political and cultural dispositions toward it. And at that time, we wrote that same-sex marriage was just beginning to make its way into legitimacy—with rights that had been established in Vermont and that had come and gone in Hawaii. But, we said, while its promise was significant, it continued to be *unpopular* with the general public. The Defense of Marriage Act that stipulated that marriage can only include one man and one woman had been passed in the 1990s in the U.S. Congress and signed by President Bill Clinton. In public opinion poll after poll, the population was opposed. Quite opposed.

We have been paying close attention to the gay marriage debates, but when we updated our section on same-sex marriage and saw how far we had come in the past decade, we were amazed. Today, a *majority* of people indicate support or acceptance of same-sex marriage. Among young people, the support is quite large. In some regions, such as New England, the acceptance is broadly held, and five of the six states there have laws granting marriage rights to same-sex couples. The main legal argument in favor of same-sex marriage is that such a ban constitutes gender discrimination.

Keep in mind: the astonishing rise of same-sex marriage rights has received opposition from an influential and vocal minority. Nothing makes that clearer than our map of same-sex rights, figure 5.7. You'll see that as of 2011 there were a number of states where gay and lesbian citizens have gained marriage rights or where marriage rights are observed from other states, but you'll see something else: more than thirty states have explicitly established "defense of marriage" laws that are designed to oppose same-sex marriage. The battle will, no doubt, continue, but the tide has risen remarkably in the past decade, and we believe there is no turning back.

Another issue tied closely to the improvement of same-sex marriage rights has been a small but emerging awareness of *heteronormativity*—or the assumption that whether we build marriages with same-sex people or other-sex people, what's best is to use the heterosexual model. As you'll read in the pages that follow, some progressive activists and scholars are concerned that the emphasis on same-sex marriage inadvertently gives legitimacy to the chaste, docile, and materially oriented and highly gendered form of marriage that emerged in the nineteenth century. Starting in the nineteenth century, marriage was the centerpiece to a view where family functions as a private social safety net that is the sole and best road to prosperity. Its success was explicitly dependent on a gendered division of labor. The irony in the interim years since our earlier edition is that a marriage movement dedicated to strengthening (heterosexual) marriage and encouraging more people to participate was the drum-beat of cultural conservatives who were as passionately opposed to same-sex marriage. What continues to be left out of these oppositional conversations are views of alternative ways to create a caring and secure world for all people.

We wrote extensively in the first edition on how marriage as an institution relies on the "joint social construction of gender and sexuality"; nowadays we use the term *heteronormativity* to make that point. So while the ascendancy of same-sex marriage rights constitutes a greater legal and cultural recognition of "sexual diversity," it has also sharpened many critics' awareness of heteronormativity. The concept of heteronormativity helps critics observe the way in which heterosexuality as well as gender organizes our social institutions! Think of something as ordinary as when your college president, for example, stands up and introduces his wife each time he speaks to the community. This act, while nicely acknowledging his wife's help and support, unwittingly reinforces heteronormativity since it takes as its assumption that a "good spouse" is central to doing business well and is key to performing a public role. It doesn't work the same way when one's partner is same-sex or when the speaker is a woman, not a man. Presumably when public figures thank their spouses in public their spouse has already heard it, so the message seems to be for the audience.

Gender difference and gender gaps. In our first edition, we wrote of the way that men's and women's social and sexual privileges had become increasingly similar over time, and in this edition, we note that the convergence continues. In chapters 2 and 3 we discuss a host of sexual practices—whether we are talking about masturbation, oral sex, or at what age men or women report their first sexual experiences—that reveal considerable "convergence." In chapter 4, updated reports of who has sex outside of (heterosexual) marriage demonstrate similar convergence, especially for younger generations. This is in keeping with larger trends, such as the near parity of men and women in the labor force and the rise in women's economic power in the form of wages.

But gender difference in the social world has not disappeared. In nearly all corners of life, including sexuality, gendered patterns continue to be a feature of experience—even in the way men and women have experienced changes. What to make of it? We argued in our previous edition that on a simple level it shows us just how much gender and gendered statuses are socially constructed. But the specific trends have led us to the conclusion that the changes we report are more of a *difference in kind* than simply a *difference in degree*. In chapter 5, for example, we write about how high-profile sexual scandals are portrayed in recent years. We have no scarcity of cases, nor of variety. The scandals have men at the center, but what has changed has been the narrative around the scandals. In the past, women have been portrayed as "victims" (if wives) and "bimbos" if a third party. Now—in contrast to the 1980s and 1990s—women in these stories are portrayed as heroic and even ironic, as we review several recent dramas. Meanwhile, we noticed that instead of men being treated as "randy playboys" or understandably "naughty," they are more likely to be portrayed as foolish, weak, and an embarrassment. The scandals are gendered, just gendered differently.

What's Our Big Idea?

What has remained the same is that readers of this book will gain useful explanations for why the notion that "men are from Mars, women are from Venus" is misleading, inaccurate, and sometimes downright silly. A good example of this comes from a colleague who told us a funny story of channel surfing. *Loveline*, a cable television talk show about sex and relationships, caught her eye. On it, the "relationship expert" host claimed that when a woman's estrogen (a sex-related hormone) is high, she is at her most loving, passive, and receptive for her partner's vigorous sexual attention. In other words, the speaker was suggesting that love and passivity are physiologically linked for a woman. Put another way, a woman's emotional and sexual response is dictated by her ovulation cycle. The implication of this line of thinking: the more sexually passive a woman is, the more she really loves you. We wonder, did the host (who was a guy) mean that if a woman is active or aggressive during sex, she really isn't in love or receptive? And what about when both sex partners are women, and both are high on estrogen? How in the world do these "naturally passive" women bring themselves to actually get any sexual activity done? Did the speaker have data to indicate that women who have higher-than-average estrogen levels are more loving and receptive than other women are? Of course not. Not only is the biological information about estrogen incorrect in this case (the story is complicated, but estrogen appears to stimulate aggression, not passivity, as we discuss in chapter 1) but also this account relies on biological sex differences to interpret sexual behavior. There are much better data that indicate that our culture's social scripts, not estrogen levels, influence women's sexual behavior and dictate passivity under some circumstances. We assure you that "receptivity" increases when sexual partners are skillful at making love, not when estrogen reaches some magical level.

What distressed our friend most while watching the show was the camera's pan of the audience. It revealed women and men alike nodding in agreement with the remarks of the speaker. Indeed, the show and its "talk" about estrogen and women's sexual passivity are another contribution to our culture's sexual scripts. What may be more evident after reading this book is how such talk about women's sexuality also defines and constrains sexual expression for men. It is all too commonplace to think of men and women as fundamentally different and to use biology to account for social behaviors.

Since we last published this book, some helpful books have appeared that help to connect the experience of bodies (and sexuality) with the experience of gender. For example, *Gendering Bodies* (Crawley, Foley, and Shehan 2008) gives a lively account of how gendered messages about bodies—think about slang used for penises, for example—and the social world shape our physical bodies, how we relate to our bodies, and how the world relates to us based on our bodies. With our book, we retain the focus on examining gender and human sexuality together—and we hope that we make it evident that neither can be examined separately. Gender and sexuality are an exciting and entertaining combination but also a serious area of study. There are important human consequences that follow from the ways in which sexuality is organized around gender—and gender around sexuality. Consequences range from how some people get punished for unusual behavior while others do not, to how medical advice and research proceeds or how social resources are spent, to how much men and women are willing to bend themselves out of shape so as to fit in to social norms.

Take a recent news story about a woman at age sixty-three who, through the miracle of modern technology, gave birth to a baby. Certainly the story provoked gossip and curiosity in both mainstream media and the tabloids. But the issues around the debate zero in on the link between gender and sexuality. The most obvious issue is, Why was this woman sanctioned so intensely for having a baby at her mature age? Why do men who father children after age sixty receive, at least, a bit of congratulatory nudging to the effect of "We didn't know you still had it in you!" while women are labeled "sick" or "selfish"? The double standard is fairly obvious, and it is a valuable jumping-off point for thinking about gender and sexuality. A less obvious issue that we would invite students to consider is what produces in people, like this particular mother and her partner, the desire to reproduce (again) so much so that she is willing to go to extraordinary effort and expense to produce this child? This aspect of the case reminds us of the rather remarkable intersection between biological capacity for producing children and a socially constructed strong preference for motherhood as an identity-confirming role. So powerful is the appeal of motherhood—from a social perspective—that this woman lied about her age to her doctor and paid big bucks so that she could override nature and social convention to enact what must have been for her a central affirming role in her life. Was her act a product of "nature" or of "culture"?

Although instructors and students who read this book will enjoy the feminist perspectives we take, this book is not about feminisms per se but about analytic tools for understanding gender and sexuality. We owe a tremendous debt to the intellectual contributions of various feminisms to the area of gender and sexuality. In the 1960s and 1970s, feminists brought personal, everyday experiences to the political world and drew attention to logically inconsistent arguments, such as the argument that it is okay for men but not for women to have children after age sixty. Feminist approaches have challenged assumptions about gender and sexuality that are either implicit or explicit in explanations of social phenomena. As time has progressed, other feminisms have served as a guidepost for improving (and raising questions about) a variety of theoretical approaches to social behavior, including social constructionism, symbolic interactionism, conflict theory, functionalism, exchange theory, and rational choice theory. Feminist approaches in the past decade have helped us focus more on social, racial, economic, and transglobal gender comparisons as well as various kinds of sexual inequality and have provided a platform for highlighting *intersectionality*—the way our multiple statuses operate simultaneously—that is not just theoretical but practical. The intellectual skepticism that has emerged from feminist thinkers enables us all to think about how—and why—gender and sexuality have been constructed.

Sexuality and gender studies have *also* advanced tremendously with the study of gay and lesbian experiences. Same-sex relationships involve doing sex that is, by definition, for nonprocreative reasons or, in other words, for pleasure only. Public arguments against homosexuality are influenced by negative attitudes toward sex that is an act of intimacy and pleasure. In many ways, the fight for civil rights undertaken by gay and lesbian rights organizations and others has highlighted our cultural ambivalence about sex for pleasure. It also has highlighted the different social response to gay men on the one hand and lesbians on the other (which we address in our book). Homosexuality, like all other sexualities, is caught up with and complicated by different societal attitudes about men's and women's sexualities.

How Did We Write This Book?

How did we write this book? As sociologists who teach and do research but also often write and speak to general audiences, we integrated evidence and anecdote, theory and experience to engage our readers. We used experience with our students—at Framingham State University and the University of

Washington—to think through important questions that are on the minds of students. We help students investigate their curiosity about where images of gendered sexual differences come from, in whose interest they operate, and how social context influences the performance of gender in sexual settings. We offer new ways for students to think about gender and sexuality. We remind the reader with data and examples that the social construction of sexuality is a part of everyone's experience—whether they are actively involved in sexual relationships or not. With our own students in mind—undergraduates we've encountered in general sociology courses as well as in more specialized courses on gender, family, or sexuality—we revised this book in ways to make it current, personal, and reliable. We hope to teach students to think like sociologists about gender and sexuality.

What were our personal motivations for getting involved in this area? While we have presented our professional reasons for writing about gender and sexuality, quite honestly, a couple of things in our personal backgrounds also helped shape us into scholars interested in sex and gender. When we were children—Pepper in the early 1960s and Virginia in the 1970s—we both discovered that talking about sex was fun and a surefire way to capture people's attention. Pepper had one of the youngest consciousness-raising reading groups ever, as she and a bunch of eleven-year-old girls would gather in her parents' basement and discuss and study her mother's books on human sexuality. Virginia was schooled early by her Aunt Betsy and Uncle Frank's irreverence about sex and what today would be called their "sex positivity." No subject was off limits around their breakfast table. Virginia loved for her mother to read to her from the biography of Madame de Pompadour, courtesan to King Louis XV, and she was eager to tell school friends and their parents' driving carpool all she had learned about the sexual habits of the French aristocracy. As adults, we still love to talk about sex—it is so provocative, so personally meaningful, and there are so many unanswered questions to explore. It never escapes us that getting paid to talk about orgasms in public is an unusual job. It is a pleasure, therefore, to put some of these observations and studies on paper and to share them with you. We hope that you, our readers, will share our curiosity and enthusiasm, and it is with those high expectations that we submit this book to you.

Acknowledgments

THIS IS THE SECOND EDITION of *The Gender of Sexuality* and there were many people who helped us to bring the first edition to fruition—in particular, the founders of the Gender Lens Series: Judith Howard, Barbara Risman, Mary Romero, and Joey Sprague. Our volume came out early in the life of this elaborate series, and we have been proud to be a part of it.

Judith Howard was the primary Madrina of our first edition and shared the oversight with Barbara Risman, who in turn oversaw the completion of this edition. Judy's rigor and diplomacy are always elegantly combined in equal proportions, and her continued engagement with us in the ongoing dialogue about puzzles of gender and sexuality have made us and this book better. Barbara, too, is remarkable as an editor and a colleague. She is able to challenge and push with great directness, but her gift is the support, solidarity, and recognition that she provides to colleagues. Thanks also to Steve Rutter (no relation!) who originally published this book with Pine Forge Press. We owe a debt of gratitude to the Department of Sociology at the University of Washington, a nexus for Pepper, Virginia, Judy, and Barbara.

We appreciate Rowman & Littlefield's work to bring this book forward. The late Alan McClare encouraged us to do a second edition, and we are sorry he is not here to see it. Thanks also to Sarah Stanton, Jin Yu, and Elaine McGarraugh.

From Pepper

Pepper thanks the University of Washington Sociology Department for their support of her career research and teaching interest in sexuality and in intimate relationships. As she says, "My colleagues there are first rate as scholars, teachers, and as human beings." She has been helped also over the years by many wonderful undergraduate and graduate students (including Virginia!) as teaching assistants and writing partners. In recognition of this fine department and because of the importance of study and teaching about human sexuality, Pepper has instituted the Pepper Schwartz Endowed Fellowship in Sexuality and Intimate Relationships. It is her hope that this fund will give graduate student support for a subject that has had very few directed fellowships and scholarships. If anyone would like to donate a check of even the most modest sum to this endeavor it would be deeply appreciated and can be sent to the University of Washington, Department of Sociology, Seattle, Washington 98195, and made out to the University of Washington Pepper Schwartz Fellowship.

Additionally, Pepper thanks the following people for their intellectual stewardship and friendship over the years: Janet Lever, Philip Blumstein, John Gagnon, Bill Simon, Gil Herdt, Debra Haffner, Dan Chirot, Dominic Cappello, and Helen Gouldner, some departed, but none forgotten. She is also deeply appreciative of the excellent education and support she received from Washington University in St. Louis and Yale University where she earned her BA, masters, and PhD degrees.

Of course, no one creates a productive life without huge support from friends and family. Pepper explains, "My children Cooper and Ryder have long been a source of pleasure; now, as adults, I am proud of them as people, and I seek their support and counsel regularly. Julie Blacklow is a dear lifetime friend who runs Rosebud River Ranch, a beautiful and peaceful place where I live and where horses and dogs help round out my life. I am indebted to her in a thousand ways. Finally I want to thank my partner in love and life, Fred Kaseburg. Witty wordsmith and careful reader, his take on everything, right or left brained, is invaluable to me."

From Virginia

This edition came to fruition over the first few years of Virginia's teaching at Framingham State University (FSU), after finishing her studies with Pepper at the University of Washington. The FSU Center for Excellence in Learning Teaching Scholarship and Service (CELTSS) provided support for extra time to complete this work as well as support for student assistance on the work. Virginia's student, Keith McNally, who graduated from FSU in 2011, provided many hours of assistance on this manuscript and was a joy to work with.

Thanks to FSU Department of Sociology colleagues Susan Dargan, Ira Silver, Ben Alberti, Jon Martin, and Ellen Zimmerman for their mentorship and support. FSU historian Bridgette Sheridan and FSU postcolonial literature scholar Lisa Eck are fabulous colleagues for thinking about gender and sexuality. Thanks to David Merwin of the FSU Department of Geography for building our map of same-sex civil rights and to Michelle Schmitt for her last minute help with this.

The FSU Sociology Department supported Virginia's creation of a senior sexualities seminar, Sex/Sexualities in Society, in which we were able to pilot the text of *The Gender of Sexuality* 2nd edition. Sex/Sexualities students Sally Kiss, Becca Savi, and Allison Chisholm, along with Keith McNally, helped us to sharpen the material in this book for serious sociology students.

Colleagues at the Council on Contemporary Families have also served as resources for us. Stephanie Coontz has been an energetic source of updated information about sexuality in the context of changing American families. Paula England did original work collecting and analyzing data from the Online College Dating Survey that she began at Stanford; since the publication of the last edition we have both talked to Paula often about the puzzles of knowledge and interpretation within the book. Deborah Siegel has kept us engaged in dialogues about how feminisms have changed in popular as well as academic communities. In addition, she has given Virginia a venue for sharpening arguments about the changing status of gender and sexuality at the blogsite GirlwPen.com. We also benefit from ongoing dialogues with members of Sociologists for Women in Society, whom we connect with daily thanks to their awesome listserv and journal.

Virginia also thanks Bill Grady at Battelle Centers for Public Health Research and Evaluation for sharing additional training in doing sex research. Bill, principal investigator of the National Couples Survey, his co-investigator Lisa Cubbins, and survey director Betsy Payn helped advance her thinking about doing research on sexual behavior, beliefs, and attitudes.

On a personal note, Virginia thanks John Schmitt for being an invaluable intellectual, scientific resource, and for his delightfully generous, useful, and engaging support.

Finally, Virginia wants to acknowledge the training, mentorship, and friendship from Pepper that made it possible for her to keep moving forward as a sex researcher and writer. This book is the fruit of a collaboration that couldn't be closer to perfect, in terms of shared ideas about gender and sexuality; commitment to sociological thinking; a deep belief that academic writing can be serious, interesting, and clear all at once; and a delight in the endless puzzles presented by gender and sexuality.

1

Sexual Desire and Gender

THE GENDER OF THE PERSON you desire is a serious matter, seemingly fundamental to the whole business of romance. And it isn't simply a matter of whether someone is male or female; how well the person fulfills a lover's expectations of masculinity or femininity is of great consequence, as two examples from the movies illustrate.

In the movie *Shallow Hal* (2001), the superficial Hal (played by Jack Black) has a magical experience in which instead of his usual choices of women based on beauty, butts, and breasts alone, women's inner beauty and their outer looks are transformed in his eyes. His friends, who have no such "magical powers," can't believe it when he falls for the obese but kind and loving Rosemary (played by Gwyneth Paltrow). When Hal looks at her we see a beautiful woman; when her friends look at her, they see a woman they wouldn't have lunch with, much less date. In fact, much of the movie's comedy comes from the sight gags ridiculing Rosemary's size (such as showing a titanic splash when she jumps into the pool).

Playing it both ways, the film celebrates Hal's new values. He resists his friend's taunts and their contempt for Rosemary. Hal has learned about inner beauty from his guru (played by Tony Robbins), and it requires great personal strength and integrity to cope with the fact that his dream woman doesn't fulfill community expectations for idealized, slender femininity. However, in the end, the movie itself accepts our cultural comfort with slimness: Hal's "virtuous" preference for inner beauty is rewarded with a slender Gwyneth Paltrow, who ultimately sheds her fat suit.

FIGURE 1.1
Shallow Hal poster doesn't promote the "large" Paltrow. *Shallow Hal* (2001), Twentieth Century-Fox/Photofest.

Gender-bending plot twists are at the center of the British drama *The Crying Game* (1992), which has become a film classic. In it, Fergus (played by Stephen Rea), is an Irish Republican Army underling who meets and falls in love with the lover (Dil, played by Jaye Davidson) of Jody (Forest Whitaker), a British soldier whom Fergus befriended prior to being ordered to execute him. The movie is about passionate love, war, betrayal, and, in the end, loyalty and commitment. After the execution, Fergus seeks out Jody's girlfriend in London out of guilt and curiosity. But Fergus's guilt over Jody's death is a less powerful emotion than his love for Dil, and the pair become romantically and sexually involved. In the end, although Fergus is jailed for terrorist activities, Fergus and Dil have solidified their bond and seem committed to one another.

The Crying Game's story of sexual conquest and love is familiar, but this particular story grabbed imaginations because of a single, crucial detail. Jody's girlfriend Dil, Fergus discovers, turns out to be transgender. Although Fergus is horrified when he discovers his lover is biologically different from what he had expected, in the end their relationship survives.

These movies focus on **sexual desire**. Although sex is experienced as one of the most basic and biological of activities, human beings are profoundly affected by things other than the body's urges. Who we're attracted to and what we find sexually satisfying is not just a matter of the genital equipment we're born with. Our drives and desires are not the simple outcome of a chemistry set inside our bodies. Sexual desire is simultaneously biological and socially constructed: This chapter explains *why* and *how* this happens.

However, before we delve into the whys and wherefores of sex, we need to come to an understanding about what **sex** is. Maybe this sounds like a dumb statement to you, but defining sex is not as easy a task as it may seem, because sex has a number of dimensions.

On one level, sex can be regarded as having both a biological and a social context. The biological (and physiological) refers to how people use their genital equipment to reproduce. Indeed, in a recent study of a large number of college students at the University of Texas, the students reported 237 reasons for having sex—and reproduction was not on the list (Meston and Buss 2007, in figure 1.3). Bodies make the experience of sexual pleasure available, and the intention to reproduce is, in fact, a very minor motivation for most sex acts. People have sex for fun, as a way to communicate their feelings to each other, as a way to satisfy their egos, and for any number of other reasons relating to the way they see themselves and interact with others. In fact, the Texas study came up with some pretty unique reasons, including the desire to burn calories, get rid of a headache, a ploy to make a partner feel powerful, and even to change the topic of conversation!

FIGURE 1.2
The Crying Game poster capitalizes on the shock value of the gender bending in the film. *The Crying Game* (1992), Miramax/Photofest.

At another level, sex involves both what we actually do and how we think about it. **Sexual behavior** refers to the sexual acts that people engage in. These acts not only include petting and intercourse but also seduction and courtship. While our first thoughts about sexual behavior might be about partnered sexual acts, in fact sexual behavior also involves the things people do alone for pleasure. In general, either partnered or individual sexuality is preceded by **sexual desire**, which is the combination of physical and mental motivation to engage in sexual acts. Sexual desire is that combination of forces that "turn people on." A person's **sexuality** consists of both behavior and desire.

The most significant dimension of sexuality is **gender**. Gender relates both to the biological and social context of sexual behavior and desire. We tend to believe we know whether someone is a man or a woman not because we do a physical examination and determine what their **sex** is (that is, that the person is biologically male or biologically female) but because we are picking up cues that reveal gender in our culture. We notice whether a person demonstrates masculine or feminine characteristics. Gender is *enacted*; we have expectations of what men and women should look like and act like and, when someone meets those expectations, it telegraphs whether they are male or female to the observer. Thus, animals, like people, tend to be identified as male and female in accordance with the reproductive function, but only people are described by their gender, as a man or a woman.

---

1. I was "in the heat of the moment."
2. It just happened.
3. I was bored.
4. It just seemed like "the thing to do."
5. Someone dared me.
6. I desired emotional closeness (i.e., intimacy).
7. I wanted to feel closer to God.
8. I wanted to gain acceptance from my friends.
9. It's "exciting," adventurous.
10. I wanted to make up after a fight.
11. I wanted to get rid of aggression.
12. I was under the influence of drugs.
13. I wanted to have something to tell my friends.
14. I wanted to express my love for the person.
15. I wanted to experience the physical pleasure.
16. I wanted to show my affection to the person.
17. I felt like I owed it to the person.
18. I was attracted to the person.
19. I was sexually aroused and wanted the release.
20. My friends were having sex, and I wanted to fit in.

Source: Meston and Buss 2007.

FIGURE 1.3. Top 20 of 237 reasons college students have sex: "Reproduce" is not on the list.

When we say something is **gendered** we mean that a social consensus exists in a given culture that has determined what is appropriately masculine and feminine. There are numerous social practices that create and sustain the consensus in a given society. For example, traditional marriage is a gendered institution: The definition involves a masculine part (husband) and a feminine part (wife). Gendered phenomena, like traditional marriage, gather traction over a long period of time and therefore appear "naturally" so. But, as recent debates about same-sex marriage underscore, the role of gender in marriage is the product of historical and contemporary social processes and beliefs about men, women, and marriage. There is no DNA program that determines marital roles. In examining how gender influences sexuality, moreover, you will see that gender rarely operates alone: class, culture, race, and individual differences also combine to influence sexuality.

This book explores and takes issue with the assumptions that sexuality is *naturally* gendered and rooted in biology, that men and women are *fundamentally* different sexually, and that this difference is consistent and universal across societies. Of course, what appears "natural" in one society may be very different in another. By calling the book *The Gender of Sexuality*, we challenge you to think about how even things that people tend to consider biological, like a woman's love for her baby, are influenced enormously by the social processes that determine what motherhood is all about and how motherhood is different from fatherhood. By subtitling our book *Exploring Sexual Possibilities*, we suggest that enormous variety exists—and even more variety *can* exist—in terms of how individuals, partners, and groups can organize sexuality.

Sexuality is a complex bit of business and as a result, the study of sexuality also presents methodological challenges. Sexual thoughts and behavior are typically private. Researchers must rely on what people say they want and do sexually, and these reports, as much as the desire and behavior itself, are influenced by what people believe they are supposed to feel and say. In this book, we will piece together this puzzle of acts, thoughts, and feelings with insights provided by survey research, physiological studies, ethnography, history, philosophy, and even art, cinema, and literature.

Desire: Attraction and Arousal

The most salient fact about sex is that nearly everybody is interested in it. Most people like to have sex, and they talk about it, hear about it, and think about it. But some people are obsessed with sex and are willing to have sex with anyone or anything. Others are aroused only by particular conditions and hold exacting criteria. For example, some people will have sex only if they are positive that they are in love, that their partner loves them, and that the act is sanctified by marriage. Others view sex as not much different from eating a sandwich. They neither love nor hate the sandwich; they are merely hungry, and they want something to satisfy that hunger. What we are talking about here are differences in desire. When you read those examples, though, you might notice that you have judgments about these different stances and what you believe to be normal or typical. What we are saying is that these are examples of sexual possibilities. As you have undoubtedly noticed, people differ in what they find attractive, and they are also physically aroused by different stimuli.

Many people assume that differences in sexual desire are more or less dictated by whether a person is a man or a woman. In large representative surveys about sexual behavior, men inevitably report more frequent sex, with more partners, and in more diverse ways than women do. In chapter 2, we will review that evidence. However, first we'd like to consider the approaches we might use to interpret it. Many observers argue that when it comes to sex, men and women have fundamentally different biological wiring. Others use the evidence to argue that culture has mandated and demanded marked sexual differences among men and women. We believe, however, that it is hard to tease apart biological differences and socially produced differences. As soon as a baby enters the world, he or she receives messages about gender and sexuality. In the United States, for example, disposable diapers come adorned in pink for girls and blue for boys. In case people aren't sure whether to treat the baby as masculine or feminine in its first years of life, the diaper signals them. "Baby Bangs Hair Band" is a product you can find online that is designed for "baby girls" who, per the advertisement, have everything but hair. The advertisement proclaims, "I'm not a boy!" and their hair band adds the requisite "feminine" hair so that the baby's parents can clarify things with the world. The assumption is that girl babies really are different from boy babies and the difference ought to be displayed. This different treatment continues throughout life, and therefore a sex difference at birth becomes amplified into gender difference as people mature.

Gendered experiences and guidelines have a great deal of influence on men's and women's sexual desire. As a boy enters adolescence, he hears jokes about boys' insuppressible desire. Girls are told the same thing, and they are told that their own desire is much less impulsive; therefore, it is their duty to resist because it's easier for them to forgo sex. These gender messages not only alter attitudes and behavior (such as whether a person grows up to prefer sex with a lover rather than a stranger) but also alter physical and biological experience. For example, a girl may be discouraged from fiercely competitive sports that can produce rough body contact. If she has never felt the thrill of aggressive sport or felt physically brave or powerful, it may influence how she develops physically, how she feels about her body, and even how she relates to the adrenaline rush associated with physical competition. Hypothetically, a person who is accustomed to adrenaline responses experiences sexual attraction differently from one who is not.

What follows are three "competing" explanations of differences in sexual desire between men and women: biological, evolutionary psychological, and social constructionist perspectives on sexuality. These are competing approaches because each tends to be presented as a complete explanation in itself, to the exclusion of other explanations. Our goal, however, is to provide a clearer picture of how "nature" and "nurture" are intertwined in the production of sexualities. We call this view an **integrative perspective** on sexuality.

The Biology of Desire: Nature's Explanation

No one, including us, would deny that biology is a critical factor in sexuality. Some things are ordained by our genes. For example, human beings do not fall in love with fish or sexualize trees. Humans are designed to respond to other humans. And human activity is, to some extent, organized by the physical equipment humans are born with, the concentration of nerve endings in specific erogenous zones and our access to those zones. Imagine if people had fins instead of arms or laid eggs instead of fertilizing them during intercourse. Romance would look quite different.

Although biology seems to be a constant (a component of sex that is fixed and unchanging), the social world tends to mold biology as much as biology shapes humans' sexuality. Each society develops rules for sexual conduct. Therefore, how people experience their biology varies widely. In some societies, women act intensely aroused and active during sex; in others, they are told that sexuality is an unpleasant burden that they must endure. There is little or no foreplay, intercourse is brief, and so most of these women have no concept of orgasm. In fact, women in some settings, when told about orgasm, do not even believe it exists, as anthropologists discovered in a region of Nepal. We know that orgasm is physically possible, barring damage to or destruction of the sex organs, so clearly culture (not biology) is at work in this case. Even ejaculation is culturally dictated. In some countries, it is considered healthy to ejaculate quickly and often; in others, men are told to conserve semen and ejaculate as rarely as possible. Biological capacity may not be different, but the way bodies behave during sex varies according to social beliefs and customs.

Sometimes the dictates of culture are so rigid and powerful that the so-called laws of nature can be overridden. For example, in American society biological parenthood is seen as so important that infertility treatment has become a several-billion-dollar industry. Couples use technological interventions that give them a chance to have a baby "naturally" (Rutter 1996). Recently, in England a child was born to a sixty-three-year-old woman who had been implanted with fertilized eggs. The cultural emphasis on reproduction and parenthood was so compelling that, in this case, a woman far beyond the age in which conception is generally possible went through considerable expense to fund technological interventions so that she could override biology. Amazing as that technology is, the subsequent birth of her child can be argued as even more of a psychological and cultural event than a biological one! Desire—be it for a live birth or a lot of sex—needs the right social and cultural context for it to emerge and for it to be validated. Nevertheless, some researchers have primarily focused on the biological foundations of sexual desire. They believe the endocrine system and hormones, brain structure, and genetics dictate sexual interest and arousal. Strictly biological research on sex proposes that many so-called sexual choices are not choices at all but are dictated by the body. Such a view generates enthusiasm for using drugs, like Viagra, to address "problems" with sexual desire (as we discuss in chapter 4).

The Influence of Hormones

Biological explanations of sexual desire concentrate on the role of hormones. Testosterone has the reputation of producing the essence of masculinity: it is generally used to explain male strength, aggression, and sexual potency (Fausto-Sterling 1992). Likewise, estrogen is used to explain the essence of womanhood. These biological products are markers in everyday speech for a host of assumptions about masculinity and femininity. To wit: we found a web-based article titled "No Hablo Estrogen!: Becoming Bilingual with the Opposite Sex." The implication is that the gulf between men's and women's cultures is explained by hormonal differences. While there are some "masculinizing" and "feminizing" functions for testosterone (for example, facial hair growth) and estrogen (such as soft skin tone), these are surface changes, not the creation of different propensities for love, nurturance, or bonding. A careful read of the research indicates that environment shapes hormone production as much as hormones play a role in behavior and that many presumed relationships between testosterone and masculinity and estrogen and femininity are more complex than the notion of "opposite sexes" would suggest. To start with, yes, testosterone appears to be the most important hormone for sexual function. But here's where myth and reality diverge: it is present in both men and women, it is important for sexual function in both men and women, and it functions in some hard-to-predict ways.

Testosterone is produced in the testes for men and ovaries for women; small amounts are also produced in the adrenal glands. Men have twenty to thirty times as much testosterone as women; yet women are more reactive to smaller amounts. Numerous research studies identify testosterone as an enabler for male sexual desire (Bancroft 1978; Masters, Johnson, and Kolodny 1995); others cite the link between female sexual desire and testosterone (Rako 1999). For men with low sexual desire associated with low levels of testosterone, testosterone is used to improve their **libido** (interest in sex). Testosterone is used similarly for women with low sexual desire—although as of summer 2011, the FDA was still investigating the safety of testosterone patches for women. Still, according to *Newsweek* (2005), one-fifth of all testosterone prescriptions are written for women (Kantrowitz and Wingert).

As important as testosterone is, we cannot predict a man's sexual tastes, desires, or behavior by measuring it. Indeed, for both men and women, testosterone levels are *not* associated with arousability—although it is associated with pursuing opportunities to become aroused (Tolman and Diamond 2001). Although a low level of testosterone in men is sometimes associated with lower sexual desire, this is not predictably the case. Furthermore, testosterone level does not always influence sexual performance. Indeed, in some studies, testosterone is being developed as a male contraceptive (McLachlan 2000), thus demonstrating that desire and the biological goal of reproduction need not be linked to sexual desire.

Testosterone has also been implicated in nonsexual behaviors, such as aggression. Aggression, along with sexuality, is at issue when we talk about testosterone-fueled macho men. But recent research on testosterone and aggression in men has turned the testosterone-aggression connection on its head: low levels of testosterone have been associated with aggression, and higher levels have been associated with calmness, happiness, and friendliness (Angier 1995; Keenan 2004).

Meanwhile, as we have mentioned, testosterone is also found in women, although at levels much lower than men's. The testosterone discrepancy has incorrectly been used as evidence for "natural" gender differences in sex drives. The seemingly low levels can be deceptive since women's testosterone receptors are more sensitive than men's to smaller amounts of testosterone (Kolodny, Masters, and Johnson 1979). Even more confusing, some research indicates that estrogen, which is derived from testosterone, is the more influential hormone in fueling sexual interest and human aggression. In animal research, male mice whose ability to respond to estrogen had been bred out of them lost much of their natural aggressiveness. Where does this leave us? It leaves us saying "not so fast" when we hear biological explanations that posit any single interpretation of the hormones testosterone and estrogen and their links to sexuality. It helps us recognize that a "his-versus-hers" world—even at the biological level—is not that distinct. Furthermore, as we will discuss below in more detail, testosterone levels are influenced by such environmental factors as competition, family conflict, even parental status.

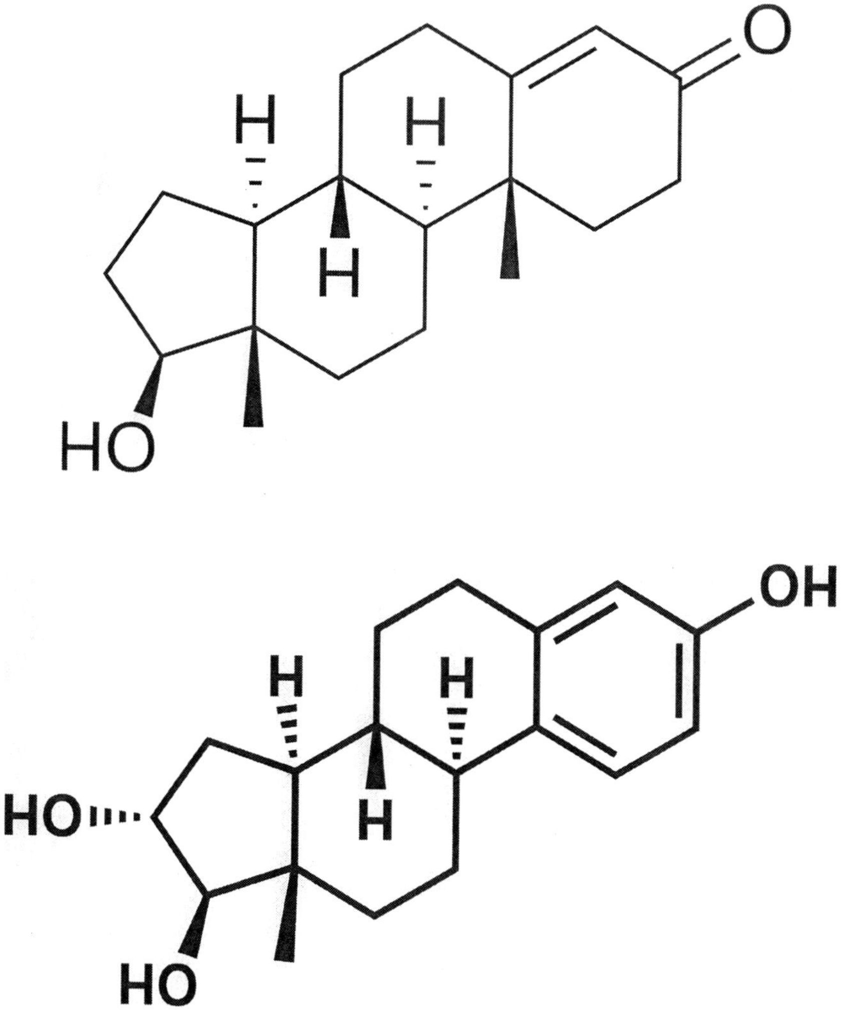

FIGURE 1.4
Testosterone and estrogen chemical composition: Nothing says sexy like these chemical compounds. http://en.wikipedia.org/wiki/File:Estriol_v2.png#filehistory; http://en.wikipedia.org/wiki/File:Testosterone.svg.

Perhaps one mistake we make about human hormones is to forget how much they fluctuate over daily, weekly, and monthly cycles. Some biologists have suspected that a woman's sexual desire may be linked to the impact of hormones as levels change during her reproductive cycle. (No evidence shows men's sexual desire to be cyclical.) Some researchers have observed that a woman's sexual desire is linked to the fertile portion of her cycle (Bullivant et al. 2004). This research is motivated by the hypothesis that sexual interest in women is best explained as the product of thousands of years of natural selection, part of the process of evolution. Natural selection would favor for survival those women who are sexually aroused during ovulation (the time women are most likely to become pregnant). These women would be reproductively successful and therefore pass on to their children the propensity for arousal during ovulation. One study in 2002 (Gangestad et al.) found this association, and found that ovulating women were more interested in alternatives to their current partner—perhaps seeking to find a "better mate" when they are fertile; yet another (Pillsworth et al. 2004) found that ovulatory shifts in desire were *not* linked to a shift from the desire for a current partner to the desire for an alternative partner. The evidence for these theories is mixed.

Table 1.1 helps summarize all these variations. It charts how testosterone and estrogen are not clearly linked to either men's or women's desire. Research shows a complicated relationship between hormones and sexuality. Hormonal fluctuations may not be the central cause of sexual behavior or any social acts; instead, social circumstances may be the cause of hormonal fluctuation. A famous series of experiments makes the point. One animal experiment took a dominant Rhesus monkey out of his environment and measured his testosterone level. It was very high, suggesting that he had reached the top of the monkey heap by being hormonally superior. Then the monkey was placed among even bigger, more dominant monkeys than he. When his testosterone was measured again, it was much lower. One interpretation is that social hierarchy had influenced the monkey's biological barometer. His

TABLE 1.1
Sexual Role of Hormones

Hormone	Influence	Weakness to Theory
Testosterone (male hormone)	Triggers sexual arousal	Also present in women and also triggers women's sexual arousal; associated with calmness, not aggression
Estrogen (female hormone)	Triggers menstrual cycle	Also present in men; associated with aggression, not calmness

testosterone level had adjusted to his social status. In this case, the social environment shaped physiology (Rose, Holaday, and Bernstein 1970). In a study of teenagers and their parents, Booth and colleagues found that testosterone levels increased for sons who were in conflict with their parents (Booth et al. 2003). The social context in these cases shaped the biological expression.

Finally, oxytocin, a hormone released in the brain, has become a favorite topic for many researchers who are teasing apart the differences among sexual desire, sexual arousal, and romantic attachment. Oxytocin is released in both men and women at orgasm—it stimulates the uterus to move semen toward fallopian tubes for fertilization and induces similar contractions in men's seminal vesicles. Psychologically, on the one hand, it stimulates desire, and on the other hand, it triggers at least temporary feelings of love and attachment. Oxytocin gives us hints that acts of sex have a social and emotional context and helps us note how closely linked what happens *between* people is to what happens *within* a person's body.

The Mechanisms of Arousal

Biological explanations of gender differences in sexuality owe a great deal to the work of Dr. William Masters and Virginia Johnson and their study of the human sexual arousal system. Unlike other researchers, who had relied on self-reports, these pioneers actually hooked up their participants to machines that could provide information on physiological responses to sexual stimuli. They based their findings on the laboratory observation of over ten thousand sexual episodes experienced by 382 women and 312 men (Masters and Johnson 1966). The research team photographed the inside of women's vaginas during arousal and observed circulatory and nipple response, and they observed the rise and fall of men's penises.

Notice that Masters and Johnson focused on bodies rather than the social and relationship contexts in which sex occurs. From the start, the research was limited to information about the mechanisms of sexuality. Remember, mechanisms—whether of sexual response or facilitating your waking up in the morning—are a useful piece of the puzzle of behavior. Rubbing your body a certain way might be a mechanism of arousal, just as setting your alarm for 9 a.m. might be a mechanism of getting up in time for class. They can tell you how to make a behavior happen, or how to change a behavior, but they cannot tell you why.

It's not hard to imagine that the responses of men and women hooked to machines and under observation might well be different from a loving couple's first (or ninety-first) sexual episode. In addition, the participants were far from "typical" or randomly selected. To the contrary, they were sexual extroverts such as prostitutes, or people who were selected for their ability to have "effective stimulation"—in other words, people able to easily masturbate to orgasm. As far as we can tell, there is no reason to believe they were representative of an average group of sexually active individuals.

Nevertheless, with this information Masters and Johnson created the new field of sex therapy, which sought to understand and modify the mechanisms of human sexual response or, as the case might be, nonresponse. The sexual therapies they developed were based on what they inferred from their data to be differences between male and female patterns of arousal and were focused above all on the ability to have an orgasm.

One of Masters and Johnson's most important observations was a sexual difference between men and women in the timing of the excitement cycle. The key difference is that men's sexual physiology has a quicker trigger. Comparing men's and women's sexual responses is like comparing sprinters (men) to long-distance runners (women). Men are excited sooner, have an orgasm sooner, relatively quickly lose their erection, and require a "refractory" period before sexual excitation and erection can begin again. This refractory period among young or exceptional men could be very brief. But for the majority of men, twenty minutes, an hour, or even a day might be necessary.

Women's sexual response cycle is, in general, a slower and more sustained proposition. The increase of blood to the genital area that accompanies arousal takes longer and remains longer after orgasm. This slower buildup may in part account for the longer time it typically takes women to be ready for sexual intercourse. Additionally, the longer time women take to reach and stay in the plateau phase theoretically makes orgasm less automatic than it is for men. However, the fact that blood leaves the genital area slowly after orgasm means that many women require little or no refractory period if re-stimulated. Consequently, Masters and Johnson described women as potentially "multiorgasmic." In other words, some women can have more than one orgasm in fairly short succession.

These physiological findings were the basis for a theory about men's and women's mating styles. Masters and Johnson considered men's more-quickly-triggered mechanisms to be at odds with the slower mechanisms of women (see figure 1.5). On the other hand, the ability of women to have more than one orgasm suggested that women might be the superior sexual athletes under certain conditions. Masters and Johnson's followers work within a model that addresses sexual problems by matching male and female sexual strategies more closely than they believe nature has done. In fact, it might be argued that Masters and Johnson's general approach to sexual counseling was to teach men to understand and cope with the slower female sexual response and to modify their own sexual response so that they do not reach orgasm before their partner is fully aroused. Masters and Johnson were really the

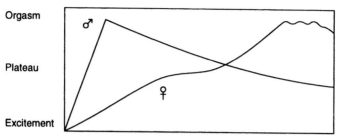

FIGURE 1.5
Mismatched sexual response of women and men.

parents of a new field: research-based sexual therapy. And, while they have been criticized for attention to the mechanics of sexual intercourse over the psychological state of the partners, their therapeutic approach did recognize that communication was the key context for making a sex life succeed or fail.

Evolutionary Psyshology

The past few decades of research on sexuality have produced a new school of human behavior-evolutionary psychology (sometimes also called sociobiology) that explains most gender differences as strategies of sexual reproduction. According to evolutionary psychologist David Buss (1995), "Evolutionary psychologists predict that the sexes will differ in precisely those domains in which women and men have faced different sorts of adaptive problems" (164). By "those domains," Buss refers to reproduction, which is the only human function that depends on a biological difference, between men and women. From the evolutionary psychologist perspective, however, myriad gender differences—from problem solving to emotion regulation—can be linked back to differences in reproductive and survival strategies for men and women.

The key assumption of evolutionary psychological theory is that humans have an innate, genetically triggered impulse to pass on their genetic material through successful reproduction. This impulse is called **reproductive fitness.** The human species, like other species that evolutionary psychologists study, achieves immortality by having children who live to the age of reproductive maturity and produce children themselves. Evolutionary psychologists seek to demonstrate that almost all male and female behavior, and especially sexuality, is influenced by this one simple but powerful proposition.

Evolutionary psychologists start at the species level. Species are divided into *r* and *K* reproductive categories. Those with *r* strategies obtain immortality by mass production of eggs and sperm. The *r* species is best illustrated by fish. The female manufactures thousands of eggs, the male squirts millions of sperm over them, and that is the extent of parenting. According to this theory, the male and female fish need not pair up to nurture their offspring. Although thousands of fertilized fish eggs are consumed by predators, only a small proportion of the massive quantity of fertilized eggs must survive for the species to continue. In the *r* species, parents need not stay together for the sake of the kids.

In contrast, humans are a *K* strategy species, and therefore, have a greater investment in each fertilized egg. Human females and most female mammals have very few eggs, especially compared to fish. Moreover, offspring take a long time to mature in the mother's womb and are quite helpless after they are born, with no independent survival ability. Human babies need years of supervision before they are independent. Thus, if a woman wants to pass on her genes (or at least the half her child will inherit from her), she must take good care of her dependent child. The baby is a scarce resource. Even if a woman is pregnant from sexual maturation until menopause, the number of children she can produce is quite limited. This limitation was particularly true thousands of years ago. Before medical advances of the nineteenth and twentieth centuries, women were highly unlikely to live to the age of menopause. Even as late as 1900 in the United States, nine of every one thousand births ended in death for the mother. In 1997, that rate was fewer than nine mothers' deaths in every 100,000 births (CDC 1999). In the past, complications from childbirth commonly caused women to die in their twenties or thirties. Where the food supply was scarce, women were less likely to be successful at conceiving, further reducing the possibility of generating offspring.

Thus, from the evolutionary psychological perspective, "men inseminate, women incubate." The human female's reproductive constraints (usually one child at a time, only so many children over a life cycle, and a helpless infant for a long period of time) shape most of women's sexual and emotional approaches to men and mating. According to the theory, women have good reason to be more selective than men about potential mates. They want to find a man who will stick around and continue to provide resources and protection to this child, at least until the child has a good chance of survival. Furthermore, because a woman needs to create an incentive for a man to remain with her, females have developed more sophisticated sexual and emotional skills specifically geared toward creating male loyalty and commitment to their mutual offspring.

Evolutionary psychologists say that differences in reproductive capacity and strategy also shape sexual desire. Buss asserts that reproductive strategies form most of the categories of desire: Older men generally pick younger women because they are more fertile; younger women seek older men who have more status, power, and resources (a cultural practice known as hypergamy) because such men can provide for their children. Furthermore, from this point of view, health and reproductive capacity make youth generally sexier, and even certain shapes of women's bodies (such as an "ideal" hip-to-waist ratio epitomized by an hourglass figure, which supposedly correlates with ability to readily reproduce) are widely preferred (Buss 1994)—despite varying standards of beauty across cultures. Likewise, men who have demonstrated their fertility by producing children are more sought after than men who have not (Buss 1994). Evolutionary psychologists even argue that intellectual endeavor, such as displays of a sense of humor, are all part of the signals of fitness that link human behavior back to reproduction, or what Geoffrey Miller refers to as the "mating mind" (2001).

According to evolutionary psychologists, men's tastes for recreational sex, unambivalent lust, and a variety of partners are consistent with maximizing their production of children. Men's sexual interest is also more easily aroused because sex involves fewer costs to them than to women, and the ability for rapid ejaculation has a reproductive payoff. On the other hand, women's taste for relationship-based intimacy and greater investment in each sexual act is congruent with women's reproductive strategies.

In a field that tends to emphasize males' "natural" influence over reproductive strategies, evolutionary anthropologist Helen Fisher (1992) offers a feminist twist. Her study of hundreds of societies shows that divorce, or its informal equivalent, occurs most typically in the third or fourth year of a marriage and then peaks about every four years after that. Fisher hypothesizes that some of the breakups have to do with a woman's attempt to obtain the best genes and best survival chances for her offspring. In both agrarian and hunter-gatherer societies, Fisher explains, women breast-feed their child for three or four years—a practice that is economical and sometimes helps to prevent further pregnancy. At the end of this period, the woman is ready and able to have another child. She reenters the mating marketplace and assesses her options to see if she can improve on her previous mate. If she can get a better guy, she will leave the previous partner and team up with a new one. In Fisher's vision, unlike the traditional evolutionary psychological view (see table 1.2), different male and female reproductive strategies do not necessarily imply female sexual passivity and preference for lifelong monogamy.

Another evolutionist, Sarah Blaffer Hrdy, bemoaned the neglect for many years of evolutionary psychologists to recognize the active—not passive—role of females in reproduction and evolution. She reports on the detailed ways in which natural selection has led mothers to be anything but passive. In *Mother Nature* (1999), she writes of the extent to which animal mothers engage in such actions as litter reduction; infanticide; or enabling siblings to destroy weaker members of the litter all as ways of maximizing fitness among the

TABLE 1.2
**Comparison of Traditional and Feminist Evolutionary Psychological
Explanations of Gender Differences in Sexuality**

Perspective	Gender Difference	Explanation
Traditional	Men seek to maximize number of progeny by changing partners as often as possible. Women seek to maximize well-being of progeny by holding on to their partners as long as possible.	Men have biological capacity to inseminate many women in a short period of time; women's biological job is to incubate and nurture young.
Feminist	Men seek to maximize progeny; women seek to maximize well-being of progeny by exchanging partners when improved options are available.	Men and women both seek to maximize number of partners and quality of partners by exchanging when improved options are available.

most promising of her offspring. Hrdy believes that evolutionary psychologists failed to note female activist roles in sexual selection because of investigator bias: the investigators simply could not think of mothers as something *different from* altruistic, nurturing, relationship-focused animals.

As a more traditional evolutionary psychologist, David Buss has emphasized the "attracting" role of women. Hrdy points out how Buss offers women the self-congratulatory notion that women today are by definition the most beautiful women in history! Why? Buss attributes present female gorgeousness to natural selection. He reasons that better-looking women will pass on their genes since these are the women who are best able to attract men and therefore have a better chance of being impregnated and surviving. (We can't help but wonder, however, if being good-looking is a key factor for raising healthy and fit children) Hrdy's research and commentary is interesting in this regard: she looks through an entirely different frame than Buss. She draws attention to neglected evidence of women's evolutionary advantages, not the least of which is the awesome strength mothering has required and the extent to which natural selection will be enhanced by strength and savvy (not just looks). She reminds us that those traits would be necessary for protecting young in a hostile environment. Evolutionary psychologists tell a fascinating but controversial story of how male and female reproductive differences might shape sexuality. To accept evolutionary psychological arguments, one must accept the premise that most animal and human behavior is driven by the instinct to reproduce and improve the gene pool. Critics note that other social science explanations can explain the differences between men and women that evolutionary psychology seeks to explain, but they are supported by more immediate, close-range evidence. We do not need to hypothesize genetic programs to account for loving and passionate attractions between humans or caretaking of the young by adults.

Consider hypergamy, the practice of women marrying men slightly older and "higher" on the social status ladder than they are. Evolutionary psychologists would say women marry "up" to ensure the most fit provider for their offspring. But hypergamy makes little sense biologically. Younger men have more years available to provide resources, and they have somewhat more sexual ability. Notably, in recent years the pattern of hypergamy has declined. For example, in England the share of women who marry younger men grew to 26 percent in the last quarter of the twentieth century. Empirically, however, hypergamy persists, even if it is malleable. Men in the United States marry on average one-and-a-half years later than women (see figure 3.3 in chapter 3 for trends in hypergamy in the United States). It is also a fact that men, overall and in nearly every subculture, have access to more rewards and status than women do. Furthermore, reams of imagery—in movies, advertising, novels, and nonfiction—promote the appeal of older, more resourceful men. Why not, when older, more resourceful men are generating the images? Social practice, in this case, overrides what evolutionary psychologists consider the biological imperative.

The Social Origins of Desire

Your own experience might convince you that biology and genetics alone do not totally control human sexuality. From the moment you entered the world, cues from the environment were telling you which desires and behaviors were "normal" and which were not. Were you told that sex was a beautiful thing between two people who loved one another? Or were you told that even sexual thoughts could lead to dangerous and immoral outcomes? Variability in teaching values and beliefs about sexuality produces people with different sexualities. Who has not had their sexual behavior influenced by their parents' or guardians' explicit or implicit rules? You may break the rules or follow them, but you can't forget them. On a societal level, in the Netherlands, for example, premarital sex is accepted for both men and women, condom ads are seen on major TV channels, and people are expected to be sexually knowledgeable and experienced. The Dutch are likely to associate sex with pleasure in this "sex positive" society. In the United States, however, people are more ambivalent about sex, especially for young people. Sex education is unfunded at the national level, while abstinence education is federally mandated to the tune of over a billion dollars. Condom ads are not allowed on network television, even though most people in the United States over the age of seventeen are sexually active. As you might imagine, feelings about sexuality are different for Americans and the Dutch. In a recent survey, for example, this question was asked in both the United States and The Netherlands: If your teenager was going to have sex with someone, would you allow them to have that experience in your home? Four-fifths of Dutch parents said they would want their child to have their sex life at home; four-fifths of Americans said absolutely not (Schalet 2004 and 2011)! Certainly, biology in the Netherlands is no different from biology in the United States, nor is the physical capacity to experience pleasure different. But in the United States, nonmarital sex for a traditional teenager is more likely to be clandestine and shameful. This may even have some unintended consequences; for example, it may be that taboos add excitement to the experience. Romanticism related to sexuality is certainly greater in the United States than in the Netherlands. In the absence of social constraint, it is possible that sex may even feel a bit mundane. These culturally specific sexual rules and experiences arise from different **norms** of sexuality and expectations of gender equality (or difference), the well-known, unwritten rules of society.

If we look at *changing* notions of men's and women's differences in desire at various points of history, we can see remarkable support for the relative weight of social versus biological influences on sexuality. Throughout history, explanations of male and female desire have varied. At times, the woman was portrayed as the stormy temptress and man the reluctant participant, as in the Bible story of Adam and Eve. In Victorian times, however, women were seen as pure in thought and deed while men were characterized as voracious sexual beasts. In the last one hundred years, we have seen the rates of masturbation for men and women become more similar: this is more evidence that sexual desire is not so much fixed as influenced by contemporary norms and permissions.

These shifting ideas about gender are the social "clothing" for sexuality. The concept of gender typically relies on a dichotomy of male versus female sexual categories, just as the tradition of women wearing dresses and men wearing pants has in the past made the shape of men and women appear quite different. Consider high heels, an on-again, off-again Western fashion. Shoes have no innate sexual function, but high heels have often been understood to be "sexy" for women, even though (or perhaps because) they render women less physically agile. (Of course, women cope. As the saying about Ginger Rogers, the 1940s movie star and dancing partner to Fred Astaire, goes, Ginger "did everything Fred did, only backwards and in high heels.") High heels are so totally understood as feminine equipment that if a man is in high heels, it is typically some sort of visual comedy gag, guaranteed to create a laugh from the audience. Alternatively, high heels are a required emblem of femininity for cross-dressing men.

Such distinctions are important tools of society; they provide guidance to human beings about how to be a "culturally correct" male or female. Theoretically, society could "clothe" its members with explicit norms of sexuality that deemphasize difference and emphasize similarity or even multiplicity. Indeed, that was the case in Maoist China, where all men and women wore black tunics and black pants. In our country, picture unisex hairstyles and men and women both free to wear skirts or pants, norms that prevail from time to time in some subcultures. What is remarkable about dichotomies is that even when distinctions, like male and female norms of fashion, are reduced, new ways to assert an ostensibly essential difference between men and women arise. Societies' rules, like clothes, are changeable. But societies' entrenched tastes for constructing differences between men and women persists, as you can see in the contrasting dancing shoes illustrated in figure 1.6.

The Social Construction of Sexuality

Social constructionists believe that cues from the environment shape human beings from the moment they enter the world. The sexual customs, values, and expectations of a culture, passed on to the young through teaching and by example, exert a powerful influence over individuals. So do social policies and even the way the economy is organized.

When Fletcher Christian sailed into Tahiti in Charles Nordhoff's 1932 account, *Mutiny on the Bounty*, he and the rest of his nineteenth-century English crew were surprised at how sexually available, playful, guilt free, and amorous the Tahitian women were. Free from the Judeo-Christian precepts and straitlaced customs that inhibited English society, the women and girls of Tahiti regarded their sexuality joyfully and without shame. The English men were delighted and, small wonder, refused to leave the island. Such women did not exist in their own society. The women back in England had been socialized within their Victorian culture to be modest, scared of sex, protective of their reputation, and threatened by physical pleasure. As a result, they were unavailable before marriage and did not feel free to indulge in a whole lot of fun after it. The source of the difference was not physiological differences between Tahitian and English women; it was sexual socialization or the upbringing that they received within their differing families and cultures. Tahitians treated sexuality seriously, and it was strongly linked to sacred rituals and religious beliefs. However, they did not believe in sexual repression, and they were not ashamed of their bodies or sexual passion.

FIGURE 1.6
Gendered fashions, real consequences: Red high heel pumps and
men's ballroom shoes. From Stockbyte/Thinkstock (women's shoes);
Jupiterimages/Goodshot/Thinkstock (men's shoes).

If we look back at the Victorian, eighteenth-century England that Nordhoff refers to, we can identify social structures that influenced the norms of women's and men's sexuality. A burgeoning, new, urban middle class created separate spheres in the division of family labor. Instead of sharing home and farm or small business, the tasks of adults in families became specialized: Men went out to earn money; women stayed home to raise children and take care of the home. Although this division of labor was not the norm in all classes and ethnicities in England at the time, the image of middle-class femininity and masculinity became pervasive. The new division of labor increased women's economic dependence on men, which further curbed women's sexual freedoms. Men, on the other hand, had more power, more privacy, and more ability to have sexual liaisons outside of the household. When gender organizes one aspect of life—such as men's and women's positions in the economy—it also organizes other aspects of life, including sex.

In a heterogeneous and individualistic culture like North America, sexual socialization is complex. A society creates an "ideal" sexuality, but different families and subcultures have their own values. For example, even though contemporary society at large may now accept premarital sexuality, a given family may lay down the law: Sex before marriage is against the family's religion and an offense against God's teaching. On a larger scale, abstinence-only sex education is preferred in numerous jurisdictions, despite indications that it is ineffective. (We will discuss sex education more fully below and in chapter 5.) A teenager who grows up in a family in which abstinence is expected may suppress feelings of sexual arousal or channel them into outlets that are more acceptable to the family. Or the teenager may react against her or his background, reject parental and community opinion, and search for what she or he perceives to be a more "authentic" self. Influences such as birth order or observations of a sibling's social and sexual expression can also influence a person's development.

As important as family and social background are, so are individual differences in response to a person's own specific background. In the abstract, people raised to celebrate their sexuality must surely have a different approach to enjoying their bodies than those who are taught that their bodies will betray them and are a venal part of human nature. Yet we cannot always predict adult sexual behavior from a person's childhood socialization or experience. Sexual sybarites and libertines may have grown up in sexually repressive environments, as did pop culture icon and Catholic-raised Madonna. Sometimes individuals whose families promoted sex education and free personal expression are content with minimal sexual expression.

Even with the nearly infinite variety of sexualities that individual experience produces, social circumstances shape sexual patterns. For example, research shows that people who have had more premarital sexual intercourse are likely to have more extramarital intercourse, or sex with someone other than their spouse (Blumstein and Schwartz 1983; Christopher and Sprecher 2000). Perhaps early experience creates a desire for sexual variety and makes it harder for a person to be monogamous. On the other hand, higher levels of sexual desire may generate both premarital and extramarital propensities. Or perhaps nonmonogamous, sexually active individuals are "rule breakers" in other areas also, and resist not only the traditional rules of sex but also other social norms they encounter. Sexual history is useful for predicting sexual future, but it does not provide a complete explanation.

To make explanations more useful, sociologists refer to societal-level explanations as the **macro** view and to individual-level explanations as the **micro** view. At the macro level, the questions pertain to the patterns among different groups. For example, in U.S. culture some women wear skirts and nearly all men do not. Why do women and men, generally speaking, differ in this way? **Social conflict** theory, which examines the way that groups gain and maintain power over resources and other groups, is often used to address macro-level questions. Questions from the conflict perspective help discover the sources of power differences: Whose interest does this custom serve, and how did it evolve? (Look to patriarchy.) What does it constrain or encourage? (Look to physical constraint.) For example, in some countries women are in Purdah—they live in private quarters in the home where visitors cannot see them. They are hidden from the sight of any man except close family members, and in some countries they may not go outside without their husband or father or adult son (or, in some places, not at all, with even those guardians). Whose purposes does this serve? Why has the custom persisted in some places and not others? When the custom changes, what social forces promote the change? What social forces resist change? When you try to answer these questions you will have to look at the history of a country, its religious teachings, who has power over whom, what reinforces that power, what counterforces exist, and what social circumstances would put those customs into question.

Symbolic interactionism deepens this macro-level view by looking at more detailed data at the micro level: How does a particular custom gain its meaning through ordinary, everyday social interaction? For example, what is really happening when a man opens a door for a woman? What changes occur when a woman resists having that door opened for her? Symbolic interactionism proposes that social rules are learned and reinforced through both small acts, such as a man's paying for a woman's dinner, and larger enactments of men's and women's roles, such as weddings, manners and advice books, movies, and television. Through such everyday social interaction, norms are confirmed or resisted. When an adult tells a little girl "good girls don't do this," or when boys make fun of her for wanting to be on the football team, or when she sees women joining a military school getting hazed and harassed, she is learning her society's rules of behavior. When junior high school boys get called "fag" when they are concerned about their clothes or like to dance, they are learning that society expects them to follow the rules of masculinity (that includes rules of heterosexuality)—or else (Pascoe 2007). These rules are learned directly—but they are also learned by every other man and woman, boy and girl, who is witness and participant to the interactions.

All these social and behavioral theories predict that biological impulses are subservient to the influence of social systems on human sexual behavior. Consider high heels again. As anyone who has done so knows, wearing high heels has physical consequences, such as flexed calves while wearing them and aching feet at the end of an evening. But nothing in the physiology of women makes wearing high-heeled shoes necessary, and the propensity to wear high heels is not programmed into women's DNA. Still, 72 percent of women wear high heels—39 percent wear them daily (APMA 2003), despite the pain they report experiencing. An evolutionary psychologist might note that any additional ways a society can invent for women to be sexy accelerate reproductive success. A symbolic interactionist would counter that most rules of sexuality go way beyond what's needed for reproductive success. Footwear has never been shown to be correlated with fertility. Instead, society orchestrates male and female sexuality so that its values are served. A social conflict theorist would go a step further and note that the enactment of gendered fashion norms, individual by individual, serves the political agenda of groups in power at the macro level.

An astounding example of gender-based social control of sexuality was the practice of binding the feet of upper-class women in China, starting around the tenth century. Each foot was bound so tightly that the last two toes shriveled and fell off. Sometimes the instep would be broken to bend the foot in the most desirable way. (Figure 1.7 provides an x-ray schema of the foot without and one with binding.) What was left was so deformed that the woman could barely walk and had to be carried. The function was to allow upper-class men to control the mobility of their women. Bound feet, which were thus associated with status and wealth, became erotically charged. Unbound feet were seen as lower class and repugnant. By the eighteenth and nineteenth centuries, even poor women participated in this practice. This practice was so associated with sexual acceptability and marriageability that it was difficult to disrupt, even when nineteenth-century missionaries from the West labeled the practice barbaric and unsafe. Only later, in 1912, did foot binding become illegal (Greenhalgh 1977).

If you think that molding the body in such ways is a relic of the past, think about plastic surgery, extreme dieting, and the abuse of steroids, and you will realize that humans continually produce diverse ways to change their bodies. How we manipulate our bodies varies; that social norms may be more powerful than an interest in health, however, seems to be a constant. A recent example shocked us: The *British Medical Journal* reported alarm over a small but growing trend of "genitoplasty," or plastic surgery to create what tabloids refer to as "designer vaginas." At a risk to a woman's capacity to experience sexual arousal, still some women elect genital surgery because, according to researchers on the topic, of commercial, media, and social pressures (Liao and Creighton 2007).

Men are not exempt from these extreme physical revisions. Young men now exercise daily to get the requisite "six-pack" musculature, and many take steroids to help them "bulk up." Chest and shoulder implants have increased so that men can have the V-shaped body that advertizing tells them they must have but that nature did not provide. Directors today have "hunks" take off their shirts in almost every romantic or adventure movie, and sometimes strip down further to show their perfectly muscled body. This is relatively new. An audience would rarely see the chest, much less the butt, of a romantic lead in the 1940s, 1950s, and 1960s. When they did, the man's body might be slim, unmuscled, and narrow shouldered. They had nothing like the idealized perfection that started appearing in advertising and movies from the 1990s. Calvin Klein, Abercrombie and Fitch, and other high-concept advertising campaigns started using half- or all-nude teenage models posed in sultry positions that only women had previously occupied. Male audiences, like female audiences before them, feel the pressure to "shape up."

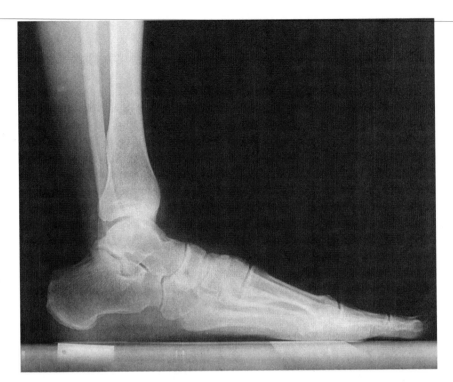

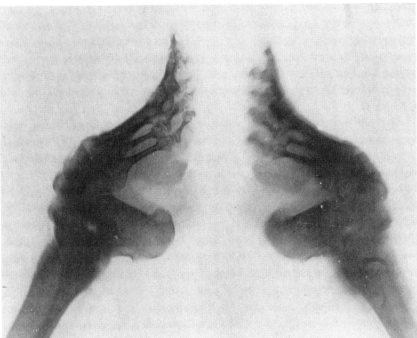

FIGURE 1.7
X-ray schema of foot without and one with binding. Before picture from Digital Vision/ Thinkstock. After picture from LOC, www.loc.gov/pictures/item/91787056/.

Social Control of Sexuality

Norms are so powerful. We know how we are "supposed" to act. In fact, most images of "liberated" sexuality involve breaking a social norm—say, having sex in public rather than in private. The social norm is always the reference point. No one escapes being influenced by their parents' and society's vision of what is sexually appropriate, and this goes beyond superficial compliance. It infiltrates our psyches, and even affects who we desire. From this point of view, sexuality is never totally "free" from its social context. For the past two centuries in North America, people have sought "true love" through personal choice in dating and mating (D'Emilio and Freedman 1988). Although this form of sexual liberation has generated a small increase in the number of mixed pairs—interracial, interethnic, interfaith pairs—the rule of *homogamy*, or marrying within one's class, religion, and ethnicity, still constitutes one of the robust social facts of romantic life. Although in recent history, there is an increased rate of interracial dating pairs, there has not been the same increased rate in interracial marriages (Joyner and Kao 2005). Freedom to choose the person one loves turns out not to be as free as one might suppose.

Despite the norm of true love currently accepted in our culture, personal choice and indiscriminate sexuality have often been construed across cultures and across history as socially disruptive. Disruptions to the social order include liaisons between poor and rich; between people of different races, ethnicities, or faiths; and between members of the same sex. Traditional norms of marriage and sexuality have maintained a given culture's social order by keeping people in familiar and "appropriate" categories. Offenders have been punished by ostracism, curtailed civil rights, or in some societies, death. Conformists are rewarded with social approval and material advantages. Although it hardly seems possible today, mixed-race marriage was against the law in parts of the United States until 1967. Today, interracial marriages are 7.5 percent of all marriages in the United States (Rosenfeld 2007). Same-sex couples were denied even the possibility of legal marriages everywhere in the United States up until 1996 (when the Hawaiian Supreme Court decision briefly made those marriages potentially legal). After many twists and turns in the path, in particular, legal decisions in Vermont, Massachusetts, Iowa, Connecticut, New Hampshire, New York, the District of Columbia, and (although rescinded later) in Maine and California, gay marriage may be a reality, but only in some parts of America. At the present time, same sex couples interested in marrying face a patchwork of states where contrasting and conflicting rights exist (discussed in chapter 5). Other countries, including Belgium, Canada, Denmark, Iceland, the Netherlands, Norway, Portugal, South Africa, Spain, and Sweden have much more consistent federal policies. Heterosexual marriage is a norm that has major social groups fighting for and against its maintenance. For same-sex couples, the stakes for marriage are not just romantic. It includes income tax breaks, health insurance benefits, and all sorts of institutional and

AN

ESSAY

ON THE

PRINCIPLE OF POPULATION,

AS IT AFFECTS

THE FUTURE IMPROVEMENT OF SOCIETY,

WITH REMARKS

ON THE SPECULATIONS OF MR. GODWIN,

M. CONDORCET,

AND OTHER WRITERS.

═══════════

LONDON:

PRINTED FOR J. JOHNSON, IN ST. PAUL'S
CHURCH-YARD.

————

1798.

FIGURE 1.8
Malthus's *The Principle of Population* (1798) linked reproduction
and economics.

community legitimacy. For those who oppose same-sex marriage, the prospect of legalizing and legitimating same-sex relationships is an attack on their concept of marriage and morality. The battle is over civil rights, but the arguments are about what people consider to be "social norms."

Some social theorists observe that societies control sexuality through the construction of a dichotomized or gendered sexuality (Foucault 1978). Society's rules about pleasure seeking and procreating are enforced by norms about appropriate behavior for men and women. For example, saying that masculinity is enhanced by sexual experimentation while femininity is demeaned by it gives men sexual privilege (and pleasure) and denies it to women. That is, the very rules that control sexual desire shape it and even enhance it. The social world could just as plausibly concentrate on how much alike are the ways that men and women experience sex and emphasize how broadly dispersed sexual conduct is across genders. However, social control turns pleasure into a scarce resource and endows leaders who regulate the pleasure of others with power.

Societies control sexuality in part because they have a pragmatic investment in it. They want to control reproduction and who reproduces. Eighteenth-century economic theorist T. R. Malthus ([1798] 1929) highlighted the relationship between reproductive practices and economics in *The Principle of Population*. According to Malthus, excessive fertility would result in the exhaustion of food and other resources. His recommendation to curb the birthrate represents an intervention into the sexual behavior of individuals for the well-being of society. A more recent example is the one-child policy in modern China. Alarmed by the predictions of famine and other disastrous consequences of rapid population growth, Mao Tse-tung and subsequent Chinese leaders instituted a program of enforced fertility control, which included monitoring women's menstrual cycles, requiring involuntary abortions, and delaying the legal age for marriage. To the state, sexual behavior isn't really an intimate, private act at all; it is a social and even economically significant activity. Such policies influence society at large, but they influence private experience as well. In China, the one-child policy has led to an increased **sex ratio** (the ratio of boys to girls in a population)—boy babies are preferred to girl babies, and methods including selective abortion and even infanticide are used to reduce the number of girls born (Cao and Lavely 2003). This in turn has led to kidnapping and trafficking of women, a growing industry of sex workers, and disruptive behavior on the part of men whose romantic options are limited because of the reduced supply of women (Hesketh, Lu, and Xing 2005). How does a society obtain the ideal number of healthy workers to create a thriving nation? How does a society produce enough people to create an army? How does it create a system in which parents control their offspring so that the state will not have to step into an expensive and impractical role?

And how do such large-scale policies influence the everyday experiences and definitions of sexuality for individuals?

Society's interest in controlling sexuality is expressed in the debates regarding sex education. The debate about sex education in grade school and high school illustrates the importance to society of both the control and meaning of sexual desire. These days the debate centers around whether "abstinence only" or comprehensive sex education is the better alternative for young people. The contrasting approaches raise the question—does formal learning about sex increase or deter early sexual experimentation? The point is that opponents and proponents of sex education all want to know how to control sexuality in young people. Those who favor comprehensive sex education hold that children benefit from early, complete information about sex, in the belief that people learn about sexuality from birth and are sexual at least from the time of puberty. The comprehensive sex education point of view is that providing young people with an appropriate vocabulary and accurate information both discourages early sexual activity and encourages safe sexual practices for those teenagers who, according to the evidence, will not be deterred from sexual activity (Sexuality Information and Education Council of the United States [SIECUS] 1995). On the other hand, abstinence-only sex education advocates are intensely committed to the belief that information about sex changes teenagers' reactions and values and leads to early, and what they believe are inappropriate, sexual behaviors (see for example, www.sexcanwait.com). Conservative groups hold that sex education, if it occurs at all, should emphasize abstinence as opposed to practical information. As we have mentioned, there has been robust government support for the conservative viewpoint. Between 1996 and 2006 the U.S. government invested over a billion dollars in abstinence-only education programs administered by the states (SIECUS 2005). Whether emphasizing knowledge or emphasizing abstinence, the programs are about managing adolescent sexual desire. Conservatives fear that education creates desire; liberals feel that information merely enables better decision making. So who is correct? In various studies, a majority of both conservative and liberal sex education programs have demonstrated little effect on whether people have sex or not. Conservatives believe these results prove the programs' lack of worth. Liberals believe the studies prove that many programs are not good enough, usually because they do not include the most important content. Furthermore, liberals point out that sex education has increased contraceptive (including condom) use, which is crucial to public health goals of reducing sexually transmitted disease and unwanted pregnancy. Other research indicates that comprehensive sex education actually tends to delay the age of first intercourse and does not intensify desire or escalate sexual behavior. There is no evidence that comprehensive sex education promotes or precipitates early teen sexual activity (Kirby et al. 2005; Kirby 2001; Alford 2003).

The passionate debate about sex education is played out with high emotions. Political ideology, parental fears, and the election strategies of politicians all influence this mode of social control. In the final analysis, however, teaching about sex clearly does not have an intense impact on the pupil. Students' responses to sex education vary tremendously at the individual level. In terms of trends within groups, however, it appears that comprehensive sex education tends to delay sexual activity and makes teenage sex safer when it happens, and that abstinence-only education tends to have only short-term benefits for preventing sex but over time the effects wear off except for one: students of abstinence-only education are less likely to use a condom when they do eventually have sex (Santelli et al. 2006; Hauser 2004).

To summarize, social constructionists believe that a society influences sexual behavior through its norms. Some norms are explicit, such as laws regulating marriage or against adult sexual activity with minors. Others are implicit, such as norms of fidelity and parental responsibility. In a stable, homogeneous society, it is relatively easy to understand such rules. But in a changing, complex society like the United States, the rules may be in flux or indistinct. Perhaps this ambiguity is what makes some issues of sexuality so controversial today.

An Integrative Perspective on Gender and Sexuality

Social constructionist explanations of contemporary sexual patterns are typically pitted against the biology of desire and the evolutionary psychological understanding of sexual selection and biological adaptations. Some social constructionists believe there is no inflexible biological reality; everything we regard as either female or male sexuality is culturally imposed (see, for example, Foucault 1978). In contrast, essentialists—those who take a biological or evolutionary psychological point of view—believe people's sexual desires and orientations are innate and hard-wired and that social impact is minimal (Buss 1994). Gender differences follow from reproductive differences. Men inseminate, women incubate; from that follows our behavior. People are born with sexual drives, attractions, and natures that simply play themselves out at the appropriate developmental age. Even if social constraints conspire to make men and women more similar to each other (as in the past decade when young men and women have had seemingly similar freedom to engage in "hooking up" or having casual sexual liaisons with friends), people's essential nature is the same: Man is the hunter, warrior, and trailblazer; and woman is the gatherer, nurturer, and reproducer. To an essentialist, social differences, such as the different earning power of men and women, are the consequence of biological difference. In short, essentialists think the innate differences between women and men are the cause of gendered sexuality; social constructionists think the differences between men and women are the result of gendering sexuality through social processes.

Using either the social constructionist or essentialist approach to the exclusion of the other can dull our understanding of sexuality. We believe the evidence shows that gender differences are more plausibly an outcome of social processes than the other way around. But a social constructionist view is most powerful when it takes the essentialist view into account. In table 1.3, we describe this view of gender differences in sexual desire as **integrative**. When we say "having sex," people will tend to think mainly of a biological function—the mechanics of tab B goes into slot A. But biology is only one part of the context of desire. Such sociological factors as family relationships and social structure also influence sex. A complex mix of anatomy, hormones, the brain, and the social world provides the basic outline for the range of acts and desires possible, but biology is neither where sexuality begins nor where it ends. Social and biological contexts link to define human sexual possibilities.

The integrative approach is based on observations from many sexuality researchers. Consider this example: A research project, conducted over four decades ago, advertised for participants, stating that its focus was how physi-

TABLE 1.3
Explanations of Male and Female Differences in Sexual Desire

Explanations	Causes of Desire	Consequences
Essentialist: Desire is biological and evolutionary.	Genetically preprogrammed reproductive functions are specific to males and females.	Male independence in reproduction and female-centered child-rearing practice and passivity are the cause, rather than the result, of gendered social institutions.
Social constructionist: Desire is sociological and contextual.	Social institutions and social interaction signal and sanction "male" and "female" gendered norms of behavior.	Support for or opposition to sex/gender-segregated reproductive and social practices depends on social definitions of men, women, and sexuality.
Integrative: Desire is contextual and physical.	Bodies, environments, relationships, families, and governments shape sexualities.	Policies address some biological differences (such as pregnancy and work) and emphasize the impact of social forces, interaction, and societal programs.

cal excitement influences a man's preference for one woman over another (Valins 1966). The researchers connected college men to a monitor that allowed them to hear their heartbeats as they looked at photographs of women models. The men were told that they would be able to hear their heartbeat when it surged in response to each photograph. A greater surge would suggest greater physical attraction. The participants were then shown a photograph of a dark-haired woman, then a blonde, then a redhead. Afterward, each man was asked to choose the picture of the woman that he would prefer to take home. In each case, the man chose the photograph of the woman who, as he believed from listening to his own speeding heartbeat, had most aroused him. Or at least the man thought he was choosing the woman who had aroused him most. In reality, the men had been listening to a faked heartbeat that was speeded up at random. The men thus actually chose the women whom they believed had aroused them most. In this case, the men's invented attraction was more powerful than their gut response. Their mind (a powerful sexual organ) told them their body was responding to a specific picture. The participants' physiological experience of arousal was eclipsed by the social context. When social circumstances influence sexual tastes, are those tastes real or sincere? Absolutely. The social world is as much a fact in people's lives as the biological world.

Now let us look at a case in which the body's cues were misinterpreted by the mind. An attractive woman researcher stood at the end of a very stable bridge (Dutton and Aron 1974). She approached men after they had walked across the bridge, engaged them in conversation, and then gave the men her telephone number—in case they had further comments, she said. Then the researcher did the same thing with another group of participants, but at the end of an unstable, swinging bridge. People tend to feel a little nervous, excited, or even exhilarated when they make their way across such a bridge. The pulse rises. Adrenaline pumps. Indeed, the anxiety response of walking across the bridge is much like the arousal response caused by meeting a desirable new person. The question was, would that anxiety confuse men into thinking that they were attracted to the woman at the end of the bridge, more so than the physiologically calm guys who met her on the stable bridge? Yes, a statistically significant, larger number of men from the swinging bridge called the woman. In this case, participants had interpreted an anxiety response as an attraction response, one compelling enough to warrant inviting a stranger on a date. The physical situation transformed the meaning of a casual meeting from anxiety to attraction, again showing the link between biological and social influences.

A very personal matter that seems to be utterly physical—penile erection, or more specifically, a man's inability to get an erection—offers another example. How might an erection be socially constructed? It is more or less understood in the United States that a penis should be hard and ready when a man's sexual opportunity is available. The importance of a ready, erect penis is punctuated by the two-billion-dollar-a-year industry in Viagra, the commercial name for a drug that aids in erection (Loe 2006). It is more or less understood that the failure to get or maintain an erection in a sexual situation has two meanings: The guy isn't "man enough," or the other person isn't attractive enough. Indeed, in *Gendering Bodies*, which explores in detail how bodies are shaped by the social world, the authors remind us that "men's sexual and reproductive bodies are also likened to machines, not as passive instruments, but rather as powerful, high-performance machines"—we use words like *drill* or *rod* or *rocket* to connote the expectation that penises are active, ready, and hard (Crawley et al. 2008, 9).

Despite the expectation that penises are at the ready, there are many explanations for why a penis may not be ready, not the least of which has been poetically explained by Shakespeare (and scientifically documented):

> Lechery, sir, [alcohol] provokes, and unprovokes; it provokes the desire, but it takes away the performance. Therefore much drink may be said to be an equivocator with lechery: it makes him, and it mars him; it sets him on, and it takes him off; it persuades him, and disheartens him; makes him stand to, and not stand to; in conclusion, equivocates him in a sleep, and, giving him the lie, leaves him. (*Macbeth*, Act II, Scene iii)

The Shakespearean speech refers to the way in which alcohol can undermine robust sexual desire by leaving the penis flaccid. The performance is not the intimate interaction of bodies in pursuit of pleasure; it is strictly focused on the penis, which ought to "stand to." The speech emphasizes the humiliation—the "mar"—for a man who fails to sustain an erection. Although the speech refers to the toll that alcohol takes on the circulatory system that assists penises in becoming erect, the discussion is about the social experience of a man failed by his penis.

Even in the absence of drinking, penises are not nearly so reliable as the mythology of masculinity and attraction would maintain. Erections appear to come and go with odd timing. For example, erections rise and fall on babies and young boys; men often wake up with erections. None of these instances has to do with machismo or sexual desire. Erections are not always evidence of romantic or sexual interest, although our culture tends to interpret them as such. But their absence or presence, which is a physical phenomenon, takes on great meaning thanks to Western culture's prevailing beliefs and norms. For example, men required to produce semen for in vitro fertilization who are unable to maintain an erection until orgasm report feeling humiliated; their partners also often report being stunned by this performance failure (Rutter 1996). Growing up in a culture that considers erectile unpredictability a problem influences the way men feel about themselves and their sexual partners, and the way sexual partners feel about them.

Endless Viagra and Levitra commercials on television reinforce the value of a penis that can "stand to." Viagra is a drug men use to facilitate erection when medical issues such as the impact of antidepressants inhibit the penis from becoming rigid. But you should understand what Viagra does and does not do: Viagra doesn't create instant erections. Sexual desire or interest in another person—or some other stimulation—is what makes the setting a sexual opportunity. The Viagra just helps the penis to participate.

Even biological research has supported the integrative perspective. Forty years ago, one team of scientists found that gay men had lower testosterone levels than a matched group of heterosexual men (Kreuz, Rose, and Jennings 1972). The traditional interpretation at the time of the study was that gay men were less "masculine" than the comparison group and that their lower testosterone levels explained why they were gay. But a group of active military men were also measured and found to be low in testosterone. The researchers were loath to believe that an unusual number of military men were gay or that military men were below average hormonally, so they found an alternative explanation for low testosterone. The researchers speculated that stress, anxiety, and similar negative emotions had temporarily lowered hormone levels in both soldiers and gay men. The stressful social context—as either a gay man living in a straight world or as a military man being bossed around constantly—had shaped a biological response, the researchers concluded. Hormones were the cart, not the horse. Biology influences desire, but social context influences biology and gives meaning to bodily sensation.

What do these studies illustrate? Sexual desire—in fact, all sexuality—is influenced by the cultural, personal, and situational. But these examples also tell us that people can't escape the biological context of sex and sexuality, nor can they rely on it. Such an integrative approach—the intimate relationship between social context and biological experience—is central to understanding sexuality.

What are the implications of using an integrative approach to sexuality? First, an integrationist will raise questions about biology when social context is emphasized as cause and will raise questions about social context when biological causes are emphasized. Second, an integrationist will examine how the biology and social context are intertwined. The point is, everything sexual and physical occurs and achieves meaning in a social context.

Sexual Identity and Orientation

Nowhere does the essentialist versus social constructionist argument grow more vehement than in the debate over **sexual identity** and sexual orientation. These terms are used to mean a variety of things. We use these terms to refer to how people tend to classify themselves sexually—either as gay, lesbian, bisexual, transgender, or straight. Sexual behavior and sexual desire may or may not be consistent with sexual identity. That is, people may identify themselves as heterosexual but desire people of the same sex—or vice versa.

It is hard to argue with the observation that human desire is, after all, organized. Humans do not generally desire cows or horses (with, perhaps, the exception of Catherine the Great, the Russian czarina who purportedly came to her demise while copulating with a stallion). More to the point, humans are usually quite specific about which sex is desirable to them and even whether the object of their desire is short or tall, dark or light, hairy or sleek.

In the United States, people tend to be identified as either **homosexual** (gay) or **heterosexual** (straight). Other cultures (and prior eras in the United States) have not distinguished between these two sexual orientations. However, our culture embraces the perspective that, whether gay or straight, one has an essential, inborn desire, and it cannot change. Many people seem convinced that homosexuality, like heterosexuality, is an essence rather than a sexual act. For essentialists, it is crucial to establish the primacy of one kind of desire or another and to build a world around that identity. People tend to assume that the object of desire is a matter of the gender of the object. That is, they think even gay men desire someone who is feminine and that lesbians desire someone who is masculine. In other words, even among gay men and lesbians, it is assumed that they will desire opposite-gendered people, even if they are of the same sex.

Historians have chronicled in Western culture the evolution of the category "homosexual" from behavior into identity (for example, D'Emilio and Freedman 1988). In the past, people might engage in same-sex sexuality, but only in the twentieth century has it become a well-defined (and diverse) lifestyle and self-definition. Nevertheless, other evidence shows that homosexual identity has existed for a long time. The distinguished historian John Boswell (1994) argued that homosexuals as a group and homosexuality as an identity have existed from the very earliest of recorded history. He used evidence of early Christian same-sex "marriage" to support his thesis.

Anthropologists have found homosexuality accepted in as many as 190 world cultures; for example, social scientist Fred Whitman (1983) has looked at homosexuality across cultures and declared that the evidence of a social type, including men who use certain effeminate gestures and have diverse sexual tastes, goes far beyond any one culture.

Biologists note homosexual behavior among nonhuman animals. Among sheep, for example, about 8 percent will be exclusively homosexual (Roughgarden 2004). (This has been a challenge for evolutionary psychologists, who emphasize reproduction as the motivation for behavior, to explain.) For humans, geneticist Dean Hamer provides evidence that sexual attraction may be genetically programmed, suggesting that it has persisted over time and been passed down through generations.

On the other side of the debate is the idea that sexuality has always been invented and that sexual orientations are socially created. A gay man's or straight woman's sexual orientation has been created by a social context. Although this creation takes place in a society that prefers dichotomous, polarized categories, the social constructionist vision of sexuality at least poses the possibility that sexuality could involve a continuum of behavior that is matched by a continuum of fantasy, ability to love, and sense of self.

The jury is still out on the scientific origins of heterosexuality and homosexuality. The most widely held conclusion among sex researchers from a variety of disciplines is that homosexuality (and heterosexuality) are related to numerous causes and are biological, genetic, and contextual; that the causes vary from individual to individual; and that probably the combination of causes for homosexuality in men are different in general from those for homosexuality in women.

The case for biological explanations for homosexuality, though, continues to grow: Studies on the brain (LeVay 1993) identified some differences in the makeup of the brains of straight and gay men. This research has been criticized because the brain samples for the gay population were taken from men who had died from AIDS, which may have systematically altered the brain structure of the men. Follow-up research on other populations tends to confirm the findings for men; less research has been done examining women's brains. Genetic research also was triggered in connection with AIDS. Hamer, while doing research at the National Institutes of Health Cancer Research Center, became interested in the genetics of sexual attraction and orientation while he was studying the heritability of Kaposi's sarcoma, a type of skin cancer that some gay men with AIDS develop. Hamer looked further into the possibility that gay men (and, in separate research, lesbians) have a genetic makeup different from that of heterosexuals (Hamer and Copeland 1994). He found a specific gene formation, identified as Xq28, that appears to be inherited through the mother's line only in gay males. The lesbian research has not thus far established a genetic link.

Hamer himself makes no claim that all attraction or arousal is genetically programmed, but his research lends support to other studies on the genetics of sexuality. For example, genetics researcher Michael Bailey and colleagues looked at identical twins (who have identical genetic material) who were reared apart. The studies found a likelihood much greater than chance that if one male twin is homosexual, the other will also be homosexual (Bailey et al. 1993). Because the twins in the study did not share the same environment, this finding suggests that the twins' common genes made them similar in their sexual orientation. Other recent genetic and twin studies have highlighted the fact that having a certain *genotype* (DNA coded for a particular characteristic, such as heart disease) does not always produce the corresponding *phenotype* (the physical expression of that characteristic, such as actually suffering from heart disease). Researchers speculate that environment and individual history influence the expression or suppression of genetic types (Wright 1995). Bailey's results suggest just this: over the past decade his studies establish about 50 percent heritability of homosexuality for men. That 50 percent means that genes are a player, but it also means that genetics aren't the only player.

These are just a few of the studies that, in some people's opinions, support the idea that homosexuality is not a choice but a naturally occurring phenomenon in a predetermined proportion of births. By extension, they believe, much human sexual desire and behavior must be biologically determined. Of course, social constructionists would disagree. But if biology does not determine whether one is heterosexual or homosexual, is sexual orientation a choice? Not exactly. The notion that sexuality is a preference supposes a person goes to a sexuality bazaar and picks out what to be today. That is not the case either. Physical and social structures and individual biography join together to produce sexual desire and behavior in an individual that may vary over time. Because of powerful social norms regarding sexuality, people are more likely to sustain a single sexual orientation throughout adulthood. The overwhelming evidence supports the idea that biology is a player in the game of sexual orientation, but it is not the only player or even captain of the team.

The Continuum of Desire

Variation among people has been examined more than changes in sexual orientation within an individual. Alfred Kinsey (see Kinsey, Pomeroy, and Martin 1948), in his pioneering studies on human sexualities in the late 1940s and 1950s, introduced the Kinsey Heterosexual-Homosexual Rating Scale (see figure 1.9). A person was coded using a zero for "completely heterosexual," a six for "completely homosexual," or a number in between to represent a more ambiguous orientation. Kinsey measured his participants' reports of interest, attraction, and explicit past experiences with both same-sex and other-sex people and figured out where his participants fit on the continuum.

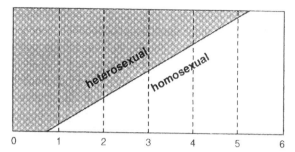

FIGURE 1.9
The sexual continuum. Based on the Kinsey Heterosexual-Homosexual Rating Scale (Kinsey, Pomeroy, and Martin 1948).

However, his measurements were more of an art than a science. One cannot weigh or calibrate sexuality so finely. But Kinsey did examine actual behavior, fantasy, intensity of feeling, and other important elements that contribute to a person's sexuality.

Although such a rating scale may be an imperfect way of providing individuals with some sort of sex score, Kinsey made the point that a dichotomous vision of sexual orientation is even more inadequate and inaccurate. The Kinsey scale still defines the polarities of sexuality as heterosexuality and homosexuality, and in that sense it is essentialist. However, it provides alternatives beyond "yes," "no," or "in denial." Kinsey opened the door to thinking in terms of the diversity of sexualities. People may use dichotomous terms in everyday life, but the idea that many people have the capacity to relate sexually to both males and females (at a single point in their life or intermittently over a lifetime) is part of the legacy of Kinsey's sex research.

By using a sexual continuum that blurs the edges of heterosexuality and homosexuality, Kinsey advanced the idea of **bisexuality**. The mere existence of bisexuality (the common term for some history of attraction to or sex with both men and women) is troubling for essentialists, who see sexuality as fixed and linked to procreation. However, biologists can show that bisexuality exists in the animal kingdom—bonobo monkeys, sheep, bison, to name a few. Evolutionary psychologists and anthropologists hypothesize that bisexuality could be useful for a group's bonding and thus have survival value (Fisher 1992). The explanation is that adults who are like aunts and uncles to children—and who are intimate with parents—provide additional support for maintaining a family. But committed essentialists do not usually buy the idea that "true" bisexuality exists. Instead, they code men and women as "true" heterosexuals or homosexuals who have some modest taste in the other direction.

Given the evidence, it is possible to believe that the biological context tends to encourage an individual to acquire one sexual orientation or another but also to believe that society exerts greater influence than biology over behavior. Kinsey's data, as well as controversial data from a small gay and lesbian subsample from the National Health and Social Life Survey (NHSLS; Laumann, Michael, and Gagnon 1994), indicate that many more people report homosexual desire and behavior than those who claim homosexuality or bisexuality as their main sexual orientation or sexual identity (see figure 1.10). Essentialists might say people who admit to homosexual behavior but deny being homosexuals are kidding themselves. Social constructionists say people are always kidding themselves; in other words, people acquire the desires and behaviors that are available and appealing. These choices will be based on personal history as well as social norms and will emerge in idiosyncratic and diverse ways across the continuum of sexuality. They will also be based on the costs and benefits in a given social system. How many people might code their fantasies differently if it were prestigious to be bisexual? Surely people's impulse to code themselves dichotomously is in part influenced by the social and emotional costs of doing otherwise.

An interesting issue that puzzles essentialists is how different homosexuality in men seems to be from homosexuality in women. Figure 1.10 demonstrates that more men than women identify as homosexual, but more women claim

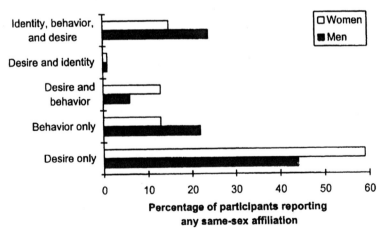

FIGURE 1.10
Same-sex behavior and homosexual identity. Data from Laumann, Michael, and Gagnon (1994).

homosexual desire and/or behavior than men in those categories. In Lever's (1994a) *Advocate* survey, as well, more men than women identify themselves as gay. Indeed, much of the sexual attraction and behavior between women is not labeled as sexual. Women hug and kiss each other with impunity, and not necessarily with specific sexual intent. They can have extended sex play in their youth, or even in adulthood, without being instantly labeled as homosexual, as men who engaged in similar behavior would be. Women are also more likely to report that a same-sex sexual episode had less to do with sexual attraction than with love.

Historically, the waters are even murkier. As Lillian Faderman illustrates in *Surpassing the Love of Men* (1981), eighteenth- and nineteenth-century women were allowed such license to love each other that they could declare truly passionate feelings for one another without labels and identities being bandied about. For example, Faderman (1981) quotes Rousseau's eighteenth-century novel *La nouvelle Héloïse*, in which Julie writes to Clair: "The most important thing of my life has been to love you. From the very beginning my heart has been absorbed in yours" (77). If these women expressed these sentiments today, observers would assume them to be homosexual. Are these the words simply of passionate friends? Essentialists would say these were lesbian lovers who did not have social permission to know who they really were. Historians and sociologists are divided as to whether these women experienced their love as sexual or romantic in the contemporary understanding of those feelings. It is difficult to label people's emotions for them after the fact and from a different historical and psychological vantage point. Just as beliefs and biases influence the way social science is conducted in the present, so such biases influence the views and interpretations of the past. We need to remember that sexual orientation, along with desire and other manifestations of sexuality, is socially constructed and culturally specific.

Psychologist Lisa Diamond might add yet another twist to our understanding of the attachment between the women in *La nouvelle Héloïse*. She has a hormonal explanation for bisexuality. The culprit is oxytocin, known as the love hormone. Oxytocin is a hormone mothers and infants release that generates suffused love and attachment feeling. But this same hormone is released in orgasm or when adults are falling in romantic love. Though it can be tied up with sexual feelings, oxytocin is not specifically about sexual desire. The oxytocin creates a path for attachment, or love. Diamond argues that this can help explain why people who identify as one sexual orientation may discover love or attraction feelings toward someone who is not the sex of the people they typically desire (Diamond 2008).

Gender as the Basis for Sexual Identity

Sexual orientation, as nearly everyone in Western culture has come to understand the phrase, signifies the identity one has based on the gender of the sexual partners one tends to pair with, either at a particular time or over a lifetime. In our culture, gender is the focus of sexual identity. But what if instead of discussing sexual identity in terms of one's preference for women or men, we referred to the various tastes one expresses for people who are funny or serious or tall or short or responsive or unresponsive to oral sex? For example, Virginia's sexuality would be "left-handed Jewish intellectual"—for male or female, this describes the people whom she tends to pair with. Pepper's sexuality would be "tall, high energy, sociable, and good looking." Instead, our culture zeroes in on which gender is doing what with which gender. Thus, the whole notion of sexual identity requires strict distinctions between men and women. The fact that the gender of sexual partners is of such great social interest highlights yet again how gender organizes the definitions of sexuality.

Few can resist gendered distinctions. But a challenge comes from **transgender** people—a variety of groups that vary from the expected link between biological sex and gender identity (for example, Male = man). **Transsexuals** are men and women who believe they were born in the wrong body. Although anatomically they are one sex, transsexuals experience themselves as the other sex, much the way we described Dil in *The Crying Game* at the beginning of the chapter, who felt like a woman but was built like a man. Sometimes transsexuals "correct" their bodies with surgery or hormone treatments. And their sexual orientations are diverse. Some male-to-female transsexuals pair with men, some with women. The same is true for female-to-male transsexuals. One male-to-female person, speaking at a sexuality conference in the 1970s, declared, "Personally, I feel it is sexist to love on the basis of gender. You love the person, whatever their sex might be!" Transsexuals offer a robust challenge to a strictly social constructionist view of gender and sexuality: On the one hand, transsexuals signal to the rest of us that all is not as it appears and that our simple gender categories don't work for everybody; however, for transsexuals their experience of their *gender* identity is *essential*—it feels as if they were born into the opposite *sex*. Especially for those who seek sex reassignment surgery, transsexuals feel convinced that they have a *true* gender and sexuality, one that defies the explicit and implicit expectations of their family and their environment. They feel that their biology must be realigned to be consistent with their mental state.

A sad story from sexuality research helps remind us of the indisputable power of biology. In the 1970s, sexologist John Money was so convinced of the complete social construction of gender and sexuality that he confidently recommended that an infant who had been damaged during his circumcision be "reassigned" to be a female. Surgeons built a vagina, and during adolescence they gave the child additional hormonal shots consistent with her assigned gender. The results of this case, and numerous others, have been told in books and media accounts. People born as males and by dint of surgical accidents reassigned as females often felt like outsiders to their assigned gender. Indeed, the alienation of these "sex reassigned" people led to depression and tragic results. For some, they found relief when their "true" underlying feeling that they were male was revealed to them.

Transgender—which includes transsexuality as well as cross-dressing, going in drag, and other gender nonconformity—allows one to consider the wide range of nonconformity that can exist beyond being a conventional man or woman.

Conclusion

There are, it seems, two arguments that help explain the way the genders express sexual desire. On the one hand are the images and statistics showing that men and women have distinct (albeit shifting) patterns of sexual expression, regardless of sexual orientation. On the other hand, the wide range of sexualities among men or among women also calls for an explanation. A continuum of passion, of desire, of sexual acts and feelings is a useful way to reconcile these phenomena. Furthermore, it helps to recognize that sexuality is socially scripted but also highly individualized. Although sexual desire tends to be described in orderly and quantifiable terms, sexual desire is a chaotic playing field on which we, as sociologists, attempt to place some order to understand it better.

Biology or, more simply stated, bodies are the site for passionate experience, even if that experience is in the brain, in the absence of actual sensations in the skin or other sexual organs. In this sense, biology is a prominent context for sexuality. However, interpersonal, biographical, social, and political contexts influence sexuality and interact with biology in surprising ways. Thus, the continuum of sexuality we propose becomes even more diverse.

In the following chapters, we examine sexuality in various realms (dating and hooking up, marriage and long-term partnerships, teenage sexuality, same-sex marriage, sexual violence, and online relationships). We will remind you that we believe the differences between men and women are not any more important than the wide range of behavior and feelings that exist among men and among women. The social world and even academic discussions of sexuality seek to set up distinct categories for understanding sexuality. But individuals rarely fit into distinct categories.

Why do we take this precaution? Because of the inaccurate self-labeling that can happen as a reader sees, or doesn't see, himself or herself in the images we present. The woman who reads that women rarely have over ten or so partners and has herself had fifty tempestuous love affairs or recreational encounters is not being told she is a man, nor is she being told that she is perverse because she is outside the middle range found in self-report survey data. Sexuality exists on a continuum. There are people whose experiences reflect either end of the continuum and people whose experiences reflect the middle. It is just as unfair to judge a sexually experienced woman as it is to judge a man who has had one sexual partner his whole life and seeks no more. Such a man is no more or less masculine than the man with five or ten sexual partners.

Sociologists, who examine overall patterns, are often criticized because people assume that the statistics of the majority are being presented as proper conduct or that other conduct is by definition abnormal. But the social scientist makes no such assumption. In fact, diversity and change in behavior are at the center of social science. Sexuality is one of the most diverse, pervasive, and enigmatic of human experiences. Therefore, far from naming a single sexuality or a dichotomous sexuality (or even a trichotomous sexuality), we may more accurately say that there are as many sexualities as there are people. Yet detecting patterns within the diversity can advance an understanding of gender, sex, and society and show how differences and similarities among groups of men and women came into being and are sustained through social practices. The categorical language of sexuality is difficult to avoid. However, we will try to avoid categorizing people or acts, and we hope you will join us in that effort.

2

Sexual Behavior and Gender

A SCENE FROM THE FILM CLASSIC *Annie Hall* (1977) provides a stereotype of gender differences in sexuality. A split screen shows Alvy Singer (played by Woody Allen) and Annie (played by Diane Keaton) as disenchanted lovers, each talking to their respective psychoanalysts about the relationship.

Alvy Singer's Therapist: How often do you sleep together?

Annie Hall's Therapist: Do you have sex often?

Alvy Singer: [*lamenting*] Hardly ever. Maybe three times a week.

Annie Hall: [*annoyed*] Constantly. I'd say three times a week.

As the writer of this scene, Woody Allen apparently views sex as a chore for a woman, who reluctantly graces her partner with hardly enough sex to sustain him. He makes frequency of sex a surrogate for desire, and women are often caricatured as having less sexual appetite than men. That attitude is reflected in jokes such as "How do you get a woman to stop wanting sex?" (Answer: "Marry her"). Jokes like that connote a shared cultural understanding that women consent to sex only as a way to land, or placate, a husband. It is commonly believed that it is men who set the pace for sex in a relationship. In survey data, the myths of men's and women's sexual difference are, to a certain extent, borne out. The gendered frequency pattern suggested by the *Annie Hall* scene also exists among same-sex couples. Gay male couples, even nonmonogamous ones, have a higher sexual frequency than lesbian couples, who may end up having genital sex infrequently. (And although all couples have less sexual frequency over the years, lesbians remain the lowest.) The patterns suggest difference, but they do not tell us why such difference exists! In fact, sometimes people take these differences as a starting point to prove that men's and women's sexuality is biologically as well as culturally different. Such a difference is a description, however, not an explanation.

In this chapter, we will explore the social sources of these differences and the ways these differences are exploited socially. We will also draw your attention to the more commonly occurring, though less often explored, sexual similarities between men and women.

The Challenge of Studying Sexual Behavior

When we look more carefully at situations like the one in *Annie Hall*, we might come up with some answers to questions about gender differences in sexuality. For example, maybe the reason that heterosexual couples with children have discrepant levels of sexual desire is biological: a nursing mother may have reduced estrogen that influences her sexual response. Or maybe the reason is socially constructed: mothers, who consistently do the lion's share of housework even when employed outside the home full time (Brines 1994), have less sexual desire because the day-to-day reality of housework and child care is exhausting. Generally when people run out of energy, sexual energy diminishes as well. Indeed, John Gottman's research on married couples shows that when husbands contribute to housework, their wives are more interested in having sex with them (1994).

These are plausible explanations, but social scientists are reluctant to commit to any of them without methodically studying the behavior and attitudes of real people.

In this chapter, we use recent and older sexuality surveys. Many examples are from the well-known National Opinion Research Center's National Health and Social Life Survey (NHSLS), as reported in Laumann, Michael, and Gagnon (1994). It continues to be one of our best, most detailed sources of information about sex in society. It is based on personal interviews with a probability sample of 3,432 U.S. women and men between the ages of eighteen and fifty-nine. The data are still a relevant reference telling us how much sexual conduct and general attitudes toward sexuality are influenced by gender, age, marital status, and other demographic characteristics. We also use examples from the American Couples survey, published in *American Couples: Money, Work, and Sex* (Blumstein and Schwartz 1983). The American Couples study used survey data and in-depth interviews in a sample of 12,066 people that included married couples, heterosexual cohabiters, and gay and lesbian couples. The focus was on relationship quality and durability across all four couple types. Because of its innovative design, *American Cou-*

ples continues to be a great data source for examining links among gender, power, and sexuality.

Another source of data comes from the Online College Social Life Survey. This is an (ongoing) national online survey of over fourteen thousand college students from nineteen universities and colleges. Paula England and other researchers at Stanford designed a survey asking college students about beliefs, attitudes, and behaviors related to hooking up and dating. The work has been supplemented by qualitative interviews, as well. (Rutter at Framingham State University and Schwartz at the University of Washington have collected data for the project.) The study provides very current information about emerging trends related to gender, sexuality, and the transition to adulthood.

This is not a book about interpreting survey data or about conducting sex research, so we will not go into great detail on those subjects. However, we caution students of sexuality to recognize the challenges of collecting and interpreting self-report data, particularly on the enigmatic topic of sexuality. Respondents may not tell the truth or remember the truth or even be sure that what they thought happened really did happen. Indeed, definitions of sexual behavior can be subjective: some of you may still recall the debate in the late 1990s about whether or not President Bill Clinton had "sex" with a White House intern. He said no under oath because in his definition of sex, oral sex didn't count. The intern and the special prosecutor questioning him about whether or not he had lied about having sex with her did believe that oral sex "counted." What do you think? Did they have sex if the activity was fellatio (oral sex)? At issue, is oral sex "having sex"?

Apparently, reasonable minds can disagree, even when there is no political disadvantage for classifying oral sex as sex. During the Clinton episode, two researchers published a survey of college students that indicated that 60 percent of them did not consider oral sex alone to be "having sex" (Sanders and Reinisch 1999). A postscript to the story: after the article was published in the *Journal of the American Medical Association*, the editor was fired for publishing this article because of its potential for influencing presidential politics (Smith 1999), adding another layer of challenge for collecting and distributing frank information about sexual behavior and beliefs (Michaels and Giami 1999). In chapter 5 we examine sex and political life in the United States in more detail. For the healthy skeptic of sexual self-reporting, survey data remain records of norms or values, if not precise accounts of deeds.

There's another puzzle in sexuality data that hints that social norms influence how men and women self-report on sexuality. In a laboratory study of college-aged students, researchers investigated whether "gender scripts" or expectations about what is proper for men or women in the sexual domain would influence patterns of response. To find out, they asked men and women to fill out a questionnaire about sexual attitudes and behavior under contrasting test conditions: In the first, they were made to feel as if the researchers would not be able to detect false or misleading answers; this condition was intended to pressure respondents into being as truthful as possible. In the other, they were made to feel as if their answers would be seen by the researcher who was administering the survey (and at risk of "performing" according to gendered expectations of sexuality). The results: when it comes to sexual *attitudes*, the two conditions were no different from each other. Men and women did not alter their responses depending upon which condition they were in. However, in terms of reported *behavior*, men and women were fairly similar in the "truth" condition, but in the "gender scripts" condition, where people might know what they had reported, men had reports of more sexual experience—such as masturbation, or earlier first intercourse—than did women. In other words, when people are taking into account how their behavior might be perceived, they may adjust their reports, even slightly, in the direction that is consistent with norms of more sexual freedom for men and for less sexual freedom for women (Alexander and Fisher 2003).

A World of Gender Difference

So, as you can see, the world makes much of gender difference: Difference between men and women is the theme on which movies, fashion, courtship, and even ideals about family structure are built. So much is made of gender difference that it is difficult to use the continuum of sexuality (that we discussed in chapter 1) rather than a dichotomous system, where men and women live in completely different sexual universes. Difficult though it may be, many researchers, including the great sociologist Erving Goffman (1977), make the point that much of what we think of as gender differences is illusory. Male and female characteristics are like two mostly overlapping distributions of physical characteristics. Think of it this way: Picture a **normal distribution**, also known as a bell curve, which represents the distribution of a particular characteristic in the general population. The units of a bell curve are characteristics—frequency of masturbation, for example—mathematically transformed into standard units. This is a good, though not perfect, tool for estimating norms and variations of those norms. Statistically, most people inhabit the fat, middle part of a bell curve. Some are a little above average, and some are a little below average. Less of the population is at either end.

Human sexuality can be displayed as a bell curve. Figure 2.1 shows one distribution for female sexuality and another for male sexuality. The line at the base of the chart, the x-axis, represents the continuum, or the range and diversity of the sexual phenomenon that has been charted onto the curve.

In Figure 2.1, you can note that a large portion of both female and male populations share much of the middle ground. This overlap is the case in almost every aspect of human experience, even sexual norms and practices. True, there are two separate distributions with two distinguishable averages (or pinnacles of the curves). However, only the small proportions of the population at either end of this double-jointed distribution are radically different from each other. The heavily shaded area in the middle is all—statistically speaking—the same. When you hear some difference described as not "statistically significant," this is what it looks like.

Sexual experience isn't all that different for men and women, but perhaps, like us, you wonder what causes men and women at one end of the continuum to be so different from other men and women at the middle or from members of the other sex at the opposite end of the continuum. You may even begin to wonder about the source of differences *among* women and among men—not simply differences *between* men and women. Finally, you may want to ask, as we do, why the world focuses on gender difference rather than similarity.

Race, Ethnicity, and Social Class

This chapter is about differences and similarities in women's and men's sexual behavior. But along with gender, people's behavior is also influenced by many other variables, such as class, race, and ethnicity—both independently and as they intersect with gender.

As difficult as it is to get reliable population samples to examine overall patterns in sexuality, obtaining sufficient numbers of respondents within demographic subcategories is even more difficult. Thus, the examination of race, class, and ethnicity along with gender influences on sexuality is a challenge.

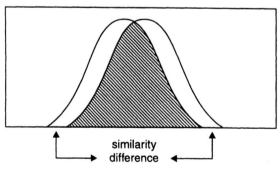

FIGURE 2.1
Overlapping distributions of men's and women's sexuality.

And even when sufficient data exist, they should be interpreted with caution, because race, class, ethnicity, and gender as variables are poorly understood and very complex. For example, when we look at someone who checks the survey box for Hispanic, we are looking at an enormous number of people who have huge cultural differences among them. Just think about it: do people from the Dominican Republic, Puerto Rico, Mexico, and Cuba really belong in the same analytic category? Nevertheless, the distinctions that we do find among different groups illustrate a crucial sociological point: social experience, more than biological inheritance, shapes sexuality. In some cases, gender overshadows other social categories; in other cases, gender combines with race, class, and ethnicity to produce variations in social and sexual norms of behavior.

Several very specific examples of sexual practices make the point. Figure 2.2 displays reported rates of masturbation by gender and by race/ethnicity, singling out white, black, and Hispanic respondents. Obviously, these divisions are very crude—whites, blacks, and Hispanics as we have just mentioned deserve to be further divided by class, by region, by national origin, and so on. (Note that "Hispanics" is the category used in the Laumann et al. survey referred to in this section. Hispanic in this case refers to people who identified as being of Spanish or Latin American origin.)

As you can see from figure 2.2, there is a gender difference: men report more masturbation than women. This finding is consistent with gendered norms of reports of sexual behavior that persist across other categories of experience, such as frequency or number of partners. But observe: black men are more similar to black, white, and Hispanic women in their reported

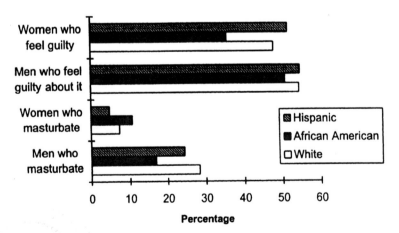

FIGURE 2.2
Masturbation practices and attitudes. Source: Laumann, et al. (1994).

levels of masturbation than they are to white and Hispanic men. That is, in the category of masturbation, black men and women have a smaller gender difference than do men and women in other racial/ethnic categories.

Now observe the sections that reflect how often people in different groups feel guilty about masturbation. About half of all those surveyed say they feel guilty about it, with one exception: only a third of black women, rather than half, say they feel guilty. The fact that black women follow a unique pattern may be the product of many cultural influences. Indeed, this result is consistent with other work that highlights a pattern of smaller gender gaps among a variety of dimensions among African Americans (Franklin 2007).

Consider another aspect of sexual behavior: duration of the most recent sexual episode (see figure 2.3). Across ethnic groups, more men than women claim that their last sexual episode lasted one hour or longer. And across ethnic groups, more women than men claim that their last sexual episode lasted fifteen minutes or less. Does this finding make sense? We think it suggests that men boast and women are demure when it comes to reporting sexual experience. Research also indicates that women are closer to the truth than men about actual time spent in intercourse, but if men are counting kissing, foreplay, undressing, and so on, their estimate might not be so off the mark. Nonetheless, the gender difference in explanations is consistent with socially constructed norms that reward men, but not women, for sexual prowess.

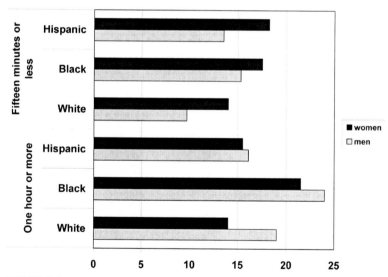

FIGURE 2.3
Duration of recent sexual encounter. Source: Laumann et al. (1994).

But what about gender differences by ethnicity? Once again, black men and women have a smaller gender difference than the other racial/ethnic groups, suggesting that the sexual scripts among African Americans tend to be less gendered than the scripts for the other groups. Hispanics are split: there is no gender difference regarding sixty-minute episodes, but fewer Hispanic men than women report the briefer, fifteen-minute episodes.

Now, look at what men and women say about giving and receiving oral sex (see figure 2.4). Whites report more oral sex than other groups; blacks report having oral sex less frequently than the other groups. Unlike our findings about duration of sex and masturbation, however, we find that oral sex brings out gender differences in reported experience by black men and women. Black men and women have a larger gender difference than whites or Hispanics. In addition, black men are quite different from white men in this graph; black women are quite different from white women. And these groups are also different from Hispanics.

Figure 2.4 reveals something even more interesting about oral sex, gender, and ethnicity. Among whites, the rates that men and women report are quite similar for both giving and receiving oral sex. Among Hispanics and even more so among blacks, however, men and women both claim receiving oral sex more often than giving it. How could this be? If they have given us accurate information, perhaps they are having oral sex with same-sex as well as opposite-sex partners. (Or perhaps there is a third party in their life!) Or it could be a definitional, cultural, and/or recall issue. We think these groups have different meanings associated with giving versus receiving oral sex. One hypothesis is that for Hispanics and blacks, giving oral sex is more of a taboo than receiving it.

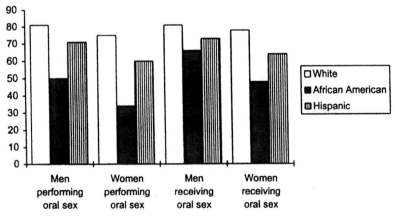

FIGURE 2.4
Oral sex in three race/ethnic categories. Source: Laumann et al. (1994).

But here is another explanation, one we find compelling. Oral sex, more so than other sexual acts, can be viewed in terms of power. Even though partners may "return the favor," it tends to be a one-way experience while it is being done. The person receiving oral sex typically feels more powerful in the moment than the person giving oral sex, even though lying back and receiving it actually makes a person quite physically vulnerable. As the examples of masturbation and duration of sexual episodes suggest, the gender difference between black men and women is smaller than between whites. Thus, black women, like black men, will express their sense of entitlement—their sense of power in the relationship—by reporting being recipients of oral sex more often than being givers of oral sex.

We can detect even more about social class, too, when we look at sexual practices. It turns out that men and women with more education are more likely to have oral sex, and yet less likely to have anal sex. Indeed, men with more education are especially more likely to *give* oral sex and women with more education are especially more likely to *receive* oral sex, according to the Laumann et al. data. We think that education provides a means for men and women to become less burdened by gendered ideas about oral sex that link oral sex with power. In contrast, men and women with less education (Billy et al. 2009) are *more likely* to have anal sex. Two explanations may hold: First, with less education, in many domains men and women are more likely to follow traditional gender scripts that may include male domination and a woman's sense of obligation to say to her partner, "yes, dear." A second is that with less education, folks also are more likely to have lower incomes and less access to birth control. Anal sex, in this case, becomes a method of birth control.

Sex is always experienced in a context that is highly specific: it is within a relationship that may be intimate or fleeting; people having sex can be of different genders or the same, different races or the same. People having sex are influenced by all these factors, and more, in varying degrees. Although from time to time in this chapter and other chapters we examine the influence of social variables such as ethnicity and class, we encourage you to raise these sociological concerns yourself as you think about all the examples of gendered sexuality that we provide.

Gendered Patterns in Sexual Practices

What people think of as the "ideal man" or the "ideal woman" is often characterized by the behavior at the extreme ends of the bell curve. Ironically, even where social forces work in concert to generate these "socially ideal" sexual norms and gender differences, few men or women achieve them. This shortfall is why so many men and women feel inadequate in the performance of feminine and masculine sexualities. Nevertheless, their expectations for gender-appropriate sexual behavior translate into many gender differences in sexual practice. As we explore below, however, men and women are generally far more alike than different.

Masturbation

We start our exploration of sexual practices with masturbation—where many of you may have started, too. As Woody Allen says, "Masturbation is sex with someone I love." It is strictly pleasure-focused, nonprocreative sex. Because it is fundamentally an individual act that is not related to bonding or reproduction, societies tend to stigmatize it. Yet this we know: masturbation is the most common of all sexual acts, especially among people outside of committed relationships. It is the least physically or emotionally dangerous, the most controllable by a person's own wishes, and the least likely to lead to misunderstandings. But masturbation is absolutely not the most socially acceptable sexual practice. Why not? The simple answer is religious taboo. Both Judaism and Christianity denounce "wasting seed," which refers to the nonprocreative character of male masturbation. Islam considers it "haraam" (forbidden) for the same reason.

As late as the nineteenth and early twentieth centuries, doctors blamed masturbation for everything from insanity to baldness, and many of those myths live on. Most of those myths were discarded over time—but some of them have not completely disappeared. One middle-aged woman told us a story from her youth that pertained directly to the power of these myths. It happened in the late 1950s, when she was eleven years old. A girlfriend came over to her house sobbing and shaking. The friend was distraught because her mother had caught her masturbating and told her she was going to go crazy and go to hell. Fortunately, the woman who was telling us this story had come from a family that believed in sex education and had given her educational materials that said masturbation was natural, common, and harmless. She let her friend read the material, and she said that it made a huge difference. Her friend was greatly reassured and comforted.

There are many stories about masturbation that have a similar theme. In Philip Roth's novel *Portnoy's Complaint* (1969), Portnoy tells how he was obsessed with masturbation until the shame crept up on him one day.

> It was at the end of my freshman year of high school—and freshman year of masturbating—that I discovered on the underside of my penis, just where the shaft meets the head, a little discolored dot that has since been diagnosed as a freckle. Cancer. I had given myself cancer. All that pulling and tugging at my own flesh, all that friction, had given me an incurable disease. (19)

Almost unbelievably, these scenes of shame continue in many households today. The stigma, particularly among those who take the Bible literally and consider masturbation a sin, is powerful. In 1994, when President Clinton's surgeon general, Joycelyn Elders, remarked that schools might teach teenagers about masturbation as a way to help them delay sexual involvement, the public uproar was so virulent that she was forced to resign. As recently as June 2007, conservative bloggers continued to complain about Elders's message: her acceptance of young people's sexual desire, according to the conservative view, constitutes recognition and encouragement of "immoral" sexual expression. Sex without an emotional connection or with no procreative intent is still apparently frowned on in U.S. society, even after the sexual revolution of the 1960s (which will be discussed in chapter 3).

Mind you, awareness has grown since Joycelyn Elders's remarks: starting in 1995, progressive cities around the country began to observe National Masturbation Month (May). And articles in mainstream publications such as *Psychology Today* examine health benefits as well as people's inhibitions regarding masturbation.

Still, public ambivalence persists, even if people's fondness for it also persists. As Laumann et al. explain when discussing their survey results on masturbation, "Masturbation has the peculiar status of being both highly stigmatized and fairly commonplace" (81). Over 60 percent of men report masturbating; more than 50 percent of women do so, too, though less frequently (Laumann et al. 1994, 81). A less scientific magazine survey in 2004 found that 81 percent of boys and 55 percent of girls started masturbating between ages ten and fifteen (Klein 2004). They start at an early age and continue whether or not they are in a committed sexual relationship. Boys may learn to masturbate at an early age because of the fortuitous friction of bed sheets or because early erections cue children to the pleasures of their own bodies. Or masturbation may begin in adolescence with the onset of more adult attractions. Whatever the critical stimulus, masturbation is pretty common. As people age, they also tend to masturbate less often.

Gender differences in frequency and prevalence of masturbation have been used by essentialists as evidence that women's sex drive is lower than men's. But social norms, including the idea that "nice girls don't touch themselves," have also been identified as the reason for the discrepancy. Think about how powerful social norms must be to convince women not to touch themselves, despite the intensely pleasurable sensation masturbation provides.

Men's and women's masturbation practices set the stage for their different approaches to sexuality in relationships. Masturbation is viewed as unavoidable for boys and men. Remember the movie *American Pie* (1999)? The very title of the movie revolves around the audience's sympathy for a teenage boy's (Jim Levenstein, played by Jason Biggs) desperation for autoerotic exploration—exploration that ultimately involved masturbating on a freshly baked (presumably somewhat cooled) pie. While some of us really love pie, the image reminds us that masturbation really puts people in touch with the fundamentals of desire.

But parents may be upset when their young daughter starts to touch herself. Since little girls—and big girls, too—are not supposed to be as sexual as boys, a girl who explores her body may alarm parents more than a boy who does the same thing (Koblinsky and Atkinson 1982). Girls may be discouraged from or punished for masturbation. They may be inculcated with the notion that sex for sex's sake is not really feminine. Parents may teach their children that sex for pleasure and release is more dangerous for women than for men because they believe that if a girl likes sex she may get pregnant or, in some locales, ruin her reputation. These worries are not passed on to men, except in the most conservative communities.

How has masturbation changed in the past thirty years? A panel study of German college students in 1966, 1981, and 1996 found that the number of men and women who masturbate increased over time, that women's first age of masturbation had become younger and more similar to men's first age of masturbation, and that men and women were more likely by 1996 than in the past to masturbate *regardless* of whether they were or ever had been sexually active (Dekker and Schmidt 2002). The changes over time among German college students (illustrated in figure 2.5) gives us more hints that where ideas about sexuality become more liberal, women's behavior will change toward doing something that they enjoy!

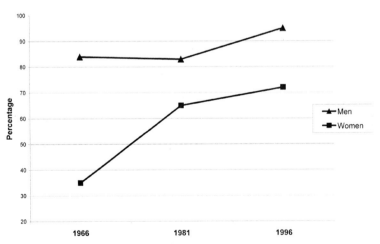

FIGURE 2.5
Masturbation rates since the 1960s. Source: Dekker and Schmidt (2002).

You can see a significant jump upward for women, yet women report masturbating less than men. Whatever the causes for this difference, less masturbation means that girls develop less sexual self-knowledge than boys do. Study after study shows a correlation between masturbation experience and women's reports of having orgasms with their intimate partner. Imagine what it is like when women enter their first relationship not having masturbated—and not having the vaguest idea about how their bodies should be touched or what thoughts are comfortable or arousing to them. Indeed, the play *The Vagina Monologues,* created by Eve Ensler, has captured attention year in and year out by drawing attention to the value and impact of women's awareness of their bodies: the frankness of the monologues provides empowerment even as it reminds us that women's genitals can still be treated with denial and euphemism as "down there." Ensler, along with the coproducers of the original show, established V-Day in 1998 to focus on women's healthy, safe sexuality; it continues to be observed around the world and is used to raise funds to support women victims of violence and abuse.

As women's desire for sexual equality has taken hold, their acceptance of masturbation has grown. Higher rates of masturbation are associated with higher rates of other sexual skills, including the ability to have orgasms. Feminist sex therapy and sex manuals for women who have been nonorgasmic teach them how to respond through masturbatory techniques. An orgasm is considered a woman's right, regardless of where and with whom she has it.

The focus on individual pleasure and the lack of concern for sex within relationships are major departures from the essentialist view of sex as procreative and the conservatives' view that sex should be properly confined to marriage. Still, a debate exists among evolutionary psychologists about what they believe is the function of orgasm: some, like Stephen Jay Gould and Elisabeth Lloyd, believe women's capacity to orgasm is just a fortunate happenstance—that it is just by random luck that women have developed this capacity. These theorists believe that it is an artifice of evolution (like an appendix) that follows from men's capacity for orgasm (Lloyd 2005). Others see women's orgasm as an adaptive bonding mechanism for women; they hold that orgasm helps to ensure that women want to have sex and that sex will enhance attachment, and that this creates the conditions for reproductive fitness at the heart of evolutionary explanations of sexuality (Margolis 2005).

However orgasm developed, it is a personal and even a commercial advantage for women and for the modern capitalist society! Not inconsequentially, an extensive video and sex-toy business for women brings in more than $8 billion a year (Auguste 2000) and is popular among middle- and upper-class women. Feminist sex shops like Good Vibrations and Toys in Babeland sell a wide variety of vibrators for single women, women in pairs with men, or women paired with other women. Women learn to respond sexually "by themselves, for themselves."

Rates of masturbation may still reveal a gender difference, but the absence of masturbation, rather than the presence of it, is more frequently being identified as a problem. In that respect, we are becoming more like the Scandinavians, who treat masturbation as a normal element of both men's and women's sexuality. To be sure, women more than men continue to be discouraged from sex for sex's sake, as observed in the next section on relational and recreational sex. But women now have social permission to be sexual, and the change has little to do with the biology of sex. Instead, it has to do with social changes that influence the sex lives of men and women. Our prediction: Even as men's and women's rates of masturbation have become more similar over the past decade, this will continue even more into the next decade.

Relational Sex versus Recreational Sex

Here's yet another sticky myth: that men generally prefer sex just for *fun*, and women only want sex for *love*. This myth has been elevated to a social norm and is believed to reflect the evolutionary psychological idea that "men inseminate and women incubate." Yet two important trends contradict this: First, it turns out that men and women *both* prefer sex in a relationship more than in a setting that is "just for fun" or "recreational" (Laumann et al. 1994)—and that *both* men and women are built for pleasure as well as reproduction. The difference is simply that recreational sex, which may occur with little emotional connection, is more acceptable to men than women if relational sex is not an option. And this difference is culturally specific: in The Netherlands, teen men and women (and their parents) are very open-minded about sex among young people—but young and old, they expect it to be in a close relationship, not a casual one (Schalet 2004). In chapters 3 and 5 we will discuss how the contrast between relational and recreational sex is expressed in the "hookup" culture. The "hookup" culture *appears* to emphasize recreational sex with "no strings attached"—but just how true is that?

The fact is, our approach to casual sex is complicated. In many places, the setting for relational sex is marriage or committed cohabitation. Furthermore, the emphasis in recent decades on reducing sexual risk taking, especially to protect against sexually transmitted diseases such as HIV, has made men as well as women more cautious. Yet over the past twenty-five years both men and women have become increasingly entitled to sexual pleasure for its own sake. To wit, as noted above, both college-aged men and women are likely to masturbate both while they are in a sexual relationship and while they are not. As suggested above, both young men and women participate in "hooking up."

Nevertheless, among the most commonly observed gender differences in the United States and in many Western countries (for example, Canada, Great Britain, France, Italy, and Scandinavian countries) is that women's sexual desire tends to be more "relational" than men's (Hatfield and Rapson 1996). That is, women's sexual desire focuses on a specific person and is ratified by love and mutual passion more so than men's. Men's sexual desire is more likely to allow for sex just for fun. A woman's sexual desire increases (or her inhibitions decrease) when she is focused on a person who cares about her rather than a person who can simply fulfill an immediate sexual need.

Some evidence from the Online College Social Life Survey on hooking up highlights the subtle contrasts between men's and women's experience. Figure 2.6 shows oral sex reciprocity in first-time sexual encounters and sexual encounters in the context of a relationship (from Armstrong, England, and Fogarty 2010). First-time encounters are far more likely to involve men's receiving oral sex, but not women's. For more developed relationships, oral sex reciprocity is much more of a norm. Another qualitative study on hooking up shows that women from middle-class families are more likely to be interested in casual encounters like "hooking up" than women from working-class families. In interviews, researchers found the difference was related to the women's level of career focus (Hamilton and Armstrong 2009). So while the majority of men also prefer relational sex (Laumann et al. 1994), more men than women seem to like recreational sex. For example, in the first half of the twentieth century, many men's sexual initiation was with a

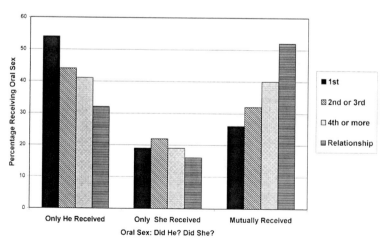

FIGURE 2.6
Gender, relationship type, and oral sex reciprocity. Source: Armstrong, England, and Fogarty (2010).

prostitute (Kinsey, Pomeroy, and Martin 1948)—later it started to decline. A recent survey in the United Kingdom even reported that men's use of female prostitutes doubled between 1990 and 2000, from 2 to just over 4 percent (Ward et al. 2005). Such practice is still lower than levels in the 1940s—and it appears to be related to travel abroad and "sex tourism." Although you can find anecdotes in the mainstream media of some instances where women pay for sex from men, this does *not* appear to be an area where men and women are approaching equality, nor does it appear that, at least for the present, many women want to have access to paid, professional sex workers. Indeed, a remarkable study of over 1,600 male sex workers around the country that examined who their customers are found no cases of women clients. There were straight men and gay men who hired male prostitutes—but no women (Logan 2010).

Figure 2.7 shows these differences, as well as men's and women's interest in two specific types of recreational sex. Although more men than women say that they find sex with a complete stranger appealing, and many more men than women say they find group sex appealing, only a very small proportion of the sample is interested in either. The proportion of men and women who prefer recreational sex may be small because of religious or personal values, family background, or a host of other reasons, not the least of which is a rational concern about sexually transmitted diseases. The proportion interested in

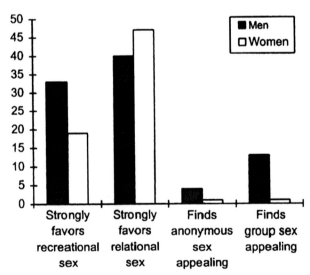

FIGURE 2.7
Attitudes toward recreational and relational sex. Data from Laumann et al. (1994).

recreational sex may be larger among special subgroups of men and women, such as urban, educated professionals whose lifestyle encourages them to delay marriage and whose advantages encourage them to feel secure about sex in uncommitted or fleeting liaisons.

Women's preference for relational sex shows up again in their limited use of prostitutes. Among those few women who have ever used a hired escort service (a hired date for the evening), if sex happens, it is rarely considered an exchange of sex for money. Instead, women see sex as an activity that was among the possibilities of the night out. The fee is for companionship; the sex is optional. Most women can hardly imagine even going so far as to hire an escort, much less pay for sex or seek sex in a totally anonymous format. It is hard to imagine finding a "Hollywood madam" who has a little black book full of female movie stars' accounts with them: both men and women movie stars have a multitude of appealing sexual options; but the women, unlike the men, don't seem to use sex for hire as one of their options.

Gender differences in relational versus recreational sexuality is further illustrated by comparing lesbian to gay male couples. Gay partners, like heterosexuals, have been raised with gendered sexual norms. But unlike heterosexual couples, both partners bring similar, rather than different, gendered norms of sexuality to the situation. The contrast between recreational sex associated with men and relational sex associated with women therefore becomes quite vivid. Although gays and lesbians, like heterosexuals, prefer relationships, the sexual norms for gay men and for lesbians differ from each other and from heterosexuals. For example, in the 1970s and 1980s gay men's magazines and subcultures touted recreational sex more than partnered sex. Since HIV and AIDS were discovered in the early 1980s, however, gay men may have shifted to preferring couplehood (Lever 1994a). There is some evidence that the popularity of gay couplehood preceded AIDS; the men of the baby boom generation (born between 1946 and 1964) were getting older and, like the rest of the country, more interested in "settling down" (Seidman 1992). Indeed, as we discuss in chapter 5, recent changes in access to and interest in same-sex marriage and civil unions foregrounds increased interest in "settling down." Although gays and lesbians have some increased access to more conventional ways to organize their personal lives; nevertheless, a significant number of gay men continue to approve of recreational sex and endorse nonmonogamy even within the context of a committed, lifetime relationship. Lesbians, on the other hand, tend to prefer sex in the context of love and relationship. In the 1990s, lesbian sex clubs started to open up that, like gay bars in their heyday, celebrate anonymous, recreational sex (Huston and Schwartz 1995), and in the 2000s women, like men, began using online services, like Craigslist, to establish quick casual liaisons. Lesbian use of Internet hookups is still lower than gay men's, but lesbians have a presence in this arena. This continues to be a peripheral movement, at the "cutting edge" of female sexuality. For the most part, lesbians, like heterosexual women, prefer sex to complement relationship goals.

To sum up, the evidence suggests that men prefer sex with someone they love but are more likely to see sex as fun for its own sake, and that women are more likely to believe sex can be enjoyable only when it has meaning, affection, and, for some, love. But let's not overstate those tendencies! Do women like quickies? Some do. As time marches on, and women are at greater liberty to express lust, the ratio of lust to love may change in women's lives. After all, even today, if you go to a male strip bar like Chippendale's, you will see women turned on by men's bodies and stuffing dollar bills in the men's G-strings—in short, behaving just as men would with female strippers. Still, the more impersonal sex is, the more likely it is that men will approve of it and women won't.

The history of sex, however, is a history of change. Although the differences in norms for men and women are striking, so are the differences between women today and women in previous eras, when women's sexual expression outside of marriage was more strictly constrained. Consider, for example, the number of women born between 1942 and 1952 who began having sex by age fifteen: 6 percent; thirty years later (for women born between 1972 and 1982), that rate was 19 percent (CDC 2007). Men today also differ from men in previous eras. For men born between 1942 and 1952, 17 percent had sex before age fifteen; 22 percent of men born between 1972 and 1982 had sex before age fifteen (CDC 2007) In fact, as figure 2.8 illustrates, men and women

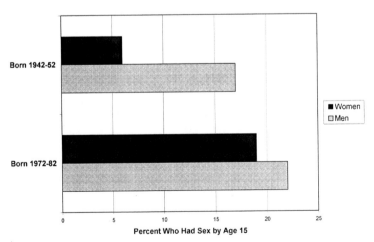

FIGURE 2.8
Narrowing the gap in sexual initiation. CDC (2007).

today are more similar to one another than men of today and men of previous eras or women of today and women of previous eras. Furthermore, you can see greater change for women than for men. But that may be in transition as well. There is now more pressure on men to be more sensitive, less predatory, and less macho in the last several decades. Legal challenges to what used to be unquestioned male sexual privilege (such as the freedom to touch or come on to women employees or co-workers, whether or not they have invited such attention) have put the sexes on more equal footing than they might have been just a few years ago. If we return to the image of the normal distribution, picture fewer and fewer men at the extreme "macho" end of the continuum and fewer women at the extreme "docile" end of the continuum. Male and female averages are still somewhat different, but over time the distributions have shifted toward a common center, and perhaps both continua have expanded to allow greater diversity in sexual expression regardless of gender.

Much of this change can be explained by societal changes: Women have gained more economic power and social influence; therefore, women's privileges have shifted. For example, in 1970, only 4 percent of wives earned more than their husbands. Today, 22 percent of wives earn more (Pew Report, 2010, New Economics of Marriage). Men and women live more similar lives in the workforce; they encounter one another professionally, and competition, respect, and colleagueship have modified their approach toward each other. Although men and women have worked together in working-class settings, the change is that now middle-class professional positions have more women in them than ever before. Additionally, today, more men have a woman supervisor or boss than has ever occurred in any previous historical period.

For a sign of a changing culture with new norms, look at images of women in Hollywood movies and on MTV. Although some people consider them caricatures of greater sexual license, these media often show a new female sexual icon. Angelina Jolie, for example, projects physical strength and courage and emotional independence in roles such as Mrs. Smith, the feisty mercenary in *Mr. and Mrs. Smith* (2005). Meryl Streep, in *It's Complicated* (2009), plays a middle-aged woman who has been left by her husband, yet remains professionally successful, well balanced, and capable of handling a love affair with her ex-husband without becoming desperate for his return.

Of course, the alert movie and television fans can counter with as many conservative images of female sexuality. In many reality television programs, such as *The Bachelor*, women vie for their "big break": to snag a husband. We get a vision of a man who seems to be sincerely looking for the woman of his dreams to marry, but we also witness a mating ritual that emphasizes the notion that a woman's path to success is paved by being chosen by the right man. Not incidentally, every woman in the group chosen to compete for his attention is tall, slim, and very sexy. One variation of *The Bachelor* had a woman choosing among "geeks"; there was no parallel program that presented geeky women to a handsome bachelor!

In the comedy film *Knocked Up* (2007), we see another vision of the conflicting elements of modern women's sexuality. Katherine Heigl, who plays Alison Scott in the film, is a young, free-spirited woman, ready to celebrate her recent big promotion with a drunken one-night stand. Her freedom to "live large" has limits though: when an accidental pregnancy ensues because of a failure of communication about contraception, her immediate assumption that she has to have the baby shows none of the struggles that a majority of women might have when faced with a pregnancy that happened after a chance encounter with a stranger. In the film, she has the baby, the baby's father (Ben Stone, played by Seth Rogan) ends up being involved and supportive, and therefore she scuttles her career and happily settles down with him to family bliss. The film's message seems to be sure, have a good time ladies, but when motherhood occurs, professional sacrifice and traditional family values are the appropriate next steps. Indeed, the filmmakers were conscious of this double standard, and, in interviews about the movie, joked about the fact that they could not even *mention* abortion, and instead referenced "rhymes with smashmortion" as the unspeakable alternative.

There are certainly conflicting models of women's sexuality in contemporary media, but perhaps the real story is that no single model of women's sexuality prevails. Instead, there seems to be the possibility of a sexual entrepreneurship unknown to previous generations of women. Women have many more paths they can take to gain a lover or to enjoy sex without gaining the obligation of a relationship. But society's emphasis on putting motherhood ahead of personal ambition, support of a partner's workforce participation ahead of one's own goals, and marriage as ultimately the best possible location for personal fulfillment still affects women more than men.

Men's roles are also not stuck in concrete. The "new man" is emerging in modern movies. For example, men are increasingly portrayed as more loyal to their partners than they would have been in the 1970s and 1980s. In *Knocked Up*, Seth Rogen's character struggles but ultimately arrives at his desire to "get the girl" and achieve the status of partner and father. Even the monogamy-challenged James Bond has had a makeover. Consider the new scruples of Pierce Brosnan's James Bond in *GoldenEye* (1996) and his subtle mooning over the ever-faithful Miss Moneypenny. Ten years later the role is even more dramatic. In *Casino Royale* (2007), Bond (played by Daniel Craig) is emotionally committed and settles down (or tries to, since tragedy, of course, is lurking around the corner) with the love of his life. This character is in sharp contrast to Sean Connery's more promiscuous, womanizing portrayals of

James Bond in the 1960s or Roger Moore's continuance of that theme decades later. In those movies of the past, when James Bond falls in love, it looks a lot more like lust than a prelude to wedding bells. A woman attracted to Bond usually has a short life span, and even if she survives, what is left is sex, not love. In essence, he doesn't get romantically trapped, but she does. His vitality is sexual; hers is sexual but also emotionally dependent. The new James Bond *does* fall in love. Still, in the 2000s, the even newer Bond has much sexual privilege. He puts his life in the hands of two women in *Casino Royale*. He has had sex with both, so they are inextricably bonded to him via sex. In previous eras, Bond had the need to conquer all women but remain free. Bond still has a lot of sexual autonomy, but this new Bond is less terrified of the power of women and portrays more vulnerability.

So here we are—witness to the narrowing of the sexual gender gap between men and women. The media is both a force toward traditionalism and innovation. The legal system is also in flux, and the news keeps us abreast about which gender rules are changing and which ones are affirmed. We are not saying that these forces have totally equalized the costs of sexual permissiveness for women and men or that women and men necessarily have the same emotional response to sex. However, the changes we have observed illustrate two important themes. First, the norms that govern women's sexuality are becoming less punitive or at least less effective. Meanwhile, norms for men have changed, but to a lesser degree. Second, this shift in rules and behavior supports the perspective that sexual desire is a social construction. Its expression varies widely according to time, place, and political climate.

Fantasy and Pornography

Another arena for examining gendered sexuality is sexual fantasy as portrayed in pornography and other material designed for sexual arousal. The first thing we know about pornography is that it is a very big business, and it is pervasive worldwide: In 2006, over $3,000 was being spent on pornography *every second*. Figure 2.9 illustrates the legal status of pornography worldwide, with a concentration of unrestricted (excluding child pornography) use in Western countries, where individual freedoms—and capitalism—are more unfettered.

Pornographers give their clients more of whatever sells best, so by looking at what is produced and bought, we can find meaningful patterns in gender differences and similarities, regardless of sexual orientation. Indeed, the use of pornography hinges on several issues: how interested women versus men are in "porn," how much the subject of porn represents men's versus women's sexuality, and the extent to which porn might actually *shape* or *influence* men's versus women's sexuality.

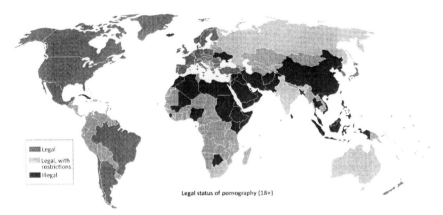

FIGURE 2.9
Legal status of pornography worldwide. (18+) Wiki Commons. http://upload.wikimedia.
org/wikipedia/commons/d/d0/Pornography_law_map.png.

Many fewer women than men say they like to use pornography for arousal (Laumann et al. 1994), as figure 2.10 shows. A more recent survey of Internet pornography usage shows a narrowing margin: 20 percent of men versus 13 percent of women report ever accessing pornography at work. Overall, 72 percent of Internet porn users are men, and 28 percent are women. To put porn use versus other activities in context, what men and women like to do on the Internet may

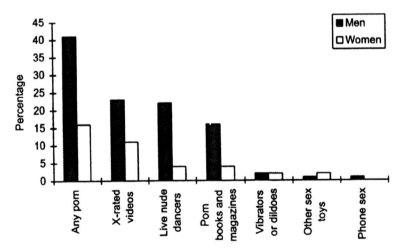

FIGURE 2.10
Preferences for pornography. Data from Laumann et al. (1994).

be somewhat different: twice as many women as men report preferring the use of Internet chat rooms.

Indeed, the content as well as the activities tend to vary for men and women. Both heterosexual and gay men's pornography tends to be graphic and sexually straightforward. Certain acts, such as partners performing oral sex and swallowing the semen, seem to be de rigueur. Both written accounts and visual representations of sex often contain themes of power and submission. Heterosexual sadomasochistic material emphasizes the erotic power of either dominating a partner or being dominated. Although subspecialties of pornography cater to a great diversity of sexual tastes, mainstream men's heterosexual pornography involves very little storytelling. Instead, it gets into "hard, fast action" right away and rarely portrays a relationship between the sexually involved actors.

Indeed, women who have used porn complain that most pornography caters to men's sexual fantasies and therefore is not usually arousing for them. They report being disgusted by the negative female imagery in films and magazines, including the use of physical power and domination by men against women. In contrast, erotic material that appeals to women often emphasizes emotional as well as physical foreplay rather than intercourse. Depictions of romance, seduction, and the growth of desire serve to make the sex itself more interesting. Indeed, this is the stuff Hollywood movies are made of, except they stop short of gynecological close-ups of vulvas and penises. The minimal availability of pornography designed by women or for women may help explain gender differences in its popularity.

In fact, women may be a big, untapped market! Women can definitely be visually aroused by images of nudity and explicit sexual acts. One study found that men *reported* more arousal than women in response to visual images, but that men's and women's actual responses (measured physiologically) were more similar than dissimilar (Schmidt and Sigusch 1970). By using a plethysmograph (a gauge attached to a penis or inserted into a vagina that monitors the amount of blood flowing to the genitals and thereby measures levels of sexual arousal), Heiman (1977) tracked the impact of erotic material. Volunteers were asked to watch sexually explicit movies and provide a self-report of their arousal. When self-reports were compared to physiological feedback, women had underreported their level of arousal as it was measured by the genital monitor. Men provided a more accurate report. Were the women not conscious of their own physiological experience? Do men and women operate with different definitions of what constitutes arousal? Or were they reluctant to admit an "improper" sexual response? In this case, men and women were physically similar, but their responses reflected social norms and stereotypes of sexuality. This finding also supports social constructionist theories of sexuality.

Women may respond to garden-variety pornography more than they let on, as we have mentioned. But women's sexual response is generated by different kinds of stimuli, as indicated by the kinds of romance books they buy or movies they order. Women's preferences seem to suggest a somewhat more relational and less mechanical approach to sexual experience than men's. For example, Ellis and Symons (1990), evolutionary psychologists who emphasize that behavior evolves to maximize reproductive capability, systematically compared men's and women's sexual fantasies. They found that women's fantasies were generally relationship oriented, focused on someone they were dating or had experienced sexually. The fantasies were full of details about the partner and the environment of the encounter. The pace was typically slow and sensual, with lots of caressing and emotional exchange. Women concentrated on foreplay rather than intercourse. In contrast, men's fantasies were more impersonal, more focused on specific sexual acts, and more likely to be populated with strangers or multiple partners. Symons (1979) thinks that for men, sex is about lust and physical gratification. In their fantasies, sex is devoid of encumbering relationships, emotional elaboration, complicated plot lines, flirtation, courtship, and extended courtship, and women are easily aroused and willing. Although Ellis and Symons use their findings to support the notion that women and men are biologically different, this pattern is equally consistent with a social constructionist view that recognizes that such a difference illustrates simply that women and men continue to behave differently. It does not tell us why. Our sexual fantasies, like our behaviors, are learned, even scripted by our environment (Hicks and Leitenberg 2001). The content of sexual fantasies may have biological features associated with it, but the preponderance of cues in the environment teach men and women that different things are sexy.

Not only are men's and women's sexual fantasies different in kind, but they appear to be different in number as well. In the NHSLS, the researchers found that 54 percent of men fantasized daily, compared to only 19 percent of women (Laumann et al. 1994). Men and women college students are a little more comparable. Hicks and Leitenberg (2001) found that college men reported on average about twice as many fantasies as women. When the researchers examined whether fantasies were romantic and about one's partner, women reported more fantasies; men on the other hand reported more fantasies about people other than their partner. Of course, self-reports may be influenced by social norms that discourage women from admitting or even recognizing sexual impulses. Still, both men and women reported fairly high rates of fantasies about someone other than their partner: 93 percent of men and 80 percent of women fantasized about someone other than their partner.

Because the inner world of an individual is created largely, if not completely, by the external world, it stands to reason that men and women, living lives differentiated by their gender, would dream and fantasize in different ways. Some more embedded reason may explain why women's fantasies are different from men's, but the proximal reasons are quite "man made." External social constraints, such as what seems properly feminine or masculine, influence imagination and behavior. To be "an admirable person," a woman is supposed to have sex only when she is in love, with only the one man who is her husband or at least her committed lover. A woman must keep her dignity, if not her virginity, so that she is not labeled "promiscuous" or, more punitively, "a slut." While the line that demarcates what constitutes promiscuity changes over time—such that nowadays women have more sexual freedom than women had in the past, a woman today will still be labeled "slut" sooner (with fewer sexual adventures) than a man will. We know that contemporary sexual expectations call on a woman, once she is in bed with an acceptable mate, to turn into a passionate, uninhibited lover. With no independent "script" or directions on how a ladylike but passionate woman is supposed to act, many women follow the model that movies and custom create: They wait for the man of their dreams to show them what to do and what kind of lover to be. While norms of sexuality and fantasies change little by little over the years, women's expectation that they mold themselves to someone else's desire persists.

Some scientists speculate that men learn to fantasize when they begin masturbating, which occurs earlier in life than women's masturbatory practice (Gagnon and Simon 1973). Furthermore, men have explicit masturbatory material, such as *Playboy* magazine, to guide their fantasies more so than women. Although women can find porn, erotic fiction, and specialty magazines, the more common form of "pornography" for women is romance novels. The consequence may be that boys and men have more experience with fantasizing, and perhaps that some of their fantasies get established when they are very young, before they have fallen in love or even know what romantic love is! They may also have greater uniformity in their fantasies and be overly focused on the highly narrow vision of erotica created by men's magazines and pornographic books. Finally, men also have few models for being today's ideally macho yet sensitive lover. They therefore may continue to rely on old-fashioned seduction scenarios involving male leadership and aggression.

One of the great writers of erotica of the twentieth century was Anaïs Nin. Her books and journals explored what she considered the feminine imagination, and while her stories and her journals of her fantasies were explicit and gave detailed attention to forbidden desires and obsessions—heterosexual as well as lesbian—the fantasies were consistent with notions that men's and women's desires are fundamentally different. Erotic books (such as those edited by Susie Bright in the 1990s and 2000s) have done more to liberate female fantasies from the traditional gender scripts. These may or may not be a reliable representation of all female fantasies, but let us assume that they represent some women's fantasies. They suggest that women have the capacity to fantasize about torrid scenarios that have nothing to do with love and that can be as bizarre and orgasm-centered as men's.

Men, on the other hand, may be more interested in fantasies centered on relationships and love than the original stereotype might suggest. In a study of men's and women's responses to romantic pornography and to more mechanical pornography, researchers found that both men and women found the romantic pornography more arousing (Quackenbush, Strassberg, and Turner 1995). Most everybody likes the combination of intimacy and sex, but social conventions encourage women to fantasize about intimate, romantic sex and not "hard core" sex. Likewise, men's imagination for "relational sex" may be neglected because norms about masculinity and virility keep those kinds of erotic stories and pictures out of erotic and pornographic materials designed for men.

In a study from the 1970s, the top fantasy for both men and women was "having sex with someone you love" (Hunt 1974). The second highest, "having sex with strangers," was appealing to twice as many men as women. This difference may not so much reflect possible fantasies or capacities for recreational sex as reflect the way the question was perceived. For example, women, much more than men, identify "stranger" with "danger," and not a sexy kind of danger. Women who might fancy a one-night stand must also intelligently evaluate the possibility that the man would be homicidal, brutal, or contemptuous and overpowering. If the fear and potential for violence that anonymous sex presents to women could be effectively removed, their fantasies might be different.

Initiation and Sexual Negotiation

Consistent with the pattern of more extensive men's influence in relationships and higher expectations of men's sexual intensity and desire, more men than women initiate sex, and more women than men refuse sex. Can we conclude that men have a stronger sex drive than women? Or has tradition, based on the theory of men's powerful drives, assigned men the job of initiating sexual courtship and given women the prerogative to accept or reject?

As table 2.1 indicates, survey respondents tend to see initiation as "men's work" and refusal as "women's work." Furthermore, Brown and Auerback (1981) found in their survey of one hundred couples that women initiate

TABLE 2.1
Sexual Initiation (In Percentages)

Statement	Men	Women
Says more likely to initiate	51	12
Says more likely to refuse	16	48
Most common function of sex	Sexual release	Love

sex for "love, intimacy, and holding," whereas men said they sought "sexual release." These are widely familiar expectations for how men and women should properly relate in heterosexual pairs. Another study highlights the power of gender beliefs on sexual initiation. Greene and Faulkner studied college students (2005) and found that women in committed relationships who supported traditional ideas about gender (or a "sexual double standard") were less likely to initiate sex than women who did not endorse traditional gender ideas.

This "norm" is so strong that women who step out of line and initiate sex "too much" often receive a nasty reaction. In the American Couples survey (Blumstein and Schwartz 1983), husbands reported negative feelings when wives showed more sexual initiative than they did. This finding is surprising for people who hold a strongly biological perspective on sexual desire. If initiation reflected only sexual appetite, it stands to reason that men would favor sex regardless of who initiates the opportunity. However, initiation is clearly also about power. Sex occurs according to men's agenda. If women initiated more, the sexual agenda might be quite different. The sexual experience, where power is skewed, is undoubtedly different from situations where power is shared. Thus, social construction, rather than biology, dictates the organization of sexual initiation and response. From a symbolic interactionist point of view, if men are the guardians of sexual frequency, they will try to initiate sex as an identity-confirming act. If women are guardians of intimacy, they will seek to have sex when it constitutes a relationship-confirming act.

Differences in initiation also occur in gay and lesbian relationships, and they often have to do with power. Gay men, like heterosexual men, are comfortable with initiating. In fact, they are so comfortable in that role that they prefer not to relinquish it. When each partner of a gay couple was asked, "who initiates sex?" in the American Couples study, both partners claimed the behavior. Initiation appears to be a measure of men's machismo and sexual competence.

However, initiation does not work the same magic for women. When lesbian couples were asked who initiates sex more often, both partners claimed that the other partner does most of the asking (Blumstein and Schwartz 1983). (Keep in mind—as we discuss later—that lesbians have higher rates of orgasm than other women.) In other words, the role of initiation seems to be

more of a man thing regardless of whether the couple is heterosexual or homosexual. In fact, both lesbian and heterosexual women tend to see initiation
as potentially too aggressive (Blumstein and Schwartz 1983). What exactly
constitutes aggression? Definitions vary, but it may include behavior ranging
from refusing to take no for an answer to asking for sex rather than allowing
it to emerge consensually.

Women who are sexually assertive learn over time that assertiveness is
not always welcomed, so most modify their behavior. This is particularly
true among lesbians. Most lesbians have had the same sexual socialization
as heterosexual women, but they also often live in a subculture that directly
opposes male standards of beauty, conduct, and acceptability for women and
masculine sexual styles such as assertiveness. Many books on lesbian couples
cite severe arguments between partners when one or the other feels she is
being "dominated" or aggressively controlled. This sensitivity exists within
the sexual realm as well, with the outcome being fewer overall initiations and
therefore less frequent sex.

If sexual assertiveness is seen as demeaning or inappropriate for women, it
makes sense that even women with intense sexual appetites will modify them.
Likewise, if sexual assertiveness is positive and rewarding for men, it makes
sense that even men who do not have a big sexual appetite will try to live up
to the current standards of masculinity and give at least an adequate gender
performance. Initiating sex may not be any more "natural" for many men
than it is for women, but the pressure to perform is different. Social conventions of gender mold individual behavior and wrap even unwilling men and
women into the gender-appropriate sexual performance.

Orgasm and Stimulation

Although orgasm and ejaculation are not synonymous for men, they
are nearly equivalent. Most men who get excited and have an erection will
experience orgasm with continued stimulation. As anyone who has had
an orgasm knows, orgasm is very reinforcing; a man is likely to repeat the
experience whenever an erection makes it possible. Some men have erectile
difficulty and a much smaller number have trouble achieving orgasm, but
when there are no dysfunctions men typically have an orgasm fairly soon
after any kind of stimulation, whether it is masturbation, intercourse, oral
sex, or some other sex act. In recent years, the issue of erectile dysfunction
has become much more visible with the introduction of Viagra and other
medications to treat "ED." It isn't clear how often men have trouble, but
one study showed that after Viagra came on the market, diagnoses of ED
doubled (Kaye and Jick 2003).

Women often learn to have orgasms later in life than men do, and a minority of women has trouble ever becoming orgasmic. As figure 2.11 illustrates, women are less likely than men to have an orgasm during sexual activity. (Notice, however, that more men report their partners having an orgasm during sex than women report having one.) Middle-class women are more likely than working-class women to have an orgasm during sex, probably because they have fewer environmental distractions and demands and more sex education (Sprecher and McKinney 1993; Richters et al. 2003). Among college students in the Online College Social Life Survey, the orgasmic gender gap persists. But the gender gap varies by relationship context—in first-time hookups, men are much more likely than women to have an orgasm, while in ongoing relationships, men's and women's frequency of orgasm is more similar, as shown in figure 2.12 (Armstrong, England, and Fogarty 2010).

Sex therapists and advice books have sought to improve women's lower rate of orgasm. Feminist critics replaced the term *frigid*—used to describe women who had never had an orgasm during sex—with *preorgasmic*. The new term reflects the belief that most women can be taught to have an orgasm, and books such as Barbach's *For Yourself*, published in the 1970s, were pathsetting in terms of opening up women's sexuality. Today, much more advice in books, on the Internet, and even on *Oprah* is available for women who want to know more about orgasm.

If orgasms constitute a central pleasure in life, it stands to reason that women would make it a priority to become orgasm experts the way men seem to be. So why are women inhibited in achieving orgasm? There are lots of reasons. First, women have less information about how to do it. Second, achieving orgasm takes practice, and women, taught to be modest and con-

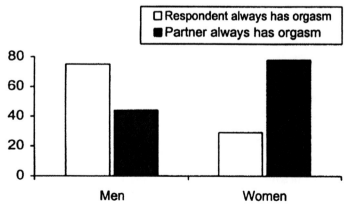

FIGURE 2.11
Orgasms during partnered sex. Data from Laumann et al. (1994).

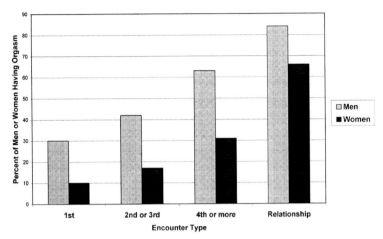

FIGURE 2.12
Gender gap in orgasm by encounter. Data from Armstrong et al. (2010).

trolled, may be inhibited about taking the time to discover how their bodies work. A third influence is the social taboo against sexual pleasure—especially by and for oneself. Remarkably, these social factors (and others) have the power to override the biological fact that orgasms feel just as good to women as they do to men and that some women can have more of them because they can be restimulated to another orgasm in a relatively short time after the first one. (Men need a longer "refractory" period.) Like men, women who have orgasms are happier in their relationships than women who do not (Byers 2005 source: *Journal of Sex Research*). In fact, one study showed that men and women described the feeling of orgasm in almost exactly the same terms (Hatfield and Rapson 1996).

No clinical name exists for men's orgasm problems (which is different from erectile dysfunction), either because so few exist, because many men do not seek therapy, or even because men who can maintain an erection for a long time gain status for their endurance. The exception to this rule is *priapism*, a painful and dangerous condition in which a man cannot lose his erection because blood will not leave the engorged penis. This problem requires medical intervention.

At first glance, men's greater ease and frequency in reaching orgasm seems biological, what with penises being so easy to locate and handle. But we believe orgasms have a learned, social element. Perhaps the first place to look for social cues that influence orgasms is the different masturbatory patterns of boys and girls. Boys gain more experience masturbating to orgasm than girls, because they start earlier. Gagnon and Simon, a creative pair of sociologists, wrote in *Sexual Conduct* (1973) that boys' ability to masturbate and their reinforcement for masturbating yield a rich, provocative, and even disturbing fantasy life. They hypothesize that one reason women masturbate less frequently than men is that women have a more minimal fantasy life. Of course, women's seemingly minimal fantasy life may be a consequence, not a cause, of less frequent masturbation. The record on pornography use and availability we discussed above also plays a role. Furthermore, women's fantasy life is devitalized by internal constraints women develop early on to be sexual in socially approved ways, just as women's reports of fantasies may be more conservative due to external constraints. Men, too, desire to be sexual in socially approved ways, but their approved ways include a less inhibited expression of sexuality.

The social constraints women are subject to have an impact on ease of orgasm, because orgasm is at least partly a mental ability. Orgasms require focus. Both men and women experience inability to climax (Rosen and Rosen 1981) when tension, worry, distraction, or the accumulated distress of previously unsuccessful attempts overshadows the experience. But most women, unlike men, face the challenge of training their body to be excited and satisfied, because they tend to have fewer orgasmic experiences through masturbation and less sexual experimentation early in life.

Furthermore, the social script for heterosexual orgasm has convinced too many people that sex is good only if both partners achieve orgasms through intercourse. Some women who report no orgasm during sexual intercourse have never tried other methods, such as manual or oral stimulation. Indeed, in a large survey of Australian adults, researchers found that the women who were least likely to have orgasms were those where intercourse was the *only* sexual activity with their partner (Richters, Visser, Rissel, and Smith 2006). When there was no oral sex or other forms of stimulation, orgasm was less common. Maybe this is because some women feel inhibited about touching themselves or being touched during lovemaking because they are worried, sometimes accurately, that it will insult their partner. Inability to climax solely through penile penetration is seen as either a rejection of the male partner or a commentary on his sexual competence. In this case, then, women's biological capacity for orgasm is overridden by social norms.

In fact, penetration may not be the easiest or the most efficient way for women to climax. The opening of the vagina is laced with nerve endings and therefore very sensitive, and the area around the cervix has a mass of nerve endings available for orgasmic stimulation. But most women climax more easily and intensely through direct clitoral stimulation. Certain sexual positions—like a woman sitting on top of her partner—make it more likely that the clitoris will be stimulated during intercourse, but direct touching or oral stimulation may be kinder to a woman's most sensitive sexual organ. Still, when custom decrees that intercourse is the lone legitimate way to have an orgasm, people will bend themselves into pretzels to try to be sexually orthodox, even at the price of the very orgasm they are seeking. We could hypothesize that lesbians are more likely to be consistently orgasmic because the requirement of intercourse is not typically present (except when lovers use equipment like a strap-on dildo); touching is more likely to be perfected and appreciated as an important avenue for lovemaking (Blumstein and Schwartz 1983).

To add to heterosexual women's dilemma, men often do not know how to touch a woman effectively. She may not know how to tell him, or have the nerve to tell him, or she may even have tried to tell him and been rebuffed. For some partners, oral sex is a satisfying alternative, but for others, it is taboo, embarrassing, or too intimate to even try. These difficulties keep many women either from finding a position during intercourse that helps them climax or from working out a sexual style that makes orgasm possible.

Women's reticence to seek effective sexual stimulation represents a distinct clash between the physical experience of sex and the social pressures that define and restrict sexual experience. A woman may consider requesting sexual acts that could stimulate her body more effectively to be sexually selfish or even unladylike. Some women avoid oral sex or other direct touching *because* it is so effective. These women may prefer a lower level of arousal rather than display themselves as out of control and therefore not "virtuous." Women may not recognize that social norms are structuring their negative response to oral sex or other alternatives to intercourse. Nevertheless, some women limit their sexual expectations accordingly and no longer try to be orgasmic all the time, or perhaps ever. This does not make sex undesirable, but it may make it somewhat less passionate or perhaps less reinforcing. Some women do not find an inability to climax frustrating, but others do, and it can diminish self-esteem, desire, or affection for a partner.

Numbers of Partners

Some research on sexual variety provides evidence that men more than women desire variety both in sexual acts and in partners (Blumstein and Schwartz 1983). In the NHSLS and General Social Survey (GSS) 1988 to 1991 studies, around 56 percent of men reported five or more partners to date; slightly less than 30 percent of women reported this many (Laumann et al. 1994).

As figure 2.13 illustrates, the gender differences in the middle range of the number of partners reported are not so high as the gender differences at the top end. Furthermore, when we look at only the youngest cohort surveyed in the NHSLS, people born between about 1964 and 1975, both women and men had more partners than older women did. Interestingly, in the youngest cohort more men than women had no sexual partners in the past year. This dif-

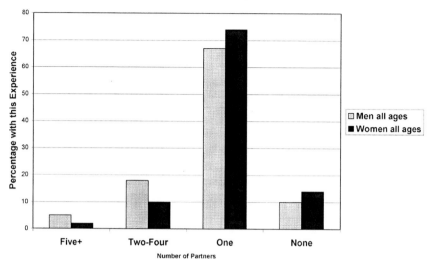

FIGURE 2.13
Number of partners in the past twelve months. Data from Laumann et al. (1994).

ference may in part be explained by women's increased sexual freedom, which gives them permission to have multiple partners as long as they don't have "too many." But it may also be a consequence of hypergamy—that is, younger women being courted by older men. Younger men don't have the same abundance of sexual opportunity early in life that women appear to have.

Evolutionary psychologists hypothesize that men naturally desire variety in partners because it helps motivate them to have sex with many women and therefore be more likely to have many offspring. In addition, perhaps having a short romantic attention span helps men to detach from a woman they already had sex with because she will not be available for reinsemination for at least nine months. A brief period of attachment allows men to turn their attention to impregnating other women.

This hypothesis is undermined, however, by women's increasing number of sexual partners over time: women and men are still different, but not as much. The other challenge is the fact that sexual interest and attention wander or decline over time for all kinds of couples, even gay couples and all kinds of partners not interested in reproduction. Gay men have consistently reported higher rates of nonmonogamy than heterosexuals or lesbian pairs, particularly before AIDS made sexual adventurousness dangerous. We might conclude that men, unfettered by heterosexual convention or by women, are innately driven to more and more partners. However, emerging sexual trends among women show similar patterns. A young lesbian is much more likely than her lesbian counterpart of twenty years ago to seek sexual experimentation with more than one partner. Furthermore, the more liberal a heterosexual woman's attitudes are about sex the more likely she is to seek and experience more than one lover. As we have discussed, differences in self-reports of sexual frequency may simply be influenced by social norms that approve the notion of men having more lovers and women having fewer.

What psychological and social impact does the number of partners have on men and women? Just as women have less experience with masturbation than men, on average, women are likely to be less sexually experienced than men prior to marriage. Divorced women tend to have additional partners between marriages (as do men), but in general the gender difference maintains for both premarital and postmarital experience. Some women have a large number of partners, but they do so in violation of both spoken and unspoken values regarding female sexual restraint, which is sometimes referred to as the *sexual double standard.* This double standard involves stronger punishments for women's sexual expression than for men's. Figure 2.13 suggests a possible result of the sexual double standard: although for men and women the numbers are small, twice as many men (5 percent) report having five or more partners than do women (2 percent).

From an evolutionary psychological perspective, the double standard is a rule of nature. Men are driven to reproduce as often as possible; women are driven to protect and nurture the few offspring they have and offer their sexual exclusivity in exchange for male support and commitment. From a social constructionist point of view, the sexual double standard serves a different purpose: men use it to obtain loyalty from women (and punish any lack of loyalty) to keep and maintain control, assure access, and establish paternity. In other words, this can be explained by the social norms that influence men's and women's response to questions about sexuality.

The sexual double standard still exists in most Western industrialized countries, even if it no longer requires wives to be virgins prior to marriage. The updated standard allows women to have sex within a nonmarital committed relationship, but having many partners is still often punished by disapproval or social isolation. A man with too many sexual conquests may be labeled a womanizer if he is heterosexual or a health risk if he is gay. But women's sexuality is rewarded mostly in the context of sexual loyalty in relationships. A particularly liberated woman may intrigue a sexually confident man, but this is not the norm.

The urban and industrialized West is notably sexually liberal and tolerant when compared to the rest of the world. In other countries or even in conservative areas in the United States, a woman with substantial sexual experience in her "past" is a woman with a dimmer marital future. This has been the story for women throughout most of history. Recall Hester Prynne, the main character in the nineteenth-century American novel by Nathaniel

Hawthorne, *The Scarlet Letter*. Prynne was ostracized and marked with the scarlet letter "A" for her nonmarital, "adulterous" sexual activity. Or think of Blanche Dubois in the 1947 Tennessee Williams play *A Streetcar Named Desire*. Blanche's plans to marry (and thereby save herself from poverty) were foiled because her sexually permissive history in a small Louisiana town followed her to New Orleans and rendered her unmarriageable.

Such social sanctions are hardly the case today in the United States; nevertheless, no equivalent female term for *stud* exists; even seemingly complementary phrases such as *femme fatale* have a more than slightly ominous tone. A star like Madonna may be able to break all the rules and gather a following because of it. But outside of Hollywood and a few other unique subcultures, a lifestyle like Madonna's could cause male contempt and anger and place a woman in a dangerous situation. At the very least, it would be difficult in most parts of the world for a woman to have all kinds of lovers and aggressively promote her own sexual agenda without getting a "bad reputation."

Models of extreme sexual prowess really represent very few women—or for that matter, men. Remember, the majority of men and women remain in the middle of the overlapping distribution of sexuality. The majority of men look at media images of hypermasculinity and ready, indiscriminate sexuality—their models of manhood include Sylvester Stallone and Arnold Schwarzenegger—and they wonder who dreams these characters up. They feel no more affinity with those images, except perhaps as fantasy heroes, than women feel about the cartoonlike antics of career celebrities like Paris Hilton or Britney Spears.

Nonmonogamy

Although both men and women typically intend to "forsake all others" when they take their wedding vows, nonmonogamy does occur. Sometimes nonmonogamy is in the form of consensual additional relationships—a practice known as *polyamory*. Polyamory refers to the conduct of multiple relationships at the same time with the consent of all parties. Other kinds of consent exist—such as understandings that nonmonogamy is "okay under some circumstances." Monogamy continues to be the assumption, however, and other kinds of arrangements are carefully negotiated.

Earlier studies indicated as many as a third to a half of married couples included an unfaithful partner, but the NHSLS estimates that only 15 percent of married people have had one nonmonogamous experience. Part of the low estimate of the NHSLS may be due to the fact that some of the interviews were conducted while the spouse was in the next room or nearby and might have overheard what the interview participant was saying about her or his nonmonogamous experiences. To wit: researchers in a study of nearly five thousand women reported that 1 percent of wives reported infidelity in the past year when the interview was face-to-face; but when the interview was on a computer, 6 percent reported infidelity (Whisman and Snyder 2007). For couples who are cohabiting the rates are higher; and for those who are dating, the rates are higher still, mainly because of a lower level of commitment or official expectation of fidelity. Many studies indicate that men are more likely than women to report an outside sexual affair or one-night stand. Some analysts explain the difference as logical: Women are more satisfied by one relationship and more committed to having only one sexual partner, especially after marriage. Men are assumed to chafe under the sexual constraints of marriage even if they abide by them. Biologists and evolutionary psychologists think these differences are perfectly compatible with different male and female reproductive strategies.

Social scientists hypothesize, however, that higher male nonmonogamy rates might be explained by the fact that women have fewer opportunities for sex outside marriage and higher costs, on average, than do husbands, as we discuss in detail in chapter 4. Consistent with this view, as women's work increases—as well as their economic independence—their rates of infidelity have increased, too (Glass 2003). Changes over time measured in survey research from 1991 to 2006 make us think that the logic of infidelity keeps changing, as men and women have different kinds of opportunities as well as cultural permission. As illustrated in figure 2.14, whether older or younger in 1991 or 2006, men reported more infidelity. But the gap for older people declined from 15 percentage points

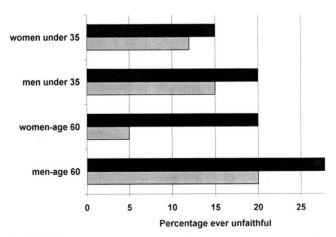

FIGURE 2.14
Infidelity by gender, time period, and age. Data from Atkins and Furrow (2008).

to 8 percentage points in a fifteen-year period: this is yet another case where we see large changes for women. The gap for younger people is less remarkable, in part because the younger women in 1991 were already closer to the men's reported rate of infidelity (Atkins and Furrow 2008).

Negative consequences may also still depress women's rates of nonmonogamy. Women are more likely to be punished for nonmonogamy and are likely to be punished more harshly. Until the 1960s, a wife's infidelity (but not a husband's) was cause for justifiable homicide in the state of Texas (Finkelhor and Yllö 1985). It is still introduced in court as a mitigating circumstance when assault or homicide has occurred (see chapter 4). Finally, women are likely to be more hesitant to take risks if they are economically dependent on their spouse. Although there is little direct evidence, when women are less economically dependent and in an egalitarian or "peer" marriage, they seem to be both more sexually frank within marriage and more similar to their men regarding nonmonogamy (Schwartz 1994).

Gendered nonmonogamy patterns persist in same-sex couples. Gay men in the 1970s and early 1980s rebelled against models of monogamy based on heterosexual marriage and asserted that a committed and happy relationship could tolerate and even profit from nonmonogamy. On the other hand, most lesbians, like most heterosexual women, believed in and enforced complete sexual fidelity in a committed relationship. Today, AIDS has made gay male monogamy much more important, although gay men are still less monogamous than heterosexual men. As an alternative to risky kinds of nonmonogamy (with sex that includes an exchange of fluids), gay men engage in nonmonogamous safe sex, including telephone sex, where men exchange fantasies but not semen, far more than lesbians or heterosexuals do. Similarly, gay male magazines and online media have an enormous amount of erotic advertising and sexually arousing stories based on the assumption of instant sexual interest between gay men who casually encounter each other. Lesbian media, on the other hand, have traditionally focused on politics rather than pornography, including the politics of sexuality and relationships. Nonmonogamy may be addressed, but it is never assumed as part of relationships. Still, lesbians are not immune to the attractions of the excitement of an outside sexual experience. In recent years we've seen more lesbians on websites that facilitate hookups. In fact, we've seen an increase in heterosexual use of websites that specifically target people looking for hookups and for infidelity. The strange paradox about nonmonogamy is that the vast majority of people who are nonmonogamous believe in monogamy! It is an area of human behavior where the flesh does seem mightier than people's principles, values, and vows.

Consent and Coercion

One of the most frequently documented differences in men's and women's sexuality is the large gap between men's and women's standards for consensual sex. This is an area where the sexual continuum appears particularly polarized. About 1 percent of sexual assault cases involve women aggressors (Sprecher and McKinney 1993). By far the most dramatic number of sexual offenses against an unwilling partner are by men against women. The rates of rape (including acquaintance rape), incest, child molestation, and sexual harassment are alarming and raise questions about our culture and its directives to men on how to be sexual and masculine (Koss et al. 1994). When these rates are examined in connection with nonsexual violence against women, including wife battering, our alarm rises. The question is whether extremes in sexual aggression and violence are a product of fundamental, inborn sex difference or a result of how men are raised and socialized in our own and other violent societies.

Rape exists worldwide and in intimate as well as political contexts. A great tragedy replays itself in the way in which violent rape against women is part of warfare. Over twenty thousand Bosnian Muslim women were raped in the 1990s during the Bosnian civil war; they were part of an ethnic cleansing strategy (Robson 1993). In 2007, the "rape hotspot" has been Congo, where even though civil war had subsided in that country, the rape culture associated with the war had taken hold. According to some observers, 27,000 *reported* sexual assaults took place in one province during 2006 (Gettleman 2007).

As the war and rape examples punctuate, the spillover across the boundary between sexuality and aggression is complex. Some observers agree with the essentialist view of male sexual domination: men are naturally aggressive, and women are less driven and more demure. Other observers look instead to the social context of sexual violence, such as the organization of young men into gangs, the use of rape as a weapon of war, the greater likelihood that a young man will be called on to fight, and fathers' desire that their sons be athletic, physical, fearless, and possess a host of other "boyish" qualities. Whether the tendency to be sexually violent is a biological and individual characteristic or a characteristic arising from social contexts and power dynamics has implications for choosing strategies to prevent, predict, and punish sexual violence.

An enormous amount of research has examined sexual violence, particularly since the early 1970s, when feminist scholars began to have some influence on selecting research topics for federal funding. A number of researchers conducted interesting studies about the attractiveness of violence to male research participants. In a study of U.S. and Canadian men, about 30 percent of men said that they were willing to intimidate, threaten, or physically coerce women into sex if they were sure they would not be caught (Briere and

Malamuth 1983). At the same time, several studies showed that men often felt women "asked for it" and put themselves in situations that made male aggression inevitable (Malamuth 1984; Koss and Leonard 1984). Predictably, women did not think men systematically put themselves at risk for being raped, nor were rape perpetrator fantasies common to women. On the other hand, only recently has sexual assault of men even been acknowledged as a reality. For example, it has been more than two decades since the Catholic Church has begun to be confronted with sexual abuse, and it continues to struggle with how to acknowledge it and respond.

As sexual violence research evolved, researchers began to study the prevalence of rape in the population, rather than studying official crime reports, prosecutions, or convictions, which tend to underestimate the problem. The rates are difficult to obtain, even in surveys where respondents' privacy is protected. In a study of college women (Koss et al. 1988), about 15 percent of women said they had been sexually assaulted. More than half of these assaults were by men the women were dating. Other researchers have found rates of sexual coercion above 27 percent among college women (Miller and Marshall 1987). Still other studies highlight rates in historically neglected groups. For example, according to Amnesty International, American Indian women face 2.5 times the risk of sexual assault than U.S. women in general, and these jurisdictions have laws that make it even less likely that such cases are ever prosecuted. Even when very conservative definitions of rape are used to exclude what some might call "unwanted sexual approaches," the evidence persistently indicates that a small but significant number of men practice sexual coercion.

Rapes against men are mostly perpetrated by other men (Forman 1982). A few studies have investigated men who reported feeling pressured into sex by women, submitting to avoid appearing less than masculine, and these are typically cases in which women applied psychological, not physical, pressure (Struckman-Johnson 1988). Emotional abuse is a serious problem with serious consequences, but it is distinct from physical assault. Most information about sexual assault by men against men is anecdotal, because same-sex sexual assaults are likely to go unreported and disbelieved. Occasionally, straight men will use sex as a way to subjugate other men in prison. The dominated man is meant to feel humiliated—and he does. A rape is not something he wants to make public. If he did, he would be violating another male requirement: being stoic and "taking it like a man."

Sexual aggression is also present between women. In fact, lesbians report instances of physically or mentally coercive sex more often than gay men do. In one study, 31 percent of lesbians and 12 percent of gay men reported forced sexual encounters (Waterman, Dawson, and Bologna 1989). Researchers tend to conclude that this difference has to do with what men or women define as aggressive. Lesbian complaints are likely to include emotional abuse as well as physical abuse. Furthermore, lesbians are more likely to be sensitized to sexual coercion and more readily identify a range of behaviors as coercive, whereas gay men are more likely to see coercion as fair play. These gendered patterns of complaint provide insight into how much more women, compared to men, are likely to be alert to aggression. As women, lesbians may be more sensitive to power inequities than gay men, because women in general tend to have less power and therefore have more experience in recognizing and attempting to rectify differences in power.

The most chilling kind of coercive sex involves underage children. Again, a gender difference exists: men are far more likely than women to see prepubescent boys or girls as sex objects. Although instances of female-perpetrated incest and child molestation occur, the offender is a man far more often (occasionally with a woman's compliance). In the United States, one estimate of the prevalence of child sexual abuse is 27 percent of all girls and 16 percent of all boys (Finkelhor et al. 1990). Notably, from 1992 to 2000 the rates appear to have declined somewhat (Finkelhor and Jones 2004).

The biological interpretation of the gender difference in child abuse requires belief that men, more than women, naturally have greater sexual desire and may have genetic propensities to molest. Social scientists have observed, however, that men are more likely to abuse children whom they did not take care of when the children were infants (Finkelhor 1984). The experience of caring for infants and small children seems to reduce the likelihood that men or women will subsequently view those children as sex objects. Symbolic interactions would explain that the caretaker status gets reinforced through the act of caring. Thus, we think that the fact that infant care is persistently relegated almost exclusively to women helps to account for the gender difference. The social organization of child care creates a location for women to connect with children more than for men.

Consequences for the child victims of sex abuse include adult depression, substance abuse, sexual problems, and a risk of being a victim or perpetrator of intimate violence as an adult. Furthermore, history of childhood sexual abuse can have consequences for adult sexuality, although those who have been sexually abused do not necessarily have sexual problems in adulthood (many victims do not). Because girls are more likely to be victims of child sexual abuse, adult women are more likely to carry the physical and emotional scars into their experience of adult sexuality. Thus, women more than men may have complex sexual inhibitions and ambivalent or negative feelings about sex because of early coerced sexual encounters. However, because men are expected to be invulnerable, boys who were sexually abused in childhood also can carry secret but severe scars from the humiliation, shame, and secrecy. In recent years, as sexual abuse by the Catholic clergy has been discovered and addressed, many young men, abused as altar boys or in other situations, have come forth to name their attackers. Their stories of pain, sexual and emotional confusion, and betrayal show what some other boys have suffered previously but had hidden as their private sorrow and shame.

Some scholars have hypothesized that the masculine proclivity to rape is natural, part of the inborn male drive to dominate. Two vastly different examples are a feminist treatise by Brownmiller, *Against Our Will: Men, Women and Rape* (1975) and an essentialist argument by Thornhill and Palmer, *A Natural History of Rape: Biological Bases of Sexual Coercion* (2000). Radical theorists, including antipornography activist Andrea Dworkin (*Woman Hating: A Radical Look at Sexuality*, 1991), have suggested that sexual penetration is always a form of rape, and thus rape is an extension of "normal" male sexuality. Some commentators argue that pornography is evidence of men's proclivity to reduce women to sexual objects. For example, law professor and activist Catherine MacKinnon (1987) states that pornography represents the theory, and rape in effect represents the practice of the misogynistic sexuality that animates men in patriarchal societies. This view isn't a thing of the past: the latest entry into this appeared in 2010 in Gail Dines's *Pornland: How Porn Has Hijacked Our Sexuality.*

Despite ample evidence that men far more than women engage in aggressive sexual behavior, including rape, there are important distinctions. First, most men do not rape. Second, in some societies rape is very rare (such as Polynesia). Rape itself may be a feature of certain cultures, through the way one-on-one interactions are organized and through the social structure of power relations. Some argue that patriarchal societies, in which men maintain greater power and privilege than women, create an environment that supports rape. Indeed, a study of domestic violence indicates that in the United States, states with more patriarchal laws (for example, laws giving men more rights and more freedom than women) have higher rates of wife assault (Dutton 1988). In societies where men and women have vastly different statuses (legally not equal and sequestered from one another), one would expect to find more rape. In fact, some cross-cultural evidence shows that rape is a consequence of sexual repression, especially in societies where women are held in contempt (see Hatfield and Rapson 1996). The more egalitarian and integrated the society, the less rape. The different rates of rape in different cultures and fluctuating rates of rape over time in the same culture suggest that society, not nature, influences men's proclivity to rape.

None of these hypotheses, however, diminishes the fact that women rarely rape. For starters, they are not physically designed to force sex. On the other hand, now that sexual harassment laws are being applied to men and women, it has become evident that women who have power sometimes pressure male co-workers or subordinates for sex (McCormick 1994). In a 2008 Louis Harris telephone survey of U.S. workers, 31 percent of women and 7 percent of men reported they had been harassed at work. While women all reported being victimized by a man, men reported being harassed by both men and women. Many fewer women than men commit sexual harassment; however, there are also fewer women than men bosses. Furthermore, the norms that cast men as sexual predators make it more likely that a man approached by a woman will be compliant; why would a man ever feel pressured into sex when he is supposed to be always ready for sex? Although women's sexual aggression seems to be less lethal than men's (i.e., not nearly so likely to be linked to homicide or brutality), the ability to force someone to have sex may have less to do with whether one is a man or a woman than with what a given culture approves as a person's sexual prerogative. Such coercion can be devastating to men and women victims alike.

Still, the majority of sexual harassment today has to do with enforcing a man's desires in a manner that confirms traditional, gendered statuses. If women had inherited a legacy of sexual privilege, would their rates of sexual harassment increase to equal men's? Now that women are nearly 50 percent of the workforce (Boushey and O'Leary 2009), will we note changes in these patterns? Alternatively, would men's rates of sexual harassment and other aggressions decline to equal women's? Until men and women experience similar opportunity to harass or victimize, the jury on the capacity to harass remains out.

Conclusion

In this chapter we asked, is sex different for men and women? Empirically, the data suggest that on average, yes, it is. As we have observed, norms of behavior and social control direct men and women toward different sexual behavior on the extremes of the continuum. We've also demonstrated that, above all, men and women want to have sex within relationships. That is, when it comes to intimacy, *men and women are much more similar than they are different.*

Historically, sexuality has changed tremendously so that we can document how malleable gendered sexual differences are over time. Recent data show us an overlapping pattern of men's and women's sexuality. In the end, sexuality takes diverse forms—not merely men's and women's, straight and gay. The configuration of these categories helps to sustain social and sexual control. When societies create categories, people are expected to fit into them. But observations show much more sexual diversity, or a "continuum of sexuality," rather than two or four boxes that people can jam themselves into. When we describe norms of sexual behavior, or a sexual script that people tend to follow, remember that social norms are simply the high point on a broadly distributed bell curve. Not only do different groups tend to overlap in the distribution of sexual acts, beliefs, and attitudes, but as the wide spread of the bell curve suggests, there is great variety within groups.

How do the norms for men's and women's sexuality influence people as they begin to be sexual? Does it make any difference in the new "hookup culture"? In the next chapter, we examine the historical and current trends of sexual behavior and sexual expression when people are not in a serious or committed relationship.

3

Uncommitted Sexual Relationships

What Does Sexual Freedom Look Like?

IS THERE SOMETHING NEW AND DIFFERENT in the way that people experience sexuality and sexual freedom now versus in the past? A couple of movies offer images of how men and women cope with sex and intimacy in uncommitted relationships these days. We return to the movie, *Knocked Up* (2007). The story of sexual adventure and an unwanted pregnancy is told from a man's (Ben Stone, played by Seth Rogen) point of view: Ben "gets lucky" with Alison Scott (played by Katherine Heigl), who is "above his market value"—he is a chubby slacker, and she is a slim and sexy young professional in her first broadcast news job. Around the same time, the movie *Juno* came out. In *Juno* sexual adventure also leads to an unwanted pregnancy—but the story is from the woman's—Juno's (played by Ellen Page)—point of view. She controls sexual initiation with her best friend Paulie Bleeker (played by Michael Cera), and when she becomes unintentionally pregnant she struggles and makes an independent decision about her pregnancy.

These pregnancy stories, one from the man's point of view and the other from a woman's point of view, have much in common—in both stories the men are good guys who want to hang in there with the woman; in both the women do not choose abortion—and resist, in varying degrees, contemplation of the concept. Indeed, when commentators viewed these movies in the summer and fall of 2007, they were puzzled to see the trend of women *not* choosing abortion in the movies. That was a shift from how sex and consequences were handled in decades past.

But the men's and women's experiences in these films were fundamentally different: not just in terms of biology but also in terms of the norms, expectations, and dilemmas they faced. This fundamental difference leads us to notice that while things have changed considerably for men and women in sexual and social relations, there is still a gap between them. The contrasting points of view—Ben's in *Knocked Up* and Juno's in *Juno*—highlight that "the more things change the more they remain the same." The women were not stigmatized as in the past, but men and women have considerably different rights and responsibilities. As we examine sexual freedom, here's what we see: women have greater license than in the past; men have greater sensitivity and flexibility in their roles. But the differences between men's and women's sexual experiences—in terms of the kinds of problems we have to solve, the meaning of sex to us, and the social consequences of our sexual behavior—persists.

In this chapter, we examine some persistent differences between men's and women's prerogatives and responses to uncommitted sexual situations. We even note fundamental changes to the *kinds* of uncommitted sexual situations available to men and women. Earlier, we referred to the continuing difference as the "sexual double standard." But it is not enough to know that there is a double standard of judgment about what is allowable for men versus women. We are asking, how wide (or narrow) is the gulf? Is it a chasm—or is it becoming less and less important?

In order to answer those questions, we review the origins and prevalence of gender differences in sexual freedom across cultures. Then we put the sex lives of singles under the microscope. We ask: How does gender influence the experience of uncommitted sex? How does uncommitted sex influence the experience of gender? Does gender play a role in controlling conduct in same-sex relationships and encounters? If so, who or what is doing the controlling? Who, if anyone, is exempt from control? And who benefits from this control? Above all, we wonder why and how gender expectations affect people who are having sex outside of the context of long-term relationship goals or expectations. We answer these questions by looking at recent data.

The Control of Sexuality: Over Time and Across Space

Most societies are not concerned about helping their citizens have a good sex life. Sexual appetite is not extolled and encouraged by governments. But neither are governments disinterested. They are concerned with fertility rates, reproduction, marriage, and divorce. Nations benefit from predictable, orderly reproduction so that they will have people to staff armies, to work in factories or service industries, and to raise the next generation to be similarly socially productive. Furthermore, the only ways most governments can afford to run a society are if parents assume the responsibility to raise children to become productive citizens and if families are organized to pass wealth from one generation to another. Some governments rely on this private strategy more than others.

It turns out that where governments share the responsibility of taking care of children—through providing family economic supports, day care, parental leave, and the like—there is greater liberality with respect to sexual experimentation. This is the case, for example, in northern European countries. The United States is an exception: we have few family economic supports, and yet sexual experimentation is quite common. (It follows that the United States has more problems associated with sexual experimentation than in northern European countries, too—such as higher rates of STDs and teen pregnancy.) Still, most societies have a history of making rules and regulations about sex that limit or even punish births outside of wedlock and prevent young people from marrying before they are capable of earning a living.

Cultures control sexuality in many different ways. Sweden and Saudi Arabia, for example, are contrasts in sexual control. Sweden, a sexually liberal country, has a long history of nonmarital sexuality, cohabitation, comprehensive sex education, and social services that assist parents with child rearing. Sweden also has a low birth rate and, like other Scandinavian countries, a very low teenage birth rate. In contrast, ultraconservative countries like Saudi Arabia believe that sex outside of marriage must be severely punished. A premarital sexual liaison constitutes a crime against family and state. It is a disruption in property relations and a crime against God. In Saudi Arabia, for example, premarital sex is punishable by lashings. Under some circumstances it could be punishable by death.

Given the consequences some societies use to keep people in line, one might conclude that premarital sex happens only in places where the social sanctions for premarital births are minimal. Curiously, countries with more liberal views of sexuality tend to have lower fertility rates (the number of children born per woman) (Jones et al. 1985). For example, the estimated total fertility rate (number of children born per woman) in Saudi Arabia in 2005 to 2010 was nearly 3.4; in Sweden, it was 1.8 (United Nations 2007). Furthermore, despite their liberal sexual climate, more progressive countries have relatively few unwanted pregnancies because of extensive, early public education regarding sex and contraception and a strong social welfare system. As we noted in chapter 1, there is convincing evidence that education is more effective than coercion for limiting unwanted reproduction.

Whether liberal or conservative, all governments have a strong influence over the way sex lives are conducted. But large and powerful institutions don't solely determine sexuality. Individual differences in desire do not neatly conform to social rules. Thus, even where severe sanctions are in place against nonmarital sexuality, the power of the flesh is awesome. That's why even in the most conservative societies, efforts to police sexuality rarely succeed completely. The tight controls may themselves encourage tabooed behavior. Strict rules over sexuality can fuel curiosity as well as fear—not to mention ignorance. A scarce resource is a tempting one. People often act before they think—and once young people have the ability to have sex, some of them will pursue their desires no matter what the personal cost. Sadly, the cost of sexual curiosity can have grave consequences when individuals are sexually active without information about safe practices or do not take into account the amount of social backlash they may face at home or by law enforcement. Politicians and religious leaders know the power of sexual desire. Even as they implore, threaten, lecture, and badger the unmarried to remain celibate until marriage, they realize that their social control agenda will not be completely successful. (After all, these same people may not have been celibate themselves until marriage!) They know that people will find a way to have sex. Therefore, one method of controlling premarital sexuality is to have a very short premarital period. In general, the more rigid the sexual code, the earlier young people are betrothed. In Saudi Arabia, the average age of women's marriage is nineteen. In contrast, in Sweden, women marry at thirty-one. Leaders would rather marry off their young than execute them for sexual transgressions. Table 3.1 summarizes births per woman in selected countries alongside the average age of first marriage for women and for men.

Each culture comes up with its own rules predicated on its own history and needs. For example, sexuality is controlled differently in contemporary China because of policies instituted to control population growth (and therefore to reduce famine and poverty in their country). In 1979, China instituted a one-child policy. Every village and town had people who were in charge of making

TABLE 3.1
Births Per Woman and Average Age of Marriage, Select Countries

Country	Total Fertility Rate (estimate 2005 to 2010)	Average Age of Marriage	
		Women	Men
Italy	1.4	30	33
China	1.7	22	24
Sweden	1.8	31	33
United States	2.0	26	27
India	2.8	21	25
Saudi Arabia	3.4	19	26
Kenya	5.0	22	26

sure couples did not have more children. Some of this population control was backed up with inexpensive and available abortions. The government also tried to slow the birthrate by reducing early partnering, which tends to create higher fertility since the age at the first committed romantic union is correlated with total family size. The government declared the legal "age of consent" (when people are free to have sex) to be twenty-two for men and twenty for women—among the oldest in the world. Other governments have different social regulations, but no matter what the system, such attempts don't work terribly well! The actual age of first sex in China was about eighteen and nineteen years old in the Durex Survey in 2005.

In sum, nearly all societies seek to control sexuality of unmarried people, they just do so in different ways. In a few parts of the world, however, the concern for sexual control reaches obsessive proportions and uses the authority of religion. For example, some Islamic countries have a policy known as **purdah**: keeping women (unmarried and married) in isolation from men and strangers. Walk down a street in Northern African countries such as Morocco or Tunisia, and you will see the fine wooden bars or latticework on windows that allow the person inside to look out but prevent the outsider from looking in. These bars are on the women's quarters in private homes. Outside, women walk around in long, dark drapes of cloth (known as chador, abbayas, or burkahs) from their heads to their toes, preventing others from seeing their bodies, faces, and in some cases, even the eyes. Women usually go out only in the company of their husband, father, brother, or mother-in-law. In most (though not all) of these societies, these practices reflect the nearly complete subordination of women in economic and other nonsexual domains. Changing values about women's right to work or right to get educated have lifted the veil in some Middle Eastern and African cities. However, the fear of uncontrolled female sexuality is still present and intransigent. Women's freedom, even their right to do what Westerners consider minimal everyday chores, such as driving to the supermarket or selling a product to a man, is highly limited. Women in such societies are thought to be too tempting, and therefore they must be covered and constrained. In these situations, women are not merely *controlled* in sexual matters, they are *defined* by sexual matters.

The degree of control of women and their sexuality usually corresponds with women's status, power, and civil rights in a given society. In strictly patriarchal countries, where women are second-class citizens, sexual control is extremely tight. In addition, women's sexuality is more guarded in societies where family name and reputation are keys to power. In these societies, the behavior of one member of a family reflects badly on all, and wealth and land are transferred through family lines. Under such conditions, 100 percent "purity" and 100 percent confidence of paternity is considered essential, and it leads to intense monitoring of women's sexual lives. Although such conservatism tends to be couched in terms of "natural" or God-given differences between men and women, biology doesn't drive the social system. If it did, the sexual rules for men and women would always be the same in different times and places regardless of the social agenda of the government and the society.

Sociologist William Goode (1969) studied the extent to which the inheritability of property predicts the prevalence of love-based or arranged marriages in a society. He looked at many different societies and categorized them in terms of how many social patterns supported the familial transfer of wealth. Not surprisingly, his research supported the idea that societies only allow love as the basis for pairing and marriage when families have nothing at stake—no land, no prestige, no political power. When family wealth is influenced by marriage choices, love and sex are controlled by older generations, and women are subjected to higher levels of patriarchal surveillance. Stephanie Coontz (2005) demonstrated just how much marriage in Western societies has become justified by love and intimacy, rather than instrumental purposes. In *Marriage: A History*, she describes how "love conquered marriage," meaning that over time, love, not social class or family liaisons, became the new standard for marriage. This new standard, creeping into the Eastern as well as the Western part of the world, is based on individualistic notions of sexual freedom and privacy that are rare in religiously based societies. Still, with the globalization of ideas through the Internet, movies, and television, Western sexual and emotional freedom has become increasingly common around the world. Even in Muslim countries with strict restrictions on women's activities—what some academic analysts refer to as gender apartheid—conservative traditions have been challenged.

Still, let us not overromanticize marriage and love in the West. While people believe in love and passion, they don't only use those emotions when choosing a marital partner. When money and property exist and are advantageous to inherit through marriage, marriage is much more likely! Today we see a linking of property and marriage in the *declining significance* of marriage. In the United States, marriage rates are higher among men and women who are more educated, and divorce rates are lower. For men and women with less property at stake, the motivation to arrange their lives around marriage tends to be smaller. Indeed, many single mothers report that they could consider marrying their baby's father—but only when they have enough money to do marriage "right" (Edin and Reed 2005).

Historical Change in the United States

The dynamics of governments, culture, and sexual control can be better understood by studying American history, too. The drive for sexual free dom in the United States started earlier than most people think. Our sexual revolution is often associated with the late 1960s, but changes in premarital sexual attitudes and behaviors started in the seventeenth century in both Europe and the United States. Historian Edward Shorter (1975) argues that as small European communities became less isolated in the sixteenth and seventeenth centuries, churches, town councils, and families exerted less control. As urban centers flourished, people sought alternatives to the traditional controlling ways of smaller, more rural communities. This period also saw a rise in individualism. With the Age of Enlightenment and the rise of capitalism, people were encouraged to think in terms of their individual futures rather than family futures. Shorter explains that the reduction in community social control led more people to express their feelings and follow their hearts rather than their parents' wishes. During this period, women and men were encouraged to respond to sentiment. In eighteenth-century novels, literary critics observe, the same story recurs: A woman, if she is middle class or upper class, is weakened by love, fainting at thoughts of the man she loves, or even a letter from him. A man (also with elevated social status) tends to be emboldened by love, even if boldness leads to tragic outcomes, such as losing a duel (Todd 1986).

Today, the United States is the most marriage-prone society in the Western world (United Nations 2001), followed by Russia and the Czech Republic. Paradoxically, as much as we love marriage, we seem unable to sustain it. Although we are more likely to marry in the United States, we are also more likely to divorce, and a full 27 percent of households today are homes of single adults (Newman 2007). It follows, then, that sex is not confined to marital unions. The United States has gone through almost every ideological position on sexuality outside of marriage since the precolonial era. Although each particular change has not always been toward greater sexual autonomy, each generation has in general conceded a more liberal stance toward sexuality. Recall the community moralists, including the New England Puritans of the seventeenth and early eighteenth centuries, who might make a sexually suspect woman wear a "scarlet letter," a badge of shame and humiliation, should she engage in nonmarital sexual relations. When the church lost authority toward the end of the eighteenth century, legal institutions continued to impose sanctions against sexual nonconformists (D'Emilio and Freedman 1988). Over time, however, the flow of history has decreased governmental interventions involving sex between consenting adults. From the turn of the twentieth century to our own time, people have fought in court for their sexual civil rights, and certain activities, such as the right of a husband and wife to do any mutually agreed-upon sexual act in their own bedroom, have been safeguarded under the legal umbrella of the right to privacy. There are notable exceptions to this protective coverage, and these have occurred in cases of interracial marriage, same-sex unions, and women's access to abortion and birth control, as discussed below.

Nonmarital sex has been less protected in general. And this is especially true for women. Societies that outlaw nonmarital sexuality impose different penalties for men and women. In general, the punishments for women's sexual transgressions are swifter, stronger, and more public than punishment for men's (heterosexual) transgressions. When teen pregnancies occur, such as when a high school boy impregnates a girl, he is rarely sanctioned and may not even have been identified. After a highly publicized cluster of seventeen pregnancies in one high school in Gloucester, Massachusetts, which had been in the news for weeks in 2008, a footnote to the news story referred to the question of who was the father. As it turned out, for several of the young women, it was the same twenty-four-year-old homeless man. Many studies from the 1990s suggest that upward of two-thirds of pregnant teen women have been impregnated by men over twenty years old (De Vita 1996). Girls, like the Gloucester teenagers, who are pregnant and unmarried are identified as a social problem, meriting study, judgment, wonder, and concern. This treatment may vary depending on the race, class, and age of the girls involved. Upper-class, younger, unmarried women who get pregnant may be pitied more than blamed, and their privacy may be respected more than the privacy of poorer women, who are suspected of being generally delinquent or linking motherhood with welfare dependency (Fields 2008).

Teenage boys in this situation are not sanctioned or particularly visible—but they also are rarely offered social support or guidance regarding their potential fatherhood. There are signs that this is changing a little bit: For example, the National Campaign to Prevent Teen and Unplanned Pregnancy launched an outreach department on their website for young men's involvement in pregnancy prevention. Their report, "It's a Guy Thing" (Marsiglio et al. 2006), notes that teenage boys are doing a better job of preventing teen pregnancy. Compared to the early 1990s, more teenage boys are taking positive health measures such as increasing their use of condoms, working to delay the first time they have sex, and decreasing the number of people they have sex with. Yet the the report notes that parents are much more likely to talk to daughters than sons about sex, sexual health, and safe sex.

How did unwanted pregnancies work out in *Knocked Up* and *Juno*—the movies we examined at the beginning of this chapter? The pregnancies were viewed as problematic but not devastating. The men seemed baffled; the women seemed focused. In these movies, the biological fathers' roles were uncertain. It was not clear whether they would feel responsible, whether they would be held accountable, or whether they would be allowed or feel compelled to participate in their children's lives. The men in these stories elected to be involved and concerned, but these fathers had far more latitude than the mothers in terms of the extent of their participation. There was, however, one crucial detail in which the men had no choice at all: the men did *not* have the choice implicitly or explicitly to keep or terminate the pregnancy. Indeed, this is an intractable puzzle with respect to abortion rights and abortion-related decisions. It highlights the way in which the biological reality of sexuality and pregnancy is still understood to dictate certain *rights*, as in the right to choose pregnancy, choose abortion, or choose adoption, as well as certain *responsibilities*, as in the inescapable physical connection between a pregnant woman and the embryo or fetus she carries.

In *Knocked Up*, the pregnant Alison—a happy, well-employed, middle-class woman—struggles with the prospect of losing her career and not having a "good provider" partner. In *Juno*, Juno is a working-class high school student, and pregnancy is not attached to her career or class dilemmas. On the other hand, the career woman who seeks to adopt Juno's baby contemplates the effect Juno's baby will have on her career, income, and heretofore carefree marriage. Sexuality intersects with the maintenance of social class, and the meanings of parenthood interact with gender and lifestyle.

Still, the intersections of sexuality, love, and class in America are relatively small compared to Europe. For example, except for the very rich, less land or wealth has been passed on through generations in this country than in European and Middle Eastern countries, and therefore little is at stake if the lineage of a child becomes unclear. Predictably, dating in the United States is more often controlled in the upper classes than in the lower classes. For example, upper-class white families still have "coming out" or debutante parties when young women make their "formal entrance into society"—that is, into the society of upper-class men who are eligible for marriage. By the mid-twentieth century, upper-class and upper-middle-class black families also created cotillions and debuts for their children, hoping to guarantee a match within class borders.

These days, however, creating class continuity by corralling rich young people into homogeneous parties and organizations is difficult—perhaps impossible. Even elite universities and institutions have become more merit-based or democratic, and diverse populations meet each other. People experiment with partners whose backgrounds are different from theirs and practice living together without the blessing or even the permission of their families. Cohabitation has been rising among all classes in the United States since the late 1960s. Cohabitation originated in lower classes (Bumpass, Sweet, and Cherlin 1989), where property rights based on marriage are less relevant. People from higher social classes are more likely than other social classes to marry and are less likely to cohabit—but a high percentage of them will live together before a legal union.

Despite the United States' long history of gradually less and less control over who becomes emotionally and sexually attached, the exceptions are notable. As recently as 1967, states outlawed interracial marriage through **antimiscegenation laws** (literally, laws against mixing genes). Antimiscegenation laws, a legacy of slavery and racism, were instituted to prevent whites from marrying blacks and other racial minorities from "mixing" sexually. The selective enforcement of antimiscegenation laws shows how sinister sexual laws tend to be: countless white men raped black women at will during and after slavery. During the late nineteenth century, while white, middle-class women were assigned the virtues of purity, chastity, and honor, white men consigned some black women to near sexual slavery. This crime was rarely punished. Only when a white man expressed love for a black woman would other men enforce the status quo by persecuting the partners. Love matches between whites and minorities were violently punished, especially when the romance was between a black man and a white woman.

During slavery and through the first half of the twentieth century, a black man could be hanged for looking at a white woman in what was perceived as a lascivious or provocative way. Thousands of lynchings of black men in the early part of the twentieth century were caused by white racist sexual paranoia. Lynchings (or mob hangings) were rationalized as a defense of white women's sexual purity and chastity (D'Emilio and Freedman 1988). You may have read about the 1955 murder of Emmett Till, a black teenager who had traveled from Chicago to spend the summer with relatives in Mississippi. Rumors that the boy had said "bye, baby" to a married white woman in a local store resulted in his murder. The brutal execution went unpunished, but it helped galvanize the civil rights movement. The incident was the proverbial "straw that broke the camel's back" because it was so representative of thousands of other vicious, racially motivated homicides that had used white sexual "purity" as an excuse for murder during slavery and the postslavery era. White paranoia was buttressed by a sexual double standard—sexual privilege for white men and sexual surveillance for men of color. Potent political and psychological support of racism and lawless vigilantes created a combined racial and sexual double standard. Women of color were also included in this twisted vision: only white women received protection, even though black women were more likely to work outside the home and were more likely to be harassed and subjected to sexual aggression.

The Shifting Double Standard

Even during periods of racist sexual backlash in the South and other regions of the United States, the twentieth-century trajectory of sexual norms and behaviors in the United States and western Europe inched slowly, if unsteadily, toward liberalization. One important phase in the process was gradual changes in formal dating rituals that began as an innovation in the 1920s and lasted through the 1950s. Dating teens, under the watchful eyes of parents, were given a certain amount of independence to meet members of the other sex. As cities grew young people could go to movies, dances, and other places of entertainment together. Parents believed that young people would make more informed marital choices if they obtained playful, independent experience with intimacy. Kissing, while scandalous in the beginning of this transition, became part of expected interactions. As relationships deepened, touching might be allowed (called "petting"), but intercourse was considered out of bounds. Boys were initiators of just about everything. They called girls for dates. They picked up the girl. They paid the check. However, this highly gendered arrangement started to unravel when gender roles became less traditional by the last quarter of the twentieth century. As the 1960s and 1970s wore on, formal dating rituals went out of fashion, and so did the concept of the absolute necessity of virginity before marriage.

Changing courtship patterns allow social scientists to observe the evolution of the gendered status of sexuality. Note the trends in figure 3.1, which shows the percentage of men and women in different cohorts (age groups) with either no sexual partners before the age of eighteen or with five or more sexual partners before the age of eighteen (Laumann, Michael, and Gagnon 1994).

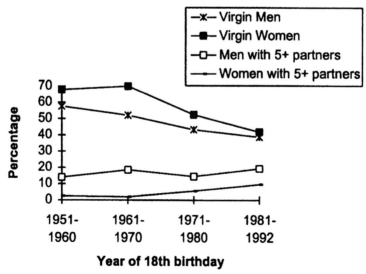

FIGURE 3.1
Trends in U.S. sexual experience by age cohort.

In a sense, the table is contrasting virgins with highly sexually active people. The big point in this graphic is that men and women have become a lot more similar in terms of having ever had sex—but there is still considerable difference between how many men and women report being *highly* sexually active. Men consistently report more partners. This difference between men and women indicates that there is less of a double standard with respect to having sex at all—but there is a persistent double standard related to having multiple partners. Still, women today are different from women in the past: The youngest women were almost four times as sexually experienced at eighteen as the oldest women in the chart. Men haven't changed as much. The youngest men look more similar to the oldest men in the chart.

In the middle years of the twentieth century—between the first wave of feminist activity aimed at women's suffrage and the second wave begun in the late 1960s—striking and sometimes pathetic stories of the sexual double standard were played out. For boys and young men to prove their manliness, they were encouraged to test their virility as early into puberty as possible. Girls, on the other hand, were admonished to maintain virginity and "save *it* for marriage." Of course, this sexual double standard presented a dilemma because it constricted the pool of available partners for boys. One adaptation was that chaste girls would be labeled "good," and girls who more clearly resembled boys in their sexual behaviors were labeled "bad." Girls who experimented with sex were considered "loose" and "easy." Anne Roiphe, a feminist activist in the 1970s who came of age during the 1950s, explained the impossibility of women's positions: The men they were dating were simultaneously cast as sexual predators, whom they had to fight off, and as protectors, whom they needed for protection from other men (Friedan et al. 1996).

Sexual attitudes were inconsistent with sexual behavior for most of the twentieth century. The famous Kinsey studies documented the increasingly liberal sexual behavior of people who went to work in the 1920s and 1930s. Kinsey, originally trained as a zoologist, changed his professional interests and interviewed hundreds of men and women about their sexual experiences and practices. Kinsey's findings shocked much of the public in 1948, when his *Sexual Behavior in the Human Male* (Kinsey, Pomeroy, and Martin 1948) reported unexpected sexual liberalism. For example, 25 percent of boys had experienced sexual intercourse by age fourteen. Still, there was mostly acclaim for his work until he published *Sexuality in the Human Female* in 1953 (Kinsey et al.). This study reported more sexual experience among women than anyone was letting on or wanted to hear. Kinsey was accused of being a liar, an incompetent scientist, and an immoral human being. Those who believed his findings were dismayed. The "good girl," groused alarmists of the day, was becoming an endangered species. Even though most of the so-called loose women had had only one premarital lover—usually the man they married—the convention of sex within marriage had been exposed as only a rule on paper; practice was something else! Kinsey's research—and the response to it—suggested that sexual behavior was more advanced than sexual attitudes in the early 1950s. Although Kinsey's methodology undoubtedly exaggerated or distorted some sexual practices and frequencies, many of his conclusions regarding sexual trends have since been confirmed by better-designed studies.

The Sexual Revolution

The pace of sexual change slowed during the more conservative 1950s and into the 1960s. It wasn't until the last years of the 1960s that an undercurrent of sexual change became an open and explicit part of the cultural landscape. In the mid-1960s, oral contraceptives—known as the Pill—became available. The Pill was the first in a set of contraceptive approaches available now that manipulate hormones in order to prevent pregnancy. Although, at least in the beginning, it was extremely difficult for unmarried women to obtain the Pill, younger generations' desire for experimentation accelerated with its availability. The commentators on the 1960s labeled the ensuing changes "the sexual revolution." The revolutionary manifesto challenged the idea that sex was respectable only in marriage and that sex was less appropriate for women than for men.

During this era, feminists examined how sexual norms, including virginity, were used to control women's sexual freedom. Even more shocking to most observers, feminists criticized marriage, a "sacred cow" of most societies. Writers reframed marriage from the ideal goal of a woman's life to an institution that was almost entirely organized for the benefit and power of men. Betty Friedan, who wrote about marriage (as experienced mostly by white, middle-class women) in *The Feminine Mystique* (1963), described the "problem that has no name": she argued that American women were kept from gaining their full human capacities. She called for a halt to early marriage and the consignment of women to housewifery. *A Strange Stirring*, Coontz's history of *The Feminine Mystique*, describes how much women from that earlier era felt this book addressed their experience (Coontz 2011). Friedan argued that women would find themselves and their power in the marketplace, not at home. During this era, age at first marriage began to rise, and the practice of cohabitation also rose. Feminists challenged the notions that women need men to be sexually satisfied and that sexual experience is incompatible with a woman's marriageability or worthiness to a man. Central to "women's liberation," as the feminist movement was first called, was the right for women to control their own bodies sexually and reproductively, both in and out of marriage. Women claimed the right to withhold (or give) sexual consent directly without fear of rape or stigma.

Reproductive rights became a central issue during this time. Women organized politically, and in 1973 were responsible for creating the climate in which the Supreme Court legalized abortion for the first time in the twentieth century, in *Roe v. Wade*. Abortion had been legal until the late nineteenth century, when the American Medical Association in conjunction with women activists concerned with protecting the purity of women lobbied Congress and changed laws in order to make it illegal. The 1973 court's liberalization of abortion policy created new legal liberties but also new arenas of disappointment. Many women found themselves seeking abortion in isolation from the men who had been equally responsible in causing the pregnancy. Feminist books of the period, such as Marilyn French's *The Women's Room* (1977), are filled with recrimination and reanalysis of gender and power relations. In *For Her Own Good* (1978), Barbara Ehrenreich and Deirdre English referred to the sexual revolution as an "ambiguous liberation": women understood that there was more sexual freedom, but they discovered that there was not more power or respect for them in the public sphere.

As feminism evolved, so did different perspectives on a feminist agenda. In particular, the concerns of women of color and lesbians were not always included in mainstream feminism. For example, when it was revealed that government-funded family-planning clinics were enforcing sterilization among young, poor women of color, white feminists were slow to respond. Middle-class feminism focused on access to abortion, but for poor women and women of color, the right of a woman to control her body also involved the right to reproduce. When conservatives tried to discredit the feminist movement by accusing feminists of being lesbians, mainstream heterosexual feminists downplayed lesbian issues, leaders, and constituents (D'Emilio and Freedman 1988). Some feminist leaders even sought to expel lesbians from feminist organizations. Gay and lesbian liberation movements fought back, and in the 1970s the National Organization of Women finally included lesbian rights in its list of goals.

In hindsight, the sexual revolution was obviously not completely revolutionary—especially for women. Many young women entered the period seeking sexual and personal freedom, only to discover that even men with very liberal politics weren't particularly feminist. For example, at a 1965 conference of the Students for a Democratic Society, a leftist group, a feminist speaker was heckled with shouts of "she just needs a good screw." Even in 2008, when Hillary Clinton was a viable presidential candidate, critics often threw gender taunts at her instead of just arguing against her positions. For example, a "Hillary nutcracker" was a popular item available in airports.

Women wanted sexual liberation to signify equality in relationships, but men often took it as an opening for sexual opportunism. Some men, who resented equality, used sexual liberation to degrade women. These entrenched feelings also impeded changes in thinking about the role of sex in romantic relationships. Men continued to interpret women's behavior through the traditional seduction scripts they had learned when they were young. Young adults in the 1960s and 1970s had been raised with traditional ideas about women's chastity and "respectability." Studies of the period showed that even among college students, the most liberal population at the time, people were sharply divided between egalitarianism and the sexual double standard. Large numbers of men and women accepted nonmarital sexuality for men as "natural" but believed in abstinence for women (Reiss 1967). Such mismatched views created resentment and emotional pain for dating pairs. Sex in the 1970s was more ambiguous, attached fewer responsibilities, and generated less understanding and sympathy between men and women. Although it may have been a minority who actually broke with the double standard or who had guilt-free recreational sex, everybody who was dating had to struggle with the confused expectations of that period.

The disappointments of the sexual revolution are not the complete picture, however. The sexual revolution was also an era of discovery. Sex became more fun for more people than ever before. Feminists wrote treatises on how women's bodies worked, how to have orgasms, and how to masturbate. More women felt freer to masturbate and enjoy sex outside of marriage or even love. Some books on these topics had a worldwide impact. *The Hite Report: A Nationwide Study of Female Sexuality* by Shere Hite (1976), and *My Secret Garden* by Nancy Friday (1973), failed as research but succeeded as consciousness-raising tools for men and women. Hite described hundreds of experiences and desires. Friday wrote a no-holds-barred account of women's diverse sexual fantasies. The detailed sexual stories signified that women could be just as sexual as men. The book explained how and when women wanted to be touched, made love to, or lusted after. Men and women gained information about what they were doing wrong sexually and what they were doing right.

Yet the sexual revolution was different for men than women. For men, the emergence and prominence of *Playboy* magazine and the "playboy image" provided an aspirational fantasy world, an opportunity to be perpetual "studs" looking for easy action. *Rabbit, Run* (1960) by John Updike typifies the sexual license men were discovering. In *Rabbit, Run*, a working-class man drops out of his family, leaving his wife, children, and then his new lover behind as he restlessly focuses on his own gratification through libertine sex. In real life, while the ideals of the sexual revolution were about "sexual abandon," unforeseen consequences included "sexual abandonment." Reams of books followed, some of which are still in print today, exploring the physical and adventurous possibilities of heterosexual and, for the first time for popular audiences, gay and lesbian sexuality. In short, the years between 1960 and the mid-1970s were a chaotic period in which sex was extolled, explained, and seemingly engaged in much more than ever in the past. But the politics of intimacy still gave men more power in relationships than women. Women still had more romantic objectives than men. The desire for more intimacy meant women were the ones who cared more in many encounters, and this greater emotional involvement, plus the fact that they were less financially independent, gave more power to their male partner. Men continued to hold better jobs, have higher pay, more political clout, and more social freedom than women. These sustained imbalances and different goals made men and women increasingly angry with each other.

By the end of the 1970s, attitudes regarding premarital sexuality had substantially changed. Virginity was no longer the badge of honor for women that it had been; loss of virginity before marriage became expected rather than mourned. During the 1980s, rates of nonvirginity among unmarried women began to equal those of unmarried men (Sexuality Information and Education Council of the United States [SIECUS] 1995). The average age at first intercourse steadily decreased for both men and women, although in recent years it has leveled off at between ages sixteen and seventeen. Men and women still have different perceptions of sexual encounters, but their agendas for sex outside of marriage have become increasingly similar. Today, at least in Western countries, sex in the context of affection is considered legitimate for both men and women in all but the most conservative of subcultures (Laumann et al. 1994).

While these sexual trends have historically varied by race and by class, there is some general convergence. In the early 1970s, black women at age eighteen had more sexual experience than white women did—over time, both groups increased in sexual experience, but those rates have increased more for whites in the two most recent decades, making the groups more similar. When nonmarital cohabitation began to increase in the 1970s, most people considered it a trend that emerged among middle-class and upper-class youth on college campuses. Instead, the trend began in lower classes and working classes and diffused up the class ladder (Bumpass et al. 1989). These days, cohabitation is common in every social class. It has become unremarkable, and it is more likely than not to precede a marriage.

Since the 1960s, individuals have increasingly claimed the right to design their own sex life. The expansion of individualism and personal autonomy in the sexual realm accompanied Vietnam War protests and abortion rights protests as well. Many observers have written that the shift to personal autonomy from tradition, obligation, and respect for one's parents was the most critical change in human relations to have happened during this period (for example, as reported in Reiss 1980:188).

Although the sexual revolution is the main story of sex in the later twentieth century, it is not the only story. U.S. society has not had a uniform shift toward personal choice. Conservative religious communities, Christian colleges, and church groups that hold a different perspective have consistently resisted it. For these groups, personal autonomy is much less important than following religious principles that include obligation to God's word as taught in the Bible, the directives of religious leadership, family values, and patriotism. Conservative movements, such as the Campus Crusade for Christ, exhort young adults to defer sex until after marriage and create social groups that draw like-minded students together to collectively support values that are generally more conservative than the majority of college students'. The general allure of religion has in fact gotten more traction in the population in general. In the 1990s, organized religion started to become very compelling again, and church affiliation and attendance increased (Stark 1996). Some political think tanks and lobbying organizations have also gotten traction. For example, during the 2000s Christian movements influenced federal policy on sex education, and funding for abstinence-only programs grew exponentially. Remarkably, this occurred despite strong countermovements that demonstrated that abstinence-only education was largely ineffective. The tension between comprehensive sex education and abstinence-only groups was highlighted again in 2008 when vice-presidential nominee Sarah Palin's teenaged daughter Bristol announced she was pregnant. Conservative organizations and religious institutions backed Palin's supportive approach to Bristol having a child while still a teenager and downgraded the importance of Bristol's lack of sex education. For liberals, the message was clearly different: teenagers, even those who are the child of a major conservative candidate, are going to have sex. Without comprehensive sex education (which includes being prepared to use a condom), an unexpected and unwanted pregnancy is more likely to occur. While vice-presidential candidate Palin seemed to indicate that all would be solved by a relatively quick marriage between her daughter and the child's father, prosex education forces fought the idea of early marriage as an inappropriate answer for accidental conceptions. The left wanted abortion to be a possible answer to a regrettable situation; the right wanted to celebrate the two young people "taking responsibility" for their actions. The nation had a tortured and angry dialogue about the situation, made all the more difficult by the soap opera that ensued among Bristol Palin, the baby's father, and the families' conflicting statements made in public. For example, after Bristol Palin had her child, she made a public statement acknowledging that abstinence-only education does not work, but then signed on as a spokesperson for abstinence.

This kind of drama happens every day on this issue. Teen sexuality is a reality, and while ages of first intercourse vary somewhat over the last several decades, the vast majority of teenagers have sex by age twenty and before marriage. As was the case for Bristol, so is the case for many Americans: "That horse is out of the barn." A 2007 report (Finer) using national data indicated that 75 percent of young people are sexually active by age twenty. And by age forty-four, 95 percent of people have had premarital sex. Abstinence simply is not a reality.

The story of the sexual revolution and its immediate aftermath in the 1970s and 1980s is primarily a change in sexual control: people became freer to have informal sexual encounters with fewer (though not zero) social and personal repercussions. Meanwhile, the double standard remained, although it was getting smaller. Opportunities for women in education and at work were accompanied by greater freedom to express themselves sexually. This freedom has recently gone way beyond whether or not a person will have premarital sex. "Hooking up," a recent phenomenon of relatively unstigmatized recreational sex for both men and women, has changed the game of premarital sexuality in both high schools and colleges. In chapter 5 we will discuss "hooking up" in greater detail. But it bears mentioning here that it refers to casual sexual encounters that are mainly undefined and that tend to be associated with people in their teens and twenties. This truly casual approach to sexuality—without courting, without dating—started to emerge in the 1970s and 1980s (Bogle 2008), when less-formal dating became more common.

Social Forces and Casual Sex

What influenced the growth of casual sex? We can look at three major social forces: technological, demographic, and sociological. The technological variable is birth control. Those born since 1962 might have trouble imagining how much their sexual behavior is influenced by easy access to birth control outside of parental or medical supervision. Birth control—including the use of condoms, withdrawal, abortion, and folk remedies—has been around for centuries. However, the fact that women could take charge of birth control with much greater reliability, especially with the Pill and the IUD (an intrauterine contraceptive device that is inserted for long periods of time), altered their sexual behavior. Both methods of birth control allow sexual intercourse with no special preparation at the time of the sexual encounter. Women using the Pill or an IUD are "ever ready" and almost always safe from pregnancy.

Sexual spontaneity and safety from pregnancy removed many traditional anxieties that had inhibited sex before the 1960s. The Pill was a green light for sex until the 1980s when HIV and AIDS were widely recognized as a deadly disease that was transmitted through sexual behaviors. AIDS is still with us (although more controllable and treatable), and men and women are more likely to use condoms because of it. Still, the Pill is the leading method of birth control for women under age thirty, and it is especially popular with women in their teens, early twenties, and women with at least a college degree (Guttmacher 2008). Figure 3.2 shows the current contraceptive choices that women who use any birth control are using in the United States (Guttmacher 2010); you can see that hormonal methods, including the Pill, Depo-Provera, vaginal ring, and Norplant, account for 35 percent of all methods.

The Pill had another major impact. Birth control became women's work and changed women's experience of sex much more than men's. The shift

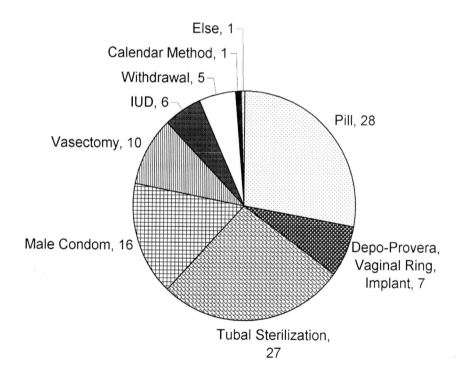

FIGURE 3.2
Method use among U.S. women using contraception (percentage). Data from Guttmacher, Facts on Contraceptive Use 2006–2008.

from condoms used by men to birth control that required female agency and a larger proportion of responsibility altered both women's approach to sex and men's attitudes toward women as sexual partners. Women have always had to be concerned about birth control, but even as it empowered women, the Pill multiplied that responsibility. Women bear the burden of unwanted pregnancy, but in previous eras, the men involved in an unwanted pregnancy sometimes took some contraceptive responsibility. In the era of high-tech birth control, men were liberated from even this tenuous tie to mutual responsibility. This didn't mean that all men were completely unconscious about birth control, and certainly many perceived themselves at least partly or in some cases equally involved in contraceptive decision making (Grady et al. 1996).

How did this technological change influence sex? Women, like men, were at greater liberty to have sex outside of commitment, but men gained power in these sexual relationships because they could feel less responsibility for unintended pregnancies. Furthermore, women's greater responsibility for birth control made it easy for the politics of reproductive rights to be cast primarily as a women's issue rather than a human issue. The reproductive consequences of sexuality were seen as primarily "her" fault.

The second force that changed the sexual world was demographics. The huge cohort of people born during the baby boom (between 1946 and 1964), especially those in the vanguard, grew up in a benign economic climate, with enormous opportunity. Many of these children were the recipients of their parents' good fortune in the best economic climate the United States had ever experienced. These first baby boomers (now in their fifties and sixties) experimented more with sex than people even a few years older than themselves. The double standard still existed, but it had lost its potency.

The size of this new cohort changed all the rules. Baby boom women and men felt a reduced urgency to marry early. Fewer people were living in small towns, and when they went to college—in greater numbers than ever before—it was like kids let loose in a candy shop! Subsequent generations—such as Generation X (born between 1961 and 1981 [Strauss and Howe 1991]), Generation Y (or Millenials, from the early 1980s until 2000 [Howe and Strauss 2000]), and beyond adjusted to the shift in age at first marriage. Today, the average age at first marriage is around twenty-eight for men, twenty-six for women (in 2010). Nearly fifty years earlier in 1960 men married around age twenty-three and women at twenty-and-a-half. (Forty years earlier—in 1920—men married at twenty-four-and-a-half, women at twenty-one.) Figure 3.3 illustrates the U-shaped historical trend from 1890 to the present; it also shows how the age gap between men and women has narrowed: in 1900, men were marrying four years later than women; in 2007 that gap was a bit more than one-and-a-half years. The numbers have risen slightly since then.

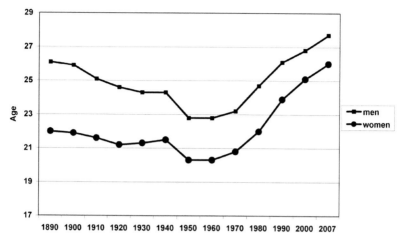

FIGURE 3.3
U.S. median age at first marriage, 1890–2007. Data from U.S. Census Bureau (2004).

College also had an impact. Not only were more young people in college in absolute terms but also the likelihood that someone would attend college increased, especially for women. In 1960, 54 percent of men who graduated from high school went on to college, compared to 38 percent of women high school graduates. By 1980 the number for women was 52 percent, and in 1999, among high school graduates 61 percent of men and 64 percent of women went on to college (NCES 2008), as illustrated in figure 3.4. As the

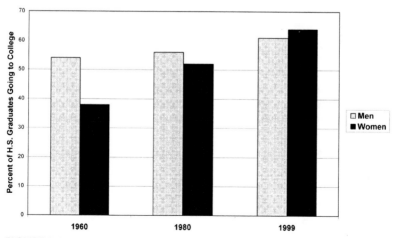

FIGURE 3.4
Growth in college attendance, change in gender composition. Data from NCES (2008).

figure shows, the proportion of all young people in college has grown. These days, there are *more* women in college than there are men (except at the most elite schools, where men are still in the slight majority). Specifically, among young people ages eighteen to twenty-four, in 1967, around two of ten women and more than three in ten men were in college; but in 2005, over four in ten women and 3.5 of ten men were enrolled (Mather and Adams 2007).

Starting in the 1960s, the longer people stayed in college and out of the marriage pool, the longer the temptation to have nonmarital sex. So just by staying in college for two or four years, young people were much more likely to lose their virginity before marriage. Furthermore, more women obtained advanced degrees, and they were likely to use these degrees in the workplace before settling down. Interestingly, the more education a woman had, the later she was likely to marry, but the reverse has been true for men. Thus, women of this era were adding on new roles: intellectual, professional, financial. Men, on the other hand, had little incentive to add to their repertoire the domestic obligations traditionally fulfilled by women, and, while men have slowly caught up—especially on child care—a gender gap in housework persists (Sullivan, Gurion, and Coltrane 2008).

In another break with tradition, few of these young people inherited family farms or family businesses, which were losing their dominant place in the economy. Some middle-class and upper-middle-class youth rejected the "safe" course of traditional jobs like accounting and engineering that they felt their parents had chosen to the detriment of "personal growth" and freedom. With neither the advantage nor burden of family economic obligations, young people started to enjoy life. As the 1970s ran into the 1980s, a growing proportion of young men and women in their twenties stayed unmarried and delayed childbearing. Those who did marry during this turbulent time were caught between traditionalism, the new promise of self-determination, and feminist critiques of marriage. The trend in delayed childbearing continues today. In 2006, the average age of a first birth was twenty-five for women; during the preceding twenty-five years the number of women over thirty giving birth doubled; over thirty-five the number tripled; and over forty the number quadrupled.

During the transition following the sexual revolution, young people, who criticized old values of loyalty, traditionalism, and duty, were predictably hard on their own relationships. Although the divorce rate in the United States had been increasing steadily since the late nineteenth century, the divorce rate took a sharp upward turn in this period (Cherlin 1992). Between 1960 and 1980, the divorce rate increased by about 250 percent. Two-thirds of all young people were married by age twenty-four in 1960, but that percentage was reversed by the 1980s: two-thirds of twenty-four-year-olds were single, never married, or already divorced (Cherlin 1992). Starting in 1980, the divorce rate leveled off to about 50 percent (Goldstein 1999), and by about 2008, the rate was closer to 40 percent.

As baby boomers aged, the marriage market became more unpredictable. Women tend to partner with men several years older, but the preboom generation had fewer men for baby boom women to choose from, and the preboom men had married earlier than those in the following generation. Baby boom women who delayed marriage in favor of education and work or whose first marriage didn't work out came back into the marriage market and found it rather sparse. Although the media vastly overestimated the problems of the marriage market in the 1980s, demographic realities still constrained women's dating options. Some women felt cheated and misled. They wanted experimentation, a career, and the freedom to leave a bad marriage and not lose out on finding a life companion eventually.

By the mid-1980s, these demographic facts, along with increasing awareness of AIDS, meant sex was associated with new kinds of anxiety, and some commentators felt the sexual climate was shifting again. The conservative influence of the 1980s; a tighter job market, born of the recession of the early 1980s; and a more dangerous disease environment created an atmosphere of caution, even if it didn't reverse sexual trends. The baby boom generation started getting older, settling down, producing children, and drifting toward greater conservatism. Furthermore, women who had attended college acquired progressive feminist ideas, but many women and men who had not gone to college or had not been involved with progressive political ideologies tended to have more traditional sexual attitudes. Although some sectors of the baby boomers remained politically liberal, younger generations reaching adulthood in the 1980s and 1990s were more conservative.

The third influence on women's changing sexuality has been the sociological and cultural context. Challenges to men's power and women's traditional roles affected men's and women's emotional engagement with one another. Roles taken for granted in the past required communication and negotiation. Men were unsure of what kind of world feminism and the sexual revolution would create. A lot of men were angry at being attacked and labeled oppressors, while another large group welcomed changes between the sexes and were enthusiastic supporters of women's new rights (Messner 1997).

In the midst of all of these changing roles and changing sexual interaction, it makes sense that a lot of the values and behaviors that were being critiqued and adjusted would cause trouble at the most intimate level of all: committed couples. Articles started to be written about the "politics of intimacy": power struggles that were played out in between two people but were related to issues of power in the wider culture (Jacobson 1989). The combination of the sexual revolution and women's growing educational and financial success meant women could be much more independent. This destabilized the traditional hierarchy of love, marriage, and family politics. Feminist issues like pay equity, abortion, divorce, and equality in the household packed a personal punch. The questions were hard to answer: What constitutes equality in the home? Who has the right to abortion? Should marriage be modified, rejected, or stay the same? Should women be treated as sexually vulnerable or as equal sexual players, no holds barred? Should men take more responsibility for sexual encounters?

Heated rhetoric flew back and forth. Debates within feminism on the costs of sexual and personal liberty were echoed by defenders of sexual and marital traditions. While feminists were concerned about the well-being of women, traditionalists were particularly spurred on by the higher divorce rates. By the 1980s, many men and women were living with the consequences of the positions they had taken earlier. Some were thrilled with the new personal latitude that the women's movement had given both men and women. Others had regrets.

Thus, three social forces—dramatic shifts in birth control technology, the demographics of the baby boom generation, and the cultural diffusion and diversification of feminism—ushered in a novel sexual era, with the promise of gender equality and a corresponding reduction of the double standard in sexuality. But utopian visions have not been completely fulfilled. Gender persists in being a principal organizing feature of sexuality today. Technological, demographic, and sociological changes linked to the baby boom generation's coming of age changed the lives of women more so than men's. Furthermore, the use of sex and sexuality as a mechanism for social control had not died; it may have been disabled a bit, but it had not died.

Frontlash and Backlash in the 1990s and Beyond

By the end of the 1970s, liberal trends in sexual behavior had turned into norms that were solidified in television situation comedies, movies, advertising, and social arrangements such as coeducational dormitories on many college campuses. The "wanton" sexual behavior that became widespread in some groups by the 1980s sent shock waves through the public, just as Kinsey's reports had shocked the public in the 1950s. And yet, just as society came to accept Kinsey's statistics through the media's discussion of his findings, our culture adjusted to the new frank and practical dialogues on sexuality that began to surface in all kinds of media. Popular icons like Oprah took graphic descriptions about sex and sexual relationships into daytime television (Illouz

2008). In the face of such obvious social change, a conservative and moralistic backlash began to grow at the dawn of the Reagan era in 1981. Conservative groups condemned premarital sex, abortion, gay rights, and women's rights, and promoted socially conservative themes. A political tactic, creating voter solidarity through calls for retrieving traditional values by Republican leadership, gained traction that persists to this day. The rallying cry was around a "silent majority" that celebrated "traditional family values" and fought for policies that turned back the clock on sexual "immorality" while promoting a return to traditional gender expectations in the family. The media used these struggles over American values to create viewership. Given the clout of a conservative and eloquent President Reagan, coverage of the sexual revolutionaries of the 1960s and 1970s was replaced by groups of resentful citizens who felt it was their time to overturn the policies of the preceding era. The Tea Party of the 2010s is the legacy of this dissent.

The family values movements linked urban decay and violence to the sexual emancipation of women; early sexual experience for men and women; and new family forms such as single-parent families, stepfamilies, same-sex partners, and heterosexual cohabiters (Coltrane 1997). There were social problems; but most sociologists felt the obvious culprit was the dramatic recession of the early 1980s and the loss of jobs in the decline of the manufacturing sector in the 1970s (Wilson 1987). The "family values" movements, however, blamed practically all social ills on changing "morality," not on economics, jobs, or politics.

Americans who had not been at the center of the sexual revolution were put off, and, at times, disgusted by the new, increasingly acceptable forms of adult social arrangements. They assumed that traditional norms had characterized the majority of U.S. households during the baby boom era of the 1950s. They believed that modern-day trends would be the downfall of the America they knew and loved. Ironically, however, the stay-at-home mom and breadwinning dad touted by family values activists have never predominated in the United States (Coontz 1992). The family values movement had a core flaw. The movement sought to sustain traditional gender roles and sexual behavior that had already irrevocably changed. It extolled a traditional family form that was becoming ever more rare because of economic necessity as well as cultural changes. Feminist ideology was not the key cause of changes in the American family, but it gained credibility, at least in part, because it was practical for the times; it suited economic needs. With change accelerated by the recession of the early 1980s, fewer than 10 percent of all U.S. households were "nuclear family" households: stay-at-home mom, employed dad, and a couple of kids. While the traditional family values cry continues to be heard today, the economy speaks more loudly: During the recession of 2009, women began to make up nearly half of our workforce for the first time, and to be breadwinners—or cobreadwinners—in 63 percent of families (Boushey and O'Leary 2009).

A particular focus of alarm for family values activists was the spread of abortion services after the 1973 *Roe v. Wade* decision, which legalized abortion during the first and second trimesters of pregnancy. This emphatically feminist and civil libertarian Supreme Court decision infuriated conservatives. It did not matter to them that abortion services were used mostly by married women. It did not matter that one reason abortion was necessary to so many young people was the fact that there were no social and economic supports to unmarried, often impoverished teens. The consequences of enduring an unwanted pregnancy were less important to these opponents of abortion than the deep need they felt to sustain traditional morality. Teenage motherhood was unfortunate, but newspaper stories quoted leaders of the antiabortion movement lacerating "immoral youth" who deserved to suffer the consequences of their behavior. Even though some antiabortion activists tried to lessen the impact on the child by creating adoption services for desperate mothers, more often than not, the best interests of the child were less than a secondary consideration during furious pronouncements against premarital sex.

During the 1980s, many people expressed anger about abortion, divorce, premarital sex, and not incidentally, women's defiant rejection of their historical classification as the upholders of purity, family, and motherhood. Despite organized interest groups' lobbying and rhetoric, however, the sexual habits of Americans continued to become increasingly diverse and permissive. A majority in the United States did not support traditional "family values"; their own lives, or their children's, had changed too much. Individualism, a foundational, constitutional principle in the United States, has deep and strong roots and was hard to trim back or cut down. The majority of people followed their hearts, not their perceptions of their ancestors' examples or their church's traditional morality. In fact, parents, churches, schools, and laws were changing to deal with the ways people now mate and marry.

What's Happening Now

For the past two decades, religious leaders' complaints about sexuality have persevered. But paradoxes persist. For example, responsive to conservative religious lobbies in the 2000s, President Bush increased money for abstinence-only education. At the same time teen sexual activity increased. We also saw the expansion of sexually frank advertising, like half-nude adolescent boys for Abercrombie and Fitch or Calvin Klein's steamy ads featuring teenagers in a three-way sexual encounter. We saw the growth—and growing alarm about—teen hookups that on the one hand looked like a natural extension of the sexual revolution and on the other hand showed ways that men and women were *still* subject to gendered norms of sexual behavior.

Something else happened. Despite the handwringing and sexual precociousness, teen pregnancy rates declined (although there was an upward blip in 2006). As abstinence-only sex education programs were discredited and the new Obama administration reduced abstinence funding, opportunities for more comprehensive sex education emerged. And good ideas—like strategies to help both girls and boys develop skills to delay sex—emerged. Resentment and resistance to the changing status of women in the workplace have also waned. When asked about the full participation of women in the workforce now, over 75 percent of Americans surveyed by *Time* agreed that this was a good thing (Boushey and O'Leary 2009). And in more categories than not, the same survey found that men and women share the same life goals.

Special Issues: Examining the Continuum

Gay/Lesbian/Bisexual/Transgender

It isn't just sex lives of heterosexuals that are controlled and influenced by culture. Gays, lesbians, bisexuals, and transgender people are remarkably subject to gendered forms of sexual control and are subject to conduct codes. Above all, our taboos against homosexuality—and our expressions of homophobia (or fear of homosexuality in ourselves or others)—come from the notion that the only way to be a good woman or a good man is to be a good heterosexual. This "heteronormativity" is what is at stake when junior high school boys call a classmate a "fag" interchangeably with a "sissy" (Pascoe 2007). These days, although gay and lesbian characters are increasingly common in mainstream television and movies, phrases like *fag* or *homo* are still used—not just against the (suspected) gay or lesbian child or adolescent—but more broadly to accent the acceptable or unacceptable appearance of masculinity at any age. The prevalence of this kind of harassment highlights how powerfully our culture clings to the link between gender and sexuality. As much as societies police heterosexuality to control marriage and reproduction, they seek to control homosexuality for similar reasons.

A major realm of control for gay men and lesbians involves access to marriage. While gays, lesbians, and sympathetic heterosexuals have joined together to successfully fight for equitable treatment in hiring and housing, access to legal validation of their relationships has been less successful. Some states, counties, and municipalities have created "civil unions" or "domestic partnerships" to give some rights and protections to same-sex and cohabiting couples that mirror aspects of marriage. And many states are engaged in serious trials over the right to marry.

At the moment gays and lesbians are still not allowed to marry in most states in the United States and are typically treated as "singles" by the state, even when couples are in a long-term, committed relationship. Marriage, from the perspective of the U.S. federal government, requires a gender difference. (See chapter 5 for more on this.) By 2011, the revolution in same-sex marriage saw six states and the District of Columbia legalize same-sex marriage. Yet, the United States still has no federal policy that ensures that those legal marriages provide true equality, and the right within states is not completely stable, either. Indeed, with a great deal of mudslinging and distortion in the subsequent political battles, two states (Maine and California) created and then rescinded same-sex marriage rights. As this book goes to press, a complex battle in the state of California (see chapter 5 for more details) has yielded a decision from a federal court against a federal law that stipulated that marriage can only include one man and one woman. The case will proceed with appeals to the Supreme Court.

Nevertheless, social attitudes toward same-sex relationships have progressed quite a bit. The relationships were tabooed and nearly invisible until forty or so years ago, but same-sex relationships have now become much more visible on television, such as the wildly popular comedian Ellen DeGeneres and her partner, Portia de Rossi, among other celebrities. Same-sex relationships are more likely to be integrated into larger, mixed communities and friendship groups as well. In the process of becoming more visible, controversies have been part of the landscape.

Most gay activists date the beginning of the gay political push for recognition and equal rights to the June 1969 riot at Stonewall Inn in Greenwich Village, New York City. At that time, gay bars, where both uncoupled and coupled gay men (and sometimes lesbians) could meet, were subjected to periodic police raids and shakedowns in the late 1960s. In general, the men would be arrested, humiliated, exposed as gay (and therefore put in danger of losing their jobs), and then let go, only to worry about when the next arbitrary raid might occur. But when the police raided the Stonewall Inn in 1969, customers resisted, and a full-fledged riot erupted. This was the start of an aggressive civil rights movement that changed the way many gay men and lesbians lived their lives. The slow movement of gays and lesbians into mainstream culture since the late 1960s has meant another very clear challenge to traditional gender norms and traditional romantic sexual scripts (D'Emilio and Freedman 1988).

Today, there is less harassment of gays and lesbians, especially in urban communities, and a much wider variety of places that gay people can use for courtship, dating, and sex. However, being single and gay is more difficult than being single and straight. First, most adolescents are exposed only to heterosexual social opportunities, especially in traditional organizations such as schools, sports, and churches. Heterosexual youth experience public pairing, organized dances, and activities in open groups of unpaired but eligible other-sex partners. This is training into "heteronormativity"—that is, the way that heterosexuality is treated as if it were a strict norm, one in which biological sex, gender, and heterosexual status are aligned. The training process socializes youth into gendered heterosexual norms: boys can do this, girls can do that. When dating begins, heterosexual youth have many people to confide in, compare notes with, and learn from.

Rarely is this social support available to gay and lesbian youth, unless they are fortunate enough to be in an environment where a gay culture is visible and where they can be "out" enough (and supported by their parents enough) to be able to participate in it. A few cities have developed gay-friendly high schools in the past several years. One challenge is that most individuals assume they are themselves straight, just as people tend to think others are straight until otherwise informed. The young person who has disconfirming evidence, such as attraction to a same-sex person or lack of attraction to the other sex, may be confused and resist this attraction. It may take years of self-examination to embrace an identity that tends to be stigmatized. As a result, many young gay people reach adulthood having dated little or having had only furtive sexual encounters in anonymous places rather than an orderly and approved dating life. Some may marry a person of the other sex, hoping that making a commitment or having children will "straighten" them out. Years later, however, these marriages usually break up, with much heartbreak all around. Some of these people first enter the gay dating market in their thirties, forties, or even fifties—unformed in their tastes and in gay social skills.

Up until the past twenty years, lesbians may have had even less experience than men because our culture discourages women from sexual experimentation. In more recent years, we've seen young women increasing their rate of same-sex sexual experimentation relative to that of men's. While there has been growing sexual freedom among women—including lesbians—there is greater sexualization among gay men. The script for women makes recognition of sexual attraction difficult because culturally it is assumed that a woman can have deep emotions for another woman and not consider it sexual or unusual. That makes it harder to recognize sexual attraction for what it is, and that misapprehension can go on for quite a while—perhaps forever. Women's friendship is affectionate and physical, and these freedoms normalize desires to hug and kiss one another. It is often hard to know who is flirting and who is merely showing deep friendship. Lesbians often tell tales of signals misread and friendships gone awry, as a woman who loves women misreads the actions of a woman who merely likes women. Of course, sometimes both women love women, and a love affair begins. Often, however, lesbians have to wait until they get to a big city or a safe environment for lesbians to meet before they learn about their sexual tastes and desires.

Today, most young lesbians and gay men learn more about homosexuality than in previous generations, thanks to the books, magazines, journals, social organizations, and especially the Internet that now help connect gay people to a gay community. But even so, being young, single, and gay is a challenge. A former student—who started coming out in junior high in the early 2000s—described it: "Junior high school is an emotional rollercoaster—if you are a heterosexual. Good luck if you are coming out. I just want to reach out to them and give them a hug." What is it like? According to the National School Climate Survey (Kosciw et al. 2009), 84 percent of middle and high school LGBT students have been verbally harassed and called names or threatened verbally due to their sexual orientation. Sixty-one percent of these students report feeling unsafe and 27 percent report having been physically harassed.

In this climate young gays and lesbians sometimes find each other in high school, become lovers, come out right away, and have parents who support their choices. But this is hardly typical. Even understanding parents are unlikely to support gay dating in the early teen years. More likely, people will try to talk young gays and lesbians out of their attraction, label it as a passing fad or fancy, or even send them into psychotherapy. Few parents will support challenging the system. In a recent nationally publicized case in 2010, a young lesbian in Mississippi tried to do just that by taking her partner to the prom. The school's prom was cancelled as a result of her request, and small alternative proms popped up to compensate. Few gays or lesbians of this age have the courage or backing to face such a harsh institutional response. Due to such experiences and deep personal alienation, suicide is about four times more common among gay than straight teens, and children from unsupportive (or "rejecting") families seem to be at greater risk for suicide attempts (Denizet-Lewis 2009).

Bisexuality

This lack of support is particularly true for people who are attracted to both men and women. There is a strong presumption in society that if a person isn't straight that must mean he or she is gay. In fact, such an essentialist assumption is a mirror image to dichotomous ideas about gender. There is little social support for bisexuality, even though quite a few people say that they are, or have been, seriously attracted to both men and women.

It isn't that we don't get exposed to stories of bisexuality. Consider the MTV reality game show entitled *A Shot at Love with Tila Tequila*. In this show, Myspace star Tila Tequila shares her house with a group of sixteen straight men and sixteen lesbian suitors who are all competing to win Tequila's heart. After an elimination in which Tila is left with a "few favorites," Tila lets her secret out that she is bisexual and the fight to "win her over" begins.

The show highlights the way that bisexuality is most understood as a war between "our side" or "their side." (It also highlights the way that women's bisexuality is frequently treated these days as a straight man's turn-on.) Kinsey's scale (see chapter 2) has resurfaced, and the concept has become hotly debated; books like Jennifer Baumgardner's *Look Both Ways* (2007) provide strong claims for the authenticity of bisexuality. The Kinsey scale suggests a continuum of sexual attractions. Although bisexuals are defined by some degree of attraction, fantasy, or experience with both sexes, rarely is there the equal intensity with men and women.

While the "authenticity" of bisexuality is a fact in the research literature, it is emotionally resisted by a majority of the population. Heterosexuals tend to deny it because they are afraid it gives people license to experiment and perhaps fall in love with the same sex—and thereby forsake family life and social approval. Gays and lesbians tend to deny it because they believe it allows men and women a way of escaping gay identity; a bisexual could always leave a same-sex partner and flee to the more comfortable heterosexual world. There is also apprehension that bisexuality might function as a "higher status," thereby undermining gay and lesbian solidarity and political clout. Above all, bisexuality threatens essentialist beliefs in a fixed and unchanging sexuality that is defined by your own gender and the gender of the ones you love. Such skepticism of the implausibility of bisexuality is reflected in researchers' categories for sexual behavior such as "situational homosexuality" (discussed in Rust 2002). The data confirm that a certain percentage of men and women have sexual experience with both sexes. Those rates vary from 5 to 20 percent (Rust 2002) depending upon what dimensions of sexuality are being measured. In sum, there is ample research to prove that bisexual behavior exists. What to make of it seems to be something of a cultural football—continually debated and left unresolved.

Bisexuality is not just an "idea" or a passing erotic play by celebrities that are looking for ways to tease their fans. The media had a field day with images of Madonna kissing Britney Spears and members of Nirvana kissing onstage. But it is hard to know what this glib sexual play means. What we do know is that a 2002 report from the Center for Disease Control found that 12 percent of women ages eighteen to forty-four reported having at least one same-sex sexual experience; that was up from 4 percent ten years earlier. The increase for men in the same time period was from 5 to 6 percent. As illustrated in figure 3.5, where in 1992 men reported more sexual freedom, women in the 2002 survey reported more sexual liberality and considerable growth in their sexual freedom.

Bisexuality complicates the dating and sexual scene. It brings up fear of contagion in this day of AIDS, and it intensifies insecurities manufactured by the dating experience. The fear of being dumped for someone else is supplemented by the apprehension that one will be the lesser attraction because she or he is the "lesser" sex. A colleague recounted his experience:

> I fell in love with her in the most complete, hopeless way. We were graduate students together; we were pals, colleagues, lovers. She was the most charismatic person. I knew she had had gay experiences. She never misled me, but I always believed, down deep, that I was too attractive to pass up and to be totally honest, that the heterosexual pull would be greater. But it wasn't. Even while we were living together, she fell in love with one of her professors and moved in with her. They are still together . . . I don't think I will love anyone again like I loved her . . . I feel misled by her—and myself.

The heartbreak he described is the same heartbreak that most of us experience—straight, gay, bisexual, or otherwise—when we create a deep

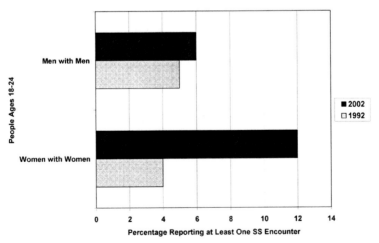

FIGURE 3.5
Same-sex sexual experience, 1992–2002. Data from Mather and Adams (2007).

romantic attachment and things come to an end against our wishes. The puzzle in this case is that we have fewer skills and know-how for dealing with the plasticity of gender and sexuality that bisexuality presents, especially given a more dichotomous view of gender and sexuality that predominates.

Transgender

When we wrote the original edition of this book in 1998, transgender was barely addressed—not that trans people didn't exist, but it was a topic that we, like many others, neglected. Today, their experience is more prominent. Transgender people, while still marginalized, are a visible part of the culture. For example, unlike a decade ago, today, gay and lesbian rights organizations include social and legal action related to transgender. Previously gay organizations now routinely identify as gay/lesbian/bisexual/transgender, or GLBT.

What is transgender? Like bisexuality, the definitions are more complex than our simple lining up of what biological sex you were born into, what gender you were raised in, and who you tend to love—either the "same sex" or the "opposite (or other) sex." Transgender people are not defined by a specific orientation; transgender can mean any identities that diverge from the gender a person was assigned at birth and can also include some combination of expression and identification with identities that are seen as "male" and "female." Transsexuals—people who seek sex reassignment surgery—can be considered part of this category. Indeed, the category includes those people who live with identities where their biological sex and their conventional gender identity are not linked in any traditional way. The emerging recognition and acceptance of these varied combinations of biology, identity, and sexual orientation suggest greater acknowledgment of the complexity of our sexual selves and the view that sexuality and gender are on a continuum.

Growing tolerance and understanding have given people more freedom to live openly as transgender. This openness has an additional impact: it offers our society an opportunity to face concerns and confusion about sex and gender. A recent story (2008) illustrates our cultural conflict on this issue. Thomas Beatie was born and raised as a woman and transformed himself in order to live as a man. Following hormone therapy and surgery, he was legally classified as a man. However, and here's where the confusion comes in, he was able to conceive and sustain a pregnancy because he had retained his female reproductive organs. Obviously interesting to both the heterosexual and homosexual public, Mr. Beatie appeared on *Oprah* and was the topic of debate across the pages of the GLBT magazine *The Advocate* as well as the conservative talk show *The O'Reilly Factor*. In each place, the dialogue reflected concern and discomfort with such a disruption of norms of sex and gender—but also norms of what it is to be a mother or a father. As Mr. Beatie explained in an article in *The Advocate*, "Our situation sparks legal, political, and social unknowns. We have only begun experiencing opposition from people who are upset by our situation. Doctors have discriminated against us, turning us away due to their religious beliefs. Health care professionals have refused to call me by a male pronoun or recognize Nancy as my wife. Receptionists have laughed at us. Friends and family have been unsupportive; most of Nancy's family doesn't even know I'm transgender." Still, Mr. Beatie reported not feeling any conflict between his identity as a man and as the gestating parent of his child. But he may be singular in that comfort with mixing the usual biological and social roles of men and women in such unprecedented fashion. The process is a challenge to beliefs about biology as destiny—or at least as a necessary component to mothering and fathering.

Sex Practices among Single People

The recent history of sexuality—from dating rituals prior to the sexual revolution to the sexual revolution's acceleration of sexual freedom and acknowledgment of sexual diversity—offers an arc that leads us to the next set of questions: What are people really *doing* when they are having sex? How much is going on outside of committed relationships? What exactly are the range of practices associated with sexual freedom? And, as always, we wonder how much men's and women's experiences have come to be more similar and how much they remain shaped by a sexual double standard.

Getting into Sex

There are so many different ways of "getting into" sex. Back in the 1950s *petting* was the word used for the slow buildup of sexual encounters that included a lot of what we might call foreplay today. The difference is that daters' foreplay these days might proceed to oral sex or intercourse, while in the 1950s anyone who ventured beyond touching would have been going way beyond common norms of sexual behavior. Petting used to be the center of young passion, although intercourse eventually occurred more often than the myth of virginity before marriage suggests. Today, *petting* is sometimes called *making out* or *hooking up*, and it involves kissing, touching, feeling, rubbing, and groping. What makes "hooking up" different is that when someone says "we hooked up," the couple may or may not have also had oral sex or intercourse.

Probably one of the more remarkable changes from past sexual courtship rituals is that these days younger and older men and women proceed quickly from first kiss to first intercourse. Before the sexual revolution of the 1960s and 1970s—and still among some groups—people talked about getting to "first base" (kissing), stopping awhile at second base (touching breasts and genitals over clothes), and getting to third base (touching nude body parts) before they had a "home run" (intercourse). Sexual permission escalated slowly between people who were "dating." Interviews with people who are in their fifties (or older) rhapsodize about the deliberate pace. For example, this woman is positively nostalgic:

> Oh, it was delicious. I remember the thrill of letting his arm hang over my shoulder and slightly, ever so slightly, touch my breast. That went on for weeks. And then I let him touch me "above the waist"—over my sweater, of course. Weeks went by, and then I let him touch me under the sweater. That was the big step for months. After a long time, he put his hand up my skirt, and we fought over that for a while until I thought it was OK. It took me the longest time to touch him— either over or under his clothes. We did this for two years before we attempted intercourse—and that was our big graduation present to each other—literally. We did it on the senior prom weekend.

These days, things go much faster. Petting is now foreplay. Touching and stimulation occur, but more commonly the expectation is that partners are preparing for intercourse. With first intercourse happening at ever-younger ages, there doesn't seem to be time for a sustained period of petting—unless it is happening at ever younger ages, but that is unlikely. Unlike earlier decades, sexual expression is now more genitally focused. In earlier decades, women had been cast as the "gatekeepers," saying "no, no, no" to intercourse. But the elimination of the need to say no made intercourse the main focus of much sexual interaction for women and men alike. This seems to be a more masculine vision of sexuality than a feminine vision, however. Women often say that they love prolonged petting and touching, but men tell of becoming enormously frustrated. Even though women extol men who take their time and kiss and touch them luxuriously, the intercourse-focused version of sex seems to have triumphed. Modern sex therapy—and our love affair with Viagra and other erectile dysfunction drugs—has fueled this change by generating sexual norms that glorify erection, penetration, and orgasm. Figure 3.6 gives us a portrait of how college students report the sexual progression in their relationships, including hookups. The graph shows that first-time encounters are more likely to be genital and less likely to include intercourse, but by the fourth encounter or in the context of a relationship, sex often includes intercourse.

Women may miss prolonged touching and foreplay, but it is quite possible that men, too, prefer more integrated sexuality that involves sensual, sustained

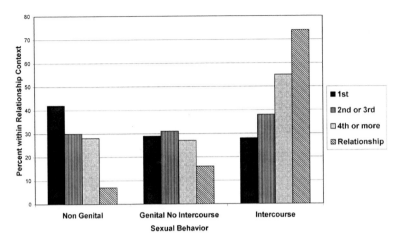

FIGURE 3.6
Sexual behavior by relationship/hookup context. Data from Armstrong et al.
(2010).

touching, as well as intercourse. However, it remains "uncool" for men to express such leisurely sexual tastes. The gendered sexual scripts that were so powerful before the sexual revolution have a tenacious hold. Old scripts regarding petting and gatekeeping have faded, but new scripts retain many gender roles that remind us that sex still occurs more according to men's than women's desires.

The intercourse model of sex is the predominant cultural sexual model; there really is not another, even if you are gay, lesbian, bisexual, or transsexual. Gays and lesbians innovate and create their own sexual scripts after having been brought up (typically) on heterosexual fantasies and priorities. As a result, alternatives to intercourse, like slowing down the escalation of sexual acts, may be occurring among gays and lesbians more than heterosexuals. For instance, gay men who are interested in sexual variety but chastened by the danger of contracting HIV have searched for turn-ons that avoid penetration or exchange of bodily fluids. Anal intercourse, one of the ways gay men might have sex, became a much less attractive behavior because if the virus was present, it was more easily transmitted through anal penetration. Public health campaigns and private commercial campaigns by condom companies emphasizing safer sex have been very successful (although not perfect) in helping gay men learn less risky ways to please each other. Large numbers of gay men have figured out how to sustain arousal and achieve satisfaction through nonpenetrative sex. Petting, erotic talk, and other methods of sexual intimacy have come back into vogue out of necessity.

Intercourse has never been the focus for lesbians. Like heterosexual women, lesbians appreciate the sensations of petting. Not having a male partner, however, has reduced the focus on penetrative sex. Most of what constitutes foreplay in heterosexual relationships is the core of lesbian lovemaking. Although penetration occurs—with fingers, a vibrator, a dildo, or some similar object for stimulating the vagina—it is not so likely to be seen as the "main event," and there's greater opportunity for more diversity in turn-ons.

First Intercourse

Age at first intercourse still tends to be around seventeen (Chandra et al 2005. Marinez et al. 2006). Nearly half of all teens (46 percent) ages fifteen to nineteen have had sex at least once. Still, at a time when there is a sense of growing sexual liberality, the number of teens who report ever having had sex declined from 49 percent in 1995 to 46 percent in 2002 for women and 55 to 46 percent for men (Abma 2004). Ten percent of teen women report their first encounter was not voluntary—while three-quarters report that it was with a boyfriend, fiancé, partner, or husband.

Even so, first intercourse is not an unproblematic, carefree event. Men still receive more admiration for sexual expertise than women, so it stands to reason that boys start having sex earlier than girls and tend to be happier about their first experiences. Several studies (Call, Sprecher, and Schwartz 1995; Laumann et al. 1994) demonstrate that people have mixed emotions about sexual initiation. These emotions are organized in part around gender; in other words, men and women have different reactions to the same act. Hollywood images of sexual outlaws like Madonna or Lady Gaga are still just a faraway fantasy to most women. Such images may appeal to men in the abstract, although in truth many men would be intimidated. Still, most young women feel less comfortable with their bodies than young men do and are more worried about the emotional connection with their partner. When a young woman feels insecure in her connection to her partner or feels too skinny, or too fat, or too flat, or too something, it is much more likely that early sexual exploration is going to be deeply disappointing.

Figure 3.7 (from NHSLS) shows men's and women's evaluations of the circumstances of their first sexual encounter. A diverse group of men and women were asked whether they would characterize their first sexual experience as something they desired, did not desire, or were forced to do. Although the majority wanted their first experience, a quarter of the women did not want intercourse their first time, three times the number of men who did not want it. A small number of women had a terrible, forced experience, and they outnumbered men who were forced by about twenty to one.

Keep in mind, however, that men's first experience may not be as ideal as the 92 percent figure suggests, nor the unwanted or forced category so small. Men are expected to enjoy intercourse no matter how disappointing

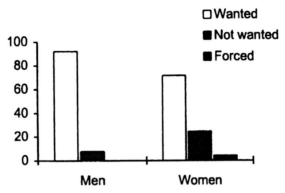

FIGURE 3.7
Evaluating first sexual experiences. Data from Laumann
et al. (1994).

or strange the experience may be. Ambivalence about sex is not expected from men. Only in some qualitative research, where they share stories about first intercourse, do men sometimes reveal that they felt trapped into a sexual situation that was not to their design or liking (as reported, e.g., in Hatfield and Rapson 1993). In the Laumann study, some of the unwanted sexual experiences of men and women included sexual activity a young person had with an adult (Browning and Laumann 2001). For men as well as women, the consequences of this early traumatic experience were hard to overcome, and men and women were likely to have challenges with sexual desire and response when they were older.

Some researchers argue that women also experience forced sex more often than the statistics reveal and that even more women did not want their first experience. Some women, the logic goes, are in denial and not really facing up to the fact that they were forced. Many young women are so accustomed to capitulating to men's desires in both sexual and nonsexual settings that it may not occur to them that their compromises are not voluntary. These commentators may be right, although it is important not to assume that women are typically sexual victims (they aren't) or that men are typically sexual aggressors (they aren't). Of course, accounts of first experiences, given retrospectively, are recreations of what happened, not firsthand observations. As with other sexual self-reports, they are hard to interpret.

In *Going All the Way* (1996), journalist Sharon Thompson presents interviews with a diverse sample of teenage girls across the United States. She shows how young women in high school sometimes trade sex when they are promised love in exchange only to find that the love doesn't follow and that the sex is something they didn't really want. The young women who were interviewed repeated statements like "I really didn't want to, but it was easier just to please him than to keep saying no" or "I figured it was going to be with someone and while I really didn't want it to be him, he convinced me that I had led him on and that I better do the right thing." Thompson shows that mostly better-educated, older, more privileged young people have the opportunity to negotiate sexual and romantic experiences on their own terms, and they have more pleasing, egalitarian outcomes. Remarkably, ten years later in *Unhooked: How Young Women Pursue Sex, Delay Love, and Lose at Both* (2007), journalist Laura Sessions Stepp offered similar observations. Based on spending time with high school women, she reported that these women *had* obtained more sexual freedom, but she observed that they *had lost* some of their opportunity for intimacy.

Why are first sexual encounters so complicated? The answer resides in the culture of sexual ambivalence that we live in. Ambivalence undermines skills and heightens unsure relations between men and women. Even the majority of women who say they wanted to have intercourse have less glowing reports of the event than men do. Ignorance and fear make many men and women less than sensitive lovers, particularly starting out. Sex requires a lot of skills—being a good lover and learning how to get pleasure for yourself requires imagination, communication, and the self-confidence to ask for what you want and to tell your partner what you like. The approval that men obtain by simply "scoring," however, makes less-than-virtuoso performances more rewarding for men than for women. The chances of dissatisfaction are increased during sexual encounters between people who don't care deeply about each other. In casual, perhaps drunken sex acts, participants aren't particularly dedicated to ensuring that it is a happy experience for both partners. It may also be true that because men still tend to be the initiators in dating and sex, women are more likely to be approached by men they don't really want to have sex with at the time. The experience is bound to be more pleasant for men and women who control the choice of partner and the timing of the event.

Many of these feelings may have to do with the presence or absence of affection in the relationship. The NHSLS data show that almost half the women who wanted intercourse had sex out of affection for their partner but that only a quarter of the men did, as indicated in figure 3.8.

Of those who didn't want sex, only 10 percent of the men and 39 percent of the women were motivated by affection. Perhaps women are more likely than men to rationalize doing something that they didn't clearly want "for love." Perhaps men are more likely than women to admit less than romantic motivations. At any rate, men and women don't appear to always be on the same page when it comes to motivations for having sex.

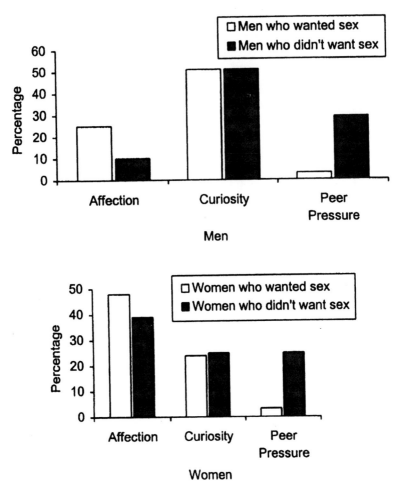

FIGURE 3.8
Reasons for first intercourse. Data from Laumann et al. (1994).

Gendered responses also appear when it comes to sexual curiosity: men were curious, women less so. When you examine the affection bars and the curiosity bars in figure 3.8, notice that a good number of women who had sex out of affection must have had sex with a guy who did it for the sake of curiosity. Even for men who didn't really want sex, curiosity and feeling "ready for it" were big reasons to do it. Note that 25 percent of the women who didn't want to have sex went forward with it anyway on account of curiosity.

About a quarter of both men and women surveyed in the NHSLS cited peer pressure as another reason they had first intercourse when they didn't want it. Today, young men and women assume they will not be virgins for very long.

Some start to feel virginity is a burdensome status they would just as soon eliminate, and so they seek out any available sexual partner.

What about pleasure? Despite the emphasis on pleasure that has characterized the modern sexual revolution, only a small number of NHSLS respondents said that their first experience was based mainly on pleasure. The men gave that answer more often than women (12.2 percent versus 2.8 percent, respectively).

What emerges from these self-reports is that young people are aroused and interested in sex, but that men's and women's motivations diverge. Fewer men than women state that they were in love with their first partner. Fewer women than men have their first experience to just see what it is like. But regardless of the gender differences, most young men and women have some key things in common. They get sexually aroused or emotionally connected, but the outcome of what happens next is often difficult for them. Equal numbers of young men and women are pushed ahead by peers before they feel good about sharing sex as their own choice.

Frequency and Sex Partners

Despite all the images of hip, never-married twenty-somethings running around bedding everything in sight, divorced people have more sex partners than young singles, and married and cohabiting people have sex most often (Laumann et al. 1994). Think about it: married people have access; single people (noncohabiting) have to put out a lot of effort to find a sex partner. Even if they are dating someone seriously, their lives aren't as synchronized as people who live together. Married people are also more likely to be on the same sexual schedule. Dating couples may not yet have worked out when and under what conditions sex will take place.

Gender differences in sexual frequency vary by marital status in another way. Single, never married men report having sex more frequently than never married women, but divorced men and women have sex at nearly the same rate. The difference in the gender gap between the two groups suggests that experience and age reduce women's inhibitions. Women who are sexually experienced may modify their earlier, more traditional vision of how committed a relationship should be before sex is part of the picture. They may be more likely to want sex for sex's sake now that they are deprived of something they were free to enjoy in marriage. Sex is like anything else: If you get used to having a good sex life, you might miss it and therefore seek it less ambivalently than never-married people do. Conversely, a marriage gone wrong usually means a deteriorated sex life. Sometimes divorced people are in a hurry to rectify an emotionally painful period. They want some love—or even what might pass for love—soon after (or before) the breakup to reassure themselves that they are still desirable. For example, in a 1995 unpublished letter to *Glamour* magazine columnists Lever and Schwartz, a person wrote,

> Our sex life was awful. He never made love to me and the few times he did it was completely unsatisfying. I stayed married because of the children but as soon as I could get divorced I did . . . the first thing I wanted to do was be touched again by someone who didn't make me cringe. I needed to feel like a desirable woman again. I slept around a lot, just to know I was sexually alive. When I finally found my present husband I wasn't so desperate anymore and I could appreciate him for what he was—a great guy and a great lover.

It may also be true that as women age, they feel less vulnerable to the double standard and the judgments that would have inhibited their sexual exploits. A number of books have surfaced by middle-aged divorced women indicating that this seems to be a time of sexual adventures without the usual worries about reputation or women's sexual norms. Pepper Schwartz wrote *Prime: Adventures and Advice about Sex, Love, and the Sensual Years* (2007), narrating the more liberated potential for people in their fifties and older. Elizabeth Gilbert's *Eat, Pray, Love: One Woman's Search for Everything across Italy, India, and Indonesia* (2007) had a similar goal to explore women's physical and spiritual autonomy; and it was followed up by a book about how her "search" was concluded by marriage that shows us a more conventional path: *Committed: A Skeptic Makes Peace with Marriage* (2010).

Dating itself, though, takes a toll, and people modify their sexual strategies the longer they are on the dating market. Men who run around like rabbits may go through a series of disappointing relationships and change their readiness to jump into bed. Women who were "looking for love in all the wrong places" often decide they would rather be celibate than disappointed. Access becomes less important than self-respect and emotional balance. As one woman in her late thirties explained, "Most of the time I would rather stay at home with a good book. I would rather be truly alone with myself than feeling alone in the middle of sex." A colleague, frustrated by women who wanted more commitment than he did, said,

> I don't want to be with someone just for fun anymore because it's never just for fun. I went out with this woman, and she was really all over me for sex. I'm human, I liked it. But I just kind of liked her and told her it wasn't going to go anywhere. To be honest I also told her that I was quite attracted to her. But I did say I was not available in any significant way. She said no problem and we had a great night. Then she called night and day for the next week, accusing me of leading her on. It just isn't worth it.

Disappointments from casual relationships and the potential for misunderstanding both make single sexuality less ideal than the media portrays it (and than many adolescents wish it to be). As figure 3.9 indicates, half the single population reports having sex only a few times a year or less (Laumann et al. 1994). Single people who participated in an international survey sponsored by a condom company (Durex 2005) reported having sex forty-nine times per year; in the same survey, married folks had sex ninety-eight times per year, and cohabiting couples reported an estimated 146 sexual encounters with each other. Sexual freedom for single people doesn't mean having lots of sex.

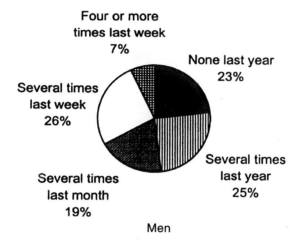

Men

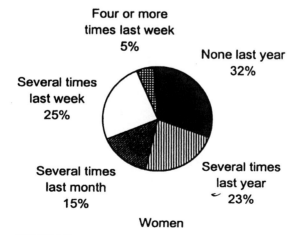

Women

FIGURE 3.9
Sexual frequency among singles. Data from Laumann et al. (1994).

The picture is somewhat different for college-aged people, eighteen to twenty-four years old, who are less likely to be encumbered by work or children and have many more partners to choose from. Figure 3.10 indicates that more than 50 percent of the youngest group was having sex at least a few times a month—though none were having sex nearly every day of the week!

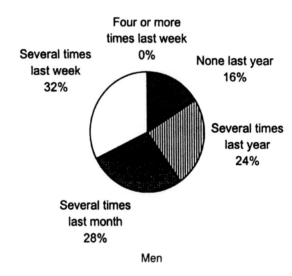

Men

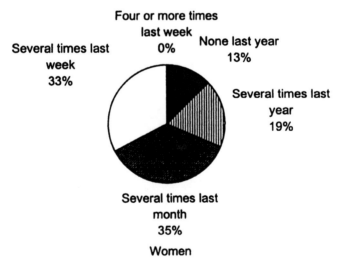

Women

FIGURE 3.10
Sexual frequency for single twenty-somethings. Data from Laumann et al. (1994).

The younger group may be more open about sex. They are in prime dating years, and sex is a high priority. The regularity of sex among the young might also be explained as a consequence of greater hormonal activity. But as we discussed in chapter 1, hormonal activity can be a response to the environment, and youth live in an environment where they are constantly meeting potential partners and falling in love or lust. These data, although not perfect, suggest that less sex is going on than the media suggest but that the young are definitely doing sex more than older people.

The rates of sexual activity also shift once we limit our observations to relationships with some level of commitment and affection (details in chapter 4). There is a "honeymoon" period in both married and nonmarried relationships. The bedazzled couple has eyes only for each other and that means significantly more sex than the two will have after the newness of the relationship has worn off. However, even committed couples tend not to have sex on a daily basis, and though their sex lives are more predictable and steady—over time the frequency of sex declines.

A dating couples study by Simpson and Gangestad (1991) found that the young couples had sex slightly less than twice a week. And Peplau, Rubin, and Hill (1977) did an imaginative study comparing couples who engaged in sex very early in the relationship with couples who delayed. The couples who had sex during the first month of the relationship had a median frequency of four or five times a week; the couples who waited longer had less sex—approximately two to three times a week at the beginning of the sexual part of the relationship. In other words, people who delay may have lower sexual needs (or comfort with sex) to begin with!

Is the experience similar for gays and lesbians? Although AIDS has changed the sexual climate for gay men, they still retain a taste for sexual variety. The AIDS epidemic has caused more gay men to resist anonymous sex and avoid meeting places (like "the baths") where men have numerous sexual encounters based on attraction and nothing else. Indeed, few bath "houses" even exist anymore. The Internet has created a new kind of sex club for gays—as well as straights—and a visit to various online sites like Craigslist is like reading a menu. Online sex trolling is mostly used by adventurous gay men, and it removes some of the uncertainty about getting hooked up with someone. Despite some of the fear of AIDS, the notion of sex as a form of play persists.

While Internet connections are also available for lesbians, they don't seem to use them as the same kind of playground. We looked at Craigslist in Boston over one four-day weekend in fall 2009. While there were over four hundred posts for men seeking men, we counted only one hundred posts for women seeking women. (These were searches for dating—not for sex-for-money, which is banned on Craigslist.)

Lesbians, like gay men and cohabiters, are subject to more frequent break-ups than married people, and so they accrue more partners over time. One recent Internet study showed that women in lesbian relationships had an average of four-year-long relationships—versus eight years for women in heterosexual relationships (including marriages, which tend to last longer). They also found that lesbians had less partnered sex than straight women in the survey—although lesbians and straight women masturbated at about the same rate (Nichols 2005). Although lesbians had sex less frequently than straight women, their sexual encounters lasted longer and were more likely to lead to orgasm. All of these patterns vary considerably by age. Younger people report more sex in all groups. Furthermore, there is a period effect: just as younger generations of heterosexual women engage in more casual sex, so casual sex is more common among younger lesbians.

Sexual Etiquette

Older rules for sex outside of marriage may have faded, but social control of sexual activity hasn't disappeared—the concept of etiquette helps capture the old news and the new news about this. *Date Etiquette* was an educational film that was shown in schools in the 1950s. It had a *Leave It to Beaver* (the 1950s situation comedy) quality to it, and it was intended to instruct young people on how to date: Who asks? Who pays? Who holds the door? Who shakes hands? The subtext of the film was a whole bunch of "don'ts" that were about not making any mistakes in the heteronormative script for how to be good at being a boy or a girl in romantic settings. There were all kinds of old-fashioned advice that had the same general principle: do not do anything to indicate a sexual self! Do not expose yourself to any romantic or sexual feelings! And that goes double if you are a woman! A good night kiss on the first date was a terrible mistake; and any kind of female independence would cost the woman her femininity and endanger a young man's masculinity.

The updated version would have to be "sexual etiquette" in which our dating landscape includes the possibility of hooking up. There is a common understanding that sex outside of marriage is not only possible but probable (replacing the common understanding that men and women just go on dates in the earlier generation). Unlike an earlier time, the things to avoid are more opaque. Above all, with the arrival of sexual etiquette, the norms signal that sexuality can be completely independent of other relationships. People are relatively free to have sex whenever and however partners agree to do so. But traditional constraints on sexuality have given way to new constraints: these involve sexual health and the reproductive consequences of sexual involvement, and these issues still get organized around gender.

Heterosexual Etiquette: Contraception, Safe Sex, and Abortion

Here's a challenge for an updated "Ms. Manners": In a dating couple, who raises the sexually transmitted disease (STD) issue or questions about birth control? In what detail and at what point in the relationship should they learn each other's views on abortion? In the context of hooking up—which is "intentionally" unplanned and low commitment by design—how do partners talk about condom use and other aspects of safe sex? Some people solve these problems by ignoring them as long as possible. At best, most people act erratically. For example, only about half of all single people use some kind of contraception the first time they have sex together (Holmes et al. 1990). Things haven't changed all that much in the past fifteen years: In 2002, adult women used a condom at first sex about 42 percent of the time, and adult men did the same about 48 percent of the time. A study done on people over forty-five for the AARP indicated that just 12 percent of single men used condoms "always" or "most of the time" and only about a third of women used them consistently (AARP 2010). On a more positive note, a Trojan condoms study reported that when teens were asked whether they used a condom the last time they had sex, 70–80 percent said yes (Willingham 2010).

As relationships proceed, partners can be inconsistent, either because they really want to escape the feeling of a condom or because they think they have assessed the risk of contracting an STD. As affection grows, partners rationalize that neither could be diseased, but of course, they don't know for sure.

A few heterosexual couples go together to the health department (or their doctor), get HIV tests to make sure they are virus free, and then proceed to use nonbarrier methods of contraception that do not affect spontaneity or enjoyment. One woman told us that she had convinced her boyfriend to go with her to receive an AIDS test. They were white, bohemian urbanites in their twenties, and both had had about a dozen lovers in the past and no same-sex experiences. Their plan was to clear any doubt about their sexual health so that they could stop using condoms during sex. The plan was sensible and, in a contemporary sense, romantic. It was a sign of the couple's commitment to each other and of their seriousness about sexual health, despite being in a fairly low-risk group. After their tests came back negative, the woman said, "I guess this means we won't be seeing other people." But the man had a different idea. "I can't promise that," he said. "I'm not planning on having sex with anyone else, but if I do, I can promise that I will use a condom." To her, his response was not sufficiently "safe." What seemed like a sexual issue had become a relationship issue—she was expecting fidelity, he couldn't promise. And as progressive as this couple had been, they were simply in a new version of that hackneyed romantic script: She wants commitment, and he wants freedom.

Even though this couple couldn't quite agree to the same rules of safe sex, they were doing better than most couples. Most heterosexuals, knowing their statistical risk is low, just assume that they will not be unlucky. Tragically, some have been wrong. While it is true that vaginal intercourse is associated with a lower risk of HIV infection, a 2008 study in *The Lancet* highlights how much it varies (Powers et al. 2008); a researcher familiar with the study remarked that heterosexual sex "can be a remarkably efficient way to transmit HIV." Sociologist Adina Nack writes about the barriers to communication about (all) STDs and sexual health in *Damaged Goods?: Women Living with Incurable Sexually Transmitted Diseases* (2008). Among barriers to communication before and after infection was the sense that women that had STDs are "sluts"—as well as the feeling that once infected they were "damaged goods."

Gay men who are dating know that the odds of infection are against them: they have been reminded of this fact for a few decades. Since the 1990s, the only group for whom the rate of HIV infection has been increasing is gay men, who account for over half of all infections. In particular, young black gay men and middle-aged white gay men are accelerating their rates of infection. Rates of infection vary depending upon region and age, but in a recent study of men who have sex with men in 21 major cities, one in five was HIV positive (CDC 2010). Gay public health campaigns have reinforced behavior change, and social action groups have worked together to promote safer sexual behaviors for their constituents. Because gay men had rarely used condoms (except as a lark) before the AIDS crisis, the campaign had to create a new habit rather than simply encourage a familiar one. Helped by the desperation of the situation, advertising eroticized condoms, showing sexy pictures of men using them and reciting slogans to reinforce the message that safe is sexy. Lesbians became part of the movement, partly as an act of solidarity. Also, most lesbians have had sexual activity with men, and 50 percent have had intercourse with a man. Also, more lesbians than heterosexual women are likely to have sex with a man who is bisexual or primarily gay and therefore they are more likely to be exposed to the virus.

No STD before AIDS has fostered this kind of behavior modification program. When herpes, also a virus, began to infiltrate heterosexual circles in the 1970s and 1980s, there was an enormous amount of media attention and public outcry; *Time* magazine made it a cover story. Like HIV, herpes is permanent, with potentially recurring episodes. It is extremely painful for some men and women (though nonsymptomatic for many), and it is potentially lethal to an infant delivered vaginally during an initial outbreak of the virus. Still, the publicity and fear about herpes did not create a revolution of safer sexual behavior.

The difference in responses to herpes and HIV were due largely to social forces. When herpes broke out, the Pill was still popular. Men had stopped carrying condoms. Couples got used to the feeling of skin against skin. Men were reluctant to use condoms. They sometimes resisted using them when asked, even though they and their partners were at risk of contracting the herpes virus and having it forever. Nothing less than a high chance of death—HIV infection—convinced many men and women to start using condoms again. But even the possibility of a lethal sexual experience hasn't convinced everyone to use condoms. A majority of college students whom Gray and Saracino (1991) studied said they tried to guess whether a new partner was likely to have HIV rather than insist on using a condom. This trend for young people persists, and more recent work emphasizes that along with having positive partner response to condoms, other important factors are condom awareness and condom skills. When college students are aware and have learned how to put one on (and take it off), they are more likely to use condoms (Barkley and Burns 2000).

Trojan, a company that produces 75 percent of U.S. condoms sold, has found a new strategy to increase condom use. They are making condoms that can be seen as "sex toys." Using the specially designed condom increases sexual pleasure more than not using it! A new product that has a technology to increase male sensitivity, called Ecstasy, has broken sales records (Willingham 2010). Other condom companies, such as Durex, Oh!, and Lifestyles, following a similar theory, have created new products based on the same idea: new products include adding vibrating penis rings to the condom package and adding warm and cold sensations. Condoms are also marketed in ways that flatter the user, with names that include Magnum, Marathon, Alpha, and so on. The innovations continue to transform a necessity into a positive advantage and to get people to buy and use these products.

Whether using condoms as sex toys or avoiding using condoms at all, immediate pleasure is a more powerful motivator for many people than future consequences. And the depth of that power is breathtaking. Customers will pay a prostitute more money not to use a condom than to use one (Lever 1994b). And people will lie about their HIV status or other disease status when they feel desperate for sex. Cochran and Mays (1990) interviewed over four hundred sexually active college students in southern California and found that 20 percent of men and 4 percent of women said they would lie, if necessary, about the results of an HIV test. They would also subvert other attempts at assessing risk: 47 percent of the men and 42 percent of the women would purposely underestimate the number of previous sexual partners if asked. Cultural norms can also play a role; for example, among

Mexican Americans if a woman proposes using a condom it is considered to be too assertive, too openly sexual (Marin et al. 1997).

Similar carelessness attends decisions about contraception. One of us has been in a women's group for over thirty years. The women meet every few months to talk about their lives, loves, careers, relationships, and marriages. At a meeting during the late 1980s, three of the single, thirty-something women were talking about the first date each of them had had in a long time. The first thing the rest of the women in the group asked was, "Did you use contraception?" The three women looked downward, and each one truthfully answered no. Stunned that they each had taken that risk, the group asked them why not. Each one said the man had refused. The men preferred no sex at all to sex with a condom. Each woman wanted to have sex so much that she decided to go ahead "just this one time." Have things changed? Not too much. But here's what we know about how things have changed for the youngest group of people having sex. Teenagers and young adults in the early 2000s increased their rate of using condoms, and they decreased their rate of unwanted pregnancy.

The women's group had encountered another interesting fact about contraception and safe sex. Discussing contraception is difficult. Whoever suggests it, the timing of when it is suggested, and how each person feels about using it is gendered and awkward. Most sex education has been directed toward women and girls on the assumption that they are more articulate about relationships than men and that they have more at stake. Young women, the logic goes, are gatekeepers of sexuality, and somehow it is up to them to protect themselves and their partner. Lever (1995) points out, however, that although young women may be good about talking about relationships and be uniquely at risk for pregnancy, the power dynamics between adolescents make it harder for a woman to prevail over a man. Young women still find it difficult to assert their rights as much as necessary, and too many are persuaded to have sex the way their guy wants.

When sex involves heterosexual intercourse, the potential reproductive consequence is a woman's burden. The pregnancy is in her body. For women, part of the cost and danger of single sex is the possibility of having to carry a baby to term, with all the life changes that go along with such a decision. Abortion is another option, and although the majority of abortion services are sought by married women, single women and their partners use it as a backup method to contraceptive failures. Before *Roe v. Wade* (1973), women pursuing abortion faced a scary proposition. Doctors who did abortions often ran a shady business and charged high fees. Entrepreneurs who did abortions without medical experience could make fatal mistakes, such as puncturing the uterus or causing infection.

People's more liberal approach to sex preceded the 1973 *Roe* decision, as did the rising trend in nonmarital pregnancies. However, when abortion became legal and safe, many more women chose to end unwanted pregnancies, which reduced the number of nonmarital births. As figure 3.11 illustrates, for teen women the abortion rate offset the birthrate up until 1990, the peak year of teen pregnancy. Yet from 1990 to 2000 teen pregnancies declined by 27 percent and teen abortions declined by 45 percent; by 2005, pregnancy rates were down even more, and abortions declined by 53 percent (Ventura, Abma, Mosher, and Henshaw 2004 and 2009).

As any one who has access to mass media knows, abortion is still very much disputed, in part, because it is a critical aspect of single (and married) women's ability to cope with unintended conception without changing her life dramatically. Single motherhood or unintended motherhood demands a level of maturity and life skills that usually takes women many decades of experience to achieve. The challenge accelerates, however, in the absence of adequate social services. Because there are no free nursery services; no inexpensive, high-quality child care; and no government-subsidized home help (which are available in some European countries); single motherhood in the United States can be an isolating, impoverishing experience. Opponents of the right to abortion have noted that the "fail-safe" of abortion makes women feel less afraid of an unintended pregnancy and therefore less cautious. Indeed,

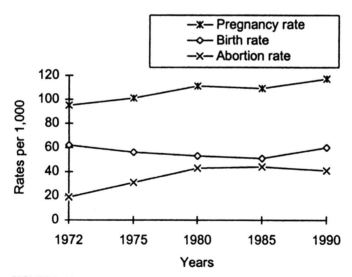

FIGURE 3.11
Teenage fertility events, rates for women ages fifteen to nineteen, 1972–1990. Data from Luker (1996).

abortion rates in the United States are much higher than in western European countries, where access to abortion is similar but child and maternal services and financial support are greater. European women and men typically receive more and better sex education than their U.S. counterparts, and their overall birthrate is lower than the U.S. birthrate. Their lower abortion rate may be due to more effective and consistent contraception usage, but it may also be lower because the social safety net in most European countries means that a woman will not suffer personal and economic disaster if she has a child.

Legal abortion may also influence men to be less concerned about conception. They know they have a fallback position against unintended fatherhood. Although some groups of adolescent men and women want to have a baby to prove their adulthood or to fulfill a need to love something "all their own," many anticipate how much having a baby will disadvantage their lives and affect their plans (Thompson 1996). In some periods of history young men were held accountable for out-of-wedlock pregnancies, and forced marriages made them generally apprehensive about premarital sex. The exception to this involved wealthy men who could prey upon poor women or women of color and experience no legal consequences. With the urbanization and industrialization of the nineteenth century, community and family influence over holding men accountable declined. A double standard emerged that condemned any woman for out-of-wedlock pregnancy. The double standard excluded male culpability or economic responsibility. Over more recent times, however, a movement has emerged that holds boys and men more accountable for supporting their children. These new policies were initiated in response to the expense children born into poverty pose to the government rather than outrage at the history of putting all of the "blame" and expense on single mothers (Lerman and Ooms 1993). Whether or not state legislatures are prochoice, they are increasingly propaternal responsibility.

Miscommunication and Sexual Privilege

The sexual revolution's legacy is the expansion of sexual variety and autonomy for singles. But the sexual revolution also left a legacy of miscommunication, misunderstanding, and abuse in the form of sexual harassment, date rape, and stranger rape. In chapter 2, we talked about gendered patterns of coerced sex. Here we return to these patterns to examine their impact on singles. We believe, however, that these problems are not a consequence of the sexual revolution but that they came to light because of the freedom to talk about sexual problems that the sexual revolution initiated.

Sexual Coercion

Some sexual interactions are not about misunderstanding or subtle differences in desire. They are about coercion, terror, shame, and self-doubt. Forced sex can occur within marriage or to married people by people other than their partners. But for singles a dilemma arises because dating situations are ambiguous, and men and women can have very different agendas. Social scripts can still set up some women to be victims rather than lovers and some men to be predators rather than suitors. We won't talk here about men with mental instability, serial rapists, sexual sadists, or the use of rape as a weapon of war. We are instead concerned with attacks by "ordinary" men in pursuit of sexual satisfaction—or the experience of dominance—on a date or at a party.

We've seen that women more than men have shifted their behavior and standards in response to the sexual revolution. An iconic 1990s film, *Thelma & Louise*, tells the story of flirtation gone very much awry. Thelma (played by Geena Davis), on a road trip with her friend Louise (played by Susan Sarandon), is emblematic of a change in women's sexual and emotional choices. She breaks away from her controlling husband and, giddy with her new freedom, feels she can freely flirt with a man in a bar. The guy she flirts with, Harlan Puckett (played by Timothy Carhart), reads her flirtation as "sluttish" sexual teasing. In his eyes, a slut loses all rights to "gentlemanly behavior and gives him the right to demand sex and take it if she refuses." Thelma's good time evaporates as she realizes he is about to rape her brutally in the bar parking lot. Louise saves her by shooting and killing the man when he refuses to take Louise's threats to shoot seriously. He cannot imagine Louise, or any woman, will have the nerve to do it. Such mismatched consciousness generated a disaster. In other circumstances, it might have just generated hurt and angry feelings.

Research supports this scenario. The more traditional a man's attitudes about women's roles, the more likely he is to feel that any sexual interest that a woman shows entitles a man to proceed to intercourse. Some research has indicated that when the woman asks the man out (contrary to tradition) or when the man pays for the date (especially when it is expensive), intercourse without the woman's consent—in other words, rape—is seen as more justifiable (Muehlenhard 1988; Muehlenhard, Friedman, and Thomas 1985). A woman who is sexually alluring is believed to be "leading a man on" (Muehlenhard and McNaughton 1988). The script for a man involves conquering such a woman to assert his masculinity. If the woman rebuffs his advances, she diminishes him and assaults his manhood. For most people, this whole scenario seems ridiculous. Who would want to have sex with someone who doesn't want it?

Most men would agree. Yet some men are still influenced by old-fashioned macho ideology. Some men still seek bragging rights about their conquests or bond with other men by talking about women in degrading terms. In the process, they become more willing to perpetrate sexual violence.

Sometimes sexual violence is even a rite of passage, a ritual a young boy goes through to show he is one of the guys. In *Makes Me Wanna Holler* (1995), journalist Nathan McCall describes the practice of seducing unsuspecting, trusting women for "trains," in which a group of men sequentially rape a woman. In one episode, some guys have abducted a teenager from the neighborhood:

> I learned that the girl was Vanessa, a black beauty whose family had recently moved into our neighborhood, less than two blocks from where I lived. She seemed like a nice girl. When I first noticed her walking to and from school I had wanted to check her out. Now it was too late. She was about to have a train run on her. No way she could be somebody's straight-up girl after going through a train. (45)

The author writes this scene out of regret and guilt, but at the time his peer group was far too powerful to resist. He thinks about saving Vanessa, but then decides, "I couldn't do that. It was too late. This was our first train together as a group. All the fellas were there and everybody was anxious to show everybody else how cool and worldly he was" (47).

Such perpetrators sometimes have no idea, even when they find themselves in court as defendants, that coercive sex violates not only the law but also ethical standards of conduct. In studies of sexual aggression and force, many men, including college men, indicate that they feel entitled to press on even when a woman doesn't consent. A large number of cases (Sprecher and McKinney 1993) show between 8 percent and 25 percent of men admitting to forcing intercourse. Even more, 30 to 50 percent, say they had used several kinds of verbal manipulation to force a woman to comply. Again, peer pressure aggravates and incites the participants.

A number of rape charges are brought every year following incidents within fraternity houses. In the 1990s, for example, a rape charge was successfully brought against some members of a fraternity at the University of Washington in Seattle. Some fraternity men found a thoroughly intoxicated woman and took turns raping her. The men believed it was her fault for getting so drunk. When they were charged with rape, they were mystified and outraged. Remarkably, even after the trial, these men still held on to their good-girl/bad-girl ideas, which give women who like to party fewer rights than women who abstain. Meanwhile, a survey of sorority women revealed that 13 percent had been in a situation that could be classified as rape; 60 percent of those rape incidents had occurred at a fraternity house or with a fraternity member; 96 percent of the incidents involved alcohol (Copenhaver and Grauerholz 1991). Year in and year out since the University of Washington case we described, similar cases get reported around the United States. A case at the University of Arkansas in fall 2009 involves familiar details: a group of fraternity men tell one story, a woman who attended a party tells another, debate ensues over what role alcohol played in the situation, and the community law enforcement is highly ambivalent (more discussion on this in chapter 5).

A study that compared fraternity men with nonaffiliated men found that the frat men reported more abusive sexual behaviors (like using drugs and alcohol to gain sexual access) and that they had more friends who supported the idea that it was reasonable to push sexual intercourse even when the woman was unwilling (Boeringer, Shehan, and Akers 1991).

What seems to happen in fraternities occurs in other homosocial (i.e., same-sex) environments, such as the military, where numerous cases of sexual harassment and sexual assaults have been publicized since the mid-1990s. In 2008, the Pentagon released a report indicating that one-third of women in the military had been sexually harassed, and 7 percent of women had received unwanted sexual contact, including assaults (Department of Defense 2011). There are more women serving in the military now than ever before. Still, an aggressive vision of male sexuality, untainted by restraint or moral judgment, becomes the standard of masculinity. The vision of "bad" or "easy" women and the notion that men have the right to treat them as tools for male bonding help promote a standard of male sexuality that, among those who embrace it, leads to a much higher likelihood of sexual coercion and rape. This likelihood puts men at risk even when they are not at fault. A famous case in 2006 pitted a young, African American college student and dancer against a Duke University lacrosse team. After "exotic" dancing at a party held for the all-male group, the dancer charged that she had been molested and raped. Later evidence proved her allegations were false. However, because the situation resembled so many others in numerous universities where rape did occur (and often where class and race advantages were in the men's favor), the case was given credibility and wide media attention. The men involved suffered great stigma, were unable to go to school, and to continue on the team for that season. They faced the possibility of jail and disgrace. They had made a less than ideal choice to hire an exotic dancer, but they were innocent of the rape charges. However, as long as rape regularly happens at homosocial parties and events, all men are put at risk of an invalid but seemingly credible charge leveled against them.

Sexual Confusion

Certainly, rates of date rape and other kinds of sexual violence are disturbing. But the matter of sexual consent is complicated. Sexual consent seems like "you just know" or you "just *think* you know." A transient working man, interviewed by a sex researcher regarding his experiences communicating about casual sex with a woman, summed it up by saying, "It's obvious, but it's really hard to know, when someone is willing to have sex with me" (Beres 2007: 93). Research has demonstrated that men and women sincerely misread each other's cues. This research argues that some of what is framed as coercion *is* coercion, but that sometimes it is more of a case of miscommunication.

Some studies examine whether miscommunication occurs because of ambiguous cues that might vary depending on gender. For example, in a laboratory study where friendly staff members interacted with both men and women participants, Abbey (1982) found that men were more likely than women to code a woman's friendliness as seductive or even promiscuous. Men who observed another man interact with a woman were more likely than women to code the man as sexually attracted to the woman. Other studies indicate that more men than women tend to code interpersonal warmth and attention as sexual. Women tend to be unaware that their actions are being labeled as flirtatious or sexual. More recent studies (Fisher and Walters 2003; Henningsen, Henningsen, and Valde 2006) continue to find support for this gendered pattern in sexual communication.

Here's the inevitable complication: Although women may in general intend to be seductive less often than men think, sometimes women are trying to be seductive. But women who intend to be seductive are not necessarily seeking intercourse. In fact, both men and women have been found to use indirect rather than straightforward approaches to show and compel sexual interest (Sprecher and McKinney 1993); being indirect is essential to seduction. Some of the strategies women used in a study of college students (Perper and Weis 1987) were seductive dressing, creating a sexual or romantic mood, using sexy or romantic talk, cuddling close, and touching.

Flirtation is certainly distinct from sexual consent. However, there are shades of meaning in between flirting and consent that may be difficult to define. Women often have a firm idea of what they mean by their acts, and they expect the person they are with to "get it." But men, who are often expected to be continuously sexually interested and ready, are unsure of how forward to be. What constitutes permission? What is offensive? Men are often more afraid of failing the first qualification (being ready and interested) than the second (being offensive or out of bounds). They may also hold on to some older definitions of what entitles them to sex, and cry, "But she was leading me on!" In the *Thelma & Louise* scenario, there is no doubt that Thelma was flirting. But from Thelma's perspective as well as Louise's, the flirtation ended when Thelma said no. For men like Harlan Puckett, who attacks Thelma, a woman's saying no does not negate the prior positive signals. Some men are baffled when their initial attempts at seduction are rebuffed; they are mystified when a woman is angry with them for insisting on what for men is the obvious next step. It is possible to accept that there are situations where a partner may be slow to comprehend that another person is saying no; this is a case of miscommunication. But being slow on the uptake is quite different from willfully ignoring or distorting the communication between adults, as occurred in *Thelma & Louise*.

In an analysis of courtroom language, legal scholar Andrew Taslitz (1999) observed that subtle uses of language—and even prohibitions against the frank language of rape—can influence juries not to convict even when there is robust evidence of the crime. If, for example, a woman engaged in "sex talk" with someone at a bar, it might be seen as obvious permission even though it was just seductive teasing. Social scripts are just too strong. In *Thelma & Louise*, Louise knew courtroom biases and took them into account when she shot Thelma's attacker. She had prior experience with the justice system and anticipated that a judge and jury would let a rapist off the hook because Thelma had been drinking and flirtatious. She didn't believe that anyone would think Thelma had actually refused—or perhaps even that Thelma had the right to refuse after her previous seductive behavior.

Men complain that it is difficult to know what consent looks like these days. A lot of men claim to believe women say no as "token resistance" on their way to saying yes. They may not be incorrect. In two studies (Muehlenhard and Hollabaugh 1988; Muehlenhard and McCoy 1991), young women were asked if they had ever said no to the guy they were with even though they had every intention to eventually have sex with him that evening. A surprisingly large number, 50 percent in the first study, 37 percent in the second, said they had. The most common reason given by the women in the first study was that they did not want to seem promiscuous. On the other hand, in a cross-cultural study of sexual consent (Sprecher et al. 1992), researchers found that 44 percent of the American women in the study had said *yes* even though they really did not want to have sex. How should we interpret this ambivalence?

Some have attempted to replace ambiguity about what constitutes consent with clear rules that any kind of no should be taken at face value. Men should assume it really means no. One attempt to clarify rights and privileges was organized by the students at Antioch College in 1992. The students sought to eliminate the gray area between consent and rape in evolving sexual situations. The path they chose was to specify that each and every sexual escalation had to receive verbal permission. Otherwise, a rape was in progress. If a woman was being kissed and her partner wanted to touch her breast, the partner would have to ask, "May I touch your breast?" Theoretically, these permissions were reciprocal. Women who wanted to touch a man would also have to ask explicit verbal permission. However, the script is clearly written with the idea of vulnerable women and more sexually aggressive men in mind.

As time passed, the Antioch rules were something of a laughingstock, as reporters discussed in 2007 when the college closed (Goldfarb 2007). The rules were comical because of the practical dilemmas within the Antioch plan. The rules didn't respond to sex as it tends to actually happen. The how, who, where, when, and why of sex are determined through social processes that begin long before people commence sexual activity; nevertheless, there is a certain happy aspect to sexual momentum that seems unfairly constrained by the Antioch rules. They imagine partners in sexual interactions to be cooler, more conscious, more in control, and more aware than most sexually aroused people. Still the notion that partners might have greater encouragement to practice talking a bit more about what they are doing isn't all bad. The Antioch rules just weren't the way to get there.

The dying out of the Antioch rules would not have surprised Melanie Beres. Using in-depth interviews with men and women, Beres (2009) describes how men and women have a complex, multistage way of reading one another's signals that includes negotiation of each step along the way, but within more familiar erotic scripts. She captures the combination of explicit (verbal) and tacit (understood) and physical (such as being undressed) ways of knowing from one of her interview subjects (John, age twenty-eight):

> Giv[ing] consent for casual sex . . . usually its pretty easy, it's either, you're making out pants are off and one or the other will say um "do you have a condom" and the other says yes or if I say yes then it's obvious . . . but if they say I'm not sure, or if I say I'm not too sure, it's an obvious just sort of [nonconsent]. (Beres 2009: 1)

Beres draws from detailed accounts of casual sex to argue that men and women do not work from such different—or gendered—scripts for sexuality. From this observation we might draw more optimism for the promise of men's and women's shared understanding of sexuality and more skepticism about excuses that draw on "gendered misunderstandings" for cases of sexual coercion.

Indeed, although we have argued that the sexual revolution helped advance women's sexual consciousness more than men's, we are wary of establishing rules that cast all men as sexual predators and all women as victims. There are three problems. One is the assumption that men are always more mature than their partners (they aren't) and that they really know when they are proceeding without heartfelt permission (they don't). Another problem is the assumption that people don't give mixed signals (they do). And finally, such rules assume that women's sexuality is so passive and unconscious that women can't be held accountable for their acts (of course, they can). Simply put, the Antioch perspective on sexuality is patronizing to women. Beres's 2009 study is a good reminder of this.

Perhaps the most regrettable aspect of the Antioch rules is that they undermined one of the key tenets of the sexual revolution: sex is pleasurable. True, the sexual revolution's hedonistic vision may have failed to anticipate some undesirable consequences of liberalized sexual norms. Nevertheless, the Antioch rules are a far cry from the sexual ideology of the 1960s and 1970s, which moved college students to fight for adult sexual privileges and had, as its foundation, a vision of sexual equality for men and women. Men and women are increasing their ability to navigate sexual communication and to coordinate the use of condoms and other forms of contraception. There's more to learn, but progress continues.

Sexual autonomy and accountability are issues that will continue to be controversial; we can't resolve the conflicts here. But be wary of solutions that inadvertently reinforce notions of gender difference. An example of a sexual harassment case will help illustrate this point: In 2006, a six-year-old Brockton, Massachusetts, boy was suspended from school for three days. The school told the boy's mother that he had placed his hand down the waistband of a girl's pants and touched her back. This was a violation of the schools sexual-harassment policy. The boy didn't even know the meaning of the word *sexual* (Ranalli and Mishra 2006). In this draconian application of sexual harassment rules, child's play devoid of sexual content was treated as if an adult were victimizing another adult. From our point of view, the punishment sends the opposite message: The boys are powerful enough, by virtue of being boys, to invite such trouble, and girls are weak enough, by virtue of being girls, to be destroyed by such trouble. The lesson glorified the notion of sexualized gender difference even among children who are presexual (in the adult meaning of the word) rather than minimizing conceptions of gender difference.

Sexual Aggression and Complicated Emotions

Many women have become politically and personally astute about the dangers in dating relationships. Still, women have a tendency to blame themselves when miscommunication occurs and to wonder if, indeed, they have behaved in a way that invited or permitted sexual aggression. In particular, if a woman consents because of verbal manipulation rather than brute force, she tends to believe that she is at fault. In addition, studies have shown that women, especially more traditional or conservative women, have some of the same beliefs about rape that men do. If a woman "led him on," if she was sexually tantalizing but then declined to go further, or if she was known for her previous sexual experiences, even other women are likely to judge her as being as much at fault as the man who pushed the issue. "Slut walks" in 2011 have been the latest effort to counter this.

Since the sexual revolution, sex has been held to the standard of mutuality. Sex is supposed to take place between people who want to have this experience together. If women do not want the sexual experience, how can they be talked into it? This is a complicated question to answer, and the answer varies situation by situation. Perhaps a better question is, why should they be talked into it? This question takes into account the fact that sexual coercion arises from "gendered" power differences on and off the sexual playing field.

The gendered power differences that influence sexual interaction are often confounded with the ambivalence people have about sex and their lack of communication skills for talking about it. In a culture that fires a U.S. surgeon general for talking in public about masturbation (discussed in chapter 2), it should come as no surprise that many people are frazzled and defensive in sexual situations. Their goal, far from love or pleasure, may be getting through the experience without humiliating themselves. They may be particularly unhappy in sexual situations when they are just beginning to date and lack sexual self-confidence, or just reentering the dating market after being in a long relationship. They may especially lose their composure when the person they are with is of a different class, ethnicity, country, or culture. Words and cues that are well understood by one group may be completely missed by another.

Sexual pressure and abuse of power is not confined to men-over-women using manipulation or force. Several cases have emerged over the last few years involving a married woman high school teacher having an affair with a male student at school. As each case has been discovered, a national debate occurs over whether this is harassment or whether the boy has just "gotten lucky." The vehemence is greater in the cases where the teacher was especially beautiful. Would people have felt the same way if this incident had involved a male teacher and a fifteen-year-old girl? Was this boy unlucky or lucky? Damaged or educated? Undoubtedly, men under pressure to have sex can feel victimized and regretful.

Another movie from the 1990s, *The Last Seduction*, illustrates this point. The main character, Bridget (played by Linda Fiorentino), has sex with a man

(Mike Swale, played by Peter Berg) in a parking lot. In the scene, we see her pushing her companion beyond his sexual limits. He was less at ease having a quickie against a chain-link fence with a stranger than she was, but it was his "manly" duty to rise to the occasion. As the movie progresses, however, it is clear that he is being victimized by her (continued) sexual aggression. His persistence in the relationship hinges on the importance for him, as a man, to be prepared to meet any sexual challenge and to overcome discomfort. (Notably, Bridget turns out to be a psychopathic killer; indeed, such sexually aggressive women characters tend to be villains in the movies.)

These pressures are not present in all societies. But in the United States, we have a volatile mix of opportunity, mixed signals, uncertain relations between the sexes, and changing gender scripts that leave men and women unsure about how to present themselves and how to interpret one another's intentions. Thus, sex between two single people has multiple meanings and expectations. It often needs much more translation than it receives. Sex, so well designed for pleasure, can be hazardous to both men and women unless mutual respect and communication become the norm rather than the exception.

The Future of Sex among Singles

The future of single sex is . . . robust. There are more singles, more years of being single, and more opportunity and social permission to engage in a whole range of sexual relationships. More people are engaging in nonmarital sex, and the age of sexual initiation has stabilized, after some years of decline. First sexual experiences in high school are not uncommon. Still, because sexual relations are so complex and sometimes painful, we often see nostalgia for easier-to-negotiate intimacy pop up in the media. This can include images of gender and sexual differences that are simplified into visions of "men from Mars and women from Venus" and send us back to essentialist, dichotomous thinking that really doesn't fit today's world.

What people want in the single sex world depends a fair amount on the stage of life. Younger, older, never married, divorced, or widowed people want the ability to have a complete sex life that may occur without marriage or even outside a committed relationship. Still, old definitions of what is respectable haven't completely faded, and so these traditional scripts cause problems for women whose suitors may not be comfortable with a more frank sexuality and for men who don't feel as bold as they are expected to be. For many, sex as a single person is a stage that will some day conclude in marriage or commitment. But for an increasing number of people, sex as a single person is not just a prelude to early marriage, nor is it the rush of sexual activities between marriages or commitment. Increasingly, singlehood, with varying degrees of sexual activity, is a way of life, and one that we expect to become more common and more diverse as time marches on. Psychologist Bella DePaulo (2006) writes about the cultural ambivalence we have about singles in the United States—still as time goes by we are optimistic. We see a culture and even public policies that, little by little, provide greater options and latitude to singles in how they live—including how they conduct their sex lives.

Conclusion

We began this discussion of uncommitted sex by asking why sexual freedom and sexual control continue to be influenced by gender. We have explored some of the factors involved in the control of men's and women's sex lives, and we have seen the influence of government policies, media, gender traditions, and even biological essentialist beliefs about how women are primarily vessels of reproduction and men have an unstoppable sexual appetite. We have seen how badly we need good communication between partners—and how social scripts make this difficult to achieve. We have noted change over time—there's more sexual opportunity for everyone, more change for women than men, and all of this results in smaller *but persistent* gender gaps.

We know that there are many traditional forces at work. Yet, why the gendered organization and experience of sexuality persists remains elusive. The answer must lie, in part, in social institutions. And no institution anchors the gendered experience of sexuality more than the time-honored institution of heterosexual marriage. Although adults spend more time than they have in the past in informal or uncommitted relationships, still most adults want some kind of steady or secure relationship in which to pursue their sexual as well as other interests. So, it is to marriage, and other kinds of more permanent coupling, that we now turn.

4

Sex and Marriage

Why Do People Marry?

IN THE 1959 MOVIE *Pillow Talk*, starring Rock Hudson and Doris Day, Hudson's buddy, played by Tony Randall, explains why he is eager to marry for the third time.

Tony Randall: Brad, as a friend I only hope one day you find a girl like this. You ought to quit all this chasing around and get married.

Rock Hudson: Why?

Randall: Why? You're not getting any younger, fellow. Oh sure, it's fun, it's exciting dancing, nightclubbing with a different doll every night, but there comes a time when a man wants to give up that kind of life.

Hudson: Why?

Randall: Because he wants to create a stable, lasting relationship with one person. Brad, believe me. There is nothing so wonderful, so fulfilling as coming home to the same woman every night.

Hudson: Why?

Randall: Because that's what it means to be adult: a wife, a family, a house. A mature man wants those responsibilities.

Hudson: Why?

Randall: Well, if you want to, you can find tricky arguments against anything. I've got to get out of here. What have you got against marriage, anyway?

Hudson: Jonathan, before a man is married he's like a tree in the forest. He stands there independent, an entity unto himself, and then he's chopped down, his branches are cut off, he's stripped of his bark, and he's thrown in the river with the rest of the logs. And this tree is taken to the mill, and when it comes out, it's no longer a tree. It's a vanity table, a breakfast nook, a baby crib, and the newspaper that lines the family garbage can.

Randall: No. If this girl [his fiancée] weren't extra special then maybe I'd agree with you. But with Jan, you look forward to having your branches cut off.

This scene caricatures marriage, but the caricature nonetheless is revealing: In this stereotype, marriage transforms a relationship into something tame, like a breakfast nook, rather than something wild, like a tree in the forest. It also suggests different statuses within marriage for men and for women, and it suggests that marriage is always the same thing; never changing, never modified by the choices of the married couple. But of course that is too simple a stereotype about an institution that has been evolving over the centuries and is evolving as we speak. For example, with the passage of same-sex marriage in several states in the United States, what we mean by marriage continues to change, just as it has for millenia. Yes, we continue to see the legacy of marriage as a *staging ground for traditional heterosexual gender performance*—especially in arguments against same-sex marriage. As for conventional, straight marriage, the performance goes like this: men submit to monogamy—if the woman is tantalizing enough to make him do it. The performance, as caricatured in *Pillow Talk*, includes associating marriage with the acquisition of property. Marriage triggers consumer events like the purchase of a home, a car, and all sorts of other big-ticket items. These days, some policymakers even hold that "investing in marriage" is an economic strategy for reducing poverty. With all the social weight and obligation of marriage, the notion of marriage as a passionate, sexual union may seem like an afterthought. And yet, passion and personal satisfaction, too, is central to contemporary expectations from marriage.

In this chapter, we examine how culture and social institutions influence sexuality in marriage. We look at the ways marriage supports a weak but still present sexual double standard, and we report on sexual practices within marriage and other committed relationships. At the end of the chapter, we consider the changing status of marriage: although the United States loves marriage, its popularity is declining. Meanwhile, the U.S. culture has become highly sexualized, but it has eroticized youth and autonomy more than commitment. Thus, we provide some ideas about the conditions under which culture can be sexualized—or sex positive—and at the same time marriage and commitment can thrive as a part of a sex-positive culture.

The Social Context of Marriage

More than four out of five adults in the United States will marry by age forty (CDC 2002). About half of all marriages end in divorce, but at least three-quarters of folks who divorce go on to remarry. These rates vary by race and social class. Although rates of marriage have declined in recent decades, the United States continues to be the most marriage- (and divorce-) prone society in the world.

Today, marriage takes on a variety of forms—dual career, long distance, traditional (i.e., husband as breadwinner, wife as homemaker), nontraditional, sexually open, sexually dead, utilitarian—each with a social meaning and a private meaning. Marriage promotes trust, predictability, reliability, commitment, and sexual exclusivity for partners. Especially since the 1950s, when marriage was idealized, marriage has increasingly been expected to fulfill its participants emotionally, socially, and sexually, like never before.

But can sexual interest be sustained in marriage? Research suggests that most married people are satisfied with their sex life together. Figure 4.1 displays patterns of sexual frequency by length of marriage. Despite the decline in frequency over time, 65 percent of couples still have sex more than once a week

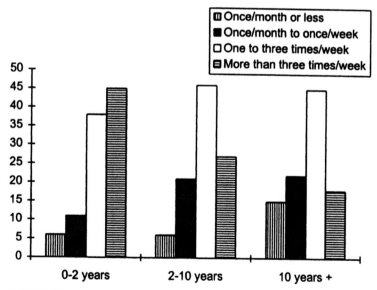

FIGURE 4.1
Sexual frequency by length of (heterosexual) marriage. Data from Blumstein and Schwartz (1983).

after ten years of marriage. Despite living in a hypersexualized culture, people appear to easily satisfy their sexual needs within committed relationships.

Do they remain together because marriage offers greater opportunities for sex than the single life does? Or do couples' needs and expectations decline as the marriage wears on? There is some truth to both ideas. Marriage is in fact "sexier" than dating relationships: Married people and long-term cohabiters have sex more frequently than singles, mostly because they have access to a partner every night. But marriage and sex within a marriage can also become boring and inconvenient as partners age, become more familiar, and as life events occur (especially having children). In truth, the actual experience of marriage usually diverges from both the romantic expectation of constant eroticism *and* the pessimistic expectations of the death of passion. Figure 4.2 describes patterns of sexual frequency by relationship type. Note that married and cohabiting couples have more sex than singles or divorced people. Paradoxically, it seems that increased commitment, in the form of cohabitation, improves sexual frequency; but moving on to marriage, which shows even more commitment, apparently reduces the frequency of sex. This may partially be explained by the fact that cohabiters tend to be younger and their relationships are also younger on average, but the reasons that people decide to cohabit are different from those that help people decide to get married, and so the groups are somewhat different from one another. Meanwhile, never-married women report more sex than never-married men. It looks like marriage tends to amplify and even produce gender differences that are less apparent in other adult social arrangements.

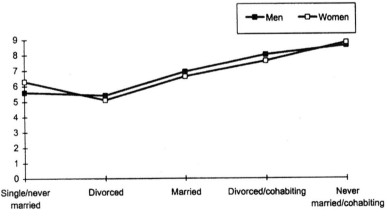

FIGURE 4.2
Sexual frequency by (heterosexual) relationship type. Data from Laumann et al. (1994).

Gender, Ethnicity, and Sexual Orientation

Whatever the impact of marriage on adults' intimate lives, most people want to pair up. They will lust after the same person for quite a while and find their sexual interests bolstered by abiding affection or love. They cannot tolerate the thought of being unpaired or unmarried for their whole life. Nevertheless, a quick review of magazines at the grocery store checkout line shows that our culture emphasizes women's desire to marry and men's desire to stay single. But this is all just a stereotype again of men's sexuality rather than the reality of what men really want. Despite the image of the reluctant groom, men marry voluntarily and eagerly. Most men who divorce will eventually (usually quickly) remarry. However popular marriage-bashing may be in bars and locker rooms, the truth is that most men want to be married more so than women. In fact, across all races and ethnic groups, men desire marriage and remarriage more than women (Tucker and Mitchell-Kernan 1995:157). In a 2009 *Time* magazine poll, 58 percent of men and 53 percent of women reported that marriage was very important to them. While 38 percent of men agreed that women can be happy without being married, 54 percent of women agreed with this.

The "Marriage Script": An Enactment of Gender Difference

Men like to be married because they receive multiple benefits from marriage. They gain in terms of quality of life, mental health, and professional opportunities considerably more than women who marry. Marriage also continues to be men's main avenue for social relationships. Young girls are encouraged to have intimate friends and to be socially at ease in gatherings at home or in public. Many mothers will train their daughters how to be a hostess or good friend. Women are expected to be the social directors of their home and to learn how to keep a variety of social relationships going, regardless of their marital status. Although the flow of resources between partners is complicated, overall the flow of social, material (except financial), and sexual resources is from wife to husband. Financially, while married men earn more than other men, the same is not true for married women. In other words, men gain more out of being married than women do, especially among whites. Of course, this flow of resources is not foremost in the minds or hearts of the matrimonial pair. People interact based on cultural ideals about marriage and being married—and these frequently involve gendered roles that men and women play as husband and wife (Goffman 1977).

Yet marriage has a social function, reinforcing norms and conventions; it is a social invention. Marriage constitutes a relationship between two people that is not simply different in degree; there is no natural progression to re-lationships that culminates in a socially, religiously, and legally sanctioned institution. Marriage is a relationship that is different in kind. In some ways, it has been classically defined around gender difference. The 1996 Defense of Marriage Act even legislates gender difference by endorsing states' rights to ignore marriages constituted in other states when those marriages are same-sex rather than cross-sex. The ongoing dialogue—and battles—over same-sex marriage repeatedly involve the argument that marriage requires one man and one woman fulfilling different roles in the relationship and in the family. Of equal importance is the vision that marriage is the model for the repro-duction of gendered roles for children. The battles hinge, furthermore, on a sense that only a husband and wife are appropriate parents (see chapter 5 for research on the impact of parents' gender and sexual orientation on children).

Even when individuals seek to experience marriage as something other than a social institution, the rest of the world still insists on responding to married people in the conventional manner. For example, outsiders assume that mar-ried people have promised sexual fidelity to each other and that those who are married are not available for liaisons with other people. Another example is the difficulty encountered by wives who keep their family name; they must go out of their way to inform people that they do not wish to be known by their hus-band's name. The few husbands who take the family name of a wife must make an even greater effort to inform others of this choice because it is so unusual.

Social norms for gender difference in marriage have awesome power. A married couple may begin as equal partners, but the marriage sets in motion a wife's duties to household and kids and a husband's duties to earning money for the family. Even when both partners work to earn money, as in over two-thirds of current marriages (Boushey and O'Leary 2009), more often than not the marriage tends to become polarized by gender (Schwartz 1994). As Schwartz described, the majority of couples who consider themselves egalitar-ian are actually "near peers." They end up falling into gendered patterns of domestic, economic, and emotional labor even when they don't intend to. The fact that most men earn more than most women is what typically tilts the division of responsibilities. Today, women's earnings closely approximate men's—in the typical two-earner family, women earn 42 percent of the fam-ily's income. Meanwhile, a full 63 percent of mothers—this includes single as well as married moms—are either the primary breadwinner or a coequal breadwinner with their partners (Boushey and O'Leary 2009). The gender difference in economic status persists, but it has diminished. Although men are adding to their housework portfolio (Sullivan et al. 2008), there's still a gender gap that is sometimes referred to as women's "second shift" (Hochs-child 1989).

This same set of assumptions sustains the caretaker, "mommy" status. Women carry a greater burden of domestic labor than men do, even when they are working full time and even when they are earning more than their partners (Brines 1994; Bianchi, Robinson, and Milkie 2006). The world, from hospitals to schools, assumes that mom is the primary parent. Through everyday interactions, the traditional roles of men and women are reinforced. Suburban folklore provides accounts of a father who goes to parent-teacher conferences and gets ignored in favor of the mother. Another image is of the dad who gets extra attention for volunteering time for, say, the fund-raising bake sale just for showing up. Although these are anecdotes, the message is familiar: caretaking for children is women's work. The same kinds of enactments occur regarding men's work and men's socially sanctioned roles. Almost every heterosexual couple has experienced a common reinforcement of men's provider role. After a meal out, even if she gives her credit card to the waiter, the card is likely to be returned to any man over age twelve at the table.

Another popular version of the gendered expectations about women and work comes from the tale of the "opt out revolution." In the early 2000s, news reports claimed that they had detected a trend: working women, when they can, were "opting out" of market work in favor of staying at home with the kids (Story 2005; Wallis 2004; Belkin 2003). It was a story about women's "natural" preferences. But the stories were based on anecdotes, and economist Heather Boushey (Boushey 2005; JEC 2008) put the lie to this claim. Women were not opting out; in fact, mothers—especially college-educated mothers—were going to work more than ever before.

However, during the persisting Great Recession that began in 2008, men and women (men more so than women) were losing jobs. The persistence of "opt out" stories remind us of the grip of traditional gender ideas: When women lose work, it gets interpreted as being about family and personal psychology (not about unemployment or the economy), or seen as a return to traditional gender roles (Rutter 2008). Tales of "opt out" continue to pop up in media stories, and they serve the purpose of keeping the notion that husbands "naturally" seek to earn and wives "naturally" seek to care (Stone 2007).

Daily interaction and media stories work to keep a couple in traditional gender patterns that influence intimate life, too. These everyday interactions are reinforced by cultural traditions that tend to sustain marriage as a gendered institution. Despite the feminist critique of marriage in the 1970s and changes in women's status in society and prominence in the workforce, women and men experience marriage differently. For example, men continue to be expected to initiate sex more often than women do. Although women have gained rights to sexual initiation, they walk a fine line. In couples in which wives initiate sex more than their husbands do, the husband's marital satisfaction tends to decrease (Blumstein and Schwartz 1983). As the ways to conduct marriage keep changing and becoming more and more diverse, what seems to make a difference is that partners have a shared understanding of each partner's level of comfort with shared initiation (Cupach and Metts 1991).

Heterosexual cohabitation is similar to marriage in that it tends to be a monogamous relationship of more than trivial duration and is usually founded on love and the hope for a continued future. Cohabiters and married people differ, however, in terms of economic dependence and the likelihood that children are present. Although heterosexual cohabiters often drift into polarized positions economically and domestically, the division of labor is even more divided for heterosexual marrieds. While men have improved their rates of housework, household data shows that especially when children are present, wives are in charge of the home. These stark differences are less present in cohabiting relationships (Blumstein and Schwartz 1983). When Brines and Joyner (1999) compared cohabiting to married couples they found that cohabiting relationships actually seem to work out better, and last longer, when partners share economic and household responsibilities, yet married couples were more stable when they had more traditional roles. Still even more recent research shows more diversity with respect to marital roles: increasingly, especially among more educated partners, sharing housework leads to happier marriages.

Race and the Significance of Marriage

The differences in the degree to which men and women in different ethnic groups desire marriage reveal powerful social influences. For example, Latino men desire marriage more than other men, but Latina women are also more favorably disposed toward marriage than other women. African American women are less likely than other women to express an interest in marriage. White men are the least likely to express interest in marriage or remarriage (although they are still more interested than white women), perhaps because white men on average have greater opportunities in life than men of other racial groups even without the advantage of having a wife (Tucker and Mitchell-Kernan 1995). Even so, white men continue to marry most often.

Differences in who actually gets married within different ethnic groups demonstrate that marriage is more of a social than a private institution. Prior to the 1960s, whites and African Americans were similar in terms of age of marriage and proportion married at any given time. Since then, however, the flight from marriage has been much greater among African Americans than whites. Blacks get married later in life, marriages are shorter in duration, divorce is more frequent, and remarriage is less likely than it is for whites. The explanation has much to do with gender and economics: traditional versions of marriage dictate a man be more economically dominant than a woman. Since black men's employment is positively related to marriage rates, high rates of unemployment depress the likelihood that black men will marry (Tucker and Mitchell-Kernan 1995:93). Black men, like white men, earn more than women of either race, but for African Americans, the gender difference is smaller. In fact, in 2009 we saw a 51.5 percent of African American wives earning the same or more than their husbands—compared to 36 to 40 percent for other groups (Boushey and O'Leary 2009). The size of the gender difference is crucial for understanding heterosexual marriage, which has a legacy, if not the current reality, of wives' economic dependence on their husbands. In the absence of alternative styles of marriage (such as peer marriage, which we discuss at the end of this chapter), minimal gender differences tend to minimize interest in heterosexual marriage.

Do ethnic differences in marriage influence marital sex? This is a difficult question to answer definitively, but we think so. For example, in the American Couples survey, black heterosexual pairs, which constituted less than 9 percent of the sample, had a smaller gender difference in patterns of sexual initiation and refusal (Blumstein and Schwartz 1983). Where social power is shared more equitably, so sexual entitlement may also be more similar. Back in chapter 2, we presented data showing that masturbation rates, duration of sexual episodes, and rates and patterns of giving and receiving oral sex vary with race and ethnicity, and differences in sexual patterns are not limited to these categories.

Ethnic differences appear to be driven partly by economics but also by culture and social class. For example, black women tend to be less eager to marry than women of other racial groups, perhaps because they receive fewer economic benefits. Black women are more independent, at least partially due to a history that has required full participation of these women in the workforce long before the feminist revolution of the 1960s and 1970s (Franklin 2001). Moreover, African Americans often feel, because of the history of institutionalized racism in the United States, that legal bureaucracies do not operate on their behalf and tend to be less invested in ratifying their personal or family lives. Marriage becomes a more personal event; this means African Americans are more likely to cohabit rather than marry legally—especially among the poor. Some people report that the very cost of getting married—the wedding itself and all the social expectations for a wedding—has constituted a barrier.

Cultural themes can even overcome class differences. In Latino families, for example, Catholicism is an important cultural influence. Because many Latinos are Catholic, the church's rules about sex and relationships are followed more closely among lower-income Latinos than among lower-income whites or African Americans. Few other racial groups have this kind of religious homogeneity. Thus, we would expect to find sexual commonalities among Latinos of all social classes—like lower masturbation rates—and we do. The extent to which these sexual practices are changing among Latinos is a good measure of acculturation, or the adoption of mainstream "American" trends and the rejection of traditional religious teaching.

Another example of acculturation is the increasing tendency of ethnic groups to intermarry rather than marry only one another. Chinese-Japanese marriages—unheard of in great numbers until very recently—expose two highly homogeneous groups to new values and new behaviors. Increasingly, Asian Americans are marrying the person they fall in love with rather than their parents' choice of spouse, and their rates of intermarriage with whites have been increasing (Qian and Lichter 2007). While intermarriage overall has been increasing in the past two decades, a few things seem to slow this process: When more immigrants are arriving, these "mixed" marriages decrease. In addition, people with more education are more likely to intermarry, especially among whites, Asian Americans, and Latinos.

Identity influences how people partner, but how people end up partnering also influences identity. Twine's 1996 study of heterosexual, biracial undergraduates observed that whom one pairs with was almost explicitly linked with individual ethnic identity. The study of such pairs promises to provide useful observations about the connection between the social structure and individuals' romantic and sexual imagination. Such dating has continued to increase: between 1992 and 2002 young people (in their twenties) nearly doubled their rate of interracial dating and cohabitation. Still, those couples were less likely to transition from cohabiting to marriage than same-race and same-ethnicity couples (Joyner and Kao 2005).

Same-Sex Commitment

With no legal institution of marriage available to them in most states—or a fragile access to marriages in a few—gays and lesbians can feel less societal pressure, or at least, less family pressure, to move in together, restrict sexual access to others, and make emotional commitments. Nonetheless, the urge to bond with another person is strong, as the gay marriage movement highlights. Lesbians and gay men, like heterosexuals, are socialized into the two-by-two world, and their requirements for bonding come from early socialization and a social structure that relies on pair bonding. A pair of studies reported by

Janet Lever (1994a, 1995) in the *Advocate*, a national gay and lesbian lifestyle magazine, indicated that more than 92 percent of gay men and lesbians favor being in a couple.

Indeed, the interest in commitment among gay men emerged in the contexts of AIDS and the aging of the baby boom population. Although gay men are currently more interested in commitment than they were in the 1970s, commitment doesn't necessarily include sexual exclusivity to the extent that it does for heterosexuals and lesbians.

Lesbians are more likely to value commitment and sexual exclusivity, but they have a higher than expected breakup rate (Blumstein and Schwartz 1983). In a 2005 study, lesbians reported their relationships tend to last around four years; straight women reported an average of eight years (Nichols 2005). Perhaps lesbians develop strong emotional relationships with women outside the relationship that turn quickly to sexual attraction and even extra-relationship sex. Because sex and love are ideologically united, "cheating" is more likely to prompt a breakup of the original relationship and the formation of another.

Proponents of same-sex marriage seek an institutional framework to help support and sustain same-sex relationships; this view is similar, in fact, to the proponents of strengthening marriage for heterosexuals. Without the institution of marriage, the idea of lifetime commitment, 'til death (or complicated legal extrication) do you part, is less likely, just as it is for straight cohabiters. The idea of marriage has great appeal. A 2005 Harris poll asked gays and lesbians whether they would choose marriage if it were available to them and they were in a committed relationship: 78 percent said yes. That's an overwhelming majority. What about the one in five who said no? Analysis by Egan and Sherrill (2005) showed that younger generations made same-sex marriage much more of a priority than older generations. For younger generations, the marriage equality movement was part of their introduction to the GLBT community. For older generations issues of sexual freedom and sexual health had been organizing themes. For all generations, continuing efforts to fight workplace discrimination are top action issues.

There is also some resistance to same-sex marriage within the gay/lesbian community, and it follows from our description of marriage as a heterosexual institution. While the gay liberation movement of the 1960s and 1970s was about sexual freedom and the celebration of difference, the same-sex marriage movement, to some critics, is about reproducing some of the limiting features of heterosexual culture. Sociologists Laurie Essig and Lynn Owens put their critique of same-sex marriage in context with their critique of all marriage: "Marriage is a structure of rights and privileges for those who least need them and a culture of prestige for those who already have the highest levels of racial, economic, and educational capital" (2009). Other GLBT theorists, such as Michael Bronski, take a "gay liberation" perspective that sees the movement toward convention and marriage as part and parcel of deemphasizing pleasure (2000).

The Importance of Sex in Marriage

Just as Noah lined up the animals two by two, human beings tend to pair and then weather the storms that come along. Unlike Noah's animals, however, humans today are not solely focused on the procreative bond that is at the center of "essentialist"—or biblical—explanations of sexuality. In fact, it seems that expectations of sexual compatibility and passion have escalated to the point that a marriage is often considered a failure if it does not foster sustained sexual interest and pleasure. In many centuries past and in many countries today, sexual boredom would not be an important consideration in gauging a marriage, but today sex is generally considered a central element of personal and relationship happiness. Not only do people think that they deserve great and frequent sex, but if they do not have it, they may question the strength of the rest of the relationship.

Some evidence suggests that the sexual expectations of women and men are not the same, however. In the American Couples study, women who reported that they had a mediocre or bad sex life might still rate their marriage as very good, depending on the extent to which domestic labor was shared and on other aspects of intimacy. Men were much more likely to rate their marriage as flawed if they considered their sex life poor. Research in the 2000s shows that men more so than women reported disappointment in their sex life as an "explanation" for an extramarital affair (Whisman, Gordon, and Chatav 2007).

For both sexes, particularly in younger couples, the expectation of an extremely good, if not spectacular, sex life has become a common part of committed relationships. Even couples who recognize that sexual frequency typically declines over time may struggle with this reality. "Not us," they say. Along with a dose of realism, a certain amount of romanticism is crucial to sustaining marital bonds. Despite the well-publicized rates of divorce—nearly one out of every two marriages will end in divorce—people keep marching into the institution with the blithe optimism that the likelihood of divorce is for someone else, not them. Pairs have faith that their passionate spark will not dim.

Part of the definition of couplehood in the United States and in most of the West is having sex together. Sex is seen as the validation of the relationship, proof of the couple's compatibility. One of our grandmothers liked to say that sex is the least important part of a marriage, but if the couple's sex life isn't right, nothing else is. That is, sex is a barometer for the rest of the relationship; a mundane sex life equals a mundane love. This is a common belief. Leonore Tiefer (1995), psychologist and therapist, notes that the sex therapy industry has advanced the notion that sexual disappointments augur poorly for the relationship, even though "marriage counselors and therapists say that sexual dissatisfaction is often a consequence of marital troubles rather than a cause" (14). Nevertheless, *happily* married couples can and do experience sexual problems.

The expectation of a stellar sex life and the fear of being mediocre have made twenty-first-century couples very interested in sex studies, sex books, sex movies—you name it. Everyone wants to know how he or she measures up. People wonder what normal sexual behavior is, how often others "do it," and every other detail. And these days, much of this information gets shared (and "spun") into unrealistic images of everybody else's great sex lives. The science of sex has given us a general picture of sexual behavior among married couples. But the fetish for counting undermines our understanding of the details. It also overemphasizes certain sexual activities, especially intercourse and orgasm, rather than alternatives like prolonged touching for sexual pleasure—or even more imaginative role-play.

Take the case of Viagra. Viagra is a recent star of the sex industry. Viagra is perhaps the best known of a number of drugs (there's also Cialis and Levitra, for example) used to increase blood flow to the penis. Viagra "fixes" sexual problems by generating erections. How much do we invest in making erections pop up? Sales in 2004 for Viagra, Cialis, and Levitra combined were estimated at 2.5 billion dollars—and that was a "down year" in sales (Berenson 2005). What we don't invest in to a similar degree is communication and sexual skills that may actually do the job better than the pill.

Frequent Viagra ads to the contrary, in many people's lives, as a relationship goes on, and especially as partners age, sex can become less prominent in daily life. Looking back at figure 4.1 (p. 153), you can see that after ten years, 15 percent of respondents in the American Couples survey were having sex once a month or less. For a few, sex may even become nonexistent. Part of this decline can be explained by individual differences. Part can be attributed to the relationship itself. And part of the attenuation in sexual activity is a function of habituation, fatigue, or absorption in work, child raising, or everyday issues and worries.

Remarkably, the "culture of couplehood" may help to sustain the rates of intercourse in a marriage. With marriage comes the expectation that you have to "work at it." As powerful as the dictum to "work at a relationship" is, the notion of work and the experience of sexual pleasure are rarely compatible. Nevertheless, marrieds may have some kind of "normal" sexual frequency because it is part of the definition of being married: "It's Friday night. We have to do it, like it or not!" Early in a couple's romantic career, sex is about seduction, attraction, and excitement. But within marriage sometimes it is a "duty" and, on occasion, an epiphany of commitment and closeness.

Duty isn't as bad as it sounds. Traditionally, duty has been the impetus for sustained sexual involvement within married pairs. Catholic tradition, for example, obligates couples to have sex, primarily or even solely for reproduction. In Protestant tradition, marital sex is often viewed as a "wifely duty." In Jewish rabbinical law, sex is viewed as the "husband's duty." Sex is a mitzvah—a good deed—from God, and sex on the Sabbath is a double mitzvah. Thus, sex turns out not to be a private matter at all but a matter between the couple and their god.

In legal tradition, husbands and wives have been entitled to file for divorce on the basis of "sexual abandonment." There have been other cultures in past history where lack of sexual performance constituted grounds for divorce, but cultures have been more ambivalent about how to deal with a husband who forces himself on his wife against her will. For example, even within the past thirty years (Finkelhor and Yllö 1985), a husband who forced his wife to have sex with him could not be prosecuted for rape. In some countries, this is still the case. Even in the United States, spousal rape can be a hard charge to make stick, unless the couple is legally separated or physical damage can be proved.

Straight and gay cohabiters experience patterns of sexual erosion (as well as the growth of intimacy) that are similar to—although not the same as—patterns within marriage. Cohabiters experience declines in sexual frequency over time. However, married couples start out with lower levels of sexual frequency than cohabiters do. Married couples are also more likely to have children (though increasingly, so do cohabiters), and children facilitate the decline in sexual satisfaction (from exhaustion, diminution of time together, conflict). The presence of kids also tends to generate or extend the gender gap. But the presence of children also increases the likelihood that pairs will remain together (Morgan, Lye, and Condran 1988).

In general, society is geared to support married couples and to treat other couples as more ephemeral. The very act of treating couples as permanent helps instill in couples a sense of commitment despite any disappointments in sex and other areas. With a less formal commitment and a relationship based on satisfaction more than obligation, straight and gay cohabiters are less likely to tolerate a tremendous decline in sexual frequency.

To summarize, people in long-term committed relationships—whether marriage or cohabitation—have higher rates of sexual frequency than people in shorter-term, non-co-residential relationships or no relationship at all. Married couples have more sexual opportunity and stability. Cohabiters, whether heterosexual or same-sex couples, have greater sexual frequency but more fragility.

Commitment and Passion

Does the perception that marriage suffocates passion have anything to do with the gendered quality of marriage? Recall the image from *Pillow Talk* at the beginning of this chapter. Marriage is designed for taming people. The idea that sex is tamed by commitment and that women turn from lovers into mothers and wives is a fear before marriage and for some men, an angry complaint after marriage. Men's magazines eroticize the stranger or lover, not the wife. Movies generally use the live-in partner—cohabiter or wife—as the foil for the exciting outside relationship. If a marriage is identified as vibrant and sexy at the start of the movie, it is usually endangered soon: a kidnapping, murder, or some other threat allows moviegoers to root for the husband and wife to stay together. Love stories are about searchers, beginnings, affairs, all as-yet-uncommitted lovers. Commitment and sexiness don't often go together in men's magazines or other popular media. Recent media images of married men don't produce images of virility and sexiness all the time, either: early 2000s situation comedies, *The King of Queens, Everybody Loves Raymond*, and a host of other "married with children" television programs displayed married men as losing their fitness, their sexual imagination, and their ability to be taken seriously by their wives. The wives are portrayed as scolds, often, but the husbands are portrayed as losing their sexual charms.

Meanwhile, women's magazines supplement their stories of love affairs and physical chemistry with articles about how to keep your man, how to have great sex "with the one you love," how to make love grow, how to keep your marriage sexually exciting, and so on. Romance novels always put sex in the context of eventual love and marriage—for the most part, free and unattached sexuality is not a female fantasy in magazines or in romance novels. What about narratives for men? Fewer seem to exist.

These are the stereotypes about gender differences in committed sex. To determine their validity, we can look at data regarding sexual frequency and patterns of initiation and refusal for sexual activity in heterosexual and same-sex couples.

Sexual Frequency

Although marrieds—and cohabiters—have more opportunity for sex, the change over time tells us a lot. There is an old saying that if a couple puts a penny in a jar for every time they have sex in the first year of marriage and then takes a penny out of the jar for every time they have sex the rest of the marriage, the pair will never empty out the jar. Surveys suggest that during the first year couples have a lot of sex—an average of about three times per week. Some impassioned spouses have sex every minute they can get their hands on each other. But frequency declines definitely and impressively after the early years, and every year thereafter sex gets a little scarcer, as figure 4.1 indicates.

Although the decline in sexual activity is associated with aging, novelty has a similar impact. The sex lives of fifty- and sixty-year-old newlyweds resemble younger couples' sex lives more than long-married couples their same age. And older newlyweds, like their younger counterparts, soon follow the course set for all marriages (Blumstein and Schwartz 1983; Fisher 2010). Three things are worth discussing here: The decline in frequency, the maintenance of a sex life over the long haul, and sustained emotional commitment and marital stability among some abstinent couples.

Sexual decline is generally understood as the consequence of habituation. All evidence about sexuality indicates that passion is fueled by novelty, uncertainty, achievement of someone's love, and desire. Marriage itself mitigates uncertainty and the need for achievement of someone's love. In other words, marriage reduces some of the prime motivations for sexual arousal. Women, trained to have a taste for commitment, may rely less on erotic motivations and somewhat more on relationship satisfaction. But just like men, women can become bored by predictability. Even women who find commitment sexy ultimately get distracted by the demands of daily life. Couples evolve into partners rather than lovers. The dictates of everyday life—especially those related to the care of children—diminish marital satisfaction and sexual behavior. Couples may enjoy sex as much as or even more than they did earlier in their relationship, but they just don't desire as much, or have the time or energy for each other as often. If a marriage is highly conflicted, sex may diminish so much that eventually the couple no longer even tries to have sex together. Finally, one of the partners may simply be less interested in sex than the other partner. In any case, the result is less sex in the relationship.

Even when couples enjoy sex, they tend to enjoy it somewhat less often as time goes on. In some cases, sex disappears but the marriage remains together. One man who was interviewed for an article on parenting was in a twenty-three-year marriage, in which there had been no sex for the past ten years. When asked why he, a successful lawyer and an extremely handsome man of forty-five, would stay in a marriage like this, he said,

> It's not so hard to understand. I have three amazing children who are my whole life, and who I would never leave. I have been very financially successful, and I have no desire to lose all that for myself or my children because of a messy divorce. I have a few meaningless affairs every so often when I start feeling too sorry for myself. And that makes things bearable. If I could have a good marriage with a reasonable sex life, I would do that. But I don't, and this isn't the worst of all compromises.

The belief is that when you contract marriage, "You've made your bed, so you lie in it—even if you don't lay in it!"

When sex becomes less frequent, that doesn't mean it is less pleasant. As long as couples still have sex, as long as sex is not a disaster when it happens, couples feel they are meeting the signature requirement of marriage: sex happens. When sex is extremely uncommon or absent, or when it is unpleasant or hostile, it becomes a vulnerability in the couple's life and may start to undermine the marriage.

These patterns apply to heterosexual cohabiters as well. Figure 4.3 indicates sexual frequency by length of relationship. Sexual frequency declines over time. However, sex is more frequent among long-term cohabiters than among long-term married couples (refer back to figure 4.1).

Initiation and Refusal

As we discussed in chapter 2, initiation and refusal are deeply gendered sexual customs that affect sexual frequency. Because leadership and dominance are considered masculine, men are required to take charge in various ways. One of the simpler ways of showing masculinity, as it is stereotypically defined, is to be the director of a couple's sex life.

It is also true that one of the elements of arousal is desire. For many men, their own desire tends to be a sexual cue; for many women, their partner's desire tends to be the cue. If men always initiate, they are responding to their own internal signals of desire but are then less often the recipients of lust. When women are mostly the recipients of desire, they must wait for cues from their partners to commence satisfying their own sexual appetites. Women learn to experience their partners' desire as erotic.

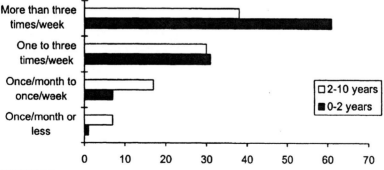

FIGURE 4.3
Sexual frequency by relationship length: Heterosexual cohabiters. Data from Blumstein and Schwartz (1983).

Despite the strong social pressures on men to initiate sex, studies have shown that men want women to initiate more than they do—just not too much. Men want to be wanted, but they don't want to give up the thrill of being the sexually dominant partner. Some data show that men like a woman to initiate often but that when she starts to initiate more than he does, satisfaction decreases (Blumstein and Schwartz 1983). Women have been given leeway to be sexual, but it is unclear how sexual they can be before men start to resent their approaches or find them "pushy" or even masculine. Desire still is supposed to begin with a man, and images of women with a strong, direct sexual desire are treated as scary.

Mass media are ambivalent about this convention. Many movies have seductive heroines, but if she is a very sexually aggressive woman, it generally ends badly for her, her partner, or both of them. A woman may show desire, but if she takes over the bedroom scene, she usually turns out to be emotionally unstable, or a double agent, as is the case in most James Bond movies. There are exceptions, but usually the woman "pays for" her version of a masculine sexual style. Samantha in *Sex and the City* was an exception— she was the very model for the "Cougar" label. She's an "older" woman with great looks, an amazing body, and an insatiable sexual appetite. Still, over the course of the TV series, she had many betrayals and she fell in love often without a "happy ending"—which in film grammar means a wedding. What of other exceptions? In the 2004 movie, *When Will I Be Loved?*, Vera Barrie (played by Neve Campbell) extends her sexual exploration outside of her relationship with her boyfriend to experiment with casual sex. She engages in numerous frank seductions in direct defiance of the conventions expected by her well-to-do Manhattan family. Even a bold story of sexuality like this one doesn't stray far, however, from gender scripts. The plot takes several twists, including the boyfriend's efforts to exploit her sexual experimentation and ultimately her use of her wits along with her sexuality to trump efforts to control her sexually.

Gendered traditions still persist when it comes to refusal. In the nineteenth century women used fear of pregnancy to justify saying no to sex with their husbands. Things have changed massively. No longer are wives expected to have headaches and be forgiven for their lesser interest in sex. Even so, refusal is still a woman's tool for controlling or responding to her partner. Similarly, a man is not supposed to refuse, even if he is in a long-term, perhaps boring, sexual relationship. The politics of modern sexuality promise to give men as much right as women to refuse sex, but in fact women sometimes feel extremely rejected when their spouses respond to advances with "I'm too tired." Women see their own right to say "I'm tired" as quite a different thing. The stereotype of men's greater sexual appetite is still alive and well. A man's refusal is seen as going against his natural instincts, whereas a woman's sexual refusal tends to be interpreted as a reflection of her natural, lesser desire. You won't see a man refuse his wife or lover in the movies unless he is angry at her, drunk, dead tired, or having an affair with someone else.

The traditional imagery of initiation and refusal recurs implicitly and explicitly in the process of sex education. Men and boys are instructed to resist their own desire. Women and girls are advised to resist the other person's desire so that they can protect themselves. These stereotypes make it difficult for men and women to experience the full range of sexual expression. The exceptions to this rule, like the heroine in Spike Lee's film *She's Gotta Have It* (1987), are so rare that the mere introduction of a lusty, demanding, unapologetic, independent female sexual initiator becomes a cultural event, and her character, not just the movie, is discussed in magazines, in newspapers, and on talk shows.

Same-Sex Pairs

According to the men-as-initiators custom, gay men should have the most sex and lesbians the least, and there is some truth to that. However, other issues complicate it. Figure 4.4 shows patterns of sexual frequency among gay men and lesbians. As with other groups, frequency declines over time. But these

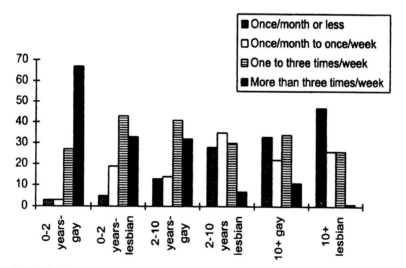

FIGURE 4.4
Sexual frequency: Gay men and lesbians. Data from Blumstein and Schwartz (1983).

statistics show that frequency is not dependent on gender but on habituation. If women's socialization to have less sex were a factor, lesbians would
have a pronounced change in sexual frequency. Gay men would not. But they
do—33 percent of gay men in relationships lasting more than ten years have
sex once a month or less. Gay couples and heterosexual cohabiters start out
with higher sexual frequency than lesbian pairs, but over time, all relationship
types move toward reduced sexual activity.

Differences between gays and lesbians in sexual frequency have several
ramifications. For instance, men in our culture—straight and gay—are
tantalized with visions of sexual variety. Rock Hudson's incredulity at Tony
Randall's pitch for marriage in the scene from *Pillow Talk* that opened this
chapter is based on the understanding that men would always prefer a variety
of romantic options to one romantic and domestic option. In various polls,
straight and gay men tend to rate the desire for variety higher than do women.
This creates a special challenge for long-term gay relationships.

If variety spikes desire among men and desire is required for initiation, gay
men in committed relationships may decrease initiation. Without the conventional marital sexual obligation, gay men in couples must find new ways to
cultivate sexual connection. Many do, with sex toys, videos, or outside partners. But others allow sexual frequency in a long-term relationship to slide.

Fulfilling the cultural expectation that men are more sexually predatory
is costly to gay men. Whereas women are perceived to temper men's desire,
men who love men theoretically have little to stop them from sexual extremes. As we've seen, gay men do in fact have higher sexual frequency and
seek greater variety than other sexual pairs. However, society's expectation
for all men also shapes homophobic views. Gay men are seen as dangerous sexual predators or as hedonists who can't be trusted, especially with
children. In reality, a prodigious sexual appetite has nothing to do with
sexual desire for children or observing other sexual norms such as choosing
socially acceptable partners.

Lesbians, like straight women, share the custom of initiating less than men
do and refusing more. With lesbians, however, if each woman expects to be
approached and both wait for the other woman to initiate, inevitably sexual
frequency slows down. Likewise, if both women feel comfortable saying no,
less sex may occur.

Additionally, many lesbians can be especially aware of sex as a source of
power. Power issues are a common theme for lesbian pairs, who tend to be
more politically aware and wary of manipulation. Because many lesbians are
in a position to reject the hierarchical nature of heterosexual relationships,
they are sensitized to any replication of those patterns. A sexually intense
partner, especially one who likes sex for its own sake, may be seen as ag-

gressive and unfeeling. Sexual gratification is not seen as a right so much as an outgrowth of a good relationship (on a good day in that relationship). "Pushing it" can be seen as a power trip or, even worse, as coercion or rape. Keep in mind, the mechanics of coercion depart from heterosexual rape; the American Couples study used any genital contact as the definition of lesbian sex, whether consensual or coercive. In couples for whom sexual aggression is a sensitive issue, sexual initiative can be complicated.

The cultural expectation for lesbians to be loving and relationship focused further complicates life. Some lesbians, especially younger women, don't fit the mold and don't want to be seen as nonsexual or passive. Young lesbians can congregate in some pretty edgy sex clubs and celebrate an adventurous single sexual life style. More conservatively, but still out of the gender script, some lesbians, as is the case with some straight women, want to date, delay commitment, and follow their career. However, these departures from the expectation that women must always link sex and love are often seen as indicating personal problems, such as having commitment or other psychological issues rather than as exercising the same rights to sexual independence and curiosity that men are free to express. A sexually adventurous lesbian may be tagged as predatory and somehow less womanly if she steps out of her gender's sexual script. Even a movie that defies that sexual image, such as *Bound*, a 1996 thriller in which a sexually aggressive, beautiful "butch" lesbian successfully pursues a woman who is being "kept" by a [male] mobster, still is essentially a love story. In it, the two women quickly become totally committed. This was a "mainstream" movie, not a lesbian movie for a primarily lesbian audience. Nevertheless, it was clearly designed to be attractive to lesbian sensibilities with a story of love above all else.

Everyday Influences on Committed Sex

In predicting sexual frequency, social scripts can shape sexual scripts. Everyday life and family events may have greater effect on a couple's sex life than anything else. After all, sex must occur in the context of the ongoing, daily lives, with demands, burdens, and triumphs that influence how pairs feel when they are in the bedroom.

All couples have external pressures that reduce sexual desire. They have everyday issues that create the biggest barrier there is to sexual frequency: anger and resentment. A preponderance of marital therapy research (i.e., Gottman 1994; Jacobson and Christensen 1996), which focuses strictly on troubled marriages, supports this assertion and explains it in terms of a *demand/ withdraw cycle* in communication. A demand/withdraw cycle is a polarizing process whereby a partner's demands for greater intimacy leads to the other partner's withdrawing and retreating. The order can also be reversed; it is as often a withdraw/demand cycle.

This pattern tends to be gendered: women are demanders, men are withdrawers. But don't confuse this imagery with some sort of essentialist vision of "men are from Mars and women are from Venus." In a significant proportion of troubled relationships, women are withdrawers and men are demanders; and the pattern occurs in same-sex relationships as well. Furthermore, research on communication patterns among healthy couples, both heterosexual and same-sex, demonstrates that demand and withdraw patterns in communication are less associated with gender and more clearly associated with power. The more powerful partner has the privilege of being withdrawn (Kollock, Blumstein, and Schwartz 1985). It may be, as marital therapist N. S. Jacobson claimed in "The Politics of Intimacy" (1989), that power influences the struggles for closeness that therapists observe in couples in their offices.

Interestingly, the demand/withdraw pattern in communication tends to be the inverse of the sexual one, where men tend to be demanders and women withdrawers. This pattern makes sense. The person with more power is more entitled, including more sexually entitled. But sex may not be particularly appealing to the person who has less power, who withdraws sexually. The other person, if offended by the sexual refusal, may retaliate by withdrawing emotionally. The less powerful partner then responds by becoming more demanding emotionally. However, to the extent that withdrawing from sex is related to power, women's power of refusal defines them as having only sexual power.

Among highly conflicted couples, sex becomes rare or nonexistent. Sometimes high-conflict couples are turned on by the regrets, apologies, and recommitment the couple has to go through to stay together. But for the most part, conflict depletes the sexual agenda rather than stokes it. Even in good relationships, sexual frequency gradually decreases. But sex usually doesn't disappear.

Emotional Complications for Heterosexuals

The demand/withdraw cycle in marriage can be exacerbated by the arrival of a first child and consolidated by subsequent children. There is substantial evidence that children depress both desire and sexual behavior (Call, Sprecher, and Schwartz 1995). One reason is that babies increase anxiety levels, but they don't produce the pleasant anxiety that lovers feel trying to impress and possess each other. No, this is the anxiety of paying bills, doing more in the same amount of time, and managing the baby schedule so it doesn't undermine work commitments.

Babies are also exhausting, and fatigue is a staunch enemy of sexual desire. People have only so much energy, and a baby who doesn't sleep through the night for a year or more creates a greater desire for sleep than for sex on the part of overwhelmed parents. Especially when children are infants, sleep deprivation falls more heavily on a mother than on a father because of the demands of breast-feeding and the social expectations of mother-focused child rearing.

A woman may love her husband as much as or more than she did before the baby came, but her energy is focused on this new human being. Indeed, a woman who isn't emotionally engrossed in her infant is treated with suspicion. Reprisals come in the details of everyday interaction, but custody battles are also illustrative. For example, in 1995 a white, single mother in her early twenties was denied custody of her infant because she was a full-time student at the University of Michigan. The baby's dad was also a white, full-time student, but his mother agreed to stay home with the baby, so the dad won out over the mom—at least until the father's mother died in 1996 (Associated Press 1996).

Husbands, though, often recognizing their baby's needs, may feel dislocated, lonely, pushed away, or even pushed out. Unless they are highly involved in their child's life (despite being discouraged by cultural norms and policies such as including no *paid* family leave when the baby arrives [Ray, Gornick, and Schmitt 2008]), they may be angry about the severe constraints on the affection and sexual relationship they were accustomed to with their spouse. Some marriages run aground in this period, and marital satisfaction typically declines by about two-thirds (Gottman and Gottman 2007). Some researchers report that husbands' affairs increase during a wife's pregnancy (Whisman, Gordon, and Chatav 2007). Prevention programs, such as Gottman's Bringing Baby Home program, help strengthen couples' friendship and reduce their criticism of each other before the baby arrives. This kind of preparation for the child's entrance into the couple's life can reduce polarization and eliminate declines in marital satisfaction.

Same-Sex Burdens

Same-sex pairs share most of the burdens of everyday life that influence heterosexuals, but there are also impediments unique to gays and lesbians. Lesbians, for example, are often under more economic pressure than other couples because two women more rarely have incomes that protect them from financial crises. In 2009, 19 percent of heterosexual women were reported to be living in poverty, while 24 percent of lesbian and bisexual women did (Quintana 2009). The gap between straight and gay men is not as large: 13 percent of straight men versus 15 percent of gay men live in poverty. The rates of poverty among same-sex and heterosexual couples with children make the point even more clearly. The poverty rate for lesbian couple families with children is 9.4 percent, while for straight (married) couple families with children, the rate is 6.7 percent. Gay couples with children, who have the benefit of the possibility of two men as earners, have the lowest rate of poverty, at 5.5 percent (Quintana 2009).

Gay men and lesbians, because they are more discriminated against than heterosexual couples, may constantly be placed in situations that stress them (Patterson 1995). Both gay and lesbian couples are more often rejected by their partner's parents and perhaps by their own than other kinds of couples. Families sometimes blame their child's lover for his or her sexual orientation. Or they will continue to treat their gay family member well but be awkward or unaccommodating toward their family member's partner. They may refuse to cooperate in major ways, perhaps by blocking child custody rights for a gay partner when the family member dies. But they may also raise barriers in pettier ways, as when they exclude a gay partner from a family photograph. Heterosexual in-laws and long-term (straight) partners may be included without a second thought. Even such seemingly small matters can lead to resentment between partners or to a cutoff from one's family (and from any of the emotional and material resources that families provide) or both.

Issues of whether to stay "closeted" or be "out" to the world become relationship pitfalls when the two partners disagree about how to handle them (Patterson and Schwartz 1994). This dilemma is heightened by the cost of being in or out. A gay man in a mainstream career may seek to remain closeted or discreet about his relationship, but his partner may feel strongly that being out is a political statement. Being closeted or out has psychological as well as economic and political consequences that can make these conflicts very intense. Over the past twenty years the age of coming out has declined, and the overall acceptance of men and women who are "out" has increased. However, the psychological distress—as indicated, for example, by how often gays and lesbians think about suicide around the time of coming out—highlights how stressful this transition is for gay and lesbian couples (Paul, Catania, and Pollack 2002)

Same-sex couples also have unique resources and strengths for committed relationships. In longitudinal research on gay and lesbian couples, John Gottman and colleagues have found that same-sex couples are better able to handle conflict, use fewer negative or hostile strategies, and are less likely to take disagreements personally (Gottman et al. 2003). In the absence of traditional gender scripts, partners are more likely to expect to have to share power and "work it out." Lesbian couples seem more likely than gay men to use both anger and humor. For gay men, their big risk is trying to avoid negativity in conflict; it is harder for gay men than other couple types to repair communication and reestablish good feelings following negativity. We suspect that the strengths of same-sex couples that Gottman found would extend to their transition to parenthood. Same-sex couples are more likely than heterosexual couples to have already built a sense of equality and friendship into their relationships, and this is essential for weathering the challenges of a child's impact on the couple.

The Concerns of Older Partners

Age may biologically depress desire, but it doesn't extinguish it. The issue of age and sexuality has grown recently—and will continue to grow. In 2008 the retiree population in the United States was 39 million, but by 2050 that population will grow to 89 million. Increasingly, elderly people will be those who came of age during or after the sexual revolution, and they are less likely to go gently into their later years. To wit: In 2009, one of us (Pepper Schwartz) became the love, sex, and relationships advice columnist for AARP, the largest membership organization in the United States (42 million people) that works as an advocacy group for older Americans. This was a brand-new position—created because love, sex, and relationships are a central part of older Americans' lives like never before, and because this generation of older Americans is freer than any prior generation to be open and frank about their interests and concerns.

Figure 4.5 demonstrates the decline in sexual frequency by age. After age sixty, frequency tends to level off to several times a month either until sexual disability becomes a factor or until a person reaches his or her seventies or eighties (Masters et al. 1995). Many people in their seventies and eighties still report sexual activity and enjoyment. The 2010 AARP national study on sexuality of people over forty-five showed that the top enemies of sex for older people were health, partner's health, and stress. But if health is held constant, and people did not stop having sex earlier in their relationship, the desire for at least some sexual activity continues. Research keeps showing us that there are massive benefits to remaining sexually active for people as they age. In fact, staying sexual will probably keep you alive longer! For example, sexually active men who have more than twenty-one "emissions" a month have lower rates of prostate cancer than men who are less sexually active (Leitzmann et al. 2004). A longitudinal study in Carphilly, Wales, shows that men who have sex more often live longer and have fewer diseases and illnesses. Women who

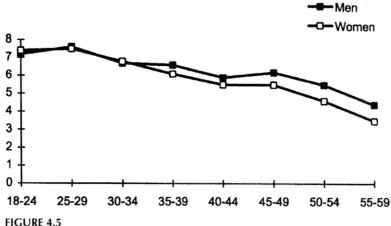

FIGURE 4.5
Sexual frequency by age. Data from Laumann et al. (1994).

have sex have better moods and can withstand pain and stress more. It lowers blood pressure and cortisol levels for everyone.

Being in a relationship *never* stops being important. The AARP study showed that men and women who had a steady partner (cohabiting, dating, or marriage) were happier with their sex lives and happier with their lives in general. And like younger people, dating and cohabiting men and women were having more sex than married people, but unlike younger people, unmarried older people were happier with their sex lives than marrieds. Who were happiest? Hispanic couples: They valued having a partner the most, had the most sex, and were most satisfied with their sex lives.

It is heartening to observe that older couples can still work on and improve their relationships. With aging and the mellowing of a long-term partnership, sex lives still have the potential to improve. The security of a marriage or a long-term commitment emboldens some partners to ask for exactly what they need and allows them to work out a mutually satisfying sexual style. Paradoxically, the consistency that tends to reduce sexual frequency also provides the conditions for sexual satisfaction through intimate negotiation.

Social Trends in Improving Committed Sex

Sexual improvement and sexual knowledge do not occur magically for pairs. Although sexual desire may emerge from a complex mixture of biology and social experience, sex is something people *learn* how to do. Consider the old joke "How do you get to Carnegie Hall?" Answer: "Practice, practice, practice!" The punch line certainly applies to improving sex between committed partners. Still, couples can be as incapable with each other after ten years of practice as they were in their first sexual encounter because sexual partners don't typically arrive in bed with an instruction manual, and giving one's partner directions can feel embarrassing or awkward. After many years, though, a couple may feel particularly stymied if much time has passed with no change or improvement. The sexual dilemma can be distressing:

> Imagine how you would feel if playing gin rummy, and playing it well, were considered a major component of happiness and a major sign of maturity, but no one told you how to play, you never saw anyone else play, and everything you ever read implied that normal and healthy people just somehow "know" how to play and really enjoy playing the very first time they try! It is a very strange situation. (Tiefer 1995:11–12)

Anybody can have sex. But good sex takes practice and communication. The matter of learning how to do sex is made complicated, however, by today's intense media climate. There is informal sexual instruction in almost every program on TV, advertisements tell the public how to dress erotically, and movies show seduction scenes and graphic sexual moves.

Sometimes the examples highlight sexual disappointments. For example, an old episode from the television show *Seinfeld* focused on oral sex. The character Elaine was dating a sexy saxophone player but was troubled that he never gave her oral sex. Later on, after she had figured out how to introduce the subject, she and her partner were excited to go test the new sexual activity. The punch line of this story was that after an episode of cunnilingus, his mouth was tired and he couldn't play the sax that night. Everyone watching understood the joke: When they had finally gotten around to oral sex, it had been an exhausting exercise that left Elaine's boyfriend's mouth numb. It was their first time having oral sex, and the pair needed more practice and more instruction.

Sexual instruction is available through seminars, videos, books, and standard textbooks. The top sex advice books on amazon.com focus on seduction—such as *The Art of Seduction* (Greene and Elffers 2003)—and technique—such as *Red Hot Touch: A Head-to-Toe Guide to Mind-blowing Orgasms* (Hanauer and Hanauer 2008). The focus on the need for extra stimulation seems to intensify each year. Long-term couples seek help with relationship issues as well as sexual dilemmas such as boredom or lifestyle obstacles to good sex. Highly popular sex advice books for couples, *The Sex-Starved Marriage* (Weiner-Davis 2003) or *Intimacy and Desire* (Schnarch 2009), are two among many that are frank and direct about the concern couples have—and the expectation that sex should support their marriage.

Social commentary and advice books on sexual issues not only illuminate problems, they may also create them. Almost every decade shows an increase in a certain kind of sexual dysfunction that disappears or vastly decreases as a new problem emerges to take its place.

Sex Advice of the 1960s

When Masters and Johnson published *Human Sexual Response* in the 1960s, few people read it but almost everyone talked about it. Even if people didn't actually read the book, and even if many therapists who were not trained by Masters and Johnson distorted their findings (Maier 2009), the book gave people permission to identify and address sexual problems in their relationships. A new specialty, sex therapy, based on Masters and Johnson's observations, advertised help to repair sexual difficulties. Long-term couples who had given up on sexual happiness now had names for the problems they were having and had a place to go for help.

Masters and Johnson's research provided the beneficial knowledge that there was no hierarchy of orgasms for women, with some types better than others. The father of psychoanalysis, Sigmund Freud, along with his followers, had declared that clitoral orgasms (rather than vaginal orgasms) were "immature" because they weren't stimulated by intercourse. From this early psychoanalytic perspective, intercourse constituted the pinnacle of sexual expression. This remained the psychological party line until Masters and Johnson's research disclosed that vaginal and clitoral orgasms are physiologically identical. This finding gave women greater permission to seek a variety of routes other than intercourse for achieving orgasm.

The change in perspective had symbolic as well as physical importance for women. Women who were married or living with someone and earning an income in the newly opened-up workforce could also see themselves as full partners in the bedroom. As independent sexual beings, they could now pursue orgasms whether or not they were having sexual intercourse. Before Masters and Johnson destroyed the idea of the superiority of vaginal orgasms, women felt guilty that they had "inferior" orgasms during masturbation or were somehow damaged goods if they couldn't be orgasmic during intercourse. Masters and Johnson told women that some orgasms might feel better than others (e.g., if a person hadn't had an orgasm for a long time and was extremely turned on or if she was being touched more expertly than usual), but that their intensity has nothing to do with whether they are produced by a penis rather than some other kind of stimulation. In fact, the pendulum of scientific opinion swung the other way. Once women were freer sexual agents, sharing personal sexual histories more freely and comparing experiences, many found that a large number of other women were more easily and more intensely orgasmic through oral sex or touching.

Masters and Johnson's groundbreaking research, which made fewer presumptions about how sex works than the Freudians had, depended on a new consciousness about how sex had been defined by men. In turn, these new authoritative, "scientific" findings were required to give women the confidence to listen to their own bodies rather than try to fit Freud's vision of "good" and "bad" orgasms. Married women could now demand sex on their own terms, much the same way they were requiring more equality in the marketplace. Nevertheless, Masters and Johnson were hardly the last word on sexual functioning. As we noted in chapter 1, the sample of men and women in their study were not particularly representative of the population.

When the first Masters and Johnson book appeared, the most common presenting complaint to sex therapists was vaginismus or dyspareunia for women and erectile failure for men. Dyspareunia is a generic term used for painful intercourse. It may have been extraordinarily common at the time because so many people were ignorant about making sure a woman was aroused before the entry of the penis or even a finger into the vagina. Insufficient natural or commercial lubricant could make penetration painful and lead to vaginismus, an involuntary clenching of the vaginal muscles that could make entry of the penis impossible or painfully difficult.

Erectile failure includes everything from total impotence (inability to get an erection) to situational erectile failure or inability to become hard enough for intercourse. Situational impotence is quite common—probably even more common than we can guess, because men with this problem may solve it privately and never seek a clinical assessment. But the "uncovering" of this fairly common problem was big news in the 1960s, and many men were encouraged to seek treatment and did. In fact, so many people sought treatment that many articles were written, musing over the possibility that erectile failure was a direct response to the women's movement and the usurping of traditional male roles and privileges. For people who believed that ready and willing sexual desire is a natural part of masculinity, even situational erectile failure was considered a disruption of the laws of nature. It was a handy "crisis" for people who objected to the women's movement. By the 2000s, there was still great interest in erectile problems, now known to everyone as "ED" (as anyone who watches television advertisements can attest to). Sources of the problem have been of less interest than getting everyone with a reticent penis to take Viagra or similar drugs.

Advice of the 1970s: More Pleasure, Our Way

In the 1970s, discussion became centered on simultaneous orgasms and multiple orgasms. As the sexual revolution extolled new sexual frontiers, many couples began to feel that simultaneous orgasm was the height of sexual competence and intimacy. After all, a couple who had been together for a while ought to be able to "come" at the same time, went the thinking. This trend was in direct response to all the discoveries about what women could do and the pressure for couples to make sex the cosmic center of their lives. In the early days of the women's movement, women were touted as sexual athletes who were entitled to all the pleasure their bodies could provide, and men's performance was measured by the ability to provide all that pleasure.

Couples sought sex therapy to learn more control and better timing. But learning to produce simultaneous orgasm was so hard (and the effort made so many people feel frustrated) that ultimately there was a backlash. A number of writers began to say that simultaneous orgasm was more trouble than it was worth (e.g., Barbach 1975).

However, the mounting pressure to be multiorgasmic, particularly for women, was tenacious. Men were told that it was now their responsibility to be more accomplished lovers, but there were few measures of how well they were doing. Giving your partner multiple rather than single orgasms was the most measurable evidence of excellence yet, and so it became the new sexual standard for couples. Producing more than one paltry orgasm gave bragging rights.

This sexual expectation eventually died down but did not entirely go away. Competitive or anxious men still use this handy yardstick to prove their sexual prowess. However, such a standard is tough to meet even for partners who know each other well, although it also places a great deal of pressure on single and dating men and women.

Advice of the 1980s: Problems, Problems, Problems

The 1980s, the beginning of the AIDS epidemic, was a much more somber sexual age. Single heterosexuals and gay men were not the only ones who began to worry about what their sexual past might do to them. The fun and games encouraged in the 1960s and 1970s stopped with a rather sudden, dull thud. Baby boomers, the largest part of the population, started settling down, marrying, and forsaking their single life and, for some, their wild and experimental pasts. It was perhaps inevitable that settling down was going to be difficult in a culture that had given them a free hand, in a culture that still touted sex from every billboard and every entertainment.

The complaint of the decade was called "inhibited sexual desire." The problem was that one or both members of the couple simply did not want to have sex with each other enough—or ever. Of course, one could only determine what was enough by making a comparison to a norm in the culture. Sometimes inhibited sexual desire turned out to be a relationship problem; desire in general was not damaged, just desire for each other. Other times, the couple, although unperturbed in everyday life, worried that they were abnormal because so little sex was going on. Therapists dedicated to the idea that everyone ought to need and want sex were only too happy to help ratify a new sexual dysfunction and try to treat it. The diagnosis of inhibited sexual desire shifted the popular fetish for counting sexual events to a fetish for pathologizing sexual events (or nonevents).

The 1990s and the New Millenium: Desire! or Desire?

In the 1990s, the sexual current again shifted. The United States has always been schizophrenic about sex, giving license and then being punitive about it. But the 1990s accelerated this tendency. As the AIDS crisis increased in ferocity, particularly among gay men, the inability of some people (both straight and gay) to curtail their sex lives in the face of overwhelming evidence of terrible danger created a new sexual therapeutic specialty. This has been the age of sexual addiction. People who could not control their sexual contacts or modify them in their own best interests were called "sex addicts." Programs were created that paralleled other addiction services, including various twelve-step approaches similar to those used in drug and alcohol addiction treatment. How many people were actually compulsive sexually and how many were, like overeaters, mired in dangerous and self-destructive practices but not psychiatrically classifiable is not clear. But again, the moment in history influenced the definition of sexual pathology and sexual health.

When concerns about levels of sexual activity are raised in therapy, more women wish to be on the celibacy end of the continuum than men. As we have mentioned, women are more likely to get engrossed in their children and put the rest of their lives and sex on a back burner. More men than women turn to sex counseling with the complaint that their partner doesn't want them anymore; more women than men complain that their partner isn't "considerate" and presses them for more sex than they want. In fact, many lesbian couples seek sex counseling when one partner wants more sex than the other. Not uncommonly, the partner who wants less sex wants very little sex or no sex at all.

This gender difference may have some biological origins, but we believe it follows from cultural practices and proscriptions and the fact that more men than women are socialized to be adventurers. Women still need more permission than men to open themselves up to an intense sexual life. For example, the research from the 1970s on "swingers" (couples who go to commercial sex clubs or advertise for couples to have sex with them) indicates that mostly the husbands convince their wives to try these experiments. Men were also more ready to quit the experiment than their wives were (Bartell 1971). It seems that once women got over the stigma of sexual liberality and nonmarital sex, they were as enthusiastic and perhaps even more adventurous than their husbands. With each passing decade, women have greater and greater sexual freedom—and more women are sexually adventuresome. In the recent Indiana University online sex survey, couples have become increasingly liberal—having more oral sex and anal sex. Men and women are experimenting more these days. Still, the same survey reported the continuing gender gap in orgasms—and perception of orgasms: men reported their women partners had orgasms 81 percent of the time; while women reported having orgasms with their partners 64 percent of the time (Herbenich et al. 2010). The sexual double standard, we argue, exists, but my how times have changed!

As women's location in the social structure shifts, for example, as they obtain more power and influence in the marketplace, they can be more autonomous sexually. Just as social conservatives have feared, growing levels of premarital sex, longer periods of sexual experience before marriage, and liberalization of female sexuality have affected the behavior of heterosexuals and lesbians. These trends are bound to shift the gendered reactions to sex in long-term relationships as well.

Outside Temptations

One of the problems that many long-term partners fear, even if it never happens to them, is nonmonogamy. We are talking about sexual liaisons outside a committed relationship, which may be a single episode, a long-term affair, or a number of affairs. Most people refer to such affairs as *cheating* or *infidelity* because they believe they are a transgression of marriage vows and that it has *moral* implications. In fact, most studies on attitudes toward nonmonogamy show that more than 85 percent of both men and women disapprove of it (e.g., Laumann, Michael, and Gagnon 1994). Affairs are a threat to marriage and, because marriage is a powerful institution that tends to preserve and expand gendered differences, a threat to gendered expectations for sexual and other experience. Infidelity is distinct from *polyamory*. While polyamory involves conducting multiple relationships at the same time with the consent of everyone involved, infidelity involves conducting relationships at the same time *without* the consent of all the parties involved.

With such high disapproval ratings, we might guess that infidelity never happens. It does. We know it from the news. We know it from our lives. Remarkably, a social networking website, AshleyMadison.com, gained prominence, millions of clients, and lots of attention in 2008 and 2009: this website is designed specifically for married people to find partners for an affair. Even so, some studies suggest that there is indeed a low rate of nonmonogamy. In the National Health and Social Life Survey (NHSLS; Laumann et al. 1994), 79 percent of men and 89 percent of women said they had been monogamous all of their marriage. A study conducted in 2006 found that 12 percent of men and 7 percent of women had had an affair in the past year (Parker-Pope 2008).

It is hard to know exactly what people are doing. As we discussed in chapter 2, the conditions under which people are asked about sexuality—and their expectations for confidentiality—influence their response. The methodologies used in some of the random sample surveys like the NHSLS may depress the actual numbers. Respondents had to pass their questionnaires back into the hands of the interviewers and thus may have been worried about anonymity. Also, some individuals may not want to talk about their affairs because they don't want to admit it to themselves, much less to some impersonal questionnaire or interviewer. Furthermore, people have varying definitions of what constitutes an affair. One national politician has said that he preferred to have only oral sex with women other than his wife so that it "wouldn't count" as an affair. Still, there is evidence that monogamy is the case in the majority of marriages and that nonmonogamy may be more feared than real.

Some groups may be more at risk for nonmonogamy than others. In fact, research data about rates of extramarital affairs may not be as informative about how much nonmonogamy occurs as they are about the relative likelihood of different groups engaging in it. The NHSLS shows that rates of affairs are higher among people in the lowest educational category (did not complete high school) and in the highest educational category (completed a graduate degree). The most conservative group were college graduates. Urban dwellers and people of low professed religiosity were more likely to have affairs than others, and very poor people were more likely to have affairs than richer people. The NHSLS found that cohabiters had many more affairs than married people, perhaps because of their lesser level of commitment and more frequent exposure to opportunities (Laumann et al. 1994). Similarly, people who have multiple marriages are more likely to have an affair than those who remain in a first marriage.

Looking at two simple variables, age and gender, suggests some ways that the sexual double standard may have changed. Let's look at two ends of the spectrum—illustrated in figure 4.6, among younger people, in newer marriages—20 percent of men and 15 percent of women report having had affairs. And how about for people over sixty? In 1991, 20 percent of men over sixty reported ever having had an affair. By 2006, that number was 28 percent. Five percent of sixty-year-old women reported ever having an affair in 1991. By 2006, that rate had tripled to 15 percent. So, for younger men and women, rates of nonmonogamy

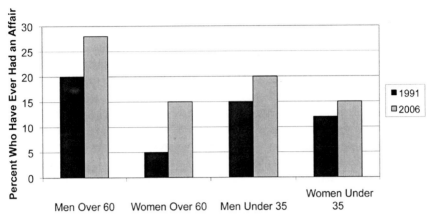

FIGURE 4.6
Nonmonogamy rates over time. Data from Atkins and Furrow (2008).

are coming closer together, though the gap persists. And for older men and women, there is a larger gap. However, more women in this age group have been changing their behavior and report having affairs. These statistics suggest a trend: Over time, women have gained license to be nonmonogamous (and to admit it in a survey interview), although only the youngest women are catching up with men in their age group.

Older men have higher rates of nonmonogamy than younger men, but younger women have higher rates than older women. Of course, this discrepancy is partly due to generation. Men who were raised in the 1940s and 1950s have more "gendered" permission for extramarital sex. But the difference is also due to the way sexual attraction is gendered. In a crude sense, younger women have a higher "market value" than older women. Their power in a committed relationship and their allure to alternative mates make them more likely to have an affair. Alternatively, men's "market value" increases as they age, in general. This is a common explanation for hypergamy—younger women marrying slightly older men. The market-value hypothesis works in the other direction, too: As women increase their economic and workplace power, the notion of women's value as achievers—just like men's value as achievers—may become influential over how free, available, and appealing women as well as men in different age groups are.

Same-sex couples are more open to affairs. What is remarkable, though, is that although same-sex couples report tolerating affairs more than straight couples, in the past twenty years the rate of people endorsing affairs seems to have declined. In a survey in the early 2000s that followed up Schwartz and Blumstein's American Couples survey, gay, lesbian, and straight people reported fewer affairs now than in the 1970s. Indeed, everybody has changed in terms of monogamy: 59 percent of gay men reported doing it (where "do it" means doing nonmonogamy)—versus 82 percent in the 1970s. Lesbians rates of nonmonogamy declined to 8 percent (Schrock 2009).

As for having any kind of open relationship, back in the 1970s, 68 percent of gay men and 34 percent of lesbians agreed to forgo monogamy, at least under some circumstances. But in the early 2000s that number was 43 percent for gay men and 5 percent for lesbians. At the other end of the spectrum, the rates of people saying "under no circumstances is it alright," went up: For all groups—including straight and gay—the numbers doubled from 43 to 80 percent. For gay men, the numbers tripled—from 13 to 44 percent. Two things are interesting about these results: First, people are staking out more conservative positions. What people actually do may vary considerably from their reported attitudes, but these changes, especially for same-sex couples, are a dramatic shift that suggests that the culture of couplehood in some ways overtakes the culture of being gay, or lesbian, or straight, and that people are more conservative sexually. The second matter of interest is that couples are having explicit, direct conversations about the threat of nonmonogamy more so than in the past. Where notions of monogamy and committed sexuality were implicit in the past, increasingly people recognize that they have to talk about their own expectations, that they can take things for granted (Schrock 2009).

For a person who discovers that a partner has betrayed his or her (explicit or implicit) understanding about fidelity, or for a person contemplating an extramarital affair despite his or her committed relationship, the general statistics are not too important. As we reported, some gay men and fewer lesbians have negotiated an agreement that outside sex is possible under discreet and limited circumstances, but the vast majority of married and cohabiting heterosexuals do not. Still, couples in the study above are more likely to talk about it, rather than make assumptions (Rutter 2009).

Plenty of couples still rely on the culture of couplehood to guide their expectations about monogamy. Ask most heterosexual married couples why they are monogamous, and they tend to find the question odd. The reply often is to the effect of, "Why get married, if you don't want to be monogamous?" or, "a marriage is built on exclusivity and trust." Quite a few people would quote scripture and Bible and say that adultery is a sin. End of story (Lawson 1988). In other words, marriage is fundamentally a social institution—affairs generate chaos. And yet, some people do go outside the relationship for sex and intimacy.

Why Do People Have Outside Sexual Relationships?

Whole books—entire careers, in fact—are devoted to the question of why people have affairs. How could someone betray a partner? As Frank Pittman (1989), a family therapist and "infidelity expert," notes, affairs are rarely about sex. Shirley Glass (2003) popularized the phrase "emotional affair" in her book *Not "Just Friends."* An emotional affair doesn't include sex, but it includes much in the way of private intimacies between lovers. Her research emphasized the complex, contemporary way that our social, professional, and intimate lives create new settings for nonmonogamy. Such affairs often start as workplace friendships, according to Glass, and become more emotionally entangled over time. So, infidelity may or may not involve sex—and explanations are complex and changing.

To understand why women have only recently been "catching up," we should recall that in many cultures and across time, a wife's infidelity has been much more harshly punished than a husband's. As a biological view of sexuality proposes, men's nonmonogamy has been considered a natural way to advance their genetic material; women's nonmonogamy undermines men's genetic investment in offspring. As a social constructionist view of sexuality proposes, women's nonmonogamy is punished as a way to control women's sexuality and fertility. In the most conservative of societies, punishment may come from religious law or current interpretations of that law to keep women from independently pursuing love, or sex in any form. In 2010, a widow was executed in Afghanistan for becoming pregnant. She was punished for having sex and not being married, and in the larger sense, for being sexual without cultural and religious permission (Sarro and Wong 2010).

Western countries also have had harsh penalties against nonmonogamy, but these have disappeared in modern times. Men were given much more license than women, of course, but looking the other way when men have affairs, however, has become less common in recent decades. During the presidency of John F. Kennedy in the early 1960s, journalists had a tacit agreement to ignore his many extramarital liaisons. Thirty years later—after the sexual revolution, the divorce revolution, and the crises of herpes and AIDS—a public figure's infidelities are seized on with gusto by the media. During his campaign for election in 1992, Bill Clinton was hounded by stories of his affairs. His presidency was marked by massive public attention because of his affair with a White House intern. Far from discreet, the discussion revolved obsessively around a semen-stained blue dress. By 2008, then New York governor Eliot Spitzer's affair revelations included information about his sexual tastes and the fact that he wore socks to bed. Notably, this was not considered "too much information" (Rutter 2011). This shift seems to have less to do with changing morality (affairs like these had been happening in the past) than with changing permission to talk about sex. The details of public figures' illicit sexual escapades is grist for the public's taste for prurient sexual tales. And marital infidelity is considered an easy "example" of bad character.

Of course, infidelity is not so simple to explain. This is a difficult phenomenon to account for, but seven major reasons, culled from Lawson (1988), Pittman (1989), Jacobson and Christensen (1996), Glass (2003), and Blumstein and Schwartz (1983), merit attention.

1. Emotional incompatibility. Sometimes a marriage turns sour, but it still remains intact. Partners grow apart; they might not even like each other anymore. But they love their children or their place in the community, or they don't want to suffer the economic losses that divorce would entail. They barely communicate anymore. If they still make love, they usually do so infrequently and more for an outlet than as an expression of intimacy. People in this category may have an extended affair or one-night stand occasionally just to regain a remnant of passion or affection in their life, even though they have no intention of breaking up their family or marriage. However, some marital therapists think such an affair can also be a way to generate a "crisis" to get out of an incompatible marriage (i.e., Jacobson and Christensen 1996).

2. Boredom. Some couples look at the person they are married to and wonder, "Is this all there is?" They miss experiencing passion or being seen again for the first time and appreciated anew. Even though sexual frequency usually declines in the course of committed relationships, sexual imagination may remain lively. People who seek affairs because their sex life has become so predictable and unexciting often cite the need for "an adventure." Or they cite the need to experience some sexual act or a rendezvous that will bring romance and excitement back into their life—or into their life for the first time. In these cases, the motive for nonmonogamy may be purely recreational. The person may or may not feel guilt about such an adventure, but in many cases, it has nothing to do with the marriage. These cases have more to do with identity and how the person feels about the need to be daring and to create a new self.

3. Sexual incompatibility. Some couples care greatly for each other but have ceased to desire each other. For instance, one woman wrote to Ann Landers complaining of having had sex with her husband for over forty years just to please him. She was now tired of it and felt she shouldn't have to have sex with him anymore. She asked Ann Landers if there was some safe place men could go and exercise their desires and leave unwilling wives alone. On the other hand, a disability may make sex physically dangerous or painful. The nondisabled partner might seek privately to see others to satisfy sexual desires the spouse cannot, or no longer wishes, to accommodate. In these cases, looking for sex outside the marriage has little to do with how loving the partners feel toward each other. Although some sex therapists work on addressing sex and disability (Foley, Kope, and Sugrue 2001), there is more commonly a reticence among physicians, therapists, and their patients to formally address the capacities and concerns about the sexuality of the disabled and to work on how to have sex when a person has a disability.

4. Anger. For many people, nonmonogamy is a way of punishing the partner for emotional slights (Lawson 1988). People who feel unloved or neglected rationalize that they have the right to seek solace elsewhere. Anger makes extramarital sex more likely in two ways: It makes making love to your partner difficult, thereby fueling a sense of deprivation; it also makes having sex outside the relationship seem like a good way to get even, especially when a direct approach is seen as impossible or ineffective. Partners who feel like they don't have the power to change things (and these might more often be women, because overall more women than men have less power in their relationship) do things in private as a secret, but satisfying, retaliation. Anger also reduces the guilt or shame of infidelity: "He treats me like dirt. I don't owe him anything."

5. Flattery (power/beauty). Sometimes nothing is wrong with the marriage. Instead, the attentions of an attractive or successful person are just too flattering to resist. The attentions of a worthy suitor may be especially tempting for someone whose self-esteem is low, especially if the spouse doesn't treat the person as attractive or exciting. The temptation is magnified if the suitor is someone the person could not have dreamed would have wanted her or him. But people who are in good relationships and who have good self-esteem can still sometimes end up having a fling or even a full-blown affair if tempted by an especially attractive, flattering person.

6. A way out. Some affairs are begun so that they can be found out and break up the relationship. A husband comes home with lipstick on his collar; he says he's someplace that he's not and knows his wife will check; or the girlfriend picks up the phone at the hotel. Many such stupid mistakes are meant to happen. Engineering a situation that will make the spouse angry is an indirect way to back out of a marriage, but it isn't rare. People who use it can't quite make up their minds to leave or can't face talking to their partners. It is easier to allow themselves to be "discovered." Occasionally, they use this method to see if their partner still loves them, if the other person will want to save the relationship, but more often they use it to bring things to the boiling point.

7. Love. Sometimes affairs are based on "true love." Probably the most common circumstance is that two people who have been thrown together a lot start out as friends and then progress to much more. Two co-workers who have been on the same team for years, learning to respect each other and like each other and trust each other, may easily fall in love (Glass and Wright 1992). Affairs between colleagues may occur when the primary relationship is satisfactory as well as when things aren't going so well at home. Or neighbors or people in the same friendship circle may learn to depend on and care for each other. Occasionally, "love at first sight" prompts an affair. Those affairs more rarely turn into the kind of relationship that lasts a lifetime. But some people who suddenly fall in love believe that they have met their "soul mate." No matter what the affair does to their home life, family, or marriage, they feel they cannot afford to let this new person go. One might guess that love would most often be the basis for an affair for women, for whom love is so important; paradoxically, some research suggests that love might be a more important motive for men's affairs. Although women are expected to have sex only when they are in love, and women's reports of sex and romance often are consistent with this social rule, men appear more likely to be "true" romantics than women (Rubin 1976) and more willing to throw away everything for love. Women are often less economically and socially independent than men and cannot disregard the financial and social upheaval such a love affair represents. They might fall in love but decide they cannot leave.

Is Nonmonogamy Gendered?

When it comes to extramarital affairs, the double standard persists in two ways: frequency and the meaning of an affair. Men and women realize different benefits and costs for sex outside the relationship, which explain why men still report being slightly freer than women to have affairs. Some men's freedom to be sexually aggressive and recreational guarantees that, at least in the heterosexual world, they would have more extramarital sex than women. Remember that the concept of adultery has historically applied only to women. Only in modem times, in some countries, has it been defined as a male trespass.

Women, on the other hand, have rarely had the standing to complain about their partner's behavior. Men's sexual acts outside the marriage may be considered deplorable, but they have never been seen, until quite recently and in only a few Western countries, as a great trespass. Even today in Western society some people wink at what they consider the built-in male sexual appetite but scowl and become punitive when a woman engages in extramarital sex. U.S. law no longer allows men to shoot nonmonogamous wives with impunity—but it used to! Depending on the judge, a wife's sexual trespass can modify an abusive or murderous husband's sentence. In a 1995 case in

Texas, the judge gave a lighter-than-expected sentence to a man who killed his wife after catching her with another man. The case gained notoriety when the judge said he was sorry to have to give this guy any jail time at all.

Women are less likely to have sex outside the marriage, but the reasons are unromantic. First, they are simply more economically insecure than men. They fear losing economic support for their children and therefore have more conservative attitudes about sexuality. Second, women tend to be raised with a concern for "reputation," which influences their appeal to men. Third, most women have been trained to be champions of family values, and their sexuality has been geared to that responsibility. Indeed, women are more religious than men, and this difference seems to be associated with parental status: a woman who is a married parent and also religious will have those factors play a role in their behavior, too. Finally, women tend to be more vulnerable to sexually transmitted disease than heterosexual men are. "Free spirits," women who are able to think of sex in recreational terms and who are financially capable of absorbing any fallout from their behavior, are rare, particularly among the married.

Both women and men still have powerfully strong feelings against nonmonogamy, which are linked in part to the family values movement. Although repressive sexual norms tend to control women's sexuality more than men's, this control is cast as a benefit to family stability, which in turn tends to be in the interest of women who are more likely to be caretakers of any children. Concern for fidelity, however, is certainly treated as a benefit to families. Thus, on the one hand, concern for marital fidelity tends to benefit women, who are less likely to have affairs and more likely to suffer economically if a marriage breaks up. On the other hand, such conservatism casts women as the stakeholders of virtue, fidelity, and family values, and this undermines a profeminist, sex-positive attitude that promotes women's independence and autonomy.

The Problem of Sustained Desire in a Divorce-Prone Society

Seattle novelist Tom Robbins begins *Still Life with Woodpecker* (1980) with a monologue about the Last-Quarter-of-the-Twentieth-Century Blues. "There is only one serious question. And that is: *Who knows how to make love stay?*" (4). More than ever before, marriage and committed relationships have become the center of intimacy and self-fulfillment. Nevertheless, long-term relationships become somewhat habituated and less sexually alluring. Many become downright mundane. In previous eras, this development didn't mean a whole lot. People stayed married no matter what. Gay people, having fewer ways in other times to meet new partners, were more likely to stay together once they found someone—fearing that they might never meet other appropriate people.

But now the centrality of sex in U.S. culture makes it hard for people to ignore a lack of sexual excitement, and this expectation exists to different degrees throughout our lives. People are told that sex is at the center of identity and a good measure of relationship quality. They believe this is their right. When sex starts to wane, spouses feel they have to find some way to either reinvigorate their sexual relationship or recast the meaning of their marriage. Otherwise, one or both partners grow dissatisfied, worried that an important part of life is being truncated, worried that vital emotional rights are being trespassed, worried that the lesser quality or quantity of sex has dire implications for the relationship's viability.

Given the sexualization of contemporary culture, people who have grown up in it have a great deal of trouble making sex a secondary consideration. People who matured prior to the sexual revolution have less trouble with the concept—partly because, with age, their sexual needs have moderated, but also because they married under different norms, values, and expectations.

We shouldn't be surprised that even though the norm of monogamy and the belief in the sanctity of marriage is still strongly held, trespasses occur. We have made much of marriage as a joining of the flesh as well as the spirit. And if trends that render men and women more sexually and emotionally similar have tamed men's right to roam, so have these trends raised women's freedom to do so. The anonymous quality of city life and jobs, the rise of the workplace as a place to encounter potential lovers, even the invention of the Internet create possibilities for women's and men's participation in extramarital sex that have never existed before. Opportunity plus an ideology of the right to sexual pleasure in marriage make extramarital sex almost a certainty for some number of people in our society.

The challenge, as we mentioned at the beginning of this chapter, is to find a way to live a sensual life that is also as committed as both partners want it to be. Sexuality, burdened by gendered sexual scripts, can slow down, leading partners to romantic alternatives. But it doesn't have to, and we are optimistic that some committed relationships are making progress out of gendered sexual scripts. While sexual imagination gets spurred on daily everywhere in the world, there is still the question of how to engage that sexual spark in marriage. Though same-sex couples have multiple ways they challenge sexual scripts, with the rise of same-sex marriage, this is a puzzle for gay as well as straight, committed pairs. Partners who are able to acknowledge and communicate about their complex, diverse, and outwardly focused sexual desires may be better equipped for the kind of honesty that a sexually energized marriage requires.

Peer Marriage: Love between Equals

As we have discussed, marriage reinforces gendered norms and conventions. But it need not do so. Does marriage also have the possibility to "undo" gendered social norms and conventions? (Risman 2004) Although social norms are resistant to change, we offer a hopeful vision.

As we see it, the dilemma of unfulfilled sexual promise in marriage has much to do with the typical absence of equality in marriage. Power imbalance is at the heart of the enactment of gender difference; indeed, marital therapy researchers observe that such imbalances are central to marital conflict (Jacobson 1989). However, marriage need not be the centerpiece of the institutionalization of gender difference. Research on egalitarian marriage, or peer marriage (Schwartz 1994), illustrates that the potential for power sharing, obligation sharing, and resource sharing in marriage is real, though not commonly enacted. Pairs with the ambition of egalitarianism often fall short, into the "near peer" category, but a few are making it. The typical scenario is the couple who believes in equality but doesn't quite achieve it. Usually, the husband "helps" his wife with the children more, and the woman "helps" her husband make economic decisions. The husband still does the major earning, and the woman still is primary parent and support staff to the family.

In peer marriage, couples have organized their emotional, sexual, economic, and parenting functions with the idea that there are no prescribed jobs or responsibilities. The key to happiness, they believe, is to experience together, and in much the same way, all things the marriage needs to accomplish. The model—whether characterized as coparenting, job sharing, or acting as a parenting and working team—is not impossible, although it is still rare. Couples who are coprincipals of their own firm and who bring their child to work with them so that they can both give care may not be ordinary, but they do exist. These couples typically have a high level of companionship, mutual respect, and a notably minimal amount of anger. Equity has its rewards.

The gendered equality and power differences of marriage and intimate relationships can influence sexual and other social practices within marriage (like housework). But peer marriages are resolutely different sexually and socially from nonegalitarian pairing. Thus, there are few examples for couples to follow, and special attention must be given to creating and sustaining shared domestic and economic responsibility. The social world tends to reinforce traditional couples far more than nontraditional and peer marriages.

Although peer marriages are not particularly common, studying these couples helps us predict social change. The prediction is the following: Where gendered power differences are minimized and committed partnerships—whether heterosexual or same-sex—use equality rather than difference as the governing principle, then satisfaction, shared sexual roles, and commitment can be better sustained. It may be that passion still diminishes over time in such a relationship. After all, if passion is often inflamed by tension, fear, uncertainty, and the desire to bridge gaps between people, then equitable marriages will be less passionate. But that doesn't mean they will be less sexually satisfying. What remains is the desire to give and receive pleasure and love—which is more likely to continue when the relationship is reciprocal in all other ways. Equity in a sexual relationship, like equity in the rest of the relationship, is about comradeship, which might sound a little less than exciting at first blush but is really the highest and best hope for a union to last fifty years or more.

At this point, our prediction is yet to be thoroughly tested. The peer marriages that have been studied (Schwartz 1994) had greater satisfaction, but they had less frequent sex than couples in near peer marriages, and far less than couples in traditional marriages. However, the partners were more balanced on initiation, and there was more experimentation and variety in sexual acts. For example, women in peer marriages were "on top" more than women in traditional relationships. Both men and women in peer marriages said that when one of them did refuse, it was not mistaken for a rejecting gesture; this meant that there were fewer angry and distancing responses. The reduced passion characteristic of peer marriages seems to relate to the burdens of everyday life (which all kinds of couples are subject to), intense work schedules, and perhaps the way sexual imaginations and desires are shaped by our culture. The sexual imagery that people are raised with nearly always includes gender differences in power and social position. Even in an egalitarian marriage, participants continue to be constrained by the sexual traditions that are part of U.S. culture. Even when the mind says, "I want to find a person who regards me as an equal and does a fair share of everything," the erotic internal script might say, "I want to be 'swept away'" or "I like it when I feel strong and competent and my partner feels helpless and innocent." In time, as these old scripts fade, new imagery may become most exciting. For example, athletic, fit women are possible sex objects to men who also believe in physical fitness, even though such an image of female beauty has probably not existed before in modern history. Or people may fantasize about closing a business deal together rather than taking care of someone or being taken care of. When such images become popular, we predict, passion will increase in peer marriages—perhaps surpassing passion in traditional marriage.

Interest in Schwartz's vision has increased. In the time since her research in the 1990s, men and women have come to share more domestic and economic responsibilities, yet the pattern persists. In the 2000s, Janet Gornick and Marcia Meyers transformed this view into a specific policy recommendation for dual-earner, dual-career families. They recommend social policies that create the opportunity not just for women to participate equally in earning, but also create incentives for men to participate equally in caring (Gornick and Meyers 2005).

Conclusion

Heterosexual marriage is a special category of intimate relationship; as it exists currently it seems to hinge on and amplify gender difference. Even as gender differences are diminishing, attachment to gender differences in marriage is a key to explaining much of the intense feeling that characterizes opposition to same-sex marriage. The reason persisting gender difference is a problem isn't a theoretical one, because gender difference tends to mean real-world power differences. Men and women do not simply have different rules they're expected to play by when it comes to sex in marriage or infidelity or the use of force in intimate relationships. Men and women have different levels of power and different privileges in the social structure. The strategy that we think best for enhancing sexuality within marriage and intimate relationships is not to erase sexuality, but instead to minimize power differences—socially, economically, politically—and create diverse new ways to experience sex in long-term relationships.

5

The Politics of Sexuality

Sex as a "Political Football"

SEXUALITY IN THE UNITED STATES is a political football. Sides team up, there's little compromise, and people love to watch the competition. There are dozens of examples of high-profile sex scandals of the rich, famous, or powerful, and no level of fame, money, or prestige protects anyone any more. Not so long ago, in 1991, one of our sitting Supreme Court justices, Clarence Thomas, went through a high-stress nomination hearing in which sex was at the center of the debate. Thomas, one of the youngest-ever nominees to the Supreme Court, is a political conservative who had advanced to the heights of jurisprudence despite the disadvantages of being raised very poor in south Georgia. But the hearing captured the country's attention because it focused on detailed allegations of sexual harassment. Law professor and former Thomas staff member Anita Hill reported that he had created a hostile work environment, with sexual innuendos and other unwelcome and professionally humiliating remarks. For example, she testified that he remarked to her that a hair in his soft drink might be a pubic hair. The allegation was one among many that demonstrated a pattern of Thomas's inappropriate sexual conduct and improper advances that undermined Professor Hill's job performance and promotions. U.S. senators, on national television, invited the country to contemplate the significance of mentioning pubic hair. This case was a consciousness-raising event for the whole country. New policies and statutes emerged in businesses and in government, and a new vocabulary for sexual issues in the workplace emerged.

But this episode had a striking downside. It humiliated almost everyone involved as political and media forces seized on the story and gave it around-the-clock coverage. The subject provided titillation that exceeded anyone's concern for sexual harassment in the workplace. For many, this bizarre scene also pitted race against gender. Even in 2007, Thomas's memoir reflected his personal bitterness about this event (Toobin 2007). Thomas was among the few African Americans at the time who had surmounted many economic and cultural obstacles to climb to such heights in government. Although his politics are dissimilar to the more liberal views held by many African Americans, his accomplishment was still an affirmation of black achievement in the historically racist United States. Anita Hill, who is also African American, found herself the "poster woman" for feminist outrage about men's many trespasses against women in—and out of—the workplace. Ultimately, many people felt the incident was a lose-lose situation. Thomas was confirmed amid skepticism, Hill's integrity was a matter of brutal public debate, and the gulf between men and women was confirmed in most people's minds. The popular image was a cartoonish, "he said, she said" split-screen reality. The skepticism and damage was so great that nearly two decades after the events, in October 2010, Thomas's wife, Virginia Thomas, telephoned Hill to ask for an "apology"; such a call emphasized how intense the pain of the episode was and how intense was the popular capacity to retain a he-said, she-said, woman-blaming narrative about the sexual harassment case. Such cartoons reflect a kind of de facto essentialism that assumes men and women are not only dramatically different but also that their interests are dramatically and *naturally* conflicting. This assumption, sometimes made strongly, sometimes weakly, dominates much of the politics of sexuality.

Newer Sex Scandals, Newer Themes

Have times moved on? The late 2000s have delivered a veritable flood of political sex scandals—but do they continue to illustrate this kind of "gulf" between men and women? Or is there something else at stake that has come along? Scan the newspaper, and you'll see multiple stories relating to sex scandals and the private sexual lives of public people. Sex sells. Political candidates use various sex scandals ("unfaithful husbands"; "sexual predators") to build a political base and, if possible, to make opponents look immoral. Let's take a look.

In spring 2008, the then-governor of New York, Eliot Spitzer, was caught visiting a high-priced prostitute at the Mayflower Hotel in Washington D.C. Spitzer, who had been an activist prosecutor against corruption on Wall Street earlier in the decade, resigned, with his wife stoically, but loyally, at his side. A year later network television featured a dramatic series featuring Julianna Margulies as *The Good Wife*. The plot seemed directly drawn from the Spitzer real-life drama. In this weekly show, the wife is strong, loyal, and building her own successful career. She remains married to her husband, who had been jailed based on corruption charges and who is in the doghouse with her based on his diverse and unfolding infidelities. The series shows her as shrewd, earnest, and continually processing the betrayals of her fallen husband. It also shows her flirting with the possibility of her own extramarital affair. In real life, Spitzer remains married and has a new career as a television news interviewer.

South Carolina's married governor, Mark Sanford, had a long-distance affair with a woman from Argentina that was exposed when he was unreachable for five days in 2009. He had told his staff to tell anyone who asked that he was "hiking the Appalachian trail." In fact, he had flown to Buenos Aires for what, as he explained in excruciating detail once discovered, was a tenderhearted farewell. When the truth came out, Sanford made claims that his lover was his soul mate but that he was trying as hard as he could to fall back in love with his wife. Mrs. Sanford was not impressed; she did not elect to stand by her man and instead initiated divorce proceedings and published a memoir. For several seasons to follow, the phrase "hiking the Applachian trail" became a fond euphemism for having clandestine sex.

Senator Larry Craig (Idaho) made headlines in 2007 when he was arrested in a Minnesota airport bathroom for sexual solicitation. According to the arresting officer, Senator Craig had "peered through a crack in a restroom stall door for two minutes and made gestures suggesting to the officer he wanted to engage in 'lewd conduct.'" After the story leaked that he had pled guilty to disorderly conduct, he recanted his plea. The senator said that his actions were misinterpreted and that he simply had a "wide stance" in the restroom. Flanked by his wife, Senator Craig proclaimed his innocence and his heterosexuality, and he persisted in his political support for antigay legislation. For months following the episode, "wide stance" was a favorite comic punch line. He has bowed out of politics and remains married.

Yet another senator, John Ensign from Nevada, had an affair with a staffer, who was the wife of a close friend—and another employee. The story had many twists and turns, including payoffs from Senator Ensign's parents and efforts to get the former staffer a job. The story came out in 2009, in fact, because the couple felt that Senator Ensign was not living up to his behind-the-scenes promises to "rectify" the situation, and they started to share the story with the news media before Senator Ensign did so. One of the curious aspects of this episode was the role that fundamentalist religion played in the life of

Senator Ensign and how it contributed to his sense of entitlement to engage in behavior that would not be acceptable to most people. We learned that his fundamentalist colleagues, part of a group of fundamentalist Christian legislators known as "the Family" who met regularly for prayer and fellowship, sought to help him through his troubles (Sharlet 2009). His wife publicly supported him throughout these revelations, and he remains married, although he resigned his office in 2011.

One of the most colorful cases was that of the 2008 presidential hopeful and former North Carolina senator John Edwards. Positioned as an advocate for the working class, Edwards campaigned widely with his wife, attorney Elizabeth Edwards. Elizabeth Edwards was a significant part of the campaign because of her policy acumen but also because of the pathos she inspired because of her struggle with metastasizing breast cancer. Behind the scenes, as we were to discover, he was conducting an affair with his campaign videographer and new-age aficionado, Rielle Hunter. The affair emerged when the tabloid the *National Enquirer* printed a story headlined "John Edwards Love Child Scandal!" complete with photos of Edwards, Hunter, and a baby. Edwards and his wife denied the claims. Edwards stated that a campaign worker fathered the child, who was complicit in the charade until he wrote his own memoir about the events (Young 2010). In the end, Edwards was disgraced and eventually conceded the truth of the *Enquirer*'s story. While his wife stood by him early on, eventually she left him. On her subsequent book tour she did not hesitate to speak about the betrayal she felt even as she spoke with conviction about the policies that Edwards had represented as a candidate and politician. In 2011 John Edwards was charged for misusing political funds to hide his affair.

What's the common thread? Very little in these stories revolves around "women as victims" in the same way that the Clarence Thomas sexual harassment case did, or even in the way that President Bill Clinton's affair with his young intern back in the 1990s did. Although many of the cases involve a stoic wife standing by her man, the narrative has three prominent characteristics. First, we are aware of an enormous amount of **detail** of the emotional and sexual content of these stories. We know that Eliot Spitzer wore socks during sex; Mark Sanford elected to share that he had delayed doing what he called the "ultimate act" for many months in his affair; Larry Craig found describing his bathroom habits by referencing a "wide stance" as a reasonable alternative to describing his sexual customs; and John Ensign's story included descriptions of heartfelt discussions about his sexuality with some of his senate colleagues. John Edwards's story eventually included information about private sex videos made of Edwards and Hunter during her pregnancy. The level of detail seems unremarkable given the extent to which sexuality is the centerpiece of so much other media and advertising.

Despite the casual explicitness of these stories, the second characteristic is the implicit **assumption** that sexual expression outside of heterosexual marriage is *always* wrong. Wives' forbearance and loyalty provides an image of marriage's importance above all else. Even when Mrs. Sanford, the first lady of South Carolina, left her husband, it was connected to her belief in marriage—and in a Christian god. Not only do the men promptly express their dedication to marriage and tradition, and a kind of perfunctory regret about their actions, but the story is told in the media without examining what we know about nonmonogamy or unconventional sexual desires. As sex researchers, both of us were interviewed frequently about these stories. Reporters and radio call-in guests asked, "What can we do to prevent affairs?" rather than what are these situations like and what are the reasons—wholesome as well as unhealthy—that they draw our attention.

Finally, the third characteristic is especially novel: A key theme of the coverage is that these men are profoundly **foolish**. Whereas the story of Clarence Thomas was about a powerful man who behaved (allegedly) in poor taste due to an erotic obsession, and the story of Bill Clinton was about his insatiable desire along with a young woman's comical seductiveness (for example, letting the president peek at her thong), these newer political sex scandals do not focus on the fortitude of men's sexual desire but rather the adolescent weakness and foolishness of the otherwise powerful and accomplished men involved.

Does this mean that the sexual double standard has diminished? Little in these stories is about he-said/she-said. The oppositions and dichotomies that we discussed in chapter 1 that remain pervasive are less apparent. The stories include angry wives and bitter, cuckolded husbands, but the stories are not so pointedly about sex's potential for turning women into victims. The combination of explicit sexual content with implicit traditional family values means that we carry around a kind of split consciousness about sexuality. This split consciousness pairs continued uncertainty about what the rules and expectations are with a reliance on traditional roles and institutions like marriage to help us avoid thinking about harder questions (like what to do with unconventional sexual desire). But now, the women are presented as more confident, brave, and self-reliant, as in the valorizing of Mrs. Spitzer in the television show *The Good Wife*. The men in these stories are treated as weak or naïve. They are viewed as naïve because they used poor judgment in the pursuit of their desires; they were weak willed because the situations got control over them rather than their having control over their situation. But their weakness is counterbalanced with their ability (most of the time) to hold on to their traditional marriage. This is a new twist on the old "men will be men" point of view. The brave, competent wives next to their sheepish husbands provide an image, once again, of the opposition or complementarity (rather than the equality) of men and women.

We couldn't find any political sex scandals about women: not that sex isn't something used to humiliate women. As we were writing this section, a commentator remarked that Speaker of the House Nancy Pelosi had done everything "but sell her body" to pass an important piece of health care legislation. Even this sexist remark suggests significant social change: we had a woman for the first time in history as our Speaker of the House of Representatives; likewise, it was a woman commentator who made the offensive remark. Things change, but reducing women to their sexuality is still a common slur, just as is acting as if all men are emotionally ineffectual and interpersonally stupid because they are undermined by their "naturally" more intense sex drive. What gets swept under the carpet in these discussions of sexual mischief or taboo relationships is that sex and sexuality are not inherently scandalous and scandal is not the only place discussions about sex should surface. Sex can also be about pleasure.

Ambivalent Obsession

"In the U.S., sex tends to be treated as a special topic, and there is much ambivalence: sex is romantic, but also sinful and dirty; it is flaunted but also something to be hidden. . . ." argued a sex researcher twenty-five years ago (Jones et al. 1985:59). The arguments continue to get repeated (Weeks 2009), and this "ambivalent obsession" continues to characterize sexual politics in America, as the details of the cases above suggest.

Throughout this book, you have already read quite a bit about the politics of sexuality. Politics—regarding family and individual differences, social interaction, and human bodies—influence and shape every aspect of sexuality. Though the processes can be subtle, political institutions sustain the use of gender to justify and extend the control over men's *and* women's sexuality in subtle and not-so-subtle ways. The expression "war between the sexes," for instance, implies that blame for a social problem can generally be placed on one gender or the other. From our view, it is a strategy for avoiding looking at structural forces that create dilemmas for men and women.

In 2009, we saw the publication of *The Shriver Report*, a book that reported that Americans have left the "war between the sexes" behind. The authors observed that Americans have come to recognize the important and permanent role women have in the workforce and as earners for their families. Policies that respond to this reality—such as equal pay for equal work, paid sick leave and family leave—are not yet part of the political or economic landscape.

Even in the health care reform debate a major feature of the new system was the prevention of any federal funding for access to abortion—and included the prevention of any subsidies to families that might purchase a private insurance plan that reimburses for abortion. A blogger at Talking Points Memo humorously wrote, "What would happen if a few female members of the House put in (or merely proposed) an amendment to the health care bill which stated that men would be barred by law from purchasing health insurance which covered Viagra, all hair-growth medications or procedures or transplants, etc.?" (Kurtz 2009).

Politics and Women's Bodies

So even as our sense of equality has changed, a large part of the politics of sex and gender continues to involve controlling women's bodies. Curiously, one of women's few resources, historically, has been their sexuality. When women are obliged to protect this resource, they are treated as if their sexuality is what's most valuable to them as well as to fathers, husbands, and other men in their lives. There is a self-confirming stereotype at play here—that is, a stereotype that gets validated because its prevalence requires that stereotyped individuals conform to the social expectation. As such women are cast as sexual objects and then must build a culture around defending their identity. Throughout this book, we have told the story of women either needing to worry about their virtue (as traditional rules of sexuality dictate) or waging a sexual revolution to obtain sexual and other kinds of freedom (as second-wave feminists did in the 1960s and 1970s). In other words, sexual politics keeps including struggles over how and when women get to use their bodies, how men get access to women's bodies, how women's bodies ought to look, and whether or not women get to determine their own fertility. This chapter discusses two contemporary political issues that clearly involve women's control over their own bodies: teen sexuality and sexual assault. The core of the third issue discussed in this chapter, same-sex marriage, also involves beliefs about bodies, but it is slightly different. It draws our attention to the links between gender and sexuality and reminds us that we have a political and cultural system that seeks to control women and men and limit their ways of self-expression. Same-sex marriage is an important issue in contemporary sexual politics, in part because it disturbs the long tradition that calls for gender difference as fundamental to romantic and marital unions.

Debates Past and Present

Public debate—and media sensationalism—over sexuality is not new. In fact, public debate about sexuality in North America is older than the United States.

Every era has had its own definitions of sexual deviance and its own punishments. During the colonial era, sexual sinners were taken to court, humiliated or physically punished in public, and neighbors were encouraged to spy on one another to denounce misdeeds to a panel of "judges." Any sexual activity that ventured beyond marital sex for procreative purposes was stigmatized and sometimes given harsh penalties.

During the nineteenth century, Post Office Special Agent Anthony Comstock used Congress and the newspapers to rally popular and political support for his antipornography campaign. His target was any advertisement or advice regarding contraception. Women's movements of the period, including the social purity and women's suffrage movements (D'Emilio and Freedman 1988), rallied support for Comstock. Today, this looks like an odd alliance, but in its time the two movements shared a view that women's sexuality would undermine her ability to be a respected citizen and valued partner in the society of the time. Both movements believed that sexual images, including those related to contraception, would demean women and that if procreation were not a possible consequence of sexual activity, women would be victims of more frequent sexual demands from their spouses. This logic presumed that women, deprived of the fear of pregnancy as an excuse to abstain from intercourse, would have no acceptable reason to say no to sex.

As a "moral entrepreneur" waging a values-based popular movement, Comstock was enormously effective; the United States criminalized all access to and discussion of birth control from 1873 until 1936, when the anticontraception provisions of the Comstock law were finally rescinded. Sexually suggestive images hardly disappeared, however, even during Comstock's era, and movies and advertisements frequently used sex to sell consumer goods in the early part of the twentieth century.

Other antipornography groups organized to ban portrayals of sexuality, and in the 1930s, the Legion of Decency, led by the Catholic Church, campaigned against "indecency" in the movies. A poster from the early 1930s commanded faithful Catholics to protest movies such as *The Trumpet Blows* (1934), about a matador and a bandit competing for the same woman. The poster advised, "The absolutely unwholesome and unattractive George Raft is the 'hero,' loose in his relationship with women and a thorough no-account. . . . It is unfit for any decent person to see or approve. . . . Protest to Paramount Studios, Hollywood, California. Protest to George Raft, same address" (*Time* 1934). In this period, Hollywood adopted many of its rules and rating systems (D'Emilio and Freedman 1988). Clearly, the United States has a history of suppressing sexual imagery that some groups consider pornography only to find sexuality expressing itself in new ways and in new places, to be subject to conservative suppression yet again.

In recent decades, other controversies have taken center stage. For example, the ongoing demonstrations for and against abortion and the shocking assassinations of physicians and other personnel who provide abortion services have persisted from the early 1990s into the late 2000s. The issues have been framed as fetal rights versus women's rights. Who benefits from this perspective? For the political right, the issue devolves into a litany of blame for women who seek abortions and demonizes physicians who help them. Meanwhile, the political left presents images of women victimized first by the lack of easily administered, safe, and automatic birth control methods and, second, when birth control fails, by their harassment at abortion clinics. Politicians take their pro- or antichoice positions, and women's bodies and their sexuality become the subject of heated and sensational debate. But less is actually done to improve access to birth control, to improve sex education for teens and communication between men and women, to empower women sexually, or to train men to take more responsibility for the consequences of their sexual acts.

In the controversy over gays and lesbians in the military, national security is pitted against nonheterosexual desire and behavior. In 1993, the United States passed the "Don't Ask Don't Tell" policy that was then President Clinton's way of compromising these two sides. The policy, which has been in effect for eighteen years, mandated the discharge of openly gay, lesbian, or bisexual members of the U.S. armed services. The policy supposedly protected gay service people—if they were closeted. In theory, if a gay person didn't "tell," the policy suggested, the military wouldn't "ask." This theory, however, didn't seem to work. Many gay people who were not voluntarily "out" were still hounded out of the military. The policy persisted despite studies (National Defense Research Institute 1993) demonstrating that unit cohesion, morale, military readiness, or national security are not affected negatively by openly gay people serving.

The costs of this policy in the first ten years were estimated to range between 190 million to 364 million dollars (Korb 2009). Throughout the 2000s reports arose year in and year out about highly skilled and very scarce Middle East specialists who were ejected from their military service for being openly gay. In other words, for as long as this policy has been maintained, it has in practice meant a preference for avoiding open homosexuality over a preference for the military's efficiency or efficacy.

But feelings and beliefs change. By 2006, three in four service members reported being comfortable with someone who is gay or lesbian (Zogby International 2006), and one in four reported knowing someone in their unit who is gay or lesbian. Census reports indicated that sixty-five thousand service members and one million veterans are gay. The public overwhelmingly accepted the idea of gays serving openly in the military, including majorities of conservatives and churchgoers.

This brings us back to sexuality as a political football: the story of enormous progress and change in attitudes reached a crescendo when in 2008 a socially liberal Democrat, Barack Obama, was elected president of the United States. Obama pledged to repeal "Don't Ask Don't Tell." By fall 2010, the U.S. House of Representatives passed legislation to move repeal forward. Also in fall 2010, a federal judge ordered a ban on the "Don't Ask Don't Tell" policy—but the White House continued to disagree. So, two years after Obama's election, "Don't Ask Don't Tell" has remained in place. The reason? Not attitudes. Not evidence. The reason was politics. In December 2010, the Senate finally voted to repeal, and Obama signed the law. Yet through more bureaucratic delays, debates, and foot dragging, final halt to Don't Ask Don't Tell occurred in September 2011.

In all these polarized debates over sex, we wonder, is there room for the private experience of sexual pleasure? Or is sex necessarily part of a political tug-of-war over traditional forms of gender and a rigid link between gender and sexuality? Does this ambivalence about sexuality ultimately reflect a collective ambivalence about sexuality as a source of pleasure? Some observers and pundits continue to use gender as a tool for pathologizing youthful sexual expression. Others seek to increase autonomy in sexual expression and to enhance tolerance for sexual diversity. To explore this further, we turn to our first issue, teenage sexuality, with the observation that true progress has occurred in this arena even though it has become a favorite political football.

Teenage Sexuality, Hooking Up, and Emerging Adulthood

The publication of the Kinsey reports in 1948 and again in 1953 stimulated anxiety in a number of ways, but one important source of public stress was the fear that the books would promote youthful, unconventional, nonmarital sexual experimentation. And, although it had little to do with the Kinsey publications, teens have embarked on sexualized lives earlier and with greater freedom in the past. They have also embarked on sexual careers, and reported about it, with greater equality across genders. Men and women's sexual histories are increasingly similar today. In the 1940s and early 1950s, Kinsey reported that fewer than 6 percent of American women had had sex by age sixteen—but 21 percent of American men said they had had sex by age sixteen. As you can see in figure 5.1, by 2002, nearly half of all teens (46 percent) had had sex at least once (Abma et al. 2004). Where we had widely different rates of sexual experience reported by men versus women in the past, today there's no gender gap.

Things have changed for teens—and they've changed a lot more for women than for men. So . . . what's all the fuss? Is it about teen sexuality—or about women becoming as frank and sexually active as men? Adult

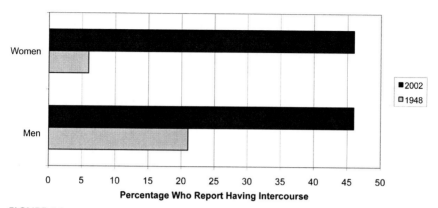

FIGURE 5.1
Changes in percentage of teens who report sexual experience. Data from Kinsey et al. (1948; 1953) and Abma (2004).

commentary has labeled teen sexuality as impulsive, irresponsible, and a narcissistic trend that is out of control, but the alarm would seem to be associated with the greater increase in women's—not men's—sexual freedom. Could it be that teens are demonized as morally wayward because women have been admitting to engaging in sex at levels that are increasingly similar to men's? The persistent "gender gap" in acceptance of women's and men's sexuality is what we have referred to as the double standard. Worry about women's sexuality continues to be about teen pregnancy, but as those rates have declined, additional worry has focused on contemplating whether the newest trend of "hooking up" has different consequences for men than for women. The answer to that question is complicated, as we discuss below. The larger message is this: The worry itself serves to keep a diminished sexual double standard alive and kicking.

The double standard is not the only contradiction attending teen sexuality. Teens may be having sex earlier, but they did not create the seductive adult clothing made for preteens or the ad campaigns with seductive thirteen-year-olds. Calvin Klein and Anthropologie ads for jeans, T-shirts, fragrance, and a host of other seductive images present teens as having the sexy bodies that "everybody" wants. From here, contradictions multiply. On the one hand, prosecutors press statutory rape charges on behalf of girls who look thirty but are in fact fifteen. On the other, the culture urges those same young girls to be as sexy as they can and tells fashion models they are over the hill at twenty-one. Our vision of sexiness is essentially based on the barely pubescent body, and yet the barely pubescent body is taboo.

While worry about teen sexuality has been around for most of the twentieth century and earlier (see Mintz 2004), two big trends are especially important in the twenty-first century. One is the phenomenon of **hooking up**. While teens have been having casual sex and nonformal "dating" since at least the 1970s (Bogle 2008), the phenomenon of "hooking up" refers to junior high school, high school, and college-aged people who engage in sexual encounters that are *not* part of any kind of defined relationship, beyond, perhaps, being "friends with benefits" (Denizet-Lewis 2004). Since "hooking up" started to be covered in the media under that phrase it has been a specific target for parents, politicians, and educators to focus on when they are wringing their hands about "kids today." The rates for college student hookups give us some context and offer a puzzle. Hooking up tends to be understood as anything "ranging from kissing to having sex" (Glenn and Marquardt 2001:13). The Online College Social Life Survey (introduced in chapter 2) found that 72 percent of fourteen thousand men and women from nineteen colleges and universities reported at least one college hookup by their senior year in college. Two in five engaged in three or fewer hookups, another two in five engaged in four to nine hookups, and the remainder had at least ten hookups, as you can see in figure 5.2 (Armstrong, England, and Fogarty 2010). Here's the tricky thing: does this tell us that a lot of intercourse is happening? No, given the widely ranging definitions of hooking up. But it does tell us something about sexual exploration and its presence in the lives of teens.

With the rise of "hooking up," some researchers have examined whether it is a site for doing gender the same way that other sexual patterns have been. An examination of the Online Social Life "hooking up" data showed that the

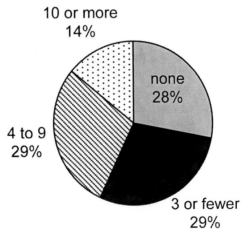

FIGURE 5.2
How often do college students hook up? Data from Armstrong et al. (2010).

double standard may be found elsewhere in terms of what people are *doing* sexually. As discussed in chapter 3, researchers asked, "Who has orgasms in hookups and relationships?" and found that whether in a first-time hookup or a relationship, men had more orgasms. The gap narrowed when people were reporting on dating relationships, or serial hookup relationships. Similarly, men were much more likely than women to be the only ones to receive oral sex in a first hookup (Armstrong et al. 2010). We can speculate that this relates to skills (as the investigators' qualitative interviews suggested) or social permission to enjoy sex, or socially learned preferences for what different people like to do. The hooking-up studies also indicate that men and women report finding their encounters pleasurable at a more similar rate; just not similarly orgasmic. Finally, other research shows that hooking up is not correlated with psychological distress any more or less than sex in a committed relationship—or no sex at all (Eisenberg et al. 2009). The same study found that more men than women reported having casual sex—but there weren't gender differences in terms of any harms or benefits. So, the empirical differences in behavior suggest that doing sex still ends up being different for men than for women even in the seemingly liberated setting of college hookups.

The second big trend is the phenomenon of **emerging adulthood** (Arnett 2006)—or the extension of adolescence well into the twenties. (Some scholars refer to it as "transition to adulthood.") Adolescence is new enough. But emerging adulthood extends adolescence and takes a surprising and unfamiliar form (to many adults). During emerging adulthood young people are less focused on "settling down"—either in a relationship or in a job—and are more likely to explore different relationships through cohabitation, trying out different jobs, and extending their years of education (when they can). Emerging adulthood can last until twenty-six or even thirty years old. In connection with this, sexual panic has widened, for example, with concern about unwanted pregnancies among women in their twenties, as well as in their teens (see for example "The Fog Zone" at the National Campaign to Prevent Teen and Unwanted Pregnancy). So, while the rate of unplanned pregnancy has declined in the population at large, and has declined considerably among teens, the rate of unplanned pregnancy among women in their twenties has increased in recent years (as illustrated in figure 5.3).

Recall the demographic changes that created the sexual revolution in the 1960s and 1970s? They involved greater prosperity, more men and women attending college, and greater cultural permission to explore diverse relationships and approaches to sexuality. In the twenty-first century the rise of emerging adulthood as a new life stage is a consequence of the necessity for more schooling for students to get ahead and the high cost of education without economic supports to help pay for it.

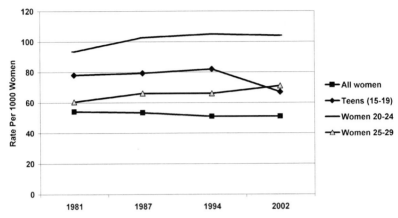

FIGURE 5.3
Unplanned pregnancy rates in the United States, 1981–2002. Adapted from Henshaw (1998) and Finer and Henshaw (2006).

The combination of these two trends (hooking up and emerging adulthood) has consequences for health *and* for intimacy. Young people, who live in a world of contradictory messages regarding sexuality along with a lack of support for their health and well-being, also occupy a world where intimacy is easier to accomplish than finding any structural support (jobs, funding for education) for their transition to adulthood. Sex is also more glamorized. Meanwhile, both intimacy and the business of becoming an adult lack clear definition more so than any other time in our recent past.

Adolescence and Families

Before emerging adulthood, the life stage known as **adolescence** emerged in the last century. The notion of adolescence is quite modern, and it laid the groundwork for lengthening the period of preadulthood. Not so coincidentally, teenage sexuality surfaced as a public issue just as the phase of life known as adolescence was recognized. Over the past 150 years, the age of puberty for both boys and girls has dropped from around seventeen to around eleven or twelve (Rutter 1995), as a consequence of improved health and nutrition among youth. Yet youths don't legally become adults until their late teens. This interval between puberty and adulthood is a stage of life that had not existed biologically or socially until the mid-twentieth century. Following even more social change in the second half of the twentieth century, emerging adulthood began to be identified in the 1990s and added to the uncertainty of how to treat youth or what to think about their sexuality.

A unique feature of adolescence is youths' sexual maturity without social maturity. The contrast is apparent when one observes the bedroom of a twelve-year-old girl who looks eighteen. She might still treasure stuffed animals or posters of horses or dollhouses. And yet this same child is at least partly aware of the allure she holds for boys and men, and she may be eager to test her new powers of enchantment. Not surprisingly, parents are appalled and scared at this turn of biology—especially when it comes with rebellion against the restrictions they deem appropriate for a twelve-year-old. Some psychologists have observed that the presence of a sexually mature youth living at home has itself produced tension and some negative interactions between parents and teens. Parents do not accept a teen or preteen's seductive behavior, and they often try to place restrictions on quasi-adult dress and adult freedoms. Parent's ineffectiveness at protecting their children from fast-track sexuality can cause major conflict in the household and sometimes even parental depression (Steinberg 1994). In other periods of history, a child old enough to be sexually active would be married or betrothed and out of the household. But today, youth tend to remain at home well past puberty (during emerging adulthood), often until their twenties, when they finally complete their education.

In contemporary society, because puberty comes earlier but marriage comes later, a young person may experience sexual and romantic longing with no "socially acceptable" outlet for quite a long time. As teens mature and begin to have sexual relationships, they tend to resent parental interference or constraint. Parental judgments and controls might not be too insufferable for the children (and the rebellion too difficult for the parents) if they lasted for only a short time before the launch into true independence. But many families experience severe challenges to parental authority. At the very least, parents tend to feel that when someone lives in their home, he or she needs to follow house rules, both moral and practical (such as when the kids are due home at night) (Schalet 2004). As guardians of their children, they are concerned for their teenagers' safety and well-being. And they also may find it threatening to lose control over their children. In response, adolescents tend to feel that these rules infringe on their rights as human beings to live according to their own judgments and desires.

Some teenagers respect and honor their parents' wishes. They may agree that it is in their best interest to curtail sexual desire and wait to have sex until they are older or married. Some parents may respond to teens' emerging sexual curiosity with support and the information they need to remain safe and self-confident. But other families fight about sexuality with everything they can muster. Fights can be over the new tools of texting, the Internet, Facebook, and other networking gadgets such as "smart phones." Parents can't control all of it, and sometimes, not any of it. Not surprisingly, many households with teenagers in them also harbor conflict and psychological distress.

In some families, competition between parent and child may arise. Adult insecurities can emerge as aging adults worry about being displaced as sexual beings by their younger, sexier offspring and grieve over the loss of their own youth. Some research has shown that parents of a same-sex adolescent (fathers who have a son or mothers who have a daughter) experience a decline in psychological well-being and even temporarily lose sexual interest in their spouse (Steinberg 1994).

For a variety of reasons, then, many parents in the United States become ambivalent about teen sexuality. Parents in one study showed how they were not supportive of teen sexual activity because they simply did not believe it was possible for young people to "fall in love" or have serious feelings for one another. They were more likely to respond to teen sexual activity as being about a "war between the sexes" rather than part of meaningful, close relationships that include sexual activity (Schalet 2004). Such ambivalence is present at the societal level. Teens are perceived as having great sexual opportunity and even feared or resented because of it. However, teen sex tends not to be nearly so active as adults imagine nor nearly as pleasing as sex between more experienced adults.

The State of Teen Sexual Behavior

The early onset of adolescence and the increased autonomy of young people have left teens with little guidance regarding sexuality and relationships. The consequences are serious: Teenage childbearing undermines the futures of the mothers and the children; sexually transmitted diseases (STDs) undermine hope for a healthy adulthood for many sexually active teens. In addition, a compelling body of research indicates that teen sexuality can be experienced in negative ways, undermining teens' self-esteem, and that it frequently involves coercion or harassment.

Addressing the needs of teenagers has been undermined by adults' obsessive negative attention to teen sex and neglect of most other aspects of teen life. Ironically, contrary to many popular media stories, teens aren't having a great deal of sex. Often they will try intercourse once and then not try it again until they are older (Rubin 1990). The average age of first intercourse for men and women is around seventeen; but more than two in five of teens—ages fifteen to nineteen—report having had no sex in the past year (Mosher, Chandra, and Jones 2005). Even teens who remain sexually active are generally not as active as adults, and they tend to be serially monogamous—one exclusive sexual relationship at a time—just like adults.

Much examination of youthful sexuality relates to unwanted and teen pregnancies. As discussed in chapter 3, teen pregnancy reached a generational high around 1991, fueling much panic at that time that has remained in our consciousness, even if pregnancy rates have declined. Luker (1996) reported that 11 percent of women experienced pregnancy before the age of nineteen. But in 2005 the rate had steadily declined for a decade-and-a-half to 5 percent (Guttmacher 2010). While teen pregnancy has declined significantly, our rate is higher than in any other comparable developed economy, as illustrated in figure 5.4. How does this happen? Are teens simply irresponsible? A lot of factors combine to make these unwanted pregnancies persist. For example, teens often believe that they can't get pregnant the first time they have sexual intercourse, but they can—and they do. To state the obvious, pregnancy happens to women, not men, and thus generates a not entirely helpful focus on changing teenage women's behavior rather than intervening about sexual knowledge.

Much of the concern about teen sexuality was fueled by the rise in out-of-wedlock births that started about forty years ago; it was more common among teens but increasingly so among adults, as well. When you look at figure 5.5 you can see that teen births happened a lot more often in the baby boom years of the 1950s, and have declined since then, with a short-term rise around 1990.

But the figure also shows you that while teen births declined overall, those births were increasingly likely to be to an *unmarried* teenager. Back in the 1950s teen births were much more likely to be to women who married young, as was common in that period of time. From the 1960s to the 1990s, the proportion of teenage mothers who weren't married changed from 25 percent

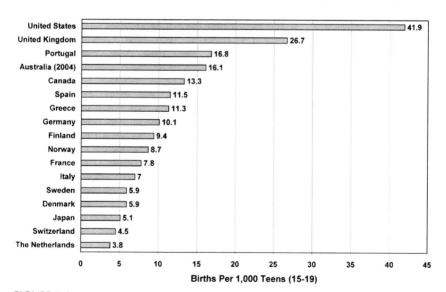

FIGURE 5.4
International comparisons: Teen birth rates. Data from United Nations Statistics Division (2006).

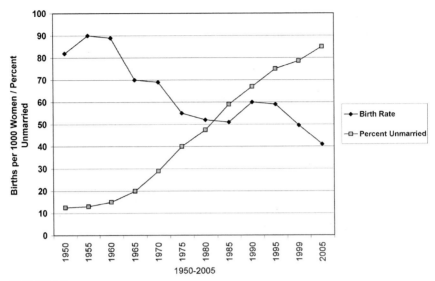

FIGURE 5.5
Births to teen women/proportion unmarried. CDC (2000; 2007).

to 75 percent of all teenage mothers (Luker 1996). This was an enormous stimulus for panic among many policymakers. Meanwhile, the trend has only continued in the same direction: while teen birthrates have declined since the early 1990s, the percentage of those births that were to unmarried women was around 85 percent in 2005 (as illustrated in figure 5.5) and was 86 percent in 2007. Meanwhile, in 2006 nearly 40 percent of *all births* were to unmarried women (at all ages)—a rate that continues to increase (CDC 2007).

In the context of growing numbers of unwed mothers, conservatives decry the perceived epidemic of teen motherhood, but the facts are more complicated. In the United States and western Europe, there has been what demographers call a major fertility transition or a substantial change in fertility rates. A fertility rate refers to the number of children born per woman (on average). The result has been a steady decline in the rate of reproduction to replacement (two children for every woman, or a fertility rate of two) or below-replacement levels (fewer than two children for every woman). As you can see in figure 5.6, in the United States, fertility has declined steadily since the early nineteenth century, with the exception of the post–World War II baby boom era. People have fewer children, causing the population of some groups—particularly better-educated, richer, and mostly white groups—actually to shrink.

As you can see, in the 1950s the rate was about three-and-a-half: by the end of the first decade of the twenty-first century, the rate was about two.

How to sum up all these trends? Teen pregnancy has declined, just like pregnancy rates in the population. Although women at all ages are having more children outside of marriage, this is especially the case among teens and even

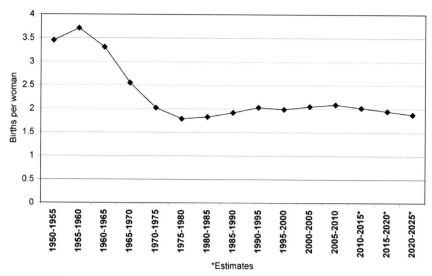

FIGURE 5.6
Changing fertility in the United States. United Nations (2008) (World Population Prospects: 2008 Revision).

people in their twenties. Keep in mind that the teens who are having babies tend to be older—eighteen or nineteen. In other words, the image of "children having children" applies to a small proportion of teenage women having babies.

Plenty of the people who are raising the alarm about teen pregnancy know that, in sheer numbers, there is no such thing as an "epidemic" of teenage pregnancy. But arousing an outcry over rising teen pregnancy rates is of political value, just as it was to Comstock in the nineteenth century. Mention teen mothers, and numerous U.S. voters start paying attention. Politicians spark citizens' outrage and use it to get votes by associating teen motherhood with welfare and casting these women as cynically producing unwanted children whom they cannot support economically.

But is the rising *proportion* of teenage mothers who are not married a legitimate cause for concern? Given U.S. policies that continue to rely on traditional marriage to solve a host of social problems, the political logic is evident. Parenthood out of wedlock used to be so stigmatized that families on both sides applied every pressure possible to make sure a woman married the father of her child. The old phrase "shotgun wedding" was real enough in some parts of the country. But the ability to compel teenagers to marry evaporated as love triumphed over more pragmatic standards for choosing a mate, such as being "a good provider" and "a solid member of society." In 2010 a national survey reported that 64 percent of teen men and 71 percent of teen women agreed that it is "OK for an unmarried female to have a child" (CDC 2010). The story made headlines nationally, but it is only the most recent point in a steady change in young people's norms.

The sexual revolution and the women's movement were both preaching independence and individual decision making for women. Parents who wanted to force marriage on pregnant teens received little help from law enforcement agencies. Of course, forcing marriages does not promote the well-being of teen mothers or their offspring. Authorities are not particularly good at either helping establish paternity or making sure child support gets paid. Furthermore, poverty, unemployment, and low wages make it difficult for young fathers to provide the support the government might like to see them deliver. The welfare system evolved to help support some of these young families to ensure that children did not suffer unduly for their parent's lack of preparation. Despite political rhetoric to the contrary, unwed teen motherhood has not grown as a result of welfare to these needy young people. In fact, welfare payments declined in real (inflation-adjusted) value over the period when rates of unwed teen motherhood grew. Political movements seeking to encourage young, unwed mothers to marry in order to solve their problems have put the cart before the horse: their poverty isn't caused by lack of marriage; their unmarried status is more of an outcome of poverty, given that men in poor communities have few good job opportunities available to them.

What about psychology? Although poverty is a common correlate for teenage motherhood, it isn't the only one. An influential 1994 book by Mary Pipher, *Reviving Ophelia,* showed how teenage women who become mothers are undermined early on by basement-level self-esteem. Although hopelessness and poverty are often experienced together, Pipher found that a future orientation was not always associated with economic advantages. The "baby boom in Gloucester, Massachusetts" highlights this picture. In 2008, seventeen young women from the same high school were pregnant, and went on to have their babies; the event captured the nation for its tabloid qualities but also because it raised the puzzle of what causes teen pregnancy (besides sex). While Gloucester is mainly working class and was in the midst of an economic downturn, these women reported seeking identity and connection as they pursued a path of early motherhood. Regardless of their economic status, women who can see a future and who think well of themselves, profiled in several chapters of *Going All the Way* (Thompson 1996), are often able to abstain from sex or to protect themselves from unwanted pregnancy. But most teenage mothers, bereft of parental support or overwhelmed by the pleasure of romance in a life that has few other pleasures, look to their child for love and community.

And what about the fathers? The mainstream news coverage of the Gloucester baby boom included exactly one line about fathers: "'We found out that one of the fathers is a 24-year-old homeless guy,' the principal says, shaking his head." Even today, young unmarried men have been given license to have sex without fear of stigma. At the beginning of the sexual revolution, teenage men's rate of sexual experience was substantially higher than women's, as illustrated in figure 5.1. But while men's rate of sexual experience has increased over the past several decades, it has not increased as much as women's. Perhaps in middle- or upper-middle-class homes, where parents fight to protect their child's future career and social status, a son's sexuality is seen as just as dangerous to his future prospects as a daughter's. But even in families where the future holds promise because of their social class, daughters, not sons, seem to receive the more dire warnings about sex outside of marriage. Regardless of class, the consequences of teen sexuality continue to be more costly for women than for men.

This imbalance may be changing somewhat, but it is less because of a sudden recognition that young men are and should be equal partners in sexual responsibility, and more because of the teen sex "blame game." Over the 1990s, men were brought into the equation by conservative political forces that saw new possibilities for spreading moral blame and sharing social costs of teen pregnancy. An odd coalition of feminists and the "new right" created an image of the unwed young father as a predatory young male, knowledgeable and malevolent, who was really to blame for all this teenage pregnancy and should be severely punished. He should be made to support his children. However, many of these young men, like the women they have paired with, had limited prospects in the job market (Lerman and Ooms 1993; Sum et al. 2008).

Some recognition of teen fathers and their need for nonstigmatizing help, guidance, and assistance has occurred in the most recent decade. As mentioned in chapter 3, less judgmental movements to address young men's risks of teen pregnancy began appearing in the late 1990s—with many states investing in helping young men prevent early or unwanted fatherhood. In 2006 the National Campaign to Prevent Teen and Unplanned Pregnancy's report, "It's a Guy Thing" (Marsiglio et al. 2006), noted that teenage boys are doing a better job of preventing teen pregnancy since the early 1990s.

Who cares about whether it is conservatives or progressives bringing men into the equation? The advantage of these newer, progressive approaches to teen men and pregnancy is that they emphasize communication and equality. In contrast, more conservative approaches to teen men's sexual responsibilities tend to emphasize the helplessness of young women. Undoubtedly, sexual predators are out there. And as chapter 3 pointed out, 71 percent of women claimed to have wanted their first sexual experiences; 25 percent said it was unwanted and 4 percent said it was coerced. Nevertheless, many young women participate in sex with confidence and gusto. Some of these women are canny planners of their own lives—even if one doesn't agree with their values or goals—and most teenage women are not victims or potential victims of predatory young men. Like women in other age groups, some teenage women are attracted to older men; many find the interest of an older guy flattering. Some women know the young men with whom they have sex because they grew up together and are friends. It is also important to remember that some of these older men are still teenagers or are barely in their twenties themselves. Finally, increasingly, young women reject seduction or obtain the information necessary to contracept effectively—and to have safe sex.

The idea of raising social costs and concern for the sexual activity of young men to induce them to abstain or use birth control is sensible. But seeing men as predators is a simplification and in many cases an injustice. Feminist columnist Katha Pollitt (1996) made the point clearly: "Construing teen sex as all victimization seems more compassionate than construing it, like Newt Gingrich [then Speaker of the House of Representatives], as all sluttishness. But do we really want to say that a 15-year-old girl is always and invariably incapable of giving consent to sex with her 18-year-old boyfriend?" (9). What kind of logic would lead us to assume that all young men somehow know more about what they are doing than young women do? Men ought to be accountable for sexual activity, but they ought not to be automatically vilified for being sexual any more than women should be vilified for the same behavior.

Our view is that a very real social concern—teen sexuality—has been used to advance the sex-negative and sex-punitive agendas of various religious and political groups. Young men and women should not produce babies before they are ready to be parents, and young people should have a shot at an unfettered youth and productive adulthood. But the vision that teenagers should be nonsexual, especially in a hypersexualized society, is simply unrealistic. Abstinence may be a reasonable suggestion to younger teenagers, particularly in conservative neighborhoods or in communities that are unified in their support of them, but in most U.S. and European urban areas, this stance is simply unrealistic.

Sexuality Education

Societies such as Sweden, where sex education starts early with full public support, have much lower rates of teen pregnancy than we do in the United States. Admittedly, Sweden is different from us in other important ways: It has fewer people in poverty, it is more homogeneous culturally, and it has a vast social safety net for all citizens. Sweden has a record of profamily social policies aimed at gender equality in families (Ray, Gornick, and Schmitt 2008), along with a record of prosex education policies that emphasize that parenthood should be voluntary (Gauthier 1996). But in the United States, people still act as if sex is the exclusive privilege of married people, even though everyone knows that unmarried people have sex. Sex education for youth would surely improve the sexual quagmire teens seem to be in today. Sex education for adults would help, too, so that citizens might understand that sex is neither dangerous nor shameful.

The broadest way to think of the political battles over sexuality education is between abstinence-only education versus comprehensive sex education. Remarkably, at the same time that teens are being blamed for unrestrained sexuality and an excess of illegitimate births, little in the way of comprehensive sex education or services for teens exists across the United States. For example, virginity for its own sake is still prized in many communities, especially for daughters. This moral code, somewhat more flexible for adults, is highly charged when it concerns teenage sons and daughters. Even though research (Kirby et al. 1994; Bearman and Bruckner 2005) indicates that the "just say no" and abstinence campaigns tend to increase, rather than decrease, risk of unprotected sex, powerful lobbies have installed many of these programs in churches and school systems. As we discussed in chapter 1, the United States invested more than a billion dollars over the decade starting in 1996 (SIECUS 2005) in abstinence-only sex education. In particular, studies show that while students of abstinence only delay sex longer than students of comprehensive sex education, they end up having premarital sex—but are *less* likely to use condoms or seek STI counseling.

These programs tend also to be conservatively gendered, reconnecting female virginity with marriageability and presenting definitions of propriety that are different for men than for women. The Heritage Keepers Program (abstinence-only education) instructs students, "Females need to be careful with what they wear, because males are looking! The girl might be thinking fashion, while the boy is thinking sex. For this reason girls have an added responsibility to wear modest clothing that doesn't invite lustful thoughts" (SIECUS 2008). Not only have programs like these been shown to fail to promote abstinence (Child Trends 2003), the gender stereotypes included in them have been shown to be harmful to girls and women (Tolman 1999). Such assumptions about men—that they are "only interested in sex"—are harmful to men, as well.

Not all abstinence movements are premised on the double standard. Some religious groups preach abstinence for both sexes and apply sanctions equally. But, in general, social conservatives still see women as more vulnerable than men, see them as incapable of making sexual decisions, and believe that purity is the natural preference of and ideal for young women. Thousands of years of controlling women's sexuality does not quietly fade away. With such a view, women's vulnerability leads to a belief we discuss in the next section that women are in a sense "at fault" for "inviting" sexual assault.

Even if conservatives did not take issue with comprehensive sex education as a means for reducing pregnancy and delaying sexual initiation, they would have another argument against it. Conservatives believe that parents should control the family, not the government. Therefore, parents should decide what information a child should have about sexuality. Liberals, on the other hand, believe that all children deserve good information about sexual health, whether or not their parents elect to provide their children with it.

From the public health point of view, sex education ensures that young people who engage in sex will do so more safely. Public health professionals who believe in "healthy" sexuality emphasize the benefits of sex education to young people. They will have thought more about their own motives and goals and their responsibility to a partner and thus be prepared to act carefully. Furthermore, sexuality education seems to reduce sexual abuses, including sexual harassment and coercion among teenagers. Groups taking this position—such as the Sexuality Information and Education Council of the United States (SIECUS); Planned Parenthood; and the American Association of Sex Educators, Counselors, and Therapists (AASECT)—recognize that teens will continue to experiment with sexuality but believe education may delay some sexual experimentation. For many professionals, however, the main benefit of sex education is to teach young people how to communicate about sex. The goal is to help people treat one another humanely and to reduce the amount of shame, guilt, and manipulation in sexual relationships.

Where is the debate over sex education now? Although the number of sex education programs has increased since the 1970s, the goals have become more diverse, and program efficacy is undermined by a lack of consensus and, in some cases, a lack of quality materials or well-trained instructors (Yarber 1994; Fields 2008). Policymakers have generally seen the growth in sexual activity among teenagers as a reason to limit services for sexually active young people. Although sex education (of any kind) is not the culprit for young people's increased—or decreased—sexual activity, nevertheless the fear persists that sex education legitimizes teen sex. Vocal bands of parents have succeeded in locking sex education courses out of many school districts. In some, they have substituted "chastity" programs, which are often programs based on religious ethics and traditional gender roles. While abstinence funding at the federal level has decreased in the Obama administration, it has not been eliminated.

Teen Health

The public debate on teen sexuality has focused squarely on teen pregnancy—as if sex were all that teenagers were doing with their spare time (Dryfoos

1990). Politicians and opinion leaders moralize about youthful promiscuity and the tax burden it entails for supporting the babies of unwed teen mothers. Worried parents are galvanized by political fund-raisers who tell them that each and every family is vulnerable to teen pregnancy unless their party's platform of moral renewal is adopted. Of course, such policymakers emphasize their compassion for teens, but it is instructive to note just how little attention they pay to other health costs of teenage sexuality besides pregnancy.

All the concern about teen sexuality has caused health institutions to provide reproductively focused health care to the exclusion of other kinds. Teens in the United States are enormously underserved (Dryfoos 1990). We complain that youth are obese and unhealthy, but programs like Safe Passage that offer full-service schools that combine education with health, mental health, and social and family services—that have worked in demonstration projects—still cannot get adequate funding. Paradoxically, the fear of teen sexuality has reduced teen health services rather than sharpening them.

Even sex-related health problems are inadequately addressed by services to youth. Sexually transmitted infections are higher in the United States than in comparable developed countries and involve about one in four young people (CDC 2009). The rate slowed in the same period of time that teen pregnancy slowed, but it has remained at a high level. Untreated STIs, especially pelvic inflammatory disease (PID) and chlamydia, threaten women's fertility. PID can cause horrific pain as well as major complications, including damage to the urinary tract and the reproductive organs. Chlamydia may be asymptomatic, but it can end a woman's reproductive future. Although infertility rates in the population in general are declining (CDC 2005), they are growing among poor people and the youngest portion of the U.S. population (Scritchfield 1995; CDC 2005).

Case Study: HPV Vaccine. Our ambivalence about women's health and sexual health is highlighted in the debate that surfaced about the HPV vaccine. The 2000s have seen a new debate around girls, women, and sexual health surrounding the HPV vaccine known commercially as Gardasil. HPV—genital human papillomavirus—is the cause of most cases of cervical cancer and genital warts. A vaccine has been developed to prevent HPV—or at least four strains of it—when given to girls before they become sexually active. Even a cancer-preventing (or reducing) vaccine isn't enough, though, to quell the opportunism of moral entrepreneurs set on using anything related to girls' sexuality as an excuse to proselytize about morality. Conservative groups, including the Family Research Council and Focus on the Family, have opposed this cancer-fighting vaccine, claiming it promotes promiscuity by reducing the threat of STIs that are linked to cancer (Family Research Council 2007).

Where are boys and young men in all of this? Although boys and men also carry HPV, research on treating men for HPV, or preventing HPV in men, has lagged behind. So has communication about it. The double standard operates here as well: although men can (and do) get genital warts, they are less affected by HPV, and their role in HPV transmission has been neglected (Nack 2010).

Although the history of medicine can be said, without much distortion, to be the treatment of male problems (Ehrenreich and English 1978; Lorber 1997), an enormous amount of consciousness raising has changed a total blindness to the specific problems of adult women—if not to teens. A women's health movement grew up in the 1960s and 1970s, marked in part by the publication in 1973 of the first edition of *Our Bodies, Ourselves* by the Boston Women's Health Book Collective. The newest edition was published in 2005, *Our Bodies, Ourselves: A New Edition for a New Era*. The Boston Women's Health Collective has also published editions on pregnancy, birth, and menopause.

Turning teenage sexuality into a political issue may be an inevitable consequence of the relatively new, extended stage of adolescence and emerging adulthood. Ambivalent and punitive attitudes toward youthful sexuality are useful to many politicians who stir up parental fears and then offer comforting but unrealistic promises that voting for them will turn back the clock. But rarely does any of this politicization translate into health and other services for young people. Often political solutions involve trying to keep our dichotomized, gendered sexual scripts especially alive for teenagers.

Sexual Assault

Sexual assault is hardly a new issue. Although rape did not historically exist in some cultures, such as Polynesia, sexual assault of women is found across many cultures and across time. What is new about sexual assault is not only greater public and political awareness in the United States but also a level of political activism that has changed the way people discuss and define it, the way police departments react, and the way many women—and men—now regard their own vulnerability in sexual situations. In this section, we describe several political movements associated with sexual assault, examine the issues surrounding accusations of assault and date rape, and discuss recent developments that can contribute to resolving some puzzles related to sexual assault.

Sexual assault is difficult to study: Victims are not always willing providers of data because of the stigma and self-doubt associated with this crime. Furthermore, only in the past thirty years have we developed a recognition of—and any response to—acquaintance rape, also known as date rape. It has taken even longer to draw attention to the issue of same-sex sexual assault. But we do know that sexual assault is not randomly distributed. Overwhelmingly, sexual assault involves men victimizing women. Furthermore, among gays and lesbians, the rate of assault is higher among men than women, even when men are also victims. In this sense, it is a crime at the intersection of sexuality and gender. From an essentialist view, it is a consequence of men's testosterone and their predatory nature (Thornhill and Palmer 2000). From a constructionist view, it is a consequence of the social permission men have to dominate women and their need to reinforce that status. These interpretations do not "explain away" the problem. Instead, these approaches point to different strategies for reducing rates of sexual assault.

Even though men are victimized less often than women, the way male victimization is treated highlights the way that gender is central to the practice and attitudes toward rape. In many states, until recently, the definition of rape explicitly excluded the possibility that a man could be a victim: the crime was defined as gender specific. The consequence of such statutes—and practices of disbelief—is to further highlight the stigma of rape and to identify women's status as being defined by vulnerability and men's status as being defined by an incapacity to ever be vulnerable (Weiss 2008).

It is not always clear when or even whether efforts to reduce sexual victimization will have the desired effect. It is possible that the discourse on sexual threats maintains fearfulness among women (Hollander 1997; Glassner 2000), just as the legal process of prosecuting assaults may discourage victims from speaking out. The specter of sexual assault does indeed render many women fearful of walking alone at night, even in statistically safe areas. Encounters with the legal system and other institutions that are ambivalent about handling sexual assault have inhibited women as well. Finally, ambivalence about same-sex sexuality has multiplied the challenges for addressing same-sex sexual assault: victims may feel doubly inhibited where there continue to be social prohibitions against homosexuality, or law enforcement may be incredulous or simply avoid such cases due to homophobia.

Feminist versus Patriarchal Positions

The feminist movement is largely responsible for consciousness raising regarding the sexual assault of women. Since the late 1960s, feminist activists have struggled to obtain resources to aid victims of assault, legislation to aid the prosecution of sexual crimes, and legislation to define as crimes such acts as husband-wife rape and sexual harassment in the workplace, and efforts continue today. In 2008, a landmark piece of federal legislation—the Debbie

Smith Act—strengthened and improved the tools used for investigating un-solved rapes by improving funding for using DNA to solve cases.

This cause was publicized starting in the late 1970s by the efforts of Cath-erine MacKinnon and Andrea Dworkin, who worked to increase awareness of how certain cultural images and practices foster violent attitudes. They vo-ciferously opposed pornography as a way to reduce misogynistic violence to-ward women. Parts of this movement are quite controversial since the Dwor-kin-MacKinnon approach holds the view that women must be protected from predatory men and that most men are potentially predatory. Many feminists reject this belief, but curiously it has support among Christian conservatives. Other feminist groups, as we discuss below, disagree with MacKinnon's and Dworkin's emphasis on women as victims and take issue with attitudes that are often viewed as antagonistic to sexuality.

The feminist movement originally battled the status quo, or patriarchy, a system of power relations in which (some) men hold power at the expense of (some) women. This status quo was part of the sexual revolution—and part of the limits of the sexual revolution, too. Whereas feminists in the early stages of the sexual revolution were committed to polymorphous and liberated sexuality for all adults, as time progressed, other feminists noticed that sexual liberation tended to maintain men's sexual and social domi-nance (Seidman 1992). But divisions by gender are not the only status quo that has been hard to subvert; sexual assault has also been more tolerated when women of color and poorer women are victims. The criminal justice system, from cops to courts, has been slow to abandon its entrenched skep-ticism regarding sexual assault. Defense lawyers have, in the past, been free to use a woman's friendly behavior, past sexual history, or style of dress as evidence to contradict the claim of victimization. Even on college campuses today, we see simultaneously efforts to combat and educate students about sexual assault, along with a reluctance to prosecute and expel men respon-sible for assaults. We see competing dialogues about holding perpetrators accountable, when administrators mull over whether in a "hookup" culture, alcohol use is a mitigating factor. In 2010 research and advocacy group, The Center for Public Integrity, reported that colleges underreport the incidence of sexual assault on campus and rarely expel men found responsible for sexual assault.

Looking back on rifts that persist today. A case from the 1980s illustrates the conflict between feminist and patriarchal perspectives. Andrea, aged twenty-four, from Gardner, Massachusetts, was at a New Year's Eve party where she met her friend's brother, David Partridge. David offered to drive his sister and Andrea home but dropped his sister off first. At Andrea's, he invited himself in for coffee, and then the evening took a dark turn. A *Time* magazine account continues: "I trusted [David's sister]. Why not trust him," Andrea says. "He had been so nice, so polite, all evening long." Once inside, Andrea alleges, he forced her to perform a variety of sex acts. She decided to prosecute. It turned out that Partridge had got out on parole on a rape conviction only six days before he met Andrea. People at the party testified for the defense that they had seen the couple talking that night and Andrea drinking. A jury acquitted Partridge (Dowd 1983:28).

In this story, Andrea was brave enough to attempt to prosecute. Her courage was, no doubt, bolstered by an explicit feminist agenda to hold men accountable for sexual violence. But society's resistance to the agenda was also evident. The jury found that Andrea's ostensibly unguarded behavior mitigated criminal intent or behavior. Twenty years after this episode, women continue to receive advice to avoid provocative dress or activities—or else suffer the consequences.

For feminists, the challenge was to get judges and juries to listen to women and to believe their accounts of assault. Defenders, tapping the sentiments of patriarchy and the status quo, have been able simply to use a woman's gender and sexuality to explain away the crime of sexual assault. The news article about Andrea's case went on to note that defense lawyers have been fond of using the nineteenth-century French writer Balzac's statement on rape: "One cannot thread a needle when the needle doesn't stand still" (Dowd 1983). From this point of view, by definition sex cannot *possibly* occur without a woman's consent. Furthermore, rape is seen as the biological act of penetration.

Since the early 1980s, however, feminist efforts to document and do research on rape have raised consciousness and prompted policy changes regarding sexual assault on college campuses, in local statutes, and in law enforcement procedures. Additional movements relating to sexual assault against women have also emerged. Some of these reforms have been so successful—or at least visible—that a countervoice among feminists has emerged, expressing concern about a view on sexual assault (and sexual harassment and pornography) that appears too ready to define women as victims and sexuality as inherently dangerous.

While sexual assault is a persistent social problem, the dilemma remains where to draw the line between seduction and coercion. Interpersonal violence, including sexual assault, often includes emotional (or psychological) abuse. The issue of what is sexual assault is a crucial public health, safety, and legal issue. But it is possible that the very question (and the skepticism it allows) distracts from addressing the problem. Still, we believe that such questions can't be sidelined on the way to work for recognizing, addressing, and ending the problem. When emotional abuse is included in the definition of sexual crime, the door is open for a range of interpretations. Emotional abuse is a real and damaging method of coercion that involves systematic humiliation, badgering, and control of one person by another (Johnson 2009). However, identifying what constitutes systematic humiliation or control has been difficult. For some, the systematic humiliation of women starts with the culture at large, in which, for example, images of half-clothed women are used to sell everything from cigarettes to cars. However, because such images are so diffuse, cannot all women claim victimization? And if all women claim victimization, how can a legal system make judgments regarding relative seriousness?

Increasingly, researchers have been able to confirm theories of emotional abuse and validate measures of emotional abuse through study (e.g., Jacobson and Gottman 1998; Murphy and Hoover 2001; Johnson 2009). Such recognition, has grown as part of state and national initiatives. For example, in 2008 Vermont passed a Domestic Violence Omnibus bill that took into account nonbodily harm, as well as use of power and control over the victim; 2010 saw a similar law passed in the state of Minnesota, where coordinated community response to domestic violence has been pioneered.

Free speech feminist approaches. While the understanding of emotional abuse has advanced, a debate about definitions of assault has fractured feminist advocacy. One faction, whom we refer to as free-speech feminists, takes issue with the continued identification of women as victims with little power or individual responsibility in social interactions that involve sex and gender. The late feminist leader Betty Friedan was quoted on the "Feminists for Free Expression" website: "To suppress free speech in the name of protecting women is dangerous and wrong." The questions raised by free-speech feminists are serious, and important, and are intended to focus attention on women's empowerment, autonomy, and sexual freedom. But even as antipornography and antiassault feminists were finding allies among Christian conservatives, so free-speech feminists were at risk of being coopted by some libertarians who minimize the seriousness or even the existence of sexual assault as a substantial social problem and barrier to gender equality.

Free-speech feminism has been concerned with specific issues such as censorship of pornography and social trends that, according to some free-speech feminists, involve casting women as perpetual victims; that is exactly what Friedan's quotation addresses. Although Friedan was a senior feminist from the pre–baby boom era, this issue has been taken up in a younger generation that followed radical, free-love feminists of the 1960s and 1970s. Writers like Katie Roiphe (1993) began to wonder publicly whether some of the sexual assault and date rape reports weren't distorted, especially those that used very broad definitions of emotional abuse. Along with others, she noticed that some of the rhetoric of feminist activists seemed to highlight a pervasive oppression that didn't ring completely true to her. Widely publicized claims of cultural, sexist oppression by middle-class, privileged white women, Roiphe and others posited, tend to dilute the claims of the most severely victimized of women. Such suspicion of feminist assertions against men's sexual aggression have persisted into the last decade.

One critic captured the shortcomings of arguments like Roiphe's by explaining that they come from a position of confusing the work of opposing and demonizing sexual assault with opposing and demonizing men in general (Traister 2007). Still another view regarding distorted reports of abuse comes from Beres, whom we discussed in chapter 3. Melanie Beres (2009) was interested in the misperceptions of sexual assault at the center of debates about minimizing or maximizing the issue. In qualitative interviews, she garnered many accounts to support the position that intimate partners really do have the capacity to recognize what is consent—and what is not. Beres draws from detailed accounts of casual sex to argue that men and women do not work from such different—or gendered—scripts for sexuality. In a sense, Beres moves us beyond the power/gender arguments without minimizing the fact that sexual assaults, and even date rapes, happen. It may be that as time progresses, and the gulf between men and women narrows, clarity will grow.

But any growing clarity is contested: A generation before Roiphe, feminists had promoted sexual liberation, yet activists had to contend with continued sexual violence against women. Thus, feminist movements had to fight to convince law enforcement personnel to believe women and hear their accusations of sexual and domestic violence. Harkening back to more sex-positive, liberationist notions, free-speech feminists wondered if antiviolence movements were exaggerating the problems of sexual violence. Feminist writers and activists have found themselves in the odd position of battling one another rather than advancing feminist causes. Notably, the rates of rape (as reported in the section "Consent and Coercion" in chapter 2) persist in lifetime prevalence, around 20 percent. Furthermore, even mainstream institutions such as the United Nations and the U.S. armed forces continue to be exposed as venues for sexual harassment and coercion. While efforts have been focused on reducing and preventing sexual assault in the military, in 2009, sexual assault increased by 11 percent. This may be attributable to work conditions but also to better reporting and more serious investigation of complaints.

Men's movements. Although the disputes among women's movements tend to eclipse men's voices regarding sexual assault, there are several distinct men's movements. A number have arisen since the mid-1980s as a response to feminism. Some, such as the mytho-poetic movement led by Robert Bly, resent the suggestion that masculine sexuality is defined by power (Bly 1990). The men in this movement feel increasingly powerless and persecuted and tend to think that their powerlessness is as salient as women's risk of sexual violence. Through mythology and group activities, these men attempt to "reclaim" their masculinity, which they believe has been eroded by feminism.

Other men's movements, such as Men against Violence, ally themselves more closely with feminism as they seek to reduce the problem of domestic violence and sexual assault. Some of these groups recognize men's accountability and the influence of a historically patriarchal culture. They seek to change cultural practices that tend to be associated with sexual violence and promote policies that adequately punish sexual violence (Kimmel 2005).

Within profeminist men's movements, theorists and observers point out the challenges for men to actively work against patriarchy and violence that flows from a system of "hegemonic masculinity" (Connell 2005). This stance recognizes that when power relations shape the norms of femininity, they also shape norms of masculinity that not only require men's dominance over women but also men's dominance over other men.

Still other groups, see men as sometimes being unavoidably, essentially violent, and for them the struggle against violence is much like a struggle for a cure to a medical (rather than social) problem. Although these men cast themselves as profeminist, they present a dilemma to the politics of feminism. These men see masculine violence as a medical or psychological problem, one that is developed on an individual level and that requires individual solutions, like psychotherapy or self-help groups. Most feminists, however, see violence against women as a social problem. This means that individual perpetrators ought to be held accountable for crimes against women, but these crimes emerge in a patriarchal social and policy context.

Strange Bedfellows

In the history of work against violence against women, we saw specific political actions that create "strange bedfellows"—that is, a curious, unexpected pairing. In the 1980s, the Reagan administration forged an unlikely alliance with some feminists around antipornography efforts. These disparate communities were brought together by an essentialist view of sexuality: Men are fundamentally predatory, women should be protected, and women should shield themselves from men.

The common ground of these two groups is well illustrated by the Reagan administration's Meese Commission on Pornography. As part of a pledge to the Christian Right, which helped him get elected in 1980 and 1984, Ronald Reagan appointed U.S. Attorney General Edwin Meese to chair a group examining the connections between pornography and sexual violence against women. The group set aside the findings of a 1970 report by the U.S. Commission on Obscenity and Pornography, which found that exposure to pornography had little or no relationship to crime or deviance (Seidman 1992). Among the witnesses for the Meese Commission was Andrea Dworkin, the antipornography feminist who has advocated the abolition of all sexually explicit materials. This odd coalition abandoned concerns for First Amendment rights to free speech and ignored research that did not support the beliefs of antipornography advocates. It reported that men exposed to sexually explicit material and entertainment were likely to become sexual victimizers. The conservatives were interested in protecting the "virtue" of women, for whom they felt virginity and sexual purity were paramount. The antipornography feminists were interested in making the streets safe for women by means of punitive and far-reaching legislation against pornography. Feminists who wanted to protect pornography under the mantle of free speech were not enthusiastic about most commercially available sexual materials; they simply believed that the First Amendment requires support.

Like a mirror image, some factions of the men's movement joined free-speech feminists in another opportunistic (although less high-profile) alliance. Those in the men's movement who emphasized men's feelings of powerlessness and their own victimization at the hands of unfeeling fathers and critical mothers hardly feel like sexual threats. Thus, they resisted the antiporn feminists' blanket condemnation of men as potential sexual predators who get stoked up by sexually explicit material. They found common cause with a faction of feminists who believe there is more harm in censorship than in pornography.

How well did this political maneuvering advance the cause of reducing sexual assault? It depends on whom you ask. Some feminists believe the debate merely ensured that women's stories will be heard and believed. However, free-speech feminists have been alarmed at the potential for women's claims to be exaggerated and fear the resulting antifeminist backlash will undermine sympathy and legal support for women who have been horribly threatened, attacked, or coerced.

Moreover, men and women who are concerned for individual civil liberties are worried about how uncritically women's claims should be taken. We are obliged to protect the rights of individuals who are unjustly accused. But even if women's claims are ever distorted or exaggerated, we need to address the real problem of sexual assault. Sexual assault persists, even if some people misrepresent themselves.

False Prophets, False Accusations, and True Lies

In the 1960s and 1970s, researchers made many advances in the study of sexual assault and sexual abuse and generally raised consciousness about perpetrators, victims, and the consequences of the crime. In the 1980s, acquaintance rape became recognized as a rampant problem; in 1987, Miller and Marshall published a study that indicated that 27 percent of college women experienced coerced or forced intercourse during their college career. By the late 1980s and 1990s, a new issue surfaced: "false accusations" of assault. In a study of a small Midwestern city, one researcher determined that 41 percent of the allegations of sexual assault were subsequently recanted by the claimants as false allegations (Kanin 1994). At the same time, researchers were studying the reliability of eyewitness testimony and finding it, often, subject to situational or ideological influences (Loftus and Ketcham 1991).

Reviews of the recanting research argued that the data provided by Kanin and others is highly faulty (e.g., Rumney 2006). Furthermore, whatever the incidence of recanting, it does not necessarily provide evidence of false accusations, although it does invite consideration of this potential problem. Women may recant for many reasons—for instance, because they lose the courage to face an impersonal legal system or because of community pressure to protect the accused, especially when they know the alleged perpetrator. Recanting can also reflect women's feelings of guilt and shame about their sexual victimization.

The question, as we see it, is how social institutions and individuals can cope with ambiguity—or even false accusations. They are abhorrent, but we must remember that even some false accusations constitute the truth as the victims of sexual assault see it. In other cases, false accusations of a particular act, at a particular time, represent a woman's overwhelming sense of general abuse, powerlessness, and anger at being used. Continuing to take emotional abuse into account offers promise, as does skillful research that shows us how to measure what is a real incident and what anger or perception comes from a history of ugly treatment. From this point of view, a lie about the man's behavior is not to be tolerated, but at the same time it has a context that should not be ignored or discounted. Many women have less power, less opportunity, and even less sexual freedom than men have, thanks to cultural and social structures. Women need a sense of power and efficacy to reduce the gendered quality of interaction. This will alleviate anger and bitterness that can fuel attempts to equalize power differences by false accusations or exaggerations. Efforts to reduce the ambivalence we discussed earlier in this chapter about sexuality can help people to understand more clearly the difference between sex and violence. Above all, the discussion of sexual assault and false accusations of sexual assault has the unintended consequence of distracting from the central issue: preventing sexual assault. Some see the central issue as the civil rights of the accused.

In the end, efforts to reduce violence against women move forward. The political divisions are interesting because of the different theories implied by the approach to sexual assault and false accusations. Those who recognize the power of social institutions and culture to form gendered sexual styles focus on institutional change; those who posit that biology and evolution drive the gendered sexual system focus on ways to refine "natural" roles for men and women to reduce sexual violence. They will, with such essentialist beliefs, neglect men who are victims. Few people believe women or men should be made sexually compliant against their will (although some still do).

Our position is that sexual assault has to be understood in this context of real and perceived male domination. Sexual assault highlights a gendered sexual system in which men in general have more power than women and where masculinity is legitimated by expressions of power. But the gender system that gives men and women different sexual power is also responsible for those unhappy instances where men and women interpret the same "facts" terribly differently. Simultaneously, a man might think he was invited and that sex was mutual while a woman might feel helpless, overwhelmed, and coerced. In the gendered sexual system, such misunderstandings between men and women are viewed as normal and natural. And the gender systems that link sex and power can produce coercive sexual situations for men as well. Thus, popular views regarding false accusations of sexual assault seem based on a polarized sexuality that casts men as essentially predatory and women as responsible for avoiding trouble. As long as gender difference is considered fundamental to sexuality, some aggression will be cast as "misunderstandings" and some "misunderstandings" will be cast as aggression.

Same-Sex Marriage

Same-sex marriage involves sexual politics of a different sort. Instead of being focused on women's sexuality, the central, thorny dilemma is more explicitly about the importance of *gender difference* for "normal" sexuality. Gender difference is so central to traditional visions of acceptable sexuality that some people abhor and fear a sexuality that is not defined by having a man and a woman participating.

The political debate over same-sex marriage is about whether gay and lesbian partners can have the same access to social and legal support of their unions that heterosexuals gain by entering the social contract of marriage. The underpinning of the debate is the gendered status of marriage within the Judeo-Christian traditions. Although the opposition to same-sex marriage has many layers, the pet arguments of opponents to same-sex marriage revolve around a kind of normative essentialism. What does this mean? Heterosexual marriage is seen as a sexual union that requires gender difference because of the "natural" purpose of marriage: reproduction and child rearing. Same-sex marriage, by eliminating gender difference and hence reproduction by the married partners, challenges many people's religious beliefs and inflames the dialogue about changing the rules. It is "normative essentialism" because it suggests that bodies—that have the capacity to refrain from reproducing in cross-sex marriages, and that have the capacity to produce biological children (with assistance) in same-sex marriages—are only legitimately used in one particular social context.

Political distress over same-sex marriage underscores a notion we have emphasized throughout this book: gender difference is central to the social control of intimacy. Indeed, same-sex marriage provides the perfect experimental design. Only one crucial variable—gender—has been altered, and all others remain constant (love, commitment, concern for property, potential desire for children, union of two families). Varying gender in the context of marriage, it turns out, is a highly provocative innovation.

Over a decade ago, when the first edition of this book was published, the issue of same-sex marriage in the United States was on the rise; but same-sex marriage was decidedly unpopular. Despite increasing awareness and some legal progress, there were few signs of broader cultural acceptance. In 2010 the status of same-sex marriage in the United States and around the world has changed dramatically, as have attitudes in gender politics. In fact, we can't think of any area where there has been more change. Even so, same-sex marriage rights still face a heated, uphill battle.

Where Have We Been? The Legal Journey

Same-sex marriage became a front-page issue in 1996 when, citing civil rights and constitutional concerns, the Hawaii Supreme Court supported the right to marry of three same-sex couples who had previously applied for marriage licenses in Hawaii. The court argued that failure to recognize same-sex marriage was a form of sex discrimination according to the Hawaii constitution, and they sent a message to the appeals court: *Show us why denying marriage to gay people is not in conflict with our constitution—or we will legalize gay marriage!* What followed in Hawaii is similar to the back-and-forth that has happened in other U.S. states: some more domestic rights were given to same-sex couples, but in 1998 Hawaiian voters passed a constitutional amendment reserving marriage for opposite-sex couples.

Same-sex marriage also came to the political forefront during the presidential election of 1996. In subsequent elections, we have continued to see the use of same-sex marriage as a strategy to mobilize conservative voters by the "family values" lobby (that also sought to promote abstinence-only education). The centerpiece of the strategy in 1996 was the Defense of Marriage Act (DoMA), a piece of legislation designed to deny federal recognition of gay marriages. Congress passed DoMA, and President Bill Clinton, responding to polls that indicated that voters were not ready to accept gay marriage, said he was not in favor of gay marriage and signed the DoMA into law.

The DoMA is still in place—though recently (February 2011) the U.S. Attorney General abandoned defending key components of it. As a federal law, DoMA denies recognition and federal benefits to same-sex couples. The law also seeks to allay concerns of the religious right that followed from the Hawaiian case related to states rights and gender difference. The (perceived) legal puzzle of same-sex marriage went like this: If one state grants marriage rights to same-sex couples, are all states obliged to recognize same-sex marriage? The question raised issues of autonomy and states rights embedded in the U.S. Constitution and also state-to-state practices of legal reciprocity. On the one hand, each state has the right to set its own statutes about marriage. On the other hand, reciprocity has always been extended to make marriages constituted in one state legal in another (for example, age restrictions on marriage). Same-sex marriage, if legal in one state, would become valid in other states, if reciprocity continued to be the norm. DoMA was passed as a direct response. Similarly, many states passed their own DoMA statutes to avoid reciprocity and to defeat local movements in support of same-sex marriage (see figure 5.7).

Where Are We Now? Laws and Attitudes

Since the Hawaii case over fifteen years ago, significant legal activity has occurred. The map in figure 5.7 illustrates the access to same-sex marriage in the United States as of 2011.

Currently, six states (Connecticut, Iowa, Massachusetts, New Hampshire, New York, and Vermont) and the District of Columbia have same-sex marriage. Two other states acknowledge same-sex marriages performed in other states (Maryland and Rhode Island) but do not grant same-sex marriages in their states. California grants benefits of marriage to all same-sex unions, but only marriages conducted between June and November 2008 are given the title of marriage. In June of 2008 the California Supreme Court ruled that limiting marriage to cross-sex couples violated their state's constitution. But later in the year an initiative, known as Proposition 8, prohibiting same-sex marriage was passed by the voters, and the right to marriage that had existed was taken away. In the summer of 2010 another judge said that Proposition

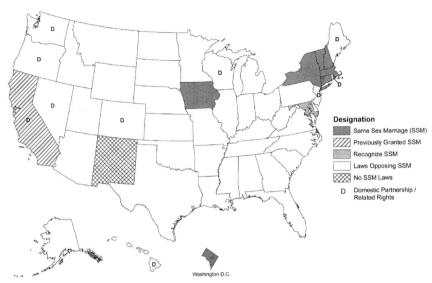

FIGURE 5.7
Same-sex civil rights in the United States as of 2011. David Merwin and Virginia Rutter, Framingham State University.

8 was unconstitutional and reinstituted gay marriage. Then, in another hearing, a judge stopped gay marriages from resuming until the case could be appealed to the California Supreme Court. The issue continues to be litigated in California. The events in California highlight how the decisive progress toward marriage for all is subject to ongoing resistance. Furthermore, the arguments center on the same arguments that were central in the DoMA: marriage requires a *gender difference*. Furthermore, so the opponents argue, marriage without gender difference threatens to undermine the entire institution of marriage itself.

What about public attitudes? In 1995 a Roper poll showed that 56 percent of Americans disapproved of gay marriage and only 30 percent approved (*Newsweek* 1995). In 2010, an ABC News poll showed that 50 percent continued to oppose gay marriage, and 47 percent approved. Furthermore, when the question included recognition of civil unions that include rights to health insurance, inheritance, and pension coverage, 31 percent opposed and 66 percent supported recognition of civil unions. Many social scientists recognize that this change is likely to continue in this direction: There is a strong correlation between age and explicit acceptance of same-sex marriage; that is, the younger a person is, the more likely s/he is to accept same-sex marriage. Moreover, in all age groups, people over time seem to become increasingly supportive of same-sex marriage.

The Debates

The politics of same-sex marriage are complicated. There are several positions regarding same-sex marriage—even among gays and lesbians. Despite the slowly growing public (and legal) acceptance of same-sex marriage, mainstream heterosexual political leaders generally tend to reject same-sex marriage. Liberals, like President Barack Obama, for example, support civil unions, but not marriage, for gays and lesbians. Some gay and lesbian activists and political leaders support same-sex marriage, but others reject it. The reasons for these positions are hardly uniform.

The fact that gays and lesbians are on both sides of the debate seems counterintuitive. However, some gays and lesbians prefer not to be involved with the state or to follow mainstream definitions and rules about intimacy. As discussed in chapter 4, older generations of gays and lesbians are less likely to put same-sex marriage on top of their agenda, while younger generations embrace same-sex marriage more often as central to their social agenda.

Gay and lesbian opponents of same-sex marriage often see it as a problematic, patriarchal institution. They feel gays and lesbians have been lucky to escape the strictures of gender roles and religious dogma about marriage and prefer not to be subjected to what is, in their estimation, a sexist and inequitable institution, as Vaid wrote in *Virtual Equality: The Mainstreaming of Gay and Lesbian Liberation* (1995). Gays and lesbians who are vocal in the campaign to receive marriage equity include couples who want the various legal benefits of marriage. In addition, some gay and lesbian civil libertarians may not want to get married themselves but feel that gay people should be vested with all the rights and obligations of heterosexual citizens.

These people join heterosexual supporters who believe that there is no God-given or "natural" shape to marriage and that same-sex marriage is in no way a sacrilege. Their position relies on the constructionist idea that social institutions, such as marriage, are created by society and therefore are appropriately modified by society. Barring some groups from enjoying the benefits of marriage is discrimination that is appropriately remedied through social engineering. In essence, courts and legislators should lead the country away from prejudice against gays and lesbians in much the same way that courts and legislation changed slavery or antimiscegenation laws that prohibited people of different races from marrying. Many people feel that marriage laws should be based on constitutional guidelines and not theology. Separation of church and state, in other words, means that religious ideas about marriage cannot be the basis for barring gays and lesbians from marriage.

The constructionist argument concludes that judges and elected officials should do the fair thing and support same-sex marriage. The powerful precedent of African American civil rights is introduced in most of the legal cases involving same-sex marriage rights: slavery, in fact, was not abolished by popular demand. Abolition was unpopular and unsupported in the South and some of the North, and religion was often used to justify discrimination based on "natural and spiritual" differences between the races. Abolitionists eventually triumphed by encouraging the government to recognize that abolition was fair in law and consistent with the mandate of the U.S. Bill of Rights. Like abolitionists, gay activists know they cannot—yet—win a popularity contest (though their cause has been gaining considerable favor). By using arguments of "constitutional right" and legal consistency, however, they hope to give gay citizens all the same opportunities and rules that other citizens have automatically.

Opponents of same-sex marriage imbed their argument in moral terms. Conservative factions claim that marriage is the cornerstone of morality and the guide to a country's ethos and social plan. Their opinion leaders hold symposia and speak in churches and on campaign trails about how same-sex marriage will degrade the sacred institution of marriage and therefore corrupt society. Like biological essentialists, these stakeholders claim that, by God's (and nature's) plan, marriage is for procreation. Two biological sexes were designed to perpetuate the species. Nature, therefore, ordains the pairing of men with women. God created two sexes to create family and, from family, create society.

Not only do we know that marriage, in practice, isn't about procreation but also that the notion of marriage as procreative has been explicitly rejected by the highest court of the United States. The Supreme Court decided in the case of *Griswold v. Connecticut* in 1965 that laws prohibiting married people from using contraceptives were antithetical to the constitutional notion of privacy (Eskridge 1996). According to this precedent, and according to the cultural shift that the Court recognized, marriage is not a procreative institution but a private one created for whatever emotional and social purposes its partners choose. Culturally, the function of marriage has become even more private since 1965; as Stephanie Coontz describes in *Marriage, A History* (2005), the great transition in marriage is that it is about love and intimacy—not about procreation, or obedience, or some other instrumental standard.

There's still another significant Supreme Court decision that is relevant to the debate. Proponents of same-sex marriage note parallels between the gay marriage ban and the antimiscegenation laws, which until 1967 prohibited marriages between individuals from different races. The premise of a ban on gay marriage is the same. A biological imperative ordains some pairs but not others. Under antimiscegenation laws, the social category of race (which was seen as a biological category) ordained that same-race pairs, but not cross-race pairs, could marry. Under laws like DoMA, the category of sex (which is seen as a biological category related to procreation) ordained that cross-sex but not same-sex pairs can marry. Of course, such bans on marriage are also a tool of social control based on prejudice—rooted in essentialism.

In the 1967 decision *Loving v. Virginia*, the ban against interracial marriage was finally lifted. Amazingly, antimiscegenation laws were still on the books late in the 1960s, illustrating the persistence of prejudices about race, religion, and gender. Laws that recognize the inalienable rights of humans are apparently not as easily agreed on as traditions based on prejudices, fears, economic systems, and class structures.

Same-Sex Parenting: Does Gender Matter?

The model of marriage as procreative and biological has some unintended irony. In reality, modern marriage is not primarily a procreative institution. A growing proportion of heterosexual, married couples do not have children (they are having fewer children later in life, or none at all). Furthermore, same-sex couples can have children, either through a temporary heterosexual alliance, fertility technology, or adoption. Yet, opponents fear that children raised by same-sex parents will suffer discrimination and even perversion; however, no evidence supports this position. There is, in fact, reason to think that children will benefit from legitimizing same-sex unions. Stable parenting pairs are endangered among all classes and subcultures in the United States. Nonetheless, the belief in marriage as an essentially procreative institution, the attachment to the primacy of having one man and one woman parent, and the fear that gay parenting is worse than heterosexual parenting have been a cornerstone of the arguments against same-sex marriage around the country.

So, what is the impact of same-sex parenting? Substantial research for several decades has highlighted minimal differences: children of same-sex parents are no better off and no worse off than their peers according to numerous studies (Golombok and Tasker 1996; Patterson 1992; Green 1987; Bozett 1987).

But, newer research in the past decade has also highlighted some differences in the lives of children of gay and lesbian parents. These newer researchers took a family diversity point of view, rather than just seeing whether gay families lived up to a straight standard. For example, Biblarz and Stacey found that daughters in these families were more popular; that boys were less aggressive and domineering; and that girls were more likely to play typically "boy games" as well as "girl games." These children were more likely to experiment with same-sex sexual activity, and the daughters to have more partners, but none were any more likely to identify as gay or lesbian as an adult or wish that they were the other sex. There were no differences in friendships, in self-esteem, or in the ability to get a job.

Still, other research has found no evidence that children need an other-sex parent for their well-being. Researchers, including Biblarz and Stacey (2010), found that two parents are better than one more often than not, but that the gender composition of the parenting team did not affect the children.

Finally, a remarkable, longitudinal study followed children of lesbian parents over twenty years and compared them with children who were raised in families with heterosexual parents. The investigators found that children of lesbian mothers were rated significantly higher in social, academic, and overall competence. They were rated significantly lower in social problems, rule breaking, and aggressive problems (Gartrell and Bos 2010). The investigators suspect the mothers had different parenting styles that may account for the differences: these moms used verbal limit-setting more often. Such research shows that lesbian mothers rely less on coercion and critical interactions with their children and have greater involvement, which may help explain the healthy psychological development of these children.

What about stigma? The researchers investigated whether these children experienced any social stigma because of their parents' sexual orientation, and four in ten reported that they did. However, the investigators found that the children who reported stigma were as psychologically well adjusted as the children who reported no stigma.

How many children are being raised by gay and lesbian parents? Estimates vary, depending upon the definition of gay or lesbian being used; demographers at the UCLA Williams Institute argue that a million gay and lesbian parents are raising around two million children. There is, therefore, reason to think that children will benefit from legitimizing same-sex unions. Stable parenting pairs are endangered among all classes and subcultures in the United States.

Legal Precedent

Without laws to safeguard the rights of both parents in a same-sex union, children's lives are often disrupted when one parent is disabled or dies—or when the parents break up. A case in Vermont foregrounds the struggle—but also highlights the progress. Two women met, fell in love, and had a civil union in Vermont in 2000 (prior to the same-sex marriage rights that eventually passed in Vermont). One of the women, Lisa, had a baby, which she raised together with her partner, Janet. When Lisa decided she did not want to live as a lesbian any more, she moved to her home in Virginia, taking her child with her. She was glad to accept child support payments from Janet, but she wanted sole custody of the child. Janet's case was perceived to be an uphill battle, given that the state of Virginia has its own version of DoMA called the Marriage Affirmation Act, which specifically nullifies any out-of-state same-sex partnerships. In 2004, Janet lost her case. However, in 2008, Janet regained joint custody of her child. The Virginia Supreme Court ruled that Lisa's moving out of state (from Vermont) in order to nullify a contract related to a child had violated the Federal Parental Kidnapping Prevention Act. On the one hand, after years of litigation, Janet had regained her rights as a mother; on the other hand, this had taken a multiyear legal fight, during which Janet had not been allowed to see her child.

It is hard to see how these battles or uncertainty about parental rights could be in the best interest of children. Heterosexual couples have a recognized biological right and adoption procedures that solidify their children's future. The issue of "traditional marriage" pales when real children, with real attachments to parents who are performing well in their obligations, suffer disrupted homes and perhaps the tragic loss of a beloved parent.

What's the future of same-sex marriage? The horizon for same-sex marriage seems to be moving in the direction of legalization. But it draws our attention back to marriage as an institution. Although marriage confers many economic and social benefits, it is far from ideal. We noted in chapter 4 that while containing many benefits for marital partners, marriage tends to reinforce traditional, gendered social practices. As such, it has some undesirable aspects. Furthermore, lifetime marriage is not an easy accomplishment for most people. As eighteenth-century social commentator Samuel Johnson noted: "It is so far from being natural for a man and woman to live in a state of marriage that we find all the motives which they have for remaining in that connection and the restraints which civilized society imposes to prevent separation, are hardly sufficient to keep them together." Gays and lesbians who seek to break away from social sexual norms may be excused for their ambivalence toward marriage. Some questions are as yet unanswered: If gay marriage is allowed, will gay and lesbian pairs who do not step up to the altar be stigmatized for abstaining from participating in this institution? And will marriage bring with it gendered performance norms that confuse rather than aid same-sex couples? That is the suspicion for those who consider that marriage is destined to be "heteronormative" for all who participate. Is this an institution that can be transformed—even more than it has—and be less polarizing?

As for the public's ambivalence about same-sex marriage, we join most other social scientists in observing that, in general, it is rooted in homophobia, the intense hatred and irrational fear of homosexual behavior and individuals, which, in turn, is related to ambivalence about sexual pleasure and a commitment to essentialist ideas about gender. Marriage is about intimacy and pleasure as much as it is about children. This is a radical and upsetting notion to many people, as we saw in case after case of political sex scandals earlier in this chapter. But, fewer people today than when we first wrote this book in the 1990s feel that way. And generation after generation, the shift is toward acceptance of same-sex marriage, gay and lesbian parenting, and less and less gender-bound ways of thinking about family.

Conclusion

We have pointed out some remarkable political battles about changes in sexual behavior and attitudes. In some ways, liberalizing forces have prevailed: people's opportunities for sexual expression have increased. At the same time, however, gendered sexuality continues to predominate in the political debate. And while this debate has focused more on women's, rather than men's, bodies, the enforcement of cultural norms affects both sexes around a host of politicized issues—including teen sex, sexual assault, and same-sex marriage.

Historian John Modell, who documented social change and continuity in *Into One's Own: From Youth to Adulthood in the United States 1920–1975*, observed that "so substantial was the repositioning of sexuality within American culture that theorists have suggested that its expression, rather than its repression, came to lie near the core of the energy that structures the society" (308). In other words, sexual expression has increased over time and with it the political battles regarding sexual expression. It is no longer about *whether* sex is openly expressed, but about *how*.

The question is whether freedom of sexual expression, for both men and women, has been advanced by political and media attention to sexuality or whether the attention has sidetracked desirable changes in sexual desire and sexual behavior. We believe that there has been progress but that true sexual freedom, unconstrained by gendered norms, has been resisted and diverted by the numerous political debates about sexuality. Clearly, much of the political controversy continues to be focused on whether or not traditional gender roles and sexualities will continue to be privileged.

Have the sexual privileges and responsibilities of women and men changed nevertheless? Yes. Have these changes brought the experiences of being a man and of being a woman closer, or allowed for greater diversity? Somewhat. Just reviewing some of the cases in this chapter we see that teen men are more likely than ever before to be targets of pregnancy prevention and awareness. But women are still at the forefront of teen sexuality panics, as we saw in the

Gloucester teen pregnancy case. Sexual assault has been a focus of men's as well as women's movements on campuses and more widely; yet (for example) campuses still hesitate to hold perpetrators accountable and tend to still seek out "excuses" like "they were both intoxiciated" or "don't forget that this is a 'hookup' culture." Recognition of men's victimization is still rare. Acceptance of same-sex marriage has grown remarkably since its legal status was introduced in the 1990s; but opposition has also become organized and vehement, as we saw with the Proposition 8 battle in California. Even more to the point of diversity, small but growing recognition of transgender, transsexual, and bisexual people gives a glimmer of a future that allows and respects greater individual choice and sexual diversity. There is reason for optimism. The public debate over sexual issues constitutes an opportunity to revise tired notions of masculinity and femininity. However, it is merely an opportunity. Social traditions—as much as biological realities—are neither immutable nor completely pliant. Political and media attention can reinforce gender differences, which may in the end be explained as a combination of social and biological forces. But this attention may also be an opportunity to promote diversity, rather than polarities, in sexual expression.

Promoting diversity in sexuality and sexual expression has not been a gentle process, nor will it be any time soon. Political battles over teen sexuality, sexual assault, and same-sex marriage continue even as we write, and sincere advocates on all sides press on with their agendas. Young people's feelings about sex are intense, caught up in their allegiance to their parents' values, their fleeting and evolving sense of their own values—in sum, who they are and who they want to be. Conservatives express alarm about nonmarital sex. Liberals feel just as strongly that their very liberty is linked to unfastening the short leash conservatives and traditionalists have imposed on sexuality—especially women's sexuality—and personal choice. These fights aren't intellectual; they are part of people's hearts and souls. No wonder they sometimes end in long, expensive court fights that the losing side never takes as a final answer—or even end in bloodshed, as we have seen in the fight over abortion rights and the assassinations of abortion doctors.

Even while sexuality is the product of social processes, it is so personal that people can have trouble moderating opinions on the subject. We forget that there are many different orientations toward sexuality and even choices out there. In the political arena, people forget that sexuality is a positive force as well as one with potential pitfalls, and that men's and women's propensities are arranged along a continuum of desire and behavior, rather than at dichotomous poles. But the sexual world is less polarized by gender than we often think it is. Social movements help us to reduce gender inequality and consider how to create a sexual life that is authentic and rewarding. As we consider what kind of sex life we want we are reminded by a truism about sex and sexuality that our most important sex organ is between our ears. As Jeffrey Weeks (2009:7) explains, "This does not mean we can simply ignore the massive edifice of sexuality which envelopes us." But it means that person by person, we ask you to be wary of positions on sexuality that rely on hidden or explicit assumptions regarding gender differences in matters sexual or otherwise. Just as you use your imagination when you think about *doing* sex, you can use it to think about the *social meanings* of it. Use it to explore sexual possibilities that lead us away from dichotomous, essentialist narratives of his/ her and straight/gay.

In the next chapter we evaluate a few very important questions about personal and social aspects of sex. The chapter will provide you with examples of how sexual issues are about similarity as well as difference and show you how to identify gendered assumptions in everyday quandaries regarding sexuality.

6

But How Do We Use What
We Know? Questions and Answers

N O BOOK EVER ANSWERS ALL THE QUESTIONS people have on any given subject. But a book on sex can feel so personal that you want to know the answers quickly! Readers ask, how does this apply to me? We understand. In fact, we feel the same way, so we added this chapter based on our students' questions.

The book so far has addressed some of the "big issues" of gender and sexuality and provided you with a framework for answering questions about sex and gender on your own. Even more valuable, we have given you ideas for how to raise new questions related to sex and sexualities.

As is often the case with the topic of sex, when people get some information—they want to know more. When we discuss sex with students, colleagues, and friends, they have endless questions about their sexuality and experiences. Indeed, after studying many of the topics that are addressed in this book, a class of college seniors was asked what they wanted more information on. Here are fourteen of their questions related to sexual function, sexual orientation, and sexual harassment, along with our responses.

Sexual Function

1. Sex is supposed to be such an important part of a man's life. What if sex isn't great or important to him?

Remember the bell curve we introduced in chapter 2? Both men and women exhibit a wide range of sexual desire, sexual frequency, and other sexual behaviors. For the most part, men and women are far more similar than they are different on various dimensions of normal sexual appetite. There is no right or wrong amount of sexual desire or activity.

We have so glorified sex in our culture that a man who doesn't think about it and do it twenty-four hours a day feels that he is somehow deflating the national average, letting down the team, and abandoning his own claim to normality. Men, in particular, have been designated as being always sexually available. Empirically, we know that men aren't always in the mood and ready for sex. But many a man who has not wanted casual sex or who has had relatively limited sexual desires has been made to feel unmasculine. The cultural expectation that men should be "ready or not" is heightened by the invention of Viagra (and other drugs that enhance or produce erection), as we discussed in chapter 1.

Women have a similar problem. For a long time, women who seemed to have intense interest in sex were considered abnormal. But today the woman who says "No, maybe later" or "I'm only interested twice a month" may be carted off to a counselor. Although no "female Viagra" has yet to be brought to market, one researched by Boehringer-Ingelheim, a German pharmaceutical company, was almost approved in 2010 by the FDA. Indeed, the work to identify a drug to enhance women's sexual readiness is of great interest to the pharmaceutical industry (Perry 2010). The push for a "pink Viagra" is, of course, contingent on either a strong demand from women to increase their sexual desire—or more problematically, medical or psychological professionals determining that a woman's lower sexual desire is necessarily troubling and evidence of a disorder.

Unfortunately, all our statistics—and the drug therapies for "treating" sexual desire—may lead us to presume a "right" amount of sex in a relationship instead of accepting that a unique pattern is appropriate for each person. That statistical norm may not even be completely reliable, as we discussed in chapter 2, because many of the people surveyed are inflating the number of times they say they have sex so they will look good to themselves and to the interviewer.

The thing to remember is that sex is like any other appetite: it can change by circumstance and over the life cycle. It can also depend on what, if any, relationship you are in. Some people are more interested in sex than others. Likewise, some people really savor food, and others can take it or leave it. But we don't pathologize that difference in eating unless someone is unhealthily over- or underweight. On the other hand, sex is supposed to be experienced a certain way, and so we chastise anyone who is brave enough or honest enough to say, I can take it or leave it. We use psychiatric problems or trauma as an explanation, even though the person's difference may not be associated with problems but simply with his or her own learning history. Thus, we have created a catch-22. We criticize men and women for too much sexual interest, and we send them to therapy for too little. The bottom line is, you don't need help unless your level of interest is so different from your partner's that you have to work on a compromise to preserve the relationship.

2. Do men and women have affairs for different reasons?

The cliché is that men have affairs for sex, and women have affairs for love. But the reality is more complicated! Men and women both have affairs for a whole bunch of different reasons! In chapter 4 we wrote about some of the various ways that people end up getting into an affair—ranging from being disappointed with their current relationship to just seeking an adventure or a stroke of a person's ego, to mention a few. Furthermore, women are catching up to men in terms of how often they have extramarital affairs. Still, a few things remain different: men are more likely to have an affair when their wife has an infant (Whisman et al. 2007). Is this because he isn't getting enough attention? Because he feels like his wife is pretty much "locked in" right now and less likely to leave him if she finds out about an affair? We don't know.

Some of why men's and women's rates and reasons for affairs are becoming more similar is because women and men are increasingly coming close to having similar levels of economic power. Indeed, research shows when women earn more, they are more likely to have an affair, just like men. But the same study gives us an idea that affairs really aren't the same for men and women (Munsch 2010). Sociologists found that when men earn less than their wives they are *more likely* to have an affair, too. The same is not true of wives who earn less than their spouses. So it looks like the affair had something to do with men's being interested in reasserting masculine power that they may have felt they lost by being the lower-earning spouse. So while men and women are becoming more similar in terms of their frequency of having affairs, men still seem to do so more. And while the wide range of reasons for having affairs for men and women incorporates issues ranging from opportunity and sexual curiosity to romance and falling in love with another person, men are still more likely to have an affair based on issues of power and opportunity more so than women.

3. Can a woman really have a "male type" sexuality and not suffer for it?

Throughout most of history, women have been punished for adopting the sexual prerogatives of men or, for that matter, even exceeding the narrow constraints of female sexuality. However, that stance is changing. One example of the narrowing of the sexual gender gap came up in question 2 (just above): the fact that women are starting to have more affairs. In younger age groups, as many women as men are nonmonogamous. Slowly but surely society's ideas about goodness and virginity, even sexual scarcity and worth, are becoming more liberal.

What is causing this change? The foundation of it is probably the availability of more dependable birth control. Most women will not have sex at will unless there is minimal or no risk of an unintended pregnancy. They may have sexual urges that they want to act on—but the fear of having a child at the wrong time or with the wrong person is a powerful argument for holding back.

Evolutionary psychologists believe that concern about motherhood and children creates a different sexual drive for women than for men. But the data belie a biological explanation. Rather, as the person who asked this question implies, there is "male type" sexuality—but it doesn't mean that it is "men's sexuality." The "male type" idea references the way people *name* a pattern of greater sexual energy and prerogative that has been associated historically with men. But this may not be a biological difference between genders. Differences in sexual energy, we observe, have been culturally mandated—and also has had utilitarian reasons for moderation or expression. Now that women have more freedom in their choice of how they live or when they reproduce, we would expect more women to have "male type" sexuality—and they do! Certainly, many women want sex only in the context of love or the hope of a further relationship; for many, that relationship has to be marriage. Some women, however, have a very "male" kind of sexuality. Before she became a mother in 1997, the pop icon Madonna certainly made it part of her act to show her ability to have sex for pleasure, often and under varied circumstances. Mind you, after she became a mother she talked about giving birth and motherhood in starkly conventional terms. Other female "sexual outlaws," women who have sex for curiosity or for pleasure rather than for love or commitment, definitely exist. Some women who are not prostitutes have had hundreds of lovers and, if they have been careful enough not to catch a sexually transmitted infection (STI), have no regrets.

How can we explain the sexuality of these women? How can these women engage in free-and-easy sex without ruining their lives? First of all, they have to be smart enough or lucky enough to avoid medical complications (as do men). Women are more at risk for many STIs than men are. Moreover, complications from those diseases can compromise a woman's fertility and make her more vulnerable to cancers. To escape the health consequences of a liberated sexuality, women have to use condoms, be fastidious about birth control, and choose partners who are also careful about their sexual health.

The women who do not suffer any stigma for their "male type" sexuality usually have many other social advantages that cause them to be exempt from the ordinary rules of the culture and the influence of social structures. They are attractive and successful professionally and therefore able to control their own destiny. They have sufficient charisma so that people don't care about their prior sexual experience. In the same way that people have idolized certain men and accepted their previous experience as just part of their power, there are now people who want to be the one who captures these women's hearts or respect. Think for a minute of the very successful, beautiful, and rich women stars, directors, and heads of studios in Hollywood. Cher, Barbra Streisand, Jessica Lange, Jennifer Aniston and others have had widely publicized affairs with other famous people, and they still remain a "catch." They, like their male counterparts, are loath to settle down, feel good about being independent, and have no problem going from one exciting relationship to another.

To do that, a woman has to be able to shuck off old images of female purity, be able to separate physical attraction from love, be confident enough to see men as companions rather than husbands, and enjoy sex for its own sake. Not as many women as men want to do that or can do it. But it is possible.

One important point. Most men aren't "sexual outlaws"—expressions of the extreme so-called male type sexuality—either. Most men—straight and gay—want sex in the context of love or attachment or commitment. Their reputation may not suffer as a woman's would for a significant history of sexual experiences, but most men, especially as they reach their late twenties and older, want more than just a no-attachment, no-strings, no-future kind of liaison. A "male type" sexuality is less common for both men and women than the polarized, gendered view of sexuality suggests.

4. Does beginning sex at an early age affect sexuality in good or bad ways? Might its effect be different for boys and girls?

There is some evidence that the younger a girl is when she first has sex the more likely she is to have been victimized. Somewhere between the ages of eleven and eighteen or so, a girl may have a woman's body but a girl's ignorance. She would have trouble understanding what an older man's intentions are or what sex is about and what the consequences of early sex might be. These mature-looking girls, and even girls who still look immature, are often flattered to have an older man's attention (even if he is only six months older). If they haven't been taught some self-protective responses, they are likely to accede to any demands—only to be shocked and disappointed.

Young boys are less commonly preyed on sexually by older girls, but they are often pushed into sex earlier than they want by peer opinion. They may also be tempted into premature sex by a girl who makes herself available so that she will be liked or given some attention. Boys aren't supposed to refuse sex of this type even if they would like to; thus, they have sex before they have much desire and often under duress. Sex of this type is disappointing, guilt producing, and altogether an alienating experience. In a 2010 study done by a research team at Indiana University, they found that 6 percent of boys and 9 percent of girls have had intercourse by age nine! Obviously, sex at this age is inappropriate, confusing, and often the result of abuse.

Of course, some young people start in early adolescence, like sex a lot, and keep at it. For some boys and girls, sex is a recreational skill, and they seem to believe that the sooner you start, the better you get. Disappointments seem to roll over them without crushing them, and they gain a sense of mastery and power by their conquests. Again, this is more culturally available to boys, who are encouraged to revel in their sexual accomplishments. But increasingly there are girls who love sex, also see experimentation as their right, and feel no shame or guilt.

Most parents, most institutions (like churches and schools), and more conventional teens don't believe that kids can like sex or know what they are doing. In the United States we think that young people can't experience real love and that sex is about raging hormones and an unavoidable battle between men and women (Schalet 2004). As a culture, we are not comfortable with early sexuality. Some cultures may assume that with puberty comes sexual encounters, but ours likes to delay sexuality as long as possible, envisioning all kinds of bad consequences (both physical and psychological) from early experience. We are particularly unwilling to think that our teenage daughters can cope with sexuality. Some data indicate that early intercourse is dangerous and damaging for some boys and girls, but many other data suggest that the real problem is not sex itself but rather the individual maturity, responsibility, and self-knowledge of the person in question. Some people benefit from early sexual experience; some people suffer.

5. *Why do men and women sometimes not use contraception, even when it is obviously necessary?*

First of all, for many sexual acts and in many situations, contraception is not necessary. Committed and monogamous gay and lesbian couples need not be concerned about contraception. Heterosexual couples who engage in comasturbation, oral sex, and other kinds of nonintercourse sexual play that leads to orgasm don't need contraception. Of course, all these groups do need protection from STIs.

When heterosexual couples are having sexual intercourse, they are usually motivated by love or passion. In the spirit of the moment, partners may be tentative about using contraception or protection, or they may be just plain irrational. It is hard, in the heat of love or lust, to modify one's behavior—even, amazingly enough, if one's future is at stake. One part of the brain is saying, "Better watch out," and the other part is saying, "Don't worry this time." That is the power of desire talking: to cast one's fate to luck and do something that has obvious possibilities for disaster.

Given human nature, perhaps the surprising thing is that anybody uses contraception or condoms for protection. The passion of the moment and the emotional awkwardness of slipping on a condom at the last moment might be deterrents. Research reviewed in chapter 3 shows that adult men use condoms the first time they have sex with someone about 42 percent of the time; women about 48 percent of the time. The Indiana University 2010 survey of sexual behavior in the United States mentioned above found that men report using condoms in general 25 percent of the time; but teen men report using condoms over 70 percent of the time! The 2010 study done by AARP (for people over forty-five) showed that only 12 percent of these men and 33 percent of women used a condom always or usually. So, perhaps young people are getting the message about protection more often and putting it in practice more often than their supposedly more mature elders.

Gender plays a role, too. Some young girls are taught that it is sexy to submit to men, that men like women who give men more pleasure and less aggravation—in this case, by having sex without a condom. Young women in particular think it is their role to submit when a boyfriend asks them to skip the condom. In some cultures even a woman in a committed relationship perceives it as inappropriate to suggest using a condom. Her fears are often well founded: her husband will think he is being accused of unfaithfulness and be furious (even if it is true), or he will feel it is morally wrong to interfere with the possibility of conception (Marin et al. 1997).

At the same time, women have been given almost all the responsibility for contraception and protection and have been made the gatekeepers for sexual intercourse—as if they are the only ones who have something to lose if things go wrong. So the very people who are less likely to feel comfortable directing the action or to be dominant in decision making, especially when young, are given all the responsibility for preventing pregnancy and STDs. Throughout life, it is women more than men who are put in a position of being pressured to abdicate these responsibilities.

However, both women and men find themselves unequipped to make contraception and protection a natural part of sexuality. Men and women can feel awkward about talking about sex. Discussing contraception and protection, much less planning for them, takes a high level of social skill and comfort with the mechanics of sexuality. And because few sexuality classes cover the topic, nearly everyone learns "on the job."

The first time a person is faced with the necessity to bring up the need for contraception is usually right in the middle of a passionate clinch. This is on-the-spot training, and it usually doesn't work. Adults and adolescents alike need to talk about condoms before (not during) sex—but if a person is not comfortable with the relationship (or there is no relationship), that talk doesn't happen. In order for condom use to be easy and comfortable, each person has to be educated about the need for protection and know that it is not an accusation of immorality but rather the right thing to do both as an act of respect for your partner—and in order to have worry-free sex.

But that is still not the standard in the United States, and this lack of preparation explains why the United States continues to have a higher rate of teenage pregnancy than other Western countries where sex education is more common. (Our rates have declined to their lowest in fifty years, but we are still higher than comparable countries, as discussed in chapter 5.) Teens and young adults are new to sexual relations and are still learning how to articulate their own interests or to enforce them. They may be too embarrassed to introduce a condom, too inexperienced to use it correctly, or insist on continued use of the condom even after they have been "going together" for a few weeks. The majority of adolescents, as we have stated, do use a condom in the beginning of a relationship—but often stop because they now trust each other and start to rely on other kinds of contraception—which may or may not be used. The problem is that only a condom will protect them from disease and pregnancy. After a while they become lax about any kind of protection—and they might be too young to realize how much they will lose if they get a disease or get pregnant. In fact, some young people have a certain fascination with the idea of seeing if their bodies actually work—if their sperm can actually impregnate someone, if their ovaries work and a baby will form. They pay a high price for finding out that their fertility is intact and their bodies work just fine.

Some people refuse to believe that education about sex and training in communication skills will actually reduce negative consequences. But research indicates that teen pregnancy rates decline when communication skills are learned and reinforced by practice in sex education programs. Unfortunately, few teens have access to such programs, and most of the programs that do exist aren't long enough to cause lasting changes in behavior. Until we teach people how to use condoms as a normal and sexy part of lovemaking, until we teach them that safe sex is better sex, we can expect depressing statistics on pregnancy and disease transmission.

While sex education of any sort doesn't solve all of the dilemmas of sexuality, the contrast between outcomes of comprehensive sex education versus abstinence-only sex education gives us an idea of how helpful knowing how to talk about it can be. Students of "just say no" abstinence-only programs delay first sex by about eighteen months; but when they eventually do have sex, they are *less likely* to use a condom or any other contraception. They don't have the psychological skills or cultural permission to protect themselves, and they do have the baggage of ambivalence or guilt about what they are doing!

In the meantime, improving communication and understanding between men and women and between partners in same-sex relationships will help people learn to show they care by taking responsibility for contraception and disease prevention. Sure, some people will still refuse to use contraceptives and protection; some will refuse to compromise sensation (even though some condoms can barely be felt); and still others will believe they are invulnerable. But changing cultural beliefs about contraception and safe sex could get most people to take precautions and have a happy, safe sex life—and that education may translate into improving those disappointing rates of condom use among older people as our young people become our middle-aged and older people.

6. I know my grandparents must have had sex when they were young. But now they are in their late seventies, and it is hard for me to think of them "doing it." Is the sex drive still alive in older people?

We didn't spend much time in this book talking about sex and aging, but we have seen the issue become much more prominent in the past decade as the baby boom generation ages and reaches midlife and beyond. One of us (Pepper Schwartz) consulted on a 2010 survey for the AARP (the largest U.S. organization representing older Americans) on the sex lives of older Americans and provides relationship advice to its members. What's the news from AARP? The frequency of sex for all people (single or coupled) age sixty and older has increased over the past ten years, and in 2010, 42 percent of men in their sixties reported having sex at least once a month, while 32 percent of women that age also reported sex at least once a month.

Why do older women have lower sexual frequencies than men? One of the differences, we think, is that women outlive their partners and are more likely to be living single at this time. When we look at *partnered* people, the difference is smaller: 63 percent of men with a partner (married, living together, or dating, age groups from forty-five and older) reported having sex one to four times a month, and 57 percent of women in this category reported having sex one to four times a month.

Sex researchers Masters and Johnson studied older as well as younger people back in the late sixties and early seventies, when they were first examining human sexual responses. They came to the conclusion that many elderly people can and do have an active sex life way into their eighties, but only under these two conditions: They must be in reasonably good health, and they must have had a continuous sex life over their lifetime.

All studies indicate that health is an important consideration. The 2010 AARP study showed that health of oneself and one's partner was the most important variable for predicting sexual frequency. Not only does bad health cause depression and otherwise diminish sexual interest, but a lot of the medications prescribed for the common diseases of older people (such as late-onset diabetes and high blood pressure) tend to suppress sexual interest or inhibit male sexual performance or female lubrication. Even without medication, natural aging processes can cause physical and psychological complications. Men, in particular, get upset when they find they need a longer time than in the past to get an erection, when the refractory period between ejaculations lengthens, and when their erections aren't as hard as they used to be. These extremely common changes may be expected, but some men get so depressed about them that they experience psychological problems that lead to more problems, including temporary or sustained erectile failure.

Another big contributing factor for men is prostate problems. The prostate is a gland that surrounds the urethra as it exits the bladder; it secretes part of the seminal fluid. Over time it becomes looser, or "boggy" as physicians like to describe. Thus, ejaculation occurs with less force. More than half of all men have had a significant prostate problem; by their eighties, almost 80 percent have had a problem. Surgery to ameliorate the problem is not uncommon. A significant number of men get prostate cancer (one in six in their lifetime). The five-year survival rate is nearly 100 percent; the ten-year survival rate is 91 percent. The growing awareness of prostate cancer has led to early detection and a range of treatment options.

Obviously, women escape this particular problem. But other facts of aging influence their sexuality. Increased risk of breast cancer, hormonal changes, and increased risk of heart disease and high-blood pressure after menopause can all depress sex drive. After menopause, women may lose some ability to produce natural vaginal lubricant, but there are dozens of different kinds of commercial lubricants, and they are a handy substitute. In addition, society's image of the sexy and desirable woman is young, not old. Older women—as well as older men—have to adjust to the idea of being sexual in a less than idealized body.

Despite these potential problems, older people can still enjoy sex. Masters and Johnson found that the single strongest predictor of continued sexual activity was past behavior. Older women lubricated more and older men had fewer erectile problems if they had continued to have sex at least every so often through life and had never stopped for a long time. Their conclusion: "use it or lose it." In other words, sometimes physical disability may follow from sexual behavior (or lack of sexual behavior) rather than cause it.

Part of the reason older people stop having sex sometimes is because they think they should. In the past decade, this attitude has declined, as the AARP study showed. Still, we tend to stereotype passion as a prerogative of the young. We even stigmatize sexually interested elderly persons as "dirty old men" or "ridiculous old ladies." Even the concept of "cougar"—older women showing sexual interest in younger men, carries with it on the one hand a sense of sexual liberation, and on the other, a kind of resistance to the notion of sexually active and enthusiastic older women. For much older people, a continuing interest in sex can even be considered evidence of senility or mental instability. There are many documented cases of nursing home personnel locking older people in their rooms so that they cannot visit each other's beds. Nursing home workers have complained to family members that their parent masturbated or masturbated too much and that steps should be taken to stop such behavior.

If older people are lucky enough to control their own destiny, to have access to a partner, and to be reasonably healthy, the data suggest that they like sex, albeit less frequently than younger folks. Some data indicate that sexual intercourse varies in married elderly persons from about once a week to about once a month, but that isn't the only or necessarily the best measure of sexual activity. A decrease in the capacity for erection or ejaculation in men doesn't necessarily mean low sexual interest or less capacity to be a good sexual partner. Quite the contrary, older women often voice pleasure in their partner's new attention to foreplay, touching, and longer, gentler sexual sessions.

Many older people have sexual fantasies and needs. Unfortunately, they have few chances to find a partner. Heterosexual women, especially, find partners scarce, because women live several more years on average than men do (which may explain why sexual activity among older men is more common than among women). Lesbians are more fortunate because they are seeking partners among other women rather than men. Lesbian sex tends to be less genitally focused than gay or heterosexual sex, and so their sexual experience may be more continuous. The good news for all older people is the advent of online dating and, lately, the specific attention to older singles on these sites. Many sites say that their fastest growing group of clients is people over fifty. This means that older people now have a way of finding each other, and fewer have to be lonely or celibate.

In general, then, although the fire of sexuality among older people may seem more like embers than a raging conflagration, there is still heat. Even people with severe medical problems, such as a serious heart condition, still maintain a sex life. In fact, some have made news by dying while "in the act." For example, the former New York state governor Nelson Rockefeller died at age seventy during a tryst with a twenty-five-year-old woman, disobeying the orders of heart specialists—who usually say that sex is fine if it is with your spouse, but with others it could be too exciting.

So don't discount your grandparents' sexuality until they are gone. And be happy for them if they are sexually active and continue to enjoy one of the delights of being alive.

Sexual Orientation

7. I still don't know where homosexuality originates. Where do you think it be-gins? Do you think it is really different for men and women?

Determining origins of homosexuality is extremely difficult. Remember, we still have people arguing over the origin of the species. Too many people are invested in competing theories—and the theories all come loaded with political implications.

This question isn't debated just in the halls of academia. The popular media debate it. In churches, temples, and synagogues, the issue is debated. It is even debated around the dinner table—sometimes quite heatedly.

Before we review the arguments regarding the origins of homosexuality, we'd like to ask why the origins of homosexuality are of concern. In other words, who cares, and why does it matter?

From our point of view, debates about homosexuality have much to do with the importance of society's attachment to gender differences. That is, even though sex typically gets done in private, people judge one another in terms of whether they conform to norms of masculinity and femininity and to the heterosexual "dos and don'ts" that are attached to being a man or a woman.

If one doesn't know the origins of homosexuality, one also doesn't know the origins of heterosexuality. Still, that is hardly ever the question that gets raised. Why? For many people, the origins of heterosexuality aren't questioned because it appears to be natural and rooted in the imperative to procreate, just as norms of masculinity and femininity seen as "natural" even though they vary dramatically from time to time and place to place.

From a theoretical point of view, the debate over the origins of homosexu-ality is tied to whether one is an essentialist or a social constructionist. But the consequences of these abstract theoretical perspectives are quite practical. The essentialist position would suggest that gay men, lesbians, and heterosexuals are born and not made. But if so, essentialists' discrimination against homo-sexuality seems cruel and unjust, like discrimination based on race, size, or ablebodiedness.

What if social constructionists are right, and homosexuality is not a natu-ral, genetic trait? It also means that *heterosexuality* is not a natural, genetic trait. Does that then mean that heterosexuality or homosexuality is a choice? Not necessarily. People can choose how they behave but have far less control over how they feel or what they desire. People do not necessarily choose to feel homosexual or heterosexual attractions.

Another issue that social constructionists draw our attention to is about how we define "homosexuality" or "heterosexuality": Is it acts? Is it fantasies?

Is it identity? Is it participation in a social movement? When homosexuality gets broken down into these questions, we find that people may have much more diverse fantasy lives than what their "identity" as straight, gay, or lesbian would suggest. In that sense, what we define as straight, gay, lesbian, or bisexual is how the categories become socially constructed.

Here's an example: children who are raised by gay or lesbian parents are more likely to experiment more widely with same-sex and cross-sex sexuality. They do not, however, seem to be much more likely to identify as gay or lesbian than kids who grew up in a heterosexual household. Is that good? Or is it neutral because children with gay parents have the same right as any other kids to have whatever sexual identity they want? The fact is that environment plays a role in some forms of sexuality, but not in whether someone ultimately feels gay, lesbian, or straight.

These two theoretical perspectives produce three popular hypotheses regarding homosexuality's origins: (1) that it is biological, caused by hormones, chromosomes, and genetic information; (2) that it is sociological, learned through lifestyle and sexual opportunity, which can happen throughout a lifetime; (3) that it is the result of various kinds of early childhood identification with men's and women's experience, formed prior to any adolescent sexual encounters. The people who say homosexuality is biological and the people who say it is the result of early childhood identification believe homosexuality is not voluntary. Gay men and lesbians no more control the direction of their sexual desires than heterosexuals do—they just experience them.

Those who have a sociological point of view are much more divided on the question of choice. Those who disapprove of homosexuality say that people decide to be gay or lesbian, and therefore deserve no protection against discrimination because they are not a special group so much as a lifestyle. Rarely do those people who disapprove of homosexuality and think that people can "choose" to be heterosexual recognize the enormous flexibility that this suggests about all our sexualities.

People who favor gay rights argue that even if gay and lesbian people establish their identities through everyday experiences and choose to follow their desires, the final product is no less legitimate a choice than heterosexual persons' becoming whatever they become. Our own stand is that whatever the path to sexual orientation, it is precognitive and nonvolitional for both heterosexuals and homosexuals. The sexual self just evolves, perhaps from biological origins for some, and further defined through a complex array of everyday choices and environmental circumstances. Furthermore, even if some choice is involved, so what? We choose our religion, and that is a protected right, no matter what we choose. In fact, the ability not to choose is also a right. The Queer movement was founded on the idea that there are many ways to be sexual and that categories themselves are inappropriate. People who call themselves queer refuse to be organized into heterosexual or homosexual identities.

We remain open to the idea that there are many paths to self-definition. There is some support for all of these theories. In fact, many scientists believe there is more than one way to become gay or lesbian. Dean Hamer's work on the inheritance of a "gay gene" (discussed in chapter 1), which shows up through the maternal line of gay men and is far more common among gay men than chance would predict, convincingly shows that for at least some gay men, homosexuality may be an inherited trait, or predisposition. Le-Vay's (1993) work on brain samples, showing different brain construction, has more critics, but there is still strong evidence that some gay men may be physiologically different from heterosexual men. Twin studies show that when one identical twin is gay the other one is more likely to be gay, too, as compared with fraternal twins. Even so, this doesn't happen anywhere near all of the time. Fred Whitman's (1983) cross-cultural data showing that certain kinds of behaviors appear in gay men but not heterosexual men the world over fuels the biological argument.

And yet some gay men and lesbians, who have no genetic marker, still feel that they were gay from their very first sexual stirrings. There is no explanation for these early feelings; they begin young and are very distinct. Some psychologists believe these feelings have been reconstructed from hindsight, but some parents report that their children, early on, have strong same-sex crushes and a greater identification with the other sex.

Some people are attracted to both sexes. Somewhere along the line they may find themselves attracted to the same sex, with no prior homosexual attractions in their young or adolescent life. Some men were happily married or dating women until midlife and then find their attractions to other men steadily growing. Or even more numerous are the women who never found women sexually alluring and then fall in love with a specific woman and sexualize that person (Schwartz and Blumstein 1976). They are as surprised as anyone else. A case in point is a woman who was married her entire adult life, had three children, but then fell in love with a woman colleague. They were both sixty at the time; neither had had a sexual fantasy about women prior to their own love affair.

Any gender difference in the origins of homosexuality is likely to be this: Women seem to be able to sexualize whomever they love; men tend to love the person they sexualize. In gay and lesbian sex surveys by the *Advocate*, 29 percent of lesbians say that they thought their sexual orientation was in part a choice, but only 4 percent of gay men indicated that they thought it was a choice (Lever 1994a, 1995). This outcome is as likely a product of gendered social processes, not fundamental gender differences. Girls, whether straight or gay, are raised to be more relationally focused than boys are, and this learning is embedded in social structures that influence how girls and boys grow up to be sexual adults. The difference between a gay sexual orientation and a lesbian sexual orientation, then, is related at least in some major way to social experience that treats boys and men one way and girls and women another.

8. I have been told that in the absence of prejudice, everyone would be bisexual. Does society impose so many rules against homosexuality because people are afraid of their own bisexuality?

Is everyone, at core, bisexual? Some people think so. But probably a whole continuum of sexual desire exists, with some people no more able to sexualize same-sex people than they can a bowling ball and some people no more able to sexualize other-sex people than they can a basketball. Still others can be turned on to either—and even to bowling balls or basketballs—depending on the circumstances. Increasingly, women are experimenting with same-sex sexual behavior, and young women have exceeded young men in recent years in their same-sex activity. It does not appear that more women are discovering that they are lesbian, but they have gained greater sexual permission for experimentation. To complicate matters, women's public same-sex sexual behavior has become a commonplace heterosexual turn-on.

Even so, society imposes many constraints on bisexuality. For example, many religious groups interpret their scriptures as prohibiting all same-sex sexuality. Governments, influenced by religious beliefs, show little tolerance for same-sex sexual activity. Many parents, even liberal ones, are nervous or panicked if their child has any kind of sexual play with a same-sex friend. It is hard to know what kind of bisexual behavior would exist in a more open society.

In many countries around the world, bisexual conduct is more tolerated and even more expected than it is in the United States. Boys in many parts of the world are not allowed to get near girls until they marry, and many boys may wait to marry until they are older and richer. Under these circumstances, same-sex experiences are expected. Other countries, such as Greece and other European and African Mediterranean countries, allow men more license with each other. American men are often shocked to see men kissing each other and holding hands in the affectionate way that women are allowed in this country. The range of same-sex contact is much broader in other parts of the world than it is in the United States.

It has also been observed in the United States that if access to the other sex is cut off, people who had no previous desire for same-sex partners develop it. The most common place this situation is noted is in prisons and reformatories. Men may take a male partner for the duration of their stay, and perhaps cease same-sex affiliation on their release. Or they may merely use another man sexually, denying that the act is homosexual. They insist that if they are the one penetrating the other sexual partner, then they are still playing the heterosexual part. And many books have noted the quasi-family and marital arrangements that girls in reform schools arrange. Some are sexualized, and some are not. It is easy, it seems, for women to love each other when necessity or opportunity presents itself.

This evidence doesn't prove that anyone can have bisexual desire or that if they have it they have equal desire for both sexes. In fact, the latter is empirically uncommon. Most people who describe themselves as bisexual still state a preference for one sex. Or they have had significant love affairs with both sexes over a lifetime and define themselves more strongly in terms of the person they are in love with now. A smaller group of men and women, however, have claimed the right to be seen as truly bisexual, retaining the ability to sexualize both sexes throughout the life cycle and not be seen, by either homosexuals or heterosexuals, as denying their true preferences.

What is so interesting about the question of bisexuality is that some gay, lesbian, and heterosexual communities have problems with the notion of bisexuality. Gay men and lesbians may feel that a person claiming bisexuality is reserving the option to be heterosexual and thereby gain the perks of being a sexual conformist. Heterosexuals may feel the same homophobia toward bisexuals that they feel toward gay men and lesbians. Sometimes, people are worried that a person who identifies as bisexual cannot be monogamous. The response from bisexual people is that straight and gay people have desires for other people outside of their committed relationships and keep them as fantasies, not actions—and most of the time they override them. Bisexuals are no different in their capacity for monogamy.

What does mark bisexuals as different from both homosexuals and heterosexuals is the fundamentally "sex positive" approach to sexuality that bisexuality seems to represent. Straight and gay people run the gamut in terms of sexual freedom and sexual expressiveness; however, bisexuals are seen as sexual outlaws (because they are seen as denying their "real" core sexual attraction) by both straight people and gay people.

So, to answer the question, more bisexuality would probably occur if we had fewer sanctions against homosexuality. The increased amount of bisexual experimentation in younger generations gives support to that view. But for bisexuality to be accepted by the larger culture, another shift would need to occur: a reduction in ambivalence or negativity regarding sexual expression and sexual freedom. Slow but steady steps are being made toward accepting homosexuality as a legitimate form of sexual expression and family building. However, the sex-positive attitudes associated with bisexuality are further behind.

9. I'm a lesbian peer educator, and people always ask who is the man and who is the woman in a gay/lesbian relationship. What do you think?

Well, the first thing we think is that you might give them a copy of our book! This kind of "heteronormativity"—or the assumption that all intimate relationships follow a consistent, seemingly natural pattern of masculine and feminine roles—persists for two very big reasons. The first is that people tend to associate the performance of gender with the performance of their sexuality; to be a good woman is to be a good heterosexual woman, to be a good man is to be a good heterosexual man. Same-sex relationships, from this point of view, must work within this paradigm and just try to make adjustments for the "lack" of a member of the other sex in the relationship.

But the second big reason is because, despite the fact that we have made a tremendous amount of progress in terms of gender equality in U.S. society, we still continue to eroticize—or think of as ultimately sexy—traditional gender roles. In our everyday lives we experience gender equality or at least aspirations to gender equality. But in our fantasy lives the sexual script of dominance and submission gets supercharged by images of a domineering, butch guy and a demure, reticent femme woman. The drama that plays in our heads is the drama that keeps straight people who might even know better asking questions like "who plays the man's role? Who plays the woman's role?" when trying to learn about the lives of gay and lesbian couples. Same-sex coupling can feel disorienting to people in a dominantly heterosexual world, where sexual fantasies revolve around the centrality of gender difference.

Now the reason the question is so challenging is that it feels—especially if you are a gay or lesbian person—dehumanizing. Whenever sexual scripts—or social scripts—blind people from seeing a situation exactly as it is (in this case seeing two women or two men as just that), it feels like hurtful stereotyping. It reminds us that the gender scripts for men and women—whether straight, gay, or lesbian—have the potential to be dehumanizing.

10. I understand why lesbians might want children, but what about gay men? Wouldn't gay men be dangerous to their own boy children?

This question might appear offensive to many readers, but well-meaning people continue to ask it. The question reflects their skepticism about gay male sexuality—and even beliefs about the dangers of heterosexual male sexuality. By far, most men, both heterosexual and gay, are not sexually interested in children. However, the question unfairly maligns gay men. Being gay is in itself not associated with child molestation or pedophilia. Both heterosexual and gay men have molested children—and seem to do so more than women (who also commit child sexual abuse, but at lower rates). We are not sure why more men than women sexualize young children. As we've mentioned, some researchers suggest that men who aren't involved in the care of infants more easily sexualize those children as they grow up. Also, men's sexual imagination is influenced by cultural and commercial emphasis on young and nubile bodies.

We are more interested in why gay men have been associated with pedophilia—what sustains the myth? Pedophilia is actually *much* more common among men who live heterosexual lives. It is assumed that when men sexually abuse boys this must be a homosexual act. But in fact pedophiles (people who sexualize children) tend to prey on both boys and girls and often are equally likely to victimize either.

The other side of the coin is that the literature on gay parenting is positive. In the 1996 trial on gay marriage in the state of Hawaii, opponents of the law tried to make the point that gay men might not be fit parents to convince the court that gay men ought not to be allowed to marry. However, all the empirical evidence presented at the trial indicated that gay men who choose to parent are as qualified as heterosexual or lesbian parents. They may tend to be somewhat more structured (disciplinarian, scheduled) than other households and perhaps have more playtime with their children, but in most ways, they are similar to other kinds of parents. Other trials since then that have occurred as a result of the gay marriage debate (Vermont, Massachusetts, and the recent federal appeal of California's Proposition 8 in San Francisco) have also brought up the issue of gay parenting, and in all cases, the evidence has revealed positive gay and lesbian parenting practices comparable, and in some cases, with better outcomes, than heterosexual parents. You can review the evidence on same-sex parenting in chapter 5.

Some of the puzzles about gay men as fathers relate to a belief that men just aren't "programmed" to nurture, but that women are. In that sense, the suspicion of gay men as fathers represents skepticism about men as care providers for their children. In chapter 5 we talked about research on the gender of the parents—done by Biblarz and Stacey (2010). They found that the gender of the parents didn't matter, but that having two parents was usually more beneficial to children than one.

There are more data, however, on heterosexual and lesbian parents. Lesbians are much more likely to have children from a previous relationship or have a personal script that guides them to motherhood even if they have no wish to be heterosexually married. Gay men, on the other hand, cannot be pregnant and often have no model of fatherhood outside of a marital union. Nevertheless, an increasing number of gay men have recently begun to consider single fatherhood or fatherhood with a gay partner. Indeed, among gay (male) partners who are married, 34 percent report raising children (versus 28 percent of married lesbians). Among gay partners who are unmarried, 7 percent are raising children (versus 26 percent of unmarried lesbians) (Sears et al. 2005).

There is no evidence that gay men are not good fathers with all the same loving and protective feelings about their children that other parents have. Most adults do not see children, especially their own, as sex objects. Gay men are no exception to this rule.

Sexual Harassment and Violence

11. Aren't some charges of sexual harassment trumped up—maybe just because the guy has a better job than the woman? Can't a woman's acts be responsible for a sexual encounter some of the time?

This is a double-barreled question: And the answer to the second part is short: yes, of course a woman can instigate a sexual encounter. In fact, in the dubious category of "you've come a long way baby," as women have increasingly come to populate nearly half the workforce, the number of claims against women have increased as well. Still, men are more likely to be the perpetrators of workplace sexual harassment.

Sexual harassment is defined as one employee making unwanted sexual advances toward another or a person's verbal or physical conduct is of a sexual nature against the wishes of another employee. The Equal Employment Opportunity Commission (EEOC) explains that sexual harassment occurs "when submission to or rejection of this conduct explicitly or implicitly affects an individual's employment, unreasonably interferes with an individual's work performance or creates an intimidating, hostile or offensive work environment."

This is serious stuff, but the good news is the rate of sexual harassment in the United States overall has declined. This may be due to improved gender equality, growing awareness of sexual harassment, the success of several high-profile legal cases punishing men for workplace sexual harassment, and the increased provision of sexual harassment prevention workshops in the workplace.

But the first part of the question about "trumped up" charges suggests that publicity about exceptional sexual harassment cases has left some people with the wrong impression about sexual harassment laws. Sometimes those laws may *seem* to have become a justification for abridging free speech. Or, they may be seen as punishing people who are awkward or inept but are not malicious or intent on undermining another person's chances to succeed.

Skepticism regarding sexual harassment claims is labeled "backlash" by activists who guard against sexual harassment, and, as we described in chapter 5, the polarization of the issue can eclipse the problem itself. Keep in mind that the cases that receive the most publicity are not a random sample of sexual harassment cases. The popular media typically pick the anomalous or exceptional cases, such as reverse sexual harassment or seemingly frivolous claims. Sex sells, and exceptional sex sells better than ordinary sex.

Sexual harassment is a hot topic partially because the law has become involved and partially because complaints have become common in university and corporate bureaucracies and are adjudicated through the courts. Sensationalized or bizarre cases aside, legitimate cases of sexual harassment are, or should be, beyond society's tolerance. Sexual harassment is really an abrogation of a person's right to work; to be in charge of their own body; and to be able to do a job without insult, humiliation, bullying, or self-doubt. Both women and men have been found guilty of demanding sexual favors from unwilling and shocked co-workers or employees, but rates of incidents by men are greater than the rate of incidents by women. However, even though the courts are far more sympathetic to sexual harassment victims than they used to be, many women feel that the reaction has been too long coming and not swift or widespread enough. Many women observe that they continue to suffer indignities and threats. Relatively few actually file suit—and then only when life is unbearable. Information about victimization, therefore, is hard to find. A U.S. Defense Department Survey conducted in 2006 found that one-third of women and 6 percent of men said they had experienced sexual harassment. The figure for women was down from a similar survey from a decade earlier (Associated Press 2008).

Some men and women feel that sexual harassment lawsuits are used as clubs by spurned women or guilty women who are not taking responsibility for their own seductive behaviors. They may readily condemn quid pro quo harassment, where a woman is given the choice to comply with sexual requests to obtain or advance in a job. But the question gets a little complicated when the scene shifts into grayer areas, like telling sexual jokes or displaying nude or sexualized photos, or other things that are clearly tasteless. But are they dangerous? Do they create a hostile work environment? That is the question firms—and courts—must contemplate. The charge of sexual harassment can raise skepticism, too, when a consensual love affair ends. Some people feel a love affair between two people of wildly different statuses and power—such as a professor and a student or a military instructor and a trainee—cannot be consensual. On the other hand, many people observe that power inequalities are extremely erotic to both parties, and were we to outlaw them, we would be unraveling many relationships.

Perhaps the issue is most clearly framed as a sociological rather than a legal question. Under what circumstances does a person have free will? When does consent seem freely given? And when does it seem coerced either directly or indirectly? We know a five-year-old can't say no to a date. But what about a woman of twenty who accepts a date with her professor? Is she free and capable of saying no? This is the kind of case that raises controversy.

The subtleties of the interactions that may be deemed sexual harassment are difficult to verify in a legalistic setting. Sociologists Judith Howard and Jocelyn Hollander, Dan Renfrow, and Judith Howard used a scene from the David Mamet play *Oleanna* to highlight the dilemma in their book, *Gendered Situations, Gendered Selves* (2011). The play opens with an undergraduate woman waiting to meet with her male professor. He proposes that she spend more time with him to improve her grade. He also keeps her waiting a very long time. Hollander and colleagues point out that the power difference between the student and the professor places her in an impossible situation, even before anything explicitly sexual or romantic becomes involved. As the play evolves, the student experiences the instructor's acts (such as suggestions to work alone and requests to make accommodations to his personal life) as improper and indicative of his abuse of his power over her, and she files a complaint of sexual harassment. Whether a "pass" has been made is never clear in the play, and it is certainly not clear to the professor. The complaint renders the professor at risk of losing his job and his good reputation. One of the observations that the playwright is making is that the student now appears to have power over the instructor. But, of course, the power gained in prosecuting a sexual harassment case is merely winning a battle. The student is still confined to a subordinate and sexualized position. Moreover, even though the professor didn't recognize the coercion involved in the interaction with the student, the power difference loaded the situation with the potential for manipulation. The professor's obtuseness regarding the power difference led directly to bitterness on the part of the student.

Women can and should be held accountable for their own acts, whether they constitute aggressive sexuality or merely adult consent. We do not see women as always the victim. A woman who has sex with a man and who later regrets it is still accountable for her acts. On the other hand, a woman's acting sexy is not license for "open season." And women who interact with powerful people, such as students directly working with a PhD adviser, should be as alert as their mentors that if a sexual relationship starts, they should alter the power relationship to maintain their free will.

Nevertheless, real life offers few clear, cut-and-dried examples. Individuals have mixed agendas, and they have their own levels of self-awareness. Ideally, that self-awareness should involve awareness about power as part of gauging sexual propriety. Most people reinterpret events to their advantage. We hope that flirting, jokes, and good-natured, but not hostile or abusive, sexual remarks will still be allowed. Playful sexual exploration makes life pleasant for many people. But sexual harassment persists. We think after a period of long-needed protection, we will reach an understanding that sexual bullies should be consistently and swiftly punished but that awkward sexual behavior should merely be corrected.

12. Do you think that people can ever accept the notion that men are sometimes victims of sexual violence, abuse, or rape?

What is interesting about your question is that we might also ask will people ever accept the *fact* (and not just the *notion*) that men are victims of abuse, including rape. According to the Bureau of Justice Statistics, 9 percent of rape victims are men. While sexuality and sexual victimization are supercharged with male privilege, that male privilege is often about men being required and expected to fulfill a role of dominance, including dominance over other men. This is so clearly the case that the FBI's database of crime statistics defines rape as "carnal knowledge of a female forcibly and against her will" (FBI 2004). In other words, a man's being forced to have sex against his will is simply not part of the definition. Such a definition has meant that people are limited by their sexual imaginations that equate men's sexuality with power, women's with victimization. But the facts are different.

Although it has taken many years and many court cases, the case of sexual abuse in the Catholic Church gives us evidence that understanding of men's and boys' vulnerabilities are coming to be understood. Starting in the 1980s, a few men began reporting their childhood and adolescent experiences of sexual abuse at the hands of their priests, a job currently only held by men. The recognition—by the families and communities, by the courts, and by the Church—took a long time, and eventually many filed cases. But in 2010, the Vatican—which is the headquarters of the world Catholic Church—took more steps forward than it had in the preceding years, starting by issuing an apology.

What's the bottom line? Will we come to recognize men as victims of sexual abuse and exploitation? We think that is happening. The sad tales of young men whose trust was betrayed by their priest (just as by any adult, especially those who are responsible for them) has awakened a nation to the fact that young men can be as vulnerable as young women. Still, because young men are often too embarrassed to bear witness against a sexual perpetrator and often hide these abuses for a lifetime, the full extent of male child sexual abuse may not be revealed.

13. What is sadomasochistic sex about? Is it always a reflection of the desire to dominate?

Sadomasochism involves gaining pleasure from inflicting pain (sadism) or receiving pain (masochism). It might help to recognize S and M on a continuum: think of spanking, tickling, and love bites as actions that can be understood as "rough sex," involving pain and pleasure that can be understood as very small versions of S and M. Moving across the continuum are acts involving, for example, bondage and domination that, to meet a classical definition of sadism or masochism, do not include consent.

In real life there are two kinds of sadomasochistic sex (S and M): playful, mutual experimentation with the eroticism of power and its evil twin, the real thing. Because domination is part of the heterosexual sexual script, which tends to provide greater privilege to men than to women, there's good reason to think about S and M from a gendered perspective. Be mindful, though, that just because S and M plays on gendered notions of power and submission in sexuality, it isn't necessarily bad. S and M can indeed reinforce gendered power relationships, but people who try S and M are not necessarily submitting to such tired scripts; in fact, S and M can be a disruption or rejection or reversal of such scripts.

Playful sadomasochism is not necessarily a degrading or sexist experience. As described by many writers in the interesting book *Pleasure and Danger: Exploring Female Sexuality* (Vance 1984), sadomasochism can be an eye-opening excursion into submission and domination. One person tries out being powerful and gets turned on by the ability to direct all the action. The paradox is that because this is a mutual act, the person can only "order" what the other person really wants to do. So the "sadist" has to understand the script that the "masochist" seeks, including what the masochist wants to exclude. If the sadist and masochist don't both understand the boundaries, the fantasy is broken. To do a "play" in which both people like the part they have, the script has to be subtly negotiated and the ritual has to be one that is reassuring to both. In such cases, partners may have a signal or a safe word when they seek to exit the "play."

The sadist may have to dress right (leather, knee-high boots, other commanding sorts of paraphernalia) and follow a set script of commands. The masochist also has to communicate to the dominant actor what acts he or she wants to experiment with so that each person's fantasies are fulfilled.

What is the appeal of this particular fantasy? For masochists, it is the loss of ego, responsibility, and resistance. They want to be directed and humbled (but only during the play). The masochist may want rough sex but indicates what is too rough. It is a challenge to achieve the thrill of submission without the risk. The sadist gets to feel omnipotent, gets exactly the sex acts that he or she wants, and knows that the partner feels pleasure in submission. Each person's fantasy nicely folds into the other person's need. One person likes to be spanked, and the other person wants the sensation of turning someone on by inflicting light pain. Such acts may not be appealing to most tastes, but so long as partners have complementary desires, a good match has been made.

But that's the play version. In the darker variant of S and M, the masochist really wants to be significantly humiliated, beaten, or frightened. Some people really get aroused by being treated as contemptible and by being abused. If they find a true sadist to oblige them, they may be in grave jeopardy. It is one thing to be tied up by someone whom you trust and who will untie you immediately if you become scared. It's quite another to be tied up by someone who really wants you to panic. The panic makes the person feel all the more worthless, far beyond what he or she needs to be sexually aroused.

Even the game may be a problem when it too clearly mirrors gender reality. When gay men or lesbians play S and M games, they need not worry about mirroring the gendered reality in the everyday world, although gender is not the only source of power difference in couples. But when heterosexual men and women play them, they risk strengthening real domination. If the man dominates the woman in real life, dominating her even more in play may be psychologically brutalizing to both parties. The man becomes a tyrant and respects the woman even less. The woman becomes merely a shadow and loses her sense of worth and peer status. If, however, the two are equals in real life they can "afford" this type of play, or if they reverse roles they can have fun experimenting with the partner's position and perks. Men may enjoy being directed rather than always being the director. Women may be turned on by literally as well as figuratively being on top.

As with all explorations, S and M sex requires the players to know why they are going somewhere and what they want to happen when they get there. If the couple likes experimentation and play, S and M doesn't have to be personally or politically dangerous. But if one person has a real need to dominate and humiliate and if the other is passive and has low self-esteem, then sadomasochistic sex is not fantasy but exaggeration. And then it's not fun.

14. Are all men potential rapists? Is the proclivity to rape wired in?

The short answer is no. The long answer is that these aren't such unreasonable questions, given that rape is overwhelmingly gendered: over 90 percent of sexual assault cases involve a male perpetrator. Furthermore, sex offenders, including rapists, child molesters, and exhibitionists, are very, very difficult to rehabilitate. In other words, sex offenders do not, in general, get better through psychiatric or psychopharmacological treatment, or even imprisonment.

Nevertheless, sexual violence may have its origins in a culture that privileges men. Patriarchal norms and individually held beliefs about men's sexual entitlements make rape and other sexual violence more likely. Thus, rehabilitating the culture to reduce gendered beliefs, sexist imagery, and the romance of sweeping a woman off her feet seems like a crucial element in reducing men's sexual violence toward women. Similarly, restructuring institutions that confer different entitlements to men than to women can further help to reduce misogynistic acts.

A small subgroup of sex offenders may in fact have a genetic or physiological basis for their pathology. Research on psychopathology in serial killers and serial rapists suggests that a very small proportion of men may be organically different from others and are truly incorrigible. They feel no remorse and are prepared to do whatever is necessary to get their next victim. These men tend to have been abuse victims themselves as children, and sometimes they have suffered a head injury at an early age, but sometimes they have completely uneventful backgrounds. In either case, this very small subset of rapists has displayed the pathology of having no remorse from a very early age. Even for these "biologically different" cases, however, culture, learning history, and social structures are the more likely culprits for why they are fixated on victimizing women or engaging in sexual victimization rather than other kinds of victimization.

Conclusion

We have come to the end of our discussion of gender and sexuality—but certainly not to the end of the topic, or your study of it! We hope that the questions raised in this book will inspire you to ask even more questions about the social organization of sexuality. We charge you now to search out and examine hidden assumptions and explicit norms regarding the role of gender in how individuals, groups, and whole nations "do" sex.

One of the questions we've raised is: Why is gender such a powerful influence over the organization of sexuality? To understand this, we have looked at cultural stereotypes that presume sexuality is naturally gendered and rooted in biology, that men and women are different sexually, and that this difference is consistent and universal across societies. In a simple sense, you have seen that sexual rules for men and women vary by society and region, they vary from one historical era to another, and they vary under the influence of social institutions.

Of course, not only does what appears "natural" in one society differ from other societies, but the whole idea that sexuality has a well-defined set of "natural" rules tends to serve political purposes that advance the social control of sexuality. The biological, or natural, presumption is powerful, but change continues to happen! Inroads at contesting assumptions about gender and sexuality can be seen in the visibility and modest success (as we write) of efforts to legalize same-sex marriages or the end, in 2011, after a long battle, of prohibitions against gays and lesbians in the military.

We have also looked at the everyday experience of sexuality. The rules of sexuality are not simply writ large in institutions like religions, governments, or even sexuality education programs in schools. By examining sexuality in relationships and sexual attitudes that individuals carry around and express through their behavior, we've tried to help you see how gendered sexuality gets inscribed and reinforced in daily lives of ordinary people going about their business. This individual level is powerful; relationships challenge norms as well as reinforce them.

A great example comes from a story told by a college professor we know. She told the story of how in grade school, her teacher, a Catholic nun, had instructed her class on "the birds and the bees." The teacher was explaining that when a man's hand touches a woman's breast, the woman responds sexually. Our colleague recalls, "I wondered, how does the breast know it's a *man's* hand?" She didn't take the assumption that sex requires two genders for granted, nor did she take for granted that sexual bodies "naturally" know the social rules for gendered sexuality.

By calling the book *The Gender of Sexuality*, we challenge you to think about how even things that people tend to consider biological, like reproduction, are influenced enormously by social processes. We want you to be analytic about how gender affects even the most potentially "hardwired" biological processes, such as what motherhood is all about and how motherhood is different from fatherhood. In the movie *Junior* (1995), Arnold Schwarzenegger plays a husband who becomes pregnant, thanks to the scientific creativity of Danny DeVito. The biological anomaly—a man rather than a woman incubating a baby—is only a prop for a movie full of jokes about how a man's producing a baby is a social anomaly, a twist on the cross-dressing comedies like *Mrs. Doubtfire* (1993) (in which Robin Williams dresses like an older woman to become nanny to his estranged children after a nasty custody battle that isolated him from his children) or *Tootsie* (1982) (in which Dustin Hoffman acts and dresses like a matron for a part on a soap opera). The movie *Junior* suggests that even if men were biologically capable of producing babies, they are ill-prepared socially for primary caretaking.

Biology or, more simply stated, bodies are mechanisms for passionate experience, even if that experience happens only in the brain (even in the absence of actual sensations in the skin or other sexual organs). In this sense, biology is a crucial context for sexuality. However, we know that interpersonal, biographical, social, and political contexts influence sexuality and interact with biology in surprising ways. Bodies are also mechanisms for sending sexual cues to others about sexual interest or about the social roles—of man, woman, straight, gay, or bi, or other. But how people use bodies to signal these things is learned rather than biological.

We acknowledge that sexuality and gender are powerful social constructs. Gender organizes so much of our lives, what feels "right" and comfortable. It becomes a veritable guide to how people want to live. Meanwhile, sexuality, when it intersects with gender, produces great fun—both in one's imagination and in sexual or social activity. But as comfortable as our familiar gender directives are, there are places in one's own biography where the gender role doesn't fit. At those times, sometimes in small ways, sometimes in larger ways, people will go outside the cultural rules they have been given. Breaking sexual rules, playing with gendered roles, even obeying rules or norms in your own particular way can be amusing and meaningful. People experiment with gender roles playfully, such as when someone cross-dresses on Halloween, or they experiment for some deeper congruency with the cultural permissions of the other sex, such as cross-dressing on a daily basis, and it becomes a satisfying way of life. People can enjoy sexual role-playing for a sexual encounter—or they take on the other sex's role as a way of life because it feels like a better fit to their core identity.

What makes sexuality and gender more than just amusement and fun is the presence and perpetuation of a hierarchy of "normality" that punishes anyone who deviates from traditional male or female behavior or heterosexual identification. When heterosexuals have more privilege than gays, lesbians and transgender people; or when men have more privilege than women; gender and sexuality norms become a tool to deprive people of their individuality, humanity, and citizenship.

So, what now? We hope you will continue to look at your life, your traditions, and social customs—and ask questions. Be mindful of power differences and how gender and sexual norms support those and how power differences can be reduced. Enjoy who you are and feel free to construct who you want to be. Take care of yourself and respect and value others. We wish you a happy, healthy, and responsible sex life so that collectively, we can become a positive force for sexual health and positive sexual experiences.

Bibliography

Abbey, A. 1982. "Sex Differences in Attributions for Friendly Behavior: Do Males Misperceive Females' Friendliness?" *Journal of Personality and Social Psychology* 42:830–38.

Abma, Joyce C. 2004. "Teenagers in the United States: Sexual Activity, Contraceptive Use, and Childbearing, 2002." *Vital and Health Statistics*, 23(24).

Abma, J. C., G. M. Martinez, and C. E. Copen. 2010. "Teenagers in the United States: Sexual Activity, Contraceptive Use, and Childbearing, National Survey of Family Growth 2006–2008." *Vital and Health Statistics*, 23(30).

Alexander, M. G., and T. D. Fisher. 2003. "Consequences Using the Bogus Pipeline to Examine Sex Differences in Self-Reported Sexuality." *Journal of Sex Research* 40(1): 27–35.

Alford, S. 2003. *Science and Success: Sex Education and Other Programs That Work to Prevent Teen Pregnancy, HIV & Sexually Transmitted Infections.* Washington, DC: Advocates for Youth.

Allen, Woody. 1977. *Annie Hall.* Rollins-Joffe Productions.

Angier, N. 1995. "Does Testosterone Equal Aggression? Maybe Not." *New York Times*, June 20, p. A1.

Apatow, Judd. 2007. *Knocked Up.* Universal Pictures.

American Podiatric Medical Association (APMA). 2003. "High Heels Survey." Bethesda, MD: American Podiatric Medical Association.

Armstrong, E., P. England, and A. Fogarty. 2010. "Orgasm in College Hookups and Relationships." In B. Risman, Ed., *Families as They Really Are.* New York: Norton.

Arnett, J. J. 2006. *Emerging Adulthood: The Winding Road from the Late Teens through the Twenties.* New York: Oxford University Press.

Associated Press. 1996. "Parents End Battle, Agree to Share Custody of Girl." October 18. Accessed at *LATimes.com* on April 10, 2011.

Associated Press. 2006. "British Woman to Give Birth at Age 63." May 4. Accessed at msnbc.msn.com on November 24, 2009.

Associated Press. 2008. "Pentagon Releases Sexual Harassment Data." March 14. Retrieved April 4, 2011.

Atkins, David, and James Furrow. 2008. "Infidelity is on the Rise: But for Whom and Why?" Presented at the Association for Behavioral and Cognitive Therapy, Orlando, FL, November 17.

Auguste, A. 2000. "This Toy Is Not a Toy." *Salon.com*, June 28.

Bailey, J. M., R. C. Pillard, M. C. Neale, and Y. Agyei. 1993. "Heritable Factors Influence Sexual Orientation in Women." *Archives of General Psychiatry* 50:217–23.

Bancroft, J. 1978. "The Relationship between Hormones and Sexual Behavior in Humans." In J. B. Hutchinson, Ed., *Biological Determinants of Sexual Behavior*. New York: Wiley.

Bancroft, J. 1984. "Hormones and Human Sexual Behavior." *Journal of Sex and Marital Therapy* 10:3–21.

Bancroft, J., D. Sanders, D. Davidson, and P. Warner. 1983. "Mood, Sexuality, Hormones, and the Menstrual Cycle: III. Sexuality and the Role of Androgens." *Psychosomatic Medicine* 45:508–24.

Barbach, L. 1975. *For Yourself: The Fulfillment of Female Sexuality*. Garden City, NY: Doubleday.

Barkley, T. W., and J. L. Burns. 2000. "Factor Analysis of the Condom Use Self-efficacy Scale among Multicultural College Students." *Health Education Research: Theory and Practice* 15(4):485–89.

Bartell, G. D. 1971. *Group Sex: A Scientist's Eyewitness Report on the American Way of Swinging*. New York: Wyden.

Baumgardner, Jennifer. 2007. *Look Both Ways: Bisexual Politics*. New York: Farrar, Straus and Giroux.

Bearman, P., and H. Bruckner. 2005. "After the Promise: The STD Consequences of Adolescent Virginity Pledges." *Journal of Adolescent Health*: 271–78.

Beatie, Thomas. 2008. "Labor of Love." *Advocate*, April. Retrieved June 28, 2011.

Belkin, Lisa. 2003. "The Opt-Out Revolution." *New York Times*, October 26. Retrieved March 19, 2011.

Berenson, Alex. 2005. "Sales of Impotence Drugs Fall, Defying Expectations." *New York Times*, December 4. Retrieved March 21, 2011.

Beres, M. A. 2007. "'Spontaneous' Sexual Consent: An Analysis of Sexual Consent Literature." *Feminism and Psychology* 17:93–108.

Beres, Melanie. 2009. "Sexual Miscommunication? Untangling Assumptions about Sexual Communication between Casual Sex Partners." *Culture, Health, & Sexuality* 12(1):1–14.

Bianchi, Suzanne M., John P. Robinson and Melissa A. Milkie. 2006. *Changing Rhythms of American Family Life*. New York: Russell Sage Foundation.

Biblarz, T. J., and J. Stacey. 2010. "How Does the Gender of Parents Matter?" *Journal of Marriage and Family*, February, 3–22.

Billy, J. O. G., W. R. Grady, and M. E. Sill. 2009. "Sexual Risk-Taking among Adult Dating Couples in the United States." *Perspectives on Sexual and Reproductive Health* 41(2):74–83.

Bloomberg Businessweek. 2006. "Viagra for Women?" December 28. Accessed April 25, 2010.

Blumstein, P., and P. Schwartz. 1983. *American Couples: Money, Work, and Sex.* New York: William Morrow.

Bly, R. 1990. *Iron John: A Book about Men.* Reading, MA: Addison-Wesley.

Boeringer, S. B., C. L. Shehan, and R. L. Akers. 1991. "Social Contexts and Social Learning in Sexual Coercion and Aggression: Assessing the Contribution of Fraternity Membership." *Family Relations* 40:50–64.

Bogle, Kathleen. 2008. *Hooking Up: Sex, Dating, and Relationships on Campus.* New York: New York University Press.

Booth, A., D. R. Johnson, D. A. Granger, A. C. Crouter, and S. McHale. 2003. "Testosterone and Child and Adolescent Adjustment: The Moderating Role of Parent-Child Relationships." *Journal of Developmental Psychology* 39:85–98.

Boston Women's Health Book Collective. 1973. *Our Bodies, Ourselves.* New York: Simon & Schuster.

Boston Women's Health Book Collective. 2005. *Our Bodies, Ourselves: A New Edition for the New Era.* New York: Touchstone.

Boswell, J. 1994. *Same-Sex Unions in Premodern Europe.* New York: Villard.

Boushey, Heather. 2005. "Are Women Opting Out? Debunking the Myth." Center for Economic and Policy Research, November. Retrieved March 24, 2011.

Boushey, Heather, and Ann O'Leary. 2009. "The Shriver Report: A Woman's Nation Changes Everything." Washington, DC: Center for American Progress.

Bozett, F. 1987. *Gay and Lesbian Parents.* New York: Praeger.

Briere, J., and N. M. Malamuth. 1983. "Self-Reported Likelihood of Sexually Aggressive Behavior: Attitudinal versus Sexual Explanations." *Journal of Research in Personality* 17:315–23.

Brigham Young University. 2011. National Pornography Statistics.

Bright, S., ed. 1988. *Herotica: A Collection of Women's Erotic Fiction.* Burlingame, CA: Down There.

Brines, J. 1994. "Economic Dependency, Gender, and Division of Labor at Home." *American Journal of Sociology* 100:652–60.

Brines, Julie, and Kara Joyner. 1999. "The Ties That Bind: Principles of Cohesion in Cohabitation and Marriage." *American Sociological Review* 64(3):333–56.

Bronski, Michael. 2000. *The Pleasure Principle: Sex, Backlash and the Struggle of for Gay Freedom.* New York: Stonewall Inn Editions.

Brown, M., and A. Auerback. 1981. "Communication Patterns in the Initiation of Marital Sex." *Medical Aspects of Human Sexuality* 15:105–17.

Browning, Christopher R., and Edward O. Laumann. 2001. "Sexual Contact between Children and Adults: A Life-Course Perspective." In Edward O. Laumann, Ed., *Sex, Love, and Health in America: Private Choices and Public Policies.* Chicago: University of Chicago Press.

Brownmiller, S. 1975. *Against Our Will: Men, Women and Rape.* New York: Simon & Schuster.

Bullivant, S. B., S. A. Sellergren, K. Stern, N. A. Spencer, S. Jacob, J. A. Mennella, and M. K. McClintock. 2004. "Women's Sexual Experience during the Menstrual Cycle: Identification of the Sexual Phase by Noninvasive Measurement of Luteinizing Hormone." *Journal of Sex Research* 41:82–93.

Bumpass, L., J. A. Sweet, and A. J. Cherlin. 1989. "The Role of Cohabitation in Declining Rates of Marriage." *Journal of Marriage and the Family* 53:913–27.

Burt, M. R. 1979. *Attitudes Supportive of Rape in American Culture.* Rockville, MD: U.S. Department of Health and Human Services.

Buss, D. 1994. *The Evolution of Desire: Strategies of Human Mating.* New York: Basic Books.

Buss, D. 1995. "Psychological Sex Differences: Origins through Sexual Selection." *American Psychologist* 50:164–68.

Byers, E. S. 2005. "Relationship Satisfaction and Sexual Satisfaction: A Longitudinal Study of Individuals in Long-Term Relationships." *The Journal of Sex Research* 42:113–118.

Call, V., S. Sprecher, and P. Schwartz. 1995. "The Incidence and Frequency of Marital Sex in a National Sample." *Journal of Marriage and the Family* 57:639–50.

Cao, Y., and W. Lavely. 2003. "Missing Girls in China: Numerical Estimates and Effects on Population Growth." *The China Review* 3(2):1–17.

Centers for Disease Control. 1999. "Mortality Patterns—United States, 1997," *MMWR Weekly* 48(30): August 6. Accessed January 27, 2010.

Centers for Disease Control. 2000. Births: Final Data for 1998. National Vital Statistics, March 28. Retrieved April 17, 2011.

Centers for Disease Control. 2002. "Cohabitation, Marriage, Divorce, and Remarriage in the United States." *Vital and Health Statistics* (23)22:1–93. Retrieved March 14, 2011.

Centers for Disease Control. 2005. *Sexually Transmitted Disease Surveillance Report 2004.* Atlanta, GA: . Centers for Disease Control Retrieved April 17, 2011.

Center for Public Integrity. 2010. *Sexual Assault on Campus: A Frustrating Search for Justice.* February 24. Retrieved at: www.publicintegrity.org/investigations/campus_assault/.

Centers for Disease Control. 2007. Births: Final Data for 2005. National Vital Statistic Reports, December 5. Retrieved April 17, 2011.

Centers for Disease Control. 2009. *Sexually Transmitted Disease Surveillance Report 2008.* Atlanta, GA: Centers for Disease Control. Retrieved April 17, 2011.

Centers for Disease Control. 2010. "HIV and AIDS among Gay and Bisexual Men." *CDC Fact Sheet.* Retrieved March 16, 2011.

Centers for Disease Control. 2010. "Teenagers in the United States: Sexual Activity, Contraceptive Use, and Childbearing, National Survey of Family Growth, 2006–08." National Center for Health Statistics, June 2.

Chandra, A. et al. 2005. Fertility, Family Planning, and Reproductive Health of U.S. Women: Data from the 2002 National Survey of Family Growth. *Vital and Health Statistics,* Series 23, No. 25.

Cherlin, A. 1992. *Marriage, Divorce, Remarriage.* Rev. ed. Cambridge, MA: Harvard University Press.

Chia, M., and D. A. Arava. 1996. *The Multi-Orgasmic Man: Sexual Secrets Every Man Should Know.* New York: HarperCollins.

Child Trends. 2003. *Heritage Keepers Life Skills Education.* Program Evaluation. Washington, DC: Child Trends. Retrieved at: www.childtrends.org/Lifecourse/programs/heri.htm.

Christopher, F. S., and S. Sprecher. 2000. "Sexuality in Marriage, Dating, and Other Relationships: A Decade Review." *Journal of Marriage and the Family* 62:999–1,017.

Cochran, S. D., and V. M. Mays. 1990. "Sex, Lies, and HIV." *New England Journal of Medicine* 322:774–75.

Cohen, Alex. 2008. "Web Site Makes Millions by Connecting Cheaters." NPR. Retrieved March 21, 2011.

Coltrane, S. 1997. *Gender and Families.* Thousand Oaks, CA: Pine Forge.

Comfort, A. 1972. *The Joy of Sex.* New York: Simon & Schuster.

Comfort, A. 1974. *More Joy.* New York: Simon & Schuster.

Connell, R. W. 2005. "Hegemonic Masculinity: Rethinking the Concept." *Gender and Society* 19(6):829–59.

Coontz, Stephanie. 1992. *The Way We Never Were: American Families and the Nostalgia Trap.* New York: Basic Books.

Coontz, Stephanie. 2005. *Marriage, A History: From Obedience to Intimacy or How Love Conquered Marriage.* New York: Viking.

Coontz, S. J. 2011. *A Strange Stirring: The Feminine Mystique and American Women at the Dawn of the 1960s.* New York: Basic Books.

Copenhaver, S., and E. Grauerholz. 1991. "Sexual Victimization among Sorority Women: Exploring the Link between Sexual Violence and Institutional Practices." *Sex Roles* 24:31–41.

Crawley, Sara, Lara J. Foley, and Constance L. Shehan. 2008. *Gendering Bodies.* New York: Rowman & Littlefield.

Cupach, W. R., and S. Metts. 1991. "Sexuality and Communication in Close Relationships." In K. McKinney and S. Sprecher, Eds., *Sexuality in Close Relationships.* Hillsdale, NJ: Lawrence Erlbaum.

Dekker, A., and G. Schmidt. 2002. "Patterns of Masturbatory Behavior: Changes between the Sixties and the Nineties." *Journal of Psychology and Human Sexuality* 14(2/3):35–48.

D'Emilio, J. D., and E. Freedman. 1988. *Intimate Matters: A History of Sexuality in America.* New York: Harper & Row.

Demo, D. H., and K. R. Allen. 1996. "Diversity within Lesbian and Gay Families: Challenges and Implications for Family Theory and Research." *Journal of Social and Personal Relationships* 13:417–36.

Denizet-Lewis, Benoit. 2004. "Friends, Friends with Benefits, and the Benefits of the Local Mall." *New York Times,* May 30. Retrieved March 26, 2011.

Denizet-Lewis, Benoit. 2009. "Coming Out in Middle School." *New York Times,* September 23. Retrieved March 16, 2011.

Department of Defense. 2008 Report on Sexual Assault in the Military. Retrieved March 16, 2011.

De Paulo, Bella. 2006. *Singled Out: How Singles are Stereotyped, Stigmatized, and Ignored, and Still Live Happily Ever After.* New York: St. Martin's Press.

De Vita, Carol J. 1996. "The United States at Mid-Decade." *Population Bulletin* 50(4). Washington, DC: Population Reference Bureau, Inc. March.

Diamond, L. 2008. *Sexual Fluidity: Understanding Women's Love and Desire.* Cambridge, MA: Harvard University Press.

Dotinga, Randy. 2010. "Infidelity Rises When She Makes More Than He Does." *Bloomberg Businessweek,* August 16. Retrieved April 4, 2011.

Dowd, M. 1983. "Rape: The Sexual Weapon." *Time*, September 5, 27–29.

Dryfoos, J. 1990. *Adolescents at Risk: Prevalence and Prevention*. New York: Oxford University Press.

Durex. 2005. "Give and Receive: 2005 Global Sex Survey Results."

Dutton, D. 1988. *The Domestic Assault of Women: Psychological and Criminal Justice Perspectives*. Newton, MA: Allyn & Bacon.

Dutton, D., and A. Aron. 1974. "Some Evidence for Heightened Sexual Attraction Under Conditions of High Anxiety." *Journal of Personality and Social Psychology* 30:510–17.

Dworkin, A. 1991. *Woman Hating: A Radical Look at Sexuality*. New York: Dutton.

Edwin, K., and J. Reed. 2005. "Why Don't They Just Get Married? Barriers to Marriage among the Disadvantaged." The *Future of Children* 15(2): 117–130.

Egan, Patrick, and Ken Sherrill. 2005. "Neither an In-Law Nor An Outlaw Be: Trends in Americans' Attitudes Toward Gay People." *Public Opinion Pros*. February.

Ehrenreich, B., and D. English. 1978. *For Her Own Good: 150 Years of the Experts' Advice to Women*. Garden City, NY: Anchor/Doubleday.

Eisenberg, Marla E., D. M. Ackard, M. D. Resnick, and D. Neumark-Sztainer. 2009. "Casual sex and psychological health among young adults: Is having 'friends with benefits' emotionally damaging?" *Perspectives on Reproductive Health*. 41(4): 231–37.

Ellis, B. J., and D. Symons. 1990. "Sex Differences in Sexual Fantasy: An Evolutionary Psychological Approach." *Journal of Sex Research* 27:527–55.

Ensler, E. 1996, 2007. *The Vagina Monologues*. New York: Random House.

Eskridge, W. N. 1996. *The Case for Same-Sex Marriage: From Sexual Liberty to Civilized Commitment*. New York: Free Press.

Essig, Laurie, and Lynn Owens. 2009. "What if Marriage is Bad for us?" *Chronicle of Higher Education*. October 5.

Faderman, L. 1981. *Surpassing the Love of Men: Romantic Friendship and Love between Women from the Renaissance to the Present*. New York: William Morrow.

Family Research Council. 2007. "Don't Mandate HPV Vaccine—Trust Parents." Retrieved March 26, 2011.

Farrelly, B., and P. Farrelly. 2001. *Shallow Hal*. Twentieth Century-Fox Film Corporation.

Fausto-Sterling, A. 1992. "Building Two-Way Streets: The Case of Feminism and Science." *National Women's Studies Association Journal* 4:336–49.

Federal Bureau of Investigation. 2004. *Crime in the United States 2004*. U.S. Department of Justice. Retrieved April 4, 2011.

Fields, Jessica. 2008. *Risky Lessons: Sex Education and Social Inequality*. New Brunswick, NJ: Rutgers University Press.

Finer, L. B. 2007. "Trends in Premarital Sex in the United States, 1954–2003," *Public Health Reports* 122.

Finer, L. B., and S. K. Henshaw. 2003. "Abortion Incidence and Services in the United States in 2000." *Perspectives on Sexual and Reproductive Health* 35(1):6–15.

Finer L., and S. Henshaw. 2006. *Estimates of Abortion Incidence 2001–2003*. New York: Guttmacher Institute.

Finkelhor, D. 1984. *Child Sexual Abuse: New Theory and Research*. New York: Free Press.

Finkelhor, D., and L. M. Jones. 2004. "Explanations for the Decline in Child Sexual Abuse Cases." Juvenile Justice Bulletin No. NC 199298. Washington, D.C.: Office of Juvenile Justice and Delinquency Prevention.

Finkelhor, D., and K. Yllö. 1985. *License to Rape: Sexual Abuse of Wives.* New York: Free Press.

Finkelhor, D., G. Hotaling, I. A. Lewis, and C. Smith. 1990. "Sexual Abuse in a National Survey of Adult Men and Women: Prevalence, Characteristics, and Risk Factors. *Child Abuse and Neglect* 14: 19–28.

Fisher, H. E. 1992. *Anatomy of Love: The Natural History of Monogamy, Adultery, and Divorce.* New York: Norton.

Fisher, Linda. 2010. *Sex, Romance, and Relationships: AARP Survey of Midlife and Older Adults.* AARP. May. Retrieved April 17, 2011.

Fisher, T. D., and A. S. Walters. 2003. "Variables in Addition to Gender That Help to Explain Differences in Perceived Sexual Interest." *Psychology of Men & Masculinity* 4:154–62.

Foley, Sallie, Sally A. Kope, and Dennis P. Sugrue. 2001. *Sex Matters for Women: A Complete Guide to Taking Care of Your Sexual Self.* New York: The Guilford Press.

Forman, B. 1982. "Reported Male Rape." *Victimology: An International Journal* 7:235–36.

Foucault, M. 1978. *A History of Sexuality: Vol. 1. An Introduction.* New York: Pantheon.

Franklin, Donna. 2001. *What's Love Got to Do With It? Understanding and Healing the Rift Between Black Men and Women.* New York: Touchstone Books.

Franklin, D. 2001. *What's Love Got to Do with It?: Understanding and Healing the Rift Between Black Men and Women.* New York: Touchstone.

French, M. 1977. *The Women's Room.* New York: Summit.

Friday, N. 1973. *My Secret Garden.* New York: Pocket Books.

Friday, N. 1991. *Women on Top.* New York: Pocket Books.

Friedan, B. 1963. *The Feminine Mystique.* New York: Norton.

Friedan, B., M. Carrow, C. Harrison, A. Kimbrell, F. Pittman, S. Quinn, S. Roiphe, and A. Roiphe. 1996. "Overcoming the Scars and Frustrations of Old Sex Roles, Sexual Politics and Backlash." A panel sponsored by Mount Vernon College, March 21, Washington, DC.

Friedman, Emily, and Susan Donaldson James. 2009. "Mom and Daughter Go AWOL in Lesbian Custody Case." *ABC News*, January 1. Retrieved April 6, 2011.

Fry, R., and D. Cohn. 2010. "New Economics of Marriage: The Rise of Wives." Pew Research Center Publications. Accessed March 6, 2011.

Gagnon, J. H., and W. Simon. 1973. *Sexual Conduct: The Social Sources of Human Sexuality.* New York: Aldine de Gruyter.

Gangestad, S. W., R. Thornhill, and C. E. Garver. 2002. "Changes in Women's Sexual Interests and Their Partners' Mate-retention Tactics across the Menstrual Cycle: Evidence for Shifting Conflicts of Interest." *Proceedings of the Royal Society of London* B(269):975–82.

Gartrell, Nanette, and Henny Bos. 2010. "The U.S. National Longitudinal Lesbian Family Study: Psychological Adjustment of 17-Year-Old Adolescents." *Pediatrics* 126:1–9.

Gauthier, A. H. 1996. *The State and the Family: A Comparative Analysis of Family Policies in Industrialized Countries.* Oxford: Clarendon.

Gettleman, Jeffrey. 2007. "Rape Epidemic Raises Trauma of Congo War." *New York Times,* October 7, p. A1.

Glass, S. P., and T. L. Wright. 1992. "Justification for Extramarital Relationships: The Association between Attitudes, Behavior, and Gender." *Journal of Sex Research* 29:361–87.

Glass, Shirley. 2003. *Not "Just Friends": Protect Your Relationship from Infidelity and Heal the Trauma of Betrayal.* New York: Free Press.

Glassner, Barry. 2000. *The Culture of Fear: Why Americans Fear the Wrong Things.* New York: Basic Books.

Glenn, N., and E. Marquardt. 2001. *Hooking Up, Hanging Out, and Hoping for Mr. Right: College Women on Dating and Mating Today.* New York: Institute for American Values.

Goffman, E. 1977. "The Arrangement between the Sexes." *Theory and Society* 4:301–31.

Goldfarb, Michael. 2007. "Where the Arts Were Too Liberal." *New York Times,* June 17. Retrieved March 16, 2011.

Goldstein, J. R. 1999. "The Leveling of Divorce in the United States." *Demography* 36(3):409–14.

Golombok, S., and F. Tasker. 1996. "Do Parents Influence the Sexual Orientation of Their Children? Findings from a Longitudinal Study of Lesbian Families." *Developmental Psychology* 32:3–11.

Goode, W. 1969. "The Theoretical Importance of Love." *American Sociological Review* 34:38–47.

Goodwin, Paula, Brittany McGill, and Anjani Chandra. 2009. "Who Marries and When? Age at First Marriage in the United States: 2002." NCHS Data Brief No. 19. Retrieved March 19, 2011.

Gornick, Janet C., and Marcia K. Meyers. 2005. *Families That Work: Policies for Reconciling Parenthood and Employment.* New York: Russell Sage Foundation Publication.

Gottman, J. M. 1994. *What Predicts Divorce?* Hillsdale, NJ: Lawrence Erlbaum.

Gottman, John, and Julie Schwartz Gottman. 2007. *And Baby Makes Three: The Six-Step Plan for Preserving Marital Intimacy and Rekindling Romance after Baby Arrives.* New York: Crown Publishers.

Gottman, J. M., R. Levenson, C. Swanson, K. Swanson, R. Tyson, and D. Yoshimoto. 2003. "Observing Gay, Lesbian and Heterosexual Couples' Relationships: Mathematical Modeling of Conflict Interaction." *Journal of Homosexuality,* 45(1), 65–91.

Grady, William R., Koray Tanfer, John O. G. Billy, and Jennifer Lincoln-Hanson. 1996. "Men's Perceptions of Their Roles and Responsibilities Regarding Sex, Contraception, and Childrearing." *Family Planning Perspectives,* 28:221–26.

Gray, L. A., and M. Saracino. 1991. "College Students' Attitudes, Beliefs, and Behaviors about AIDS: Implications for Family Life Educators." *Family Relations* 40:258–63.

Green, G. D. 1987. "Lesbian Mothers: Mental Health Considerations." In F. W. Bozett, Ed., *Gay and Lesbian Parents.* New York: Praeger.

Greene, Robert, and Joost Elffers. 2003. *The Art of Seduction.* New York: Penguin Group.

Greene, K., and S. L. Faulkner. 2005. "Gender Belief in the Sexual Double Standard and Sexual Talk in Heterosexual Dating Relationships." *Sex Roles* 53:239–251.

Greenhalgh, S. 1977. "Hobbled Feet, Hobbled Lives: Women in Old China." *Frontiers* 2:7–21.

Guttentag, M., and P. P. Secord. 1983. *Too Many Women? The Sex Ratio Question.* Beverly Hills, CA: Sage.

Guttmacher Institute. 2008. Improving Contraceptive Use in the United States. Retrieved March 26, 2011.

Guttmacher Institute. 2010. Parental Involvement in Minors' Abortions, State Policies in Brief. Retrieved March 26, 2011.

Hamer, D. H., and P. Copeland. 1994. *The Science of Desire: The Search for the Gay Gene and the Biology of Behavior.* New York: Simon & Schuster.

Hamilton, L., and E. Armstrong. 2009. "Gendered Sexuality in Young Adulthood: Double Binds and Flawed Options." *Gender & Society* 23:589.

Hanauer, Jaiya, and Jon Hanauer. 2008. *Red Hot Touch: A Head-to-Toe Handbook for Mind-blowing Orgasms.* New York: Broadway Books.

Hatfield, E., and R. L. Rapson. 1993. *Love, Sex, and Intimacy: Their Psychology, Biology, and History.* New York: HarperCollins College.

Hatfield, E., and R. L. Rapson. 1996. *Love and Sex: Cross-Cultural Perspectives.* Needham Heights, MA: Allyn & Bacon.

Hauser, D. 2004. *Five Years of Abstinence-Only-Until-Marriage Education: Assessing the Impact.* Washington, DC: Advocates for Youth.

Hawthorne, N. 1947. *The Scarlet Letter.* New York: Rinehart.

Heiman, J. R. 1977. "A Psychophysiological Exploration of Sexual Arousal Patterns in Females and Males." *Psychophysiology* 14:266–74.

Henningsen, D. D., M. L. M. Henningsen, and K. Valde. 2006. "Gender Differences in Perceptions of Women's Sexual Interest during Cross-sex Interactions: An Application and Extension of Cognitive Valence Theory." *Sex Roles* 54:821–29.

Henshaw, S. 1998. "Unintended Pregnancy in the United States." *Family Planning Perspectives.* 30(1): 24–29 & 46.

Herbenick, D., M. Reece, V. Schick, S. A. Sanders, B. Dodge, and J. Fortenberry. 2010. "Sexual Behavior in the United States: Results from a National Probability Sample of Men and Women Ages 14-94." *Journal of Sexual Medicine*, 7(5), 255–65.

Hesketh, T., L. Lu, and Z. W. Xing. 2005. "The Effect of China's One-Child Family Policy after 25 Years." *New England Journal of Medicine* 353:1171–76.

Hess, B. B., and M. M. Ferree, Eds. 1987. *Analyzing Gender: A Handbook of Social Science Research.* Newbury Park, CA: Sage.

Hicks, T., and H. Leitenberg. 2001. "Sexual Fantasies about One's Partner versus Someone Else: Gender Differences in Incidence and Frequency." *Journal of Sex Research* 38(1):43–50.

Hite, S. 1976. *The Hite Report: A Nationwide Study of Female Sexuality.* New York: Dell.

Hochschild, Arlie. 1989. *The Second Shift: Working Parents and the Revolution of Home* (with Anne Machling). New York: Viking Penguin.

Hollander, J. 1997. "Discourses of Danger: The Construction and Performance of Gender through Talk about Violence." University of Washington. PhD dissertation.

Holmes, K. K., P. F. Sparling, W. E. Stamm, and P. Piot. 1990. *Sexually Transmitted Diseases.* 2nd ed. New York: McGraw-Hill.

Hoon, P. W., K. E. Bruce, and B. Kinchloe. 1982. "Does the Menstrual Cycle Play a Role in Sexual Arousal?" *Psychophysiology* 19:21–27.

Howard, J. A., D. G. Renfrow, and J. A. Hollander. 2001. *Gendered Situations, Gendered Selves: A Gender Lens on Social Psychology* 2nd ed. New York: Rowman & Littlefield.

Howe, N., and W. Strauss. 2000. *Millennials Rising: The Next Great Generation.* New York: Vintage Books.

Hrdy, S. B. 1999. *Mother Nature: Maternal Instincts and How They Shape the Human Species.* New York: Random House.

Hunt, M. 1974. *Sexual Behavior in the 1970s.* Chicago: Playboy.

Huston, M., and P. Schwartz. 1995. "The Relationships of Lesbians and Gay Men." In J. T. Wood and S. Duck, Eds., *Under-Studied Relationships: Off the Beaten Track.* Newbury Park, CA: Sage.

Illouz, E. 2008. *Saving the Modern Soul: Therapy, Emotions, and the Culture of Self-help.* Berkeley: University of California Press.

Jacobson, N. S. 1989. "The Politics of Intimacy." *Behavior Therapist* 12:29–32.

Jacobson, N. S., and A. J. Christensen. 1996. *Integrative Couple Therapy: Promoting Acceptance and Change.* New York: Norton.

Jacobson, Neil, and John Gottman. 1998. *When Men Batter Women: New Insights into Ending Abusive Relationships.* New York: Simon and Schuster.

Johnson, Michael P. 2009. "Differentiating among Types of Domestic Violence: Implications for Healthy Marriages." In H. Elizabeth Peters and Claire M. Kamp Dush, Eds., *Marriage and Family: Perspectives and Complexities.* New York: Columbia University Press.

Joint Economic Committee. 2008. "Equality in Job Loss: Women Are Increasingly Vulnerable to Layoffs during Recessions." Washington, DC: Joint Economic Committee of the U.S. Congress. Retrieved April 24, 2011.

Jones, E. F., J. Darroch-Forest, N. Goldman, S. K. Henshaw, R. Lincoln, J. I. Rosoff, C. F. Westoff, and D. Wulf. 1985. "Teenage Pregnancy in Developed Countries: Determinants and Policy Implications." *Family Planning Perspectives* 17:53–63.

Jones, J. C., and D. H. Barlow. 1990. "Self-Reported Frequency of Sexual Urges, Fantasies, and Masturbatory Fantasies in Heterosexual Males and Females." *Archives of Sexual Behavior* 19:269–79.

Jordan, N. 1992. *The Crying Game.* Palace Pictures.

Joyner, Kara, and Grace Kao. 2005. "Interracial Relationships and the Transition to Adulthood." *American Sociological Review* 70:563–81.

Kanin, Eugene. 1994. "False Rape Allegations." *Archives of Sexual Behavior* 23(1):81–103.

Kantrowitz, B., and P. Wingert. 2005. "Inside the Struggle to Treat Women with Dwindling Sex Drives." *Newsweek*, October 4.

Kaplan, H. S. 1979. *Disorders of Sexual Desire.* New York: Simon & Schuster.

Kaye, J. A., and H. Jick. 2003. "Incidence of Erectile Dysfunction and Characteristics of Patients Before and After the Introduction of Sildenafil in the United Kingdom: Cross Section Study with Comparison Patients." *British Medical Journal* 326:424–425.

Keenan, T. 2004. "Bad Boys, Whatcha Gonna Do? Ask Your Mama." *Calgary Herald*, September 9, p. D3.

Kimmel, Michael. 2005. *The Gender of Desire: Essays on Male Sexuality.* Albany: State University of New York Press.

Kinsey, A. C., W. B. Pomeroy, and C. E. Martin. 1948. *Sexual Behavior in the Human Male.* Philadelphia: W. B. Saunders.

Kinsey, A. C., W. B. Pomeroy, C. E. Martin, and P. H. Gephard. 1953. *Sexual Behavior in the Human Female.* Philadelphia: W. B. Saunders.

Kirby, D. 2001. "Emerging Answers: Research Findings on Programs to Reduce Teen Pregnancy." Washington, DC: National Campaign to Prevent Teen Pregnancy.

Kirby, D., B. Laris, and L. Rolleri. 2005. *Impact of Sex and HIV Education Programs on Sexual Behaviors of Youth in Developing and Developed Countries. Youth Research Working Paper No. 2.* Research Triangle Park, NC: Family Health International (FHI).

Kirby, D., L. Short, J. Collins, D. Rugg, L. Kolbe, M. Howard, B. Miller, F. Sonenstein, and L. S. Zabin. 1994. "School-Based Programs to Reduce Sexual Risk Behaviors: A Review of Effectiveness." *Public Health Reports* 109:339–60.

Klein, A. 2004. *NOW's Love and Sex Survey.* Accessed July 10, 2006.

Koblinsky, S., and J. Atkinson. 1982. "Parental Plans for Children's Sex Education." *Family Relations* 31:29–35.

Kollock, P., P. Blumstein, and P. Schwartz. 1985. "Sex and Power in Interaction: Conversational Privileges and Duties." *American Sociological Review* 50:34–46.

Kolodny, R. C., W. H. Masters, and V. E. Johnson. 1979. *Textbook of Sexual Medicine.* Boston: Little, Brown.

Korb, Lawrence J. 2009. "The Cost of Don't Ask, Don't Tell." *Center for American Progress,* March 2. Retrieved March 26, 2011.

Koss, M. P., T. E. Dinero, C. A. Seibel, and S. L. Cox. 1988. "Stranger and Acquaintance Rape: Are There Differences in the Victim's Experience?" *Psychology of Women Quarterly* 12:1–24.

Kosciw, Joseph G., Emily A. Greytak, Elizabeth M. Diaz, and Mark J. Bartkiewicz. 2009. *2009 National School Climate Survey: The Experiences of Lesbian, Gay, Bisexual and Transgender Youth in Our Nation's Schools.* Washington, DC: Gay, Lesbian and Straight Education Network.

Koss, M. P., L. A. Goodman, A. Browne, L. F. Fitzgerald, G. P. Keita, and N. F. Russo. 1994. *No Safe Haven: Male Violence against Women at Home, at Work, and in the Community.* Washington, DC: American Psychological Association.

Koss, M. P., and K. E. Leonard. 1984. *Sexually Aggressive Men: Empirical Finding and Theoretical Implications.* N. M. Malamuth and E. Donnerstein, Eds., *Pornography and Sexual Aggression.* New York: Academic Press.

Kreuz, L. E., R. M. Rose, and J. R. Jennings. 1972. "Suppression of Plasma Testosterone Levels and Psychological Stress: A Longitudinal Study of Young Men in Officer Candidate School." *Archives of General Psychiatry* 26:479–82.

Kurtz, David. 2009. "Thought Experiment." Talking Points Memo, November 11. Retrieved March 26, 2011.

Laumann, E. O., R. T. Michael, and J. H. Gagnon. 1994. *The Social Organization of Sexuality: Sexual Practices in the United States.* Chicago: University of Chicago Press.

Lawson, A. 1988. *Adultery: An Analysis of Love and Betrayal.* New York: Basic Books.

Leitzmann, M. F., E. A. Platz, M. J. Stampfer, W. C. Willett, and E. Giovannucci. 2004. "Ejaculation Frequency and Subsequent Risk of Prostate Cancer." *JAMA* 291:1578–86.

Leland, J. 1996. "Bisexuality." *Newsweek,* July 17.

Lerman, R. I., and T. J. Ooms. 1993. *Young Unwed Fathers: Changing Roles and Emerging Policies.* Philadelphia: Temple University Press.

LeVay, S. 1993. *The Sexual Brain.* Cambridge, MA: MIT Press.

Lever, J. 1994a. "The 1994 *Advocate* Survey of Sexuality and Relationships: The Men." *Advocate: The National Gay & Lesbian Newsmagazine,* August 23, pp. 17–24.

Lever, J. 1994b. "Viewpoint: Bridging Fundamentals of Gender Studies into Safer Sex Education." *Family Planning Perspectives* 27:172–74.

Lever, J. 1995. "The 1995 *Advocate* Survey of Sexuality and Relationships: The Women." *Advocate: The National Gay & Lesbian Newsmagazine,* August 22, pp. 22–30.

Liao, L. M., and S. M. Creighton. 2007. "Requests for Cosmetic Genitoplasty: How Should Healthcare Providers Respond?" *BMJ* 334:1090–92.

Liman, Doug. 2005. *Mr. & Mrs. Smith.* Regency Enterprises.

Lloyd, E. A. 2005. *The Case of Female Orgasm: Bias in the Science of Evolution.* Cambridge, MA: Harvard University Press.

Loe, Meika. 2006. *The Rise of Viagra: How the Little Blue Pill changed Sex in America.* New York: NYU Press.

Loftus, Elizabeth, and Katherine Ketcham. 1991. *Witness for the Defense: The Accused, the Eyewitness and the Expert Who Puts Memory on Trial.* New York: St. Martin's Press.

Logan, T. D. 2010. "Personal Characteristics, Sexual Behaviors, and Male Sex Work: A Quantitative Approach." *American Sociological Review* 75(5): 679–704.

Lorber, J. 1997. *Gender and the Social Construction of Illness.* Thousand Oaks, CA: Sage.

Luker, K. 1996. *Dubious Conceptions: The Politics of Teenage Pregnancy.* Cambridge, MA: Harvard University Press.

MacKinnon, C. 1987. *Feminism Unmodified: Discourses on Life and Law.* Cambridge, MA: Harvard University Press.

Maier, Thomas. 2009. *Masters of Sex: The Life and Times of William Masters and Virginia Johnson, the Couple Who Taught America How to Love.* New York: Basic Books.

Malamuth, N. M. 1984. "Aggression against Women: Cultural and Individual Causes." In N. M. Malamuth and E. Donnerstein, Eds., *Pornography and Sexual Aggression.* New York: Academic Press.

Malthus, T. R. [1798] 1929. *An Essay on the Principle of Population as It Affects the Future Improvement of Society.* New York and London: Macmillan.

Margolis, J. 2005. *O: The Intimate History of the Orgasm.* New York: Grove Press.

Marin B. V., C. A. Gomez, J. M. Tschann, S. E. Gregorich. 1997. "Condom Use in Unmarried Latino Men: A Test of Cultural Constructs." *Health Psychology* 16:458–67.

Marsiglio, W., A. Ries, F. Sonenstein, F. Troccoli, and W. Whitehead. 2006. "It's a Guy Thing: Boys, Young Men, and Teen Pregnancy Prevention," pp. 9–100. Washington, DC: National Campaign to Prevent Teen Pregnancy.

Martinez, G. M. et al. 2006. Fertility, Contraception, and Fatherhood: Data on Men and Women from Cycle 6 (2002) of the National Survey of Family Growth. *Vital and Health Statistics,* Series 23, No. 26.

Masters, W. H., and V. E. Johnson. 1966. *Human Sexual Response.* Boston: Little, Brown.

Masters, W. H., V. E. Johnson, and R. C. Kolodny. 1995. *Human Sexuality.* 5th ed. New York: HarperCollins College.

Mather, M., and D. Adams. 2007. *The crossover in female-male college enrollment rates.* Population Reference Bureau. February. Retrieved at www.prb.org/Articles/2007/ CrossoverinFemaleMaleCollegeEnrollmentRates.aspx.

McCall, N. 1995. *Makes Me Wanna Holler.* New York: Random House.

McCormick, N. B. 1994. *Sexual Salvation: Affirming Women's Sexual Rights and Pleasures.* Westport, CT: Praeger.

McLachlan, R. I. 2000. "Male Hormonal Contraception: A Safe, Acceptable and Reversible Choice." *Medical Journal of Australia* 172:254–55.

McLanahan, Sara. 2006. "Fragile Families and the Marriage Agenda." In Lori Kowaleski-Jones and Nicholas Wolfinger, Eds., *Fragile Families and the Marriage Agenda.* New York: Kluwer Academic Press.

Messner, M. 1997. *The Politics of Masculinities: Men in Movements.* Thousand Oaks, CA: Sage.

Meston, C. M., and D. Buss. 2007. "Why Humans Have Sex." *Archives of Sexual Behavior* 36:477–507.

Meuwissen, I., and R. Over. 1992. "Sexual Arousal across Phases of the Human Menstrual Cycle." *Archives of Sexual Behavior* 2:101–19.

Meyers, Nancy. 2009. *It's Complicated.* Universal Pictures.

Michaels, S., and A. Giami. 1999. "Review: Sexual Acts and Sexual Relationships: Asking about Sex in Surveys." *Public Opinion Quarterly* 63:401–20.

Miller, B., and J. C. Marshall. 1987. "Coercive Sex on the University Campus." *Journal of College Student Personnel,* January, 38–47.

Miller, G. 2001. *The Mating Mind: How Sexual Choice Shaped the Evolution of Human Nature.* New York: Random House.

Mintz, Steven. 2004. *Huck's Raft: A History of American Childhood.* Cambridge, MA: Harvard University Press.

Modell, J. 1989. *Into One's Own: From Youth to Adulthood in the United States 1920–1975.* Berkeley: University of California Press.

Morgan, S. P., D. N. Lye, and G. A. Condran. 1988. "Sons, Daughters, and the Risk of Marital Disruption." *American Journal of Sociology* 94:110–29.

Mosher, W. D., A. Chandra, and J. Jones. 2005. "Sexual Behavior and Selected Health Measures: Men and Women 15–44 Years of Age, United States, 2002." *Advance Data from Vital and Health Statistics* 362. Hyattsville, MD: National Center for Health Statistics.

Muehlenhard, C. L. 1988. "'Nice Women' Don't Say Yes and 'Real Men' Don't Say No: How Miscommunication and the Double Standard Can Cause Sexual Problems." *Women and Therapy* 7:95–108.

Muehlenhard, C. L., D. E. Friedman, and C. M. Thomas. 1985. "Is Date Rape Justifiable?" *Psychology of Women Quarterly* 9:297–310.

Muehlenhard, C. L., and L. C. Hollabaugh. 1988. "Do Women Sometimes Say No When They Mean Yes? The Prevalence and Correlates of Women's Token Resistance to Sex." *Journal of Personality and Social Psychology* 54:872–79.

Muehlenhard, C. L., and M. L. McCoy. 1991. "Double Standard/Double Bind: The Sexual Double Standard and Women's Communication about Sex." *Psychology of Women Quarterly* 15:447–61.

Muehlenhard, C. L., and J. S. McNaughton. 1988. "Women's Beliefs about Women Who 'Lead Men On.'" *Journal of Social and Clinical Psychology* 7:65–79.

Munsch, Christin. 2010. "The Effect of Relative Income Disparity on Infidelity in Men and Women." Annual Meeting of the American Sociological Association, Atlanta, GA, August 16.

Murphy, C. M., and S. A. Hoover. 2001. "Measuring Emotional Abuse in Dating Relationships as a Multifactorial Construct." In K. D. O'Leary and R. D. Maiuro, Eds., *Psychological Abuse in Violent Domestic Relations.* New York: Springer.

Nack, Adina. 2008. *Damaged Goods?: Women Living with Incurable Sexually Transmitted Diseases.* Philadelphia: Temple University Press.

Nack, Adina. 2010. "Why This Feminist Cares about Men's Health." *Ms.* Magazine Blog, March 8. Retrieved March 28, 2011.

National Center for Education Statistics. 2008. Digest of Education Statistics, 2008. Washington, DC.

National Defense Research Institute. 1993. *Sexual Orientation and U.S. Military Personnel Policy: Policy Options and Assessment.* Rand Corporation.

National Law Journal. 1994. "Custody Restored to Lesbian." July 4.

Newman, Andrew Adam. 2007. "A Guide to Embracing Life as a Single (Without the Resignation, That Is)." *New York Times,* December 31. Retrieved March 14, 2011.

Newsweek. 1995. "Family: Time to Legalize Gay Marriage." December 11, p. 82.

Nichols, M. 2005. "Sexual Function in Lesbians and Lesbian Relationships." In I. Goldstein, C. M. Meston, S. Davis, and A. Traish, Eds., *Women's Sexual Function and Dysfunction: Study, Diagnosis and Treatment.* New York: Taylor and Francis.

Nordhoff, C., and J. N. Hall. 1932. *Mutiny on the Bounty.* Boston: Little, Brown.

Parker-Pope, Tara. 2008. "Love, Sex, and the Changing Landscape of Infidelity." *New York Times,* October 28. D1.

Pascoe, C. J. 2007. *Dude, You're a Fag: Masculinity and Sexuality in High School.* Berkeley: University of California Press.

Patterson, C. J. 1992. "Children of Lesbian and Gay Parents." *Child Development* 63:1025–42.

Patterson, D. G. 1995. "Virtual In-Laws: Kinship and Relationship Quality in Gay Male Couples." University of Washington. Unpublished master's thesis.

Patterson, D. G., and P. Schwartz. 1994. "The Social Construction of Conflict in Intimate Same-Sex Couples." In D. D. Cahn, Ed., *Conflict in Personal Relationships.* Hillsdale, NJ: Lawrence Erlbaum.

Paul, J. P., J. Catania, and L. Pollack. 2002. "Suicide Attempts among Gay and Bisexual Men: Lifetime Prevalence and Antecedents." *American Journal of Public Health* 92(8):1338–45.

Peplau, L. A., Z. Rubin, and C. T. Hill. 1977. "Sexual Intimacy and Dating Relationships." *Journal of Social Issues* 33:86–109.

Perper, T., and D. L. Weis. 1987. "Proceptive and Rejective Strategies of U.S. and Canadian College Women." *Journal of Sex Research* 23:455–80.

Perry, Susan. 2010. "Hunt (and Hype) for a 'Pink Viagra' Continues, Despite Advisory Panel's Rejection of Flibanserin." Minnpost, June 21. Retrieved April 4, 2011.

Pillsworth, E. G., M. G. Haselton, and D. M. Buss. 2004. "Ovulatory Shifts in Female Sexual Desire." *Journal of Sex Research* 41:55–56.

Pipher, M. 1994. *Reviving Ophelia: Saving the Selves of Adolescent Girls.* New York: Putnam.

Pittman, F. 1989. *Private Lies: Infidelity and the Betrayal of Intimacy.* New York: Norton.

Pollitt, K. 1996. "Motherhood and Morality." *Nation,* May 27, p. 9.

Powers, K. A., C. Poole, A. E. Pettifor, and M. S. Cohen. 2008. "Rethinking the Heterosexual Infectivity of HIV-1: Systematic Review and Meta-analysis." *Lancet Infectious Diseases* 8(9):553–63.

Qian, Z-C, and D. T. Lichter. (2007). "Social Boundaries and Marital Assimilation: Evaluating Trends in Racial and Ethnic Intermarriage." *American Sociological Review* 72:68–94.

Quackenbush, D. M., D. S. Strassberg, and C. W. Turner. 1995. "Gender Effects of Romantic Themes in Erotica." *Archives of Sexual Behavior* 24:21–35.

Quintana, Nico Sifra. 2009. "Poverty in the LGBT Community." Center for American Progress, July 1. Retrieved March 21, 2011.

Rako, S. 1999. *The Hormones of Desire: The Truth about Testosterone, Sexuality, and Menopause.* New York: Three Rivers Press.

Ranalli, Ralph, and Raja Mishra. 2006. "Boy's Suspension in Harassment Case Outrages Mother." *Boston Globe,* February 8. Retrieved March 16, 2011.

Ray, Rebecca, Janet C. Gornick, and John Schmitt. 2008. "Parental Leave Policies in 21 Countries: Assessing Generosity and Gender Equality." *CEPR Reports and Issue Briefs.* Washington, DC: Center for Economic and Policy Research (CEPR). Retrieved March 21, 2011.

Reiss, I. L. 1967. *The Social Context of Premarital Sexual Permissiveness.* New York: Holt, Rinehart & Winston.

Reiss, I. L. 1980. *Family Systems in America.* 3rd ed. New York: Holt, Rinehart & Winston.

Reitman, Jason. 2007. *Juno.* Fox Searchlight Pictures.

Richters, J., A. Grulich, R. de Visser, A. Smith, and C. Rissel. 2003. "Sex in Australia: Sexual Difficulties in a Representative Sample of Adults." *Australian and New Zealand Journal of Public Health* 27:164–70. Retrieved April 27, 2011.

Richters, J., R. Visser, C. Rissel, and A. Smith. 2006. "Sexual Practices at Last Heterosexual Encounter and Occurrence of Orgasm in a national survey." Journal of Sex Research 43(3): 217–226.

Risman, B. 2004. "Gender as a Social Structure: Theory Wrestling with Activism." *Gender & Society.* 18(4): 429–50.

Risman, B. J., C. Hill, Z. Rubin, and L. A. Peplau. 1981. "Living Together in College: Implications for Courtship." *Journal of Marriage and the Family* 43:77–83.

Robbins, T. 1980. *Still Life with Woodpecker.* New York: Bantam.

Roberts, Stephen. 1934. *The Trumpet Blows.* Paramount Pictures.

Robson, Angela. 1993. "Weapon of War." *New Internationalist* Magazine, June, Issue 244. Retrieved April 27, 2011.

Roiphe, K. 1993. *The Morning After: Sex, Fear, and Feminism on Campus.* New York: Little, Brown.

Rose, R. M., J. W. Holaday, and I. S. Bernstein. 1970. "Plasma Testosterone, Dominance Rank, and Aggressive Behavior in Male Rhesus Monkeys." *Nature* 231:366–68.

Rosen, R., and L. Rosen. 1981. *Human Sexuality.* New York: Random House.

Rosenfeld, M. 2007. *The Age of Independence: Interracial Unions, Same-Sex Unions and the Changing American Family.* Cambridge, MA: Harvard University Press.

Rotello, G. 1996. "To Have and To Hold: The Case for Gay Marriage." *Nation,* June 24, pp. 11–18.

Roth, P. 1969. *Portnoy's Complaint.* New York: Random House.

Roughgarden, J. 2004. *Evolution's Rainbow: Diversity, Gender, and Sexuality in Nature and People.* Berkeley: University of California Press.

Rubin, L. B. 1976. *Worlds of Pain: Life in the Working-Class Family.* New York: Basic Books.

Rubin, L. B. 1990. *Erotic Wars: What Happened to the Sexual Revolution?* New York: HarperCollins.

Rumney, P. N. S. 2006. "False Allegations of Rape." *Cambridge Law Journal* 65(1): 128–58.

Russell, D. E. H. 1984. *Sexual Exploitation: Rape, Child Sexual Abuse, and Workplace Harassment.* Beverly Hills, CA: Sage.

Rust, Paula C. Rodriguez. 2002. "Bisexuality: A Contemporary Paradox for Women." *Journal of Social Issues* 56(2):205–21.

Rutter, V. 1995. "Adolescence: Whose Hell Is It?" *Psychology Today,* January/February, pp. 54–66.

Rutter, V. 1996. "Who Stole Fertility?" *Psychology Today,* March/April, pp. 44–70.

Rutter, Virginia. 2008. "Opting out ain't what it used to be," *GirlwPen.com.* July 22.

Rutter, Virginia. 2009: Blog Column: "Nice Work: talking about sex-with-others—with your partner!" *GirlwPen.com.* August 31.

Rutter, Virginia. 2011. "In the Modern Sex Scandal, Boys will be Idiots." *CNN.com.* June 15.

Sanders, A. S., and J. M. Reinisch. 1999. "Would You Say You 'Had' Sex If . . .?" *Journal of the American Medical Association* 281:275–77.

Santelli, J., M. A. Ott, M. Lyon, J. Rogers, D. Summers, and R. Schleifer. 2006. "Abstinence and Abstinence-only Education: A Review of U.S. Policies and Programs." *Journal of Adolescent Health* 38(1):72–81.

Sarro, D., and Curtis Wong. 2010. "Taliban Execute Pregnant Woman." *HuffingtonPost.com.* August 8.

Schalet, Amy. 2004. "Must We Fear Adolescent Sexuality?" *Medscape General Medicine* 6(4). Retrieved April 4, 2011.

Schalet, Amy. 2011. *Not Under My Roof! Parents, Teens and the Culture of Sex.* Chicago: University of Chicago Press.

Schmidt, G., and V. Sigusch. 1970. "Sex Differences in Response to Psychosexual Stimulation by Films and Slides." *Journal of Sex Research* 6:268–83.

Schnarch, David. 2009. *Intimacy and Desire: Awaken the Passion in Your Relationship.* New York: Beaufort Books.

Schrock, Karen. 2009. "Monogamy Is All the Rage These Days." *Scientific American,* August 7. Retrieved March 21, 2001.

Schwartz, P. 1994. *Peer Marriage: Love between Equals.* New York: Free Press.

Schwartz, P. 1995. "When Staying Is Worth the Pain." *New York Times,* April 29, p. B1.

Schwartz, P. 2007. *Prime: Adventures and Advice on Sex, Love, and the Sensual Years.* New York: William Morrow.

Schwartz, P., and P. Blumstein. 1976. "Bisexuality in Women." In J. Wiseman, Ed., *The Social Psychology of Sex.* New York: Harper and Row.

Scritchfield, S. 1995. "The Social Construction of Infertility." In J. Best, Ed., *Images of Issues.* New York: Aldine de Gruyter.

Sears, R. Bradley, Gary Gates, and William B. Rubenstein. 2005. Same-Sex Couples and Same-Sex Couples Raising Children in the United States. The Williams Project on Sexual Orientation Law and Public Policy, UCLA School of Law. Retrieved April 24, 2011.

Seidman, S. 1992. *Embattled Eros: Sexual Politics and Ethics in Contemporary America.* New York: Routledge.

SIECUS (Sexuality Information and Education Council of the United States). 1995. "A Report on Adolescent Sexuality." New York: SIECUS.

SIECUS (Sexuality Information and Education Council of the United States). 2005. "A Brief History of Federal Abstinence-Only-Until-Marriage Funding." New York: SIECUS. Accessed April 25, 2010.

SIECUS (Sexuality Information and Education Council of the United States). 2005. "State Sexual and Reproductive Health Legislative Reports, Accurate as of May 2005." New York: SIECUS. Retrieved March 26, 2011.

Shakespeare, W. 1983. *Macbeth.* New York: Penguin.

Sharlet, Jeff. 2009. "Sex and Power inside 'the C Street House.'" *Salon.com*, July 21. Retrieved March 16, 2011.

Shorter, E. 1975. *The Making of the Modern Family.* New York: Basic Books.

SIECUS. 2008. "Heritage Keepers Review." Sexuality Information and Education Council of the United States Community Action Kit/Curricula Reviews: Retrieved at: www.communityactionkit.org/index.cfm?fuseaction=page.viewpage&pageid=984.

Simpson, J. A., and S. W. Gangestad. 1991. "Individual Differences in Sociosexuality: Evidence for Convergent and Discriminant Validity." *Journal of Personality and Social Psychology* 60:870–83.

Smith, T. W. 1999. "The JAMA Controversy and the Meaning of Sex." *Public Opinion Quarterly* 63(3):385–400.

Sprecher, S., and K. McKinney. 1993. *Sexuality.* Thousand Oaks, CA: Sage.

Stanislaw, H., and F. J. Rice. 1988. "The Correlation between Sexual Desire and Menstrual Cycle Changes." *Archives of Sexual Behavior* 17:499–508.

Stark, R. 1996. *The Rise of Christianity: A Sociologist Reconsiders History.* Princeton, NJ: Princeton University Press.

Steinberg, L. 1994. *Crossing Paths: How Your Child's Adolescence Triggers Your Own Crisis.* New York: Simon & Schuster.

Stepp, Laura Sessions. 2007. *Unhooked: How Young Women Pursue Sex, Delay Love, and Lose at Both.* New York: Riverhead Books.

Stone, Pamela. 2007. *Opting Out? Why Women Really Quit Careers and Head Home.* Berkeley: University of California Press.

Story, Louise. 2005. "Many Women at Elite Colleges Set Career Path to Motherhood." *New York Times*, September 20. Retrieved March 19, 2011.

Strauss, W., and N. Howe. 1991. *Generations: The History of America's Future, 1584–2069.* New York: William Morrow.

Struckman-Johnson, C. 1988. "Forced Sex on Dates: It Happens to Men, Too." *Journal of Sex Research* 24:234–41.

Sullivan, Oriel, and Scott Coltrane. 2008. "Men's Changing Contribution to Housework and Child Care." Council on Contemporary Families. Retrieved March 19, 2011.

Sum, Andrew, Joseph McLaughlin, Sheila Palma, Jacqui Motroni, and Ishwar Khatiwada. 2008. "Out with the Young and in with the Old: U.S. Labor Markets 2000–2008 and the Case for an Immediate Jobs Creation Program for Teens and Young Adults." Working paper, Northeastern University, Boston, MA.

Swidey, N. 2005. "What Makes People Gay?" *Boston Globe,* August 14, Magazine.

Symons, D. 1979. *The Evolution of Human Sexuality.* New York: Oxford University Press.

Taslitz, Andrew. 1999. *Rape and the Culture of the Courtroom.* New York: New York University Press.

Thompson, S. 1996. *Going All the Way: Teenage Girls' Tales of Sex, Romance, and Pregnancy.* New York: Hill & Wang.

Thornhill, R., and C. Palmer. 2000. *A Natural History of Rape: Biological Bases of Sexual Coercion.* Cambridge, MA: MIT Press.

Tiefer, L. 1995. *Sex Is Not a Natural Act and Other Essays.* Boulder, CO: Westview.

Time. 1934. "Religion: Legion of Decency." June 11.

Time. 1934. "Religion: Legion of Decency." June 11. Retrieved March 26, 2011.

Tizon, A. 1996. "Idaho County Fights Teen Sex using Old Fornication Law." *Seattle Times,* July 15, p. Al.

Toback, James. 2004. *When Will I Be Loved?* IFC Films.

Todd, J. 1986. *Sensibility: An Introduction.* London: Methuen.

Tolman, D. L. 1999. "Femininity as a Barrier to Positive Sexual Health for Adolescent Girls." *Journal of the American Medical Women's Association* 54:133–38.

Tolman, D., and L. Diamond. 2001. "Desegregating Sexual Research: Cultural and Biological Perspectives on Gender and Desire." *Annual Review of Sex Research* 12:33–74.

Toobin, J. 2007. "Unforgiven: Why is Clarence Thomas So Angry?" *The New Yorker* November 12.

Traister, Rebecca. 2007. "Katie Roiphe's Morning After." *Salon.com,* July 9. Retrieved April 24, 2011.

Tucker, M. B., and C. Mitchell-Kernan. 1995. *The Decline in Marriage among African Americans: Causes, Consequences, and Policy Implications.* New York: Russell Sage.

Twine, F. W. 1996. "Heterosexual Alliances: The Romantic Management of Racial Identity." In M. P. P. Root, Ed., *The Multiracial Experience: Racial Borders as the New Frontier.* Thousand Oaks, CA: Sage.

UNICEF. Netherlands Statistics. Retrieved March 27, 2011.

UNICEF. Saudi Arabia Statistics. Retrieved March 27, 2011.

United Nations. 2001. Monthly Bulletin of Statistics, April. Retrieved March 14, 2011.

United Nations. 2008. World Population Prospects: 2008 Revision. Population database. Retrieved March 28, 2011.

United Nations Department of Economic and Social Affairs, Population Division. 2007. United Nations World Population Prospects: 2006 Revision, Table A.15. New York: United Nations.

United Nations Statistics Division. 2006. *Demographic Yearbook 2006*. New York: United Nations.

U.S. Office of Technology Assessment. 1988. *Infertility: Medical and Social Choices*. Publication No. OTA BA 358. Washington, DC: U.S. Congress.

University of Texas Health Science Center at Tyler. 2007. "Hazards of High Heels," June 19, 2007. Accessed February 24, 2010.

Updike, J. 1960. *Rabbit, Run*. New York: Knopf.

Vaid, U. 1995. *Virtual Equality: The Mainstreaming of Gay and Lesbian Liberation*. New York: Anchor.

Valins, S. 1966. "Cognitive Effects of False Heart-Rate Feedback." *Journal of Personality and Social Psychology* 4:400–8.

Vance, C. S. 1984. *Pleasure and Danger: Exploring Female Sexuality*. Boston: Routledge & Kegan Paul.

Ventura, S. J., J. C. Abma, W. D. Mosher, and S. Henshaw. 2004. "Estimated Pregnancy Rates for the United States, 1990–2000: An Update." *National Vital Statistics Reports* 52(23).

Ventura S. J., J. C. Abma, W. D. Mosher, and S. K. Henshaw. 2009. "Estimated pregnancy rates for the United States, 1990-2005: an update." *National Vital Statistics Reports* 58(4):1–14.

Wallis, Claudia. 2004. "The Case for Staying Home." *Time*, March 22. Retrieved March 19, 2011.

Ward, H., C. H. Mercer, K. Wellings, K. Fenton, B. Erens, A. Copas, and A. M. Johnson. 2005. "Who Pays for Sex? An Analysis of the Increasing Prevalence of Female Commercial Sex Contacts among Men in Britain." *Sexually Transmitted Infections* 81:467–71.

Waterman, C. K., L. J. Dawson, and M. J. Bologna. 1989. "Sexual Coercion in Gay Male and Lesbian Relationships: Predictions and Implications for Support Services." *Journal of Sex Research* 26:118–24.

Weeks, Jeffrey. 2009. *Sexuality (Key Ideas)*. New York: Routledge.

Weiner-Davis, Michele. 2003. *The Sex-Starved Marriage: A Couple's Guide to Boosting Their Marriage Libido*. New York: Simon and Schuster.

Weiss, Karen G.. 2008. "Male sexual victimization: Examining men's experiences of rape and sexual assault." *Men and Masculinities*. 12: 275–98.

Whisman, M., K. C. Gordon, and Y. Chatav. 2007. "Predicting Sexual Infidelity in a Nationally Representative Sample: The Relative Contributions of Vulnerability, Stressors, and Opportunity." *Journal of Family Psychology* 21:320–24.

Whisman, M. A., and D. K. Synder. 2007. "Sexual Infidelity in a National Survey of American Women: Differences in Prevalence and Correlates as a Function of Method of Assessment." *Journal of Family Psychology* 21:147–54.

Whitehead, B. D. 1994. "The Failure of Sex Education." *Atlantic Monthly*, October, pp. 55–80.

Whitman, F. 1983. "Culturally Invariable Properties of Male Homosexualities: Tentative Conclusions from Cross-Cultural Research." *Archives of Sexual Behavior* 12:207–26.

Wietz, Paul. 1999. *American Pie*. Universal Pictures.

Williams, T. 1947. *A Streetcar Named Desire*. New York: New Directions.

Willingham, Val. 2010. "Survey documents teen condom use and U.S. sexual habits." ccn.health.com. October 4. Retrieved at: www.cnn.com/2010/HEALTH/10/04/med.teen.condom.study/index.html.

Wilson, William Julius. 1987. *The Truly Disadvantaged: The Inner City, the Underclass, and Public Policy*. Chicago: University of Chicago Press.

Wright, L. 1995. "A Reporter at Large: Double Mystery." *New Yorker* 8/7:44–50.

Wyatt, G. E. 1992. "The Sociocultural Context of African American and White American Women's Rape." *Journal of Social Issues* 48:77–92.

Yarber, W. L. 1994. "Past, Present, and Future Perspectives on Sexuality Education." In *Promoting Healthy Sexuality in Young People*. New York: SIECUS.

Yarber, W. L., and M. R. Torabi. 1994. "Public Opinion from a Rural Region about Condoms for HIV Prevention." *Wellness Perspectives: Research, Theory, and Practice* 10(2):63–75.

Young, Andrew. 2010. *The Politician: An Insider's Account of John Edwards's Pursuit of the Presidency and the Scandal That Brought Him Down*. New York: St. Martin's Press.

Zelnick, M., and F. K. Shah. 1983. "First Intercourse among Young Americans." *Family Planning Perspectives* 15:64–70.

Zogby International. 2006. "Opinions of Military Personnel on Sexual Minorities in the Military." Retrieved April 17, 2011.

Index

About the Authors

Virginia Rutter, PhD, is associate professor of sociology at Framingham State University in Framingham, MA. She has been a co-investigator of the National Couples Survey at Battelle funded by the National Institutes of Health and a public policy fellow at the Committee on Women in Science and Engineering at the National Academies of Science. She is a board member of the Council on Contemporary Families and an editor and columnist at Girl w/Pen, where she writes about gender and sexuality.

Pepper Schwartz, PhD, is professor of sociology at the University of Washington, past president of the Society for the Scientific Study of Sexuality, and past president of the National Sexuality Resource Center. She is a senior fellow at the Council of Contemporary Families and the Love, Sex and Relationship Ambassador for AARP.

3 2183 01510 1427

CPSIA information can be obtained at www.ICGtesting.com
Printed in the USA
BVOW030735151111

276113BV00002B/1/P

9 780742 570047